Revolutionary Science

The Language of the Genes
In the Blood
Almost Like a Whale
Y: The Descent of Men
The Single Helix
Coral: A Pessimist in Paradise
Darwin's Island
The Serpent's Promise

Revolutionary Science

Transformation and Turmoil
in the Age of the Guillotine

Steve Jones

PEGASUS BOOKS
NEW YORK LONDON

REVOLUTIONARY SCIENCE

Pegasus Books Ltd
148 West 37th Street, 13th Fl
New York, NY 10018

First Pegasus Books hardcover edition January 2017

ISBN: 978-1-68177-309-4

10 9 8 7 6 5 4 3 2 1

Printed in the United States of America
Distributed by W. W. Norton & Company, Inc.

To the memory of Chris Jackson,
linguist, naturalist and philosopher,
who died too soon.

Paper is made from the rags of things that did once exist; there are endless excellencies in paper.

THOMAS CARLYLE,
The French Revolution (1837)

CONTENTS

PREFACE

CONFESSIONS OF A
SOIXANTE-HUITARD

> Here perhaps is the place to fix, a little more
> precisely, what these two words, French Revolution,
> shall mean; for, strictly considered, they may have as
> many meanings as there are speakers of them.
>
> THOMAS CARLYLE, *The French Revolution*

Paris, May 1968: I was there, but not for long. It was my first experience of the city, and as I sat on the sunny steps of the Gare du Nord, I was amazed by the vitality of the scene. There was not much time to enjoy the occasion, for within an hour I was on the Métro to pick up the night train to Perpignan in the south. In the carriage, still with seats marked as reserved for *mutilés de guerre*, lingered an unfamiliar scent, perhaps a perfume, pungent but not unpleasant. It was in fact tear gas that had seeped into the tunnels from the running battles above, events of which I was then quite unaware.

After an uncomfortable night in a couchette, I lifted the blind to see a landscape of austere beauty, the foothills of the Pyrenees. There lived a most remarkable mollusc, and a month in search of that creature was an early step in what became a lifetime's research on its evolution and genetics; a subject of deep interest to a tiny, and diminishing, group of biologists.

I have returned to those mountains again and again, and now spend much of my time in a small house nearby. There I indulge in what the French call, in an inelegant but precise phrase, *vulgarisation scientifique*: writing about the natural world for a general audience. Fifty years on from my first trip to the City of Light, and more than two centuries since the Revolution of 1789, a crisis that (unlike the disturbances around my own initial visit) changed world history, this book celebrates the scientists of Paris in that era. They are not as familiar to English-speakers as they deserve to be, for their work laid the foundations of much of today's physics, astronomy, biology and chemistry. They were true revolutionaries: agents of an upheaval of understanding that had rather more effect on the future than did the bloody disturbances on the streets.

Just as remarkable (but even less well remembered) is the part that many among them played in the events of the day. Nowhere else, before or since, have members of their profession been so much involved in public affairs. The explosion on the *Quatorze Juillet* was sparked off by an unlikely alliance of technical experts and political thinkers, of *philosophes* (as scientists were then known) and *politiques*, each of whom believed that their own field illuminated the other. Together, the two groups were convinced, they would lead humankind to an era of inevitable progress.

As its system of government creaked and fell, Paris had more experimenters and theoreticians than did the rest of the planet put together. In the heady days around the fall of the Bastille, the city was saturated in science. Historians sometimes see the French Revolution as a bourgeois revolt against a corrupt and ineffective aristocracy, but in truth scientists were more involved than were bankers. Many stellar names in physics and the rest were participants in the great eruption, while several of those remembered as statesmen and grandees spent a good part of their time at the laboratory bench. Together they built a new world.

Most of those who admire the French capital today do not realise that some of its most famous icons are reminders of the way in which research then pervaded its very fabric. Visitors, alone or in a group, can opt for one of a large number of architectural, artistic or historical tours, but there are none based on the efforts of the city's scientists and engineers. Such a circuit would be worth the effort, for they would visit some unfamiliar places and would, for often unexpected reasons, also see some of Paris's best-known relics in a new light.

The obvious place for a suitably minded *flâneur* to begin his or her perambulation would be the Eiffel Tower, already a compulsory halt on the tourist trail. Opened in 1889 to celebrate the centennial of the fall of the Bastille, that audacious symbol of modernity was for four decades the tallest structure in the world. It welcomed its two hundred and fifty millionth client in 2010 to become the most visited commercial monument ever built. The place is now surrounded by desperate Eastern Europeans and North Africans, who harass visitors to buy crude casts of the structure, made in China. Neither they, nor most of their customers, are aware of its importance in the history of science.

The Tower was supposed to stand for just twenty years before its lease expired. Gustave Eiffel had from its earliest days a scheme to preserve his monument for far longer than that. 'It will', he said, 'be an observatory and a laboratory such as science has never had at its disposal', and its discoveries would ensure its survival. His scheme was a success.

The Tower, *La Dame de Fer* to the French (a name also bestowed on an equally angular and unyielding British politician and on a torture device whose victims were squeezed to death) is itself a technical marvel. It has eighteen thousand wrought-iron girders, and their ability to cope with high winds was essential to the design. Wrought iron was light and strong, and Eiffel had already designed several railway bridges on the principle that storms should be allowed to blow through rather than being fought off with massive girders. His Parisian monument was so elegantly conceived that the weight of the air bounded by its beams is greater than that of the metal used to construct it, which if melted down to fill the one hundred and twenty-five metre square of its base would be no more than six centimetres deep. Even in a severe gale, his tower sways just seven centimetres at its three-hundred-metre summit.

The structure would symbolise, said Gustave Eiffel, 'the century of Industry and Science in which we live, and for which the way was prepared by the great scientific movement of the end of the eighteenth century'. He was right, for Paris at that time was a centre of that endeavour to an extent never seen before or since, and his own edifice soon became, as he had promised, a laboratory as much as an engineering *tour de force*.

First, its architect made a pioneering estimate of wind resistance by running metal plates of different shapes and sizes down a vertical cable attached to a high point within its framework. Each was attached to a fan connected to a pen that drew a graph that showed acceleration and terminal velocity, while time was recorded with a tuning fork that inscribed a white line trace on a smoked drum. Eiffel used the data to work out the mathematical relationships between shape, size, mass and speed. In a further study of aerodynamics, at the tower's base he built the world's first functional wind tunnel. It could generate airspeeds close to those experienced by the earliest aircraft and was much used by the pioneers of aviation. Complaints about noise forced him to abandon that machine, but he built a larger version some distance away. Eiffel himself used the device in the first analysis of the physics of lift on an aircraft wing.

The monument acted as a test bed in other ways. Its iron mast contained a physiology laboratory that examined the effects of exercise on those forced to climb its steps (and such measures could be repeated today on those who survive *La Verticale de la Tour Eiffel*, a race up the 1665 treads to the top). In addition, it had a weather station used to compare winds and temperatures on the surface and in the heights (and, in a nod to modernity, has now been furnished with *éoliennes* that generate much of its electricity). It was used as an observatory when mist obscured the view from the ground, and soon the highest pressures ever achieved by man were recorded at the bottom of a three-hundred-metre steel tube of mercury that stretched from its summit to the base. Not all the experiments were a success: a hopeful aeronaut who asked permission to test a 'parachute suit' with a dummy thrown from the topmost balcony used himself as a subject instead and died at once.

A year after the tower's inauguration, the first measurements of changes in the electric charge of the atmosphere with height were made on its platforms. More remarkable – and more unexpected – a later comparison of radiation levels on the topmost gallery with those on the ground below gave the first hint of the existence of cosmic rays, a discovery that paved the way to the idea of the Big Bang. Gustave Eiffel was more than justified in his confidence in the value of his masterpiece.

Thomas Edison, who visited the architect in his tiny private apartment at the top of the edifice soon after its inauguration, conceived of a huge phonograph, which would give the Iron Maiden a voice that could be heard five miles away. It was never built.

In a rather more realistic experiment in communication, the tower was the site of the world's first radio transmission. In 1898, a signal was sent from an aerial on a high point to a receiver four kilometres away in the Panthéon, a deconsecrated eighteenth-century church. A year later, the waves crossed the English Channel, and by 1913 they reached the United States. In an early step towards a global geography, the Paris Observatory used the great iron mast as an aerial to contact the United States Naval Academy and to estimate the precise distance across the Atlantic from the differences in time recorded in the two centres.

Such advances were seen as so crucial by French military authorities that the monument's future was assured. In 1914, plans were made to blow it up if the Germans reached the city as their armies invaded but instead the tower saved Paris when its radio receiver picked up an enemy message that warned of an attack, enabling troops to be rushed in taxis to the valley of the Marne to hold the assault back. In 1967, public outcry meant that the edifice was also spared de Gaulle's audacious plan to ship it to the Montreal Exposition.

The structure acts as a monument to human ingenuity in other ways. On its beams, just below the first balcony, are inscribed the names of seventy-two French chemists, biologists, mathematicians and engineers of the era between the Revolution and its own construction, almost all those discussed in this book included. Gustave Eiffel's own career would, had there been space for later entries, no doubt have qualified him to join their number.

The view from the summit of his wrought-iron masterpiece reveals the landscape in which those eminent men made their discoveries. Even a glance downwards tells part of the story, for its foundations rest on the Champ de Mars, the launch pad of the world's first hydrogen balloon, which took to the air in 1783. Its four legs are aligned with the points of the compass and the prospect in each direction reveals new treasures.

The gardens of the Luxembourg, to the north across the

Seine, were the site of one of the first experiments in scientific agriculture. Beyond that stands the hill of Montmartre, where, in the city of metaphorical light, a spinning mirror was used as part of a device that made the first measurement of the speed of light itself. In the same direction but further away is the Musée des Arts et Métiers, the world's first museum of technology, set up in a disaffected abbey soon after the fall of the monarchy as a 'public repository of machines, models, tools, descriptions, and books of all the varieties of arts and crafts' and still much involved in the celebration of the nation's engineering genius. A kilometre or so further on is its modern equivalent, the Museum of Science and Industry at La Villette, a vast space on the site of what was once the Paris abattoir.

Southwards lie the laboratories that established the germ theory of disease and identified the agents of rabies, typhus, plague and, in recent years, AIDS. Also on view is the home of the *Société d'Arcueil*, a private laboratory set up in 1807. It had fifteen members, nine of whom became Fellows of the Royal Society of London. They included, inter alia, the inventor of bleach, the founder of biogeography, the first aerial explorer of the atmosphere, and the discoverers of the origin of meteorites, the internal biological clock and the polarisation of light.

Rather further away in the same direction is the Palace of Versailles. Its gardens had the largest plant collection in the world and were the site of an innovative experiment in genetics. An inherited shift, a mutation, appeared in a line of strawberries that suddenly produced leaves with one blade instead of three. The new form was crossed with others, and the results described, in a hint of the later emergence of genetics and evolution, in a 1766 paper entitled *On the Distinction of Species, Races and Varieties*. In 1783, to universal astonishment, the place saw the first public flight of a balloon.

The expensive fantasy's builder and owner, Louis XIV, promoted the latest technology with a series of experiments designed to impress his subjects. One used a metal burning glass a metre across to light a whole room with a candle placed at its focal point, while another demonstrated the power of electricity when, for the edification of the court, a surge of current was passed through a circle of two hundred royal guards as they held hands.

To the east of the Tower is an equally illustrious vista. Half an hour's walk away, the Academy of Sciences finds its modern home beneath the magnificent seventeenth-century dome of what was once the Collège Mazarin, the section of the University of Paris in which the great (and doomed) chemist of the revolutionary years Antoine Lavoisier studied. The building now contains the headquarters of several national academies and is a global centre for research and education. Further on in much the same direction is the Paris Observatory, whose astronomers established the shape of the Earth and instigated a survey of their nation more accurate than any other (although they failed in their plan to have the meridian that separates eastern and western hemispheres pass through the building, for the British took it to Greenwich). To add allegory to the brutal facts of physics the Paris town hall, just over the river, is decorated by a bronze statue,

La Science, which features a young lady perched on a globe, armed with a pair of dividers and with a map in her hand (every other of the dozen or so Parisian effigies dedicated to members of the profession is of a male).

On the Left Bank, in the same direction, is the Jardin des Plantes, itself decorated with a noble bronze inscribed to the *Fondateur de la Doctrine de l'Evolution* (a Frenchman, and not the bearded Englishman to whom that role is ascribed by most Britons), while in the nearby Museum of Natural History – established as one of the first acts of the new republican government – modern palaeontology was born and, rather later, radioactivity was discovered. A few hundred yards away, near today's Place de la Bastille, were laid the foundations of modern chemistry and, by the same research team, of human physiology. Those talented men also made some of the earliest studies of the effects of drugs, morphine included. Close by is the Pitié-Salpêtrière Hospital, then a prison for prostitutes and lunatics, where the first steps were taken in psychiatry and neurology.

In the opposite direction from the *Dame de Fer,* in the western suburbs, stands the International Bureau of Weights and Measures, founded in recognition of the French invention of the metric system, and still the world capital of measurement. Within its walls are the platinum bar that first defined the length of the metre, and the spherical mass that did the same for the kilogram. They have been supplemented by instruments that can measure size and weight together with power, electrical current and time to an accuracy of one part in billions. Nearby is the site of the world's first lightning conductor, erected well before the famous experiment in Philadelphia in which a kite was flown into a thunderstorm, a structure that – as we shall see – had an unexpected connection with some of the major figures behind the bloody events of July 1789.

The scientific landscape of the French capital is, without doubt, the richest in the world. Varied as it might be, most visitors are more interested in the relics of historical events. These are magnificent indeed, but quite often they too have ties with the world of research. The Louvre was the first home of the *Académie Royale de Sciences*, and of a generation of great mathematicians who established the ground rules that shape the solar system, together with the theories of chaos which explain why we will never make long-range economic or weather forecasts. They also studied the statistics of electoral systems and came up with the first hints of what became the theory of relativity. The Panthéon, a superb church in the classical manner, was after the upheaval deconsecrated to become the mausoleum of France's national heroes, those of science included. Not far away stands the Abbey Church of Saint-Germain-des-Prés, the oldest in the city. In the turbulent years of the late eighteenth century the place became the home of major advances in the chemistry of explosives (and much of it was destroyed when one of them went wrong). On the Île de la Cité, the historical heart of Paris, the Cathedral of Nôtre-Dame was itself for a time converted into a monument to rationalism, with a religion that would have one god alone, the people. The rationalists paid the price for their blasphemy when they, with several thousand others, were escorted from their cells in a nearby medieval prison, the Conciergerie, and introduced to a novel humanitarian device designed in part by the nation's Academy of Surgery.

Among the guillotine's victims were some of the foremost chemists, astronomers and mathematicians of the age. They suffered because the rebellion of the *philosophes*, in its first days an engine of progress, soon degenerated into recrimination and revenge. Many among them made the mistake of falling out with the authorities. As well as those who faced the 'national razor', others were murdered, driven to suicide, or killed in battle.

Even so, most of the survivors returned to their laboratories when the bloodshed had abated. Their efforts ensured that French science retained its powers even as the purity of the new regime's ideas gave way to dictatorship, and then to years of unstable government. The half-century or so on either side of the fall of the Bastille shows how that profession unites enemies as much as it does friends, and how science itself can survive all upheavals, whatever the fate of those who practise it.

Enough of the Revolution's monuments remain to allow the tourist (and thirty million arrive each year) to piece together its major incidents. Every guidebook describes the relics of that violent era. Those who wish to learn more can turn to the enormous literature on the period, in both English and French, with dozens of books written even since the bicentennial of 1989 to be added to the mountain of works published since the cataclysm itself.

Two among them have become classics. Thomas Carlyle's *The French Revolution* of 1837 gives a real sense of the collapse and disorder that led to the end of the monarchy (at least for those who already have a decent knowledge of the *dramatis personae* involved). It is renowned for its vivid and sometimes virulent prose. I have pillaged it for my chapter headings and more.

Charles Dickens claimed, with perhaps pardonable exaggeration, to have read *The French Revolution* five hundred times. As he put it: 'No-one can hope to add anything to the philosophy of Mr Carlyle's wonderful book', and he used its narrative as the basis of *A Tale of Two Cities*. He did decorate the plot to some degree (the *tricoteuses* were moved from knitting as they observed the machinations of the Senate to fictional seats at the foot of the guillotine), but Carlyle's influence is unmistakable. From the mid-1840s, Dickens spent much time in the French capital, which he felt to be 'a wicked and detestable place, though wonderfully attractive ... I have been seeing Paris – wandering into Hospitals, Prisons, Dead-Houses, Operas, Theatres, Concert Rooms, Burial-grounds, Palaces, and Wine Shops ... every description of gaudy and ghastly sight has been passing before me in a rapid Panorama.' Those gaudy and ghastly sights are woven into his great tale, and one or two even make it to these pages.

However, like the guidebooks, almost none of the histories, real or imagined, old or new, refer to the central part played in the occurrences of 1789 by students of the natural world, let alone to the fundamental importance of their work to today's science. Carlyle himself makes a few references to some of the key participants, but only because so many among them were embroiled in public affairs. In the same way, Simon Schama's excellent *Citizens: A Chronicle of the French Revolution*, published in the episode's bicentennial year, makes no more than a mention of the bloody fate of Antoine Lavoisier, the founder of modern chemistry and a pivotal figure in the civic affairs of the time, and deals with his research not at all.

That unique overlap between such contrasting fields of endeavour deserves commemoration, and this book is an attempt to provide it. On the way, it tries to bring one half of the story up to date.

No Need for Geniuses ranges widely, perhaps too widely, from astronomy to zoology and from farming to physics, taking in the origin of potato crisps, dynamite, and the Tour de France on the way. So active was the pursuit of knowledge in that period that many of its advances do not find a place. The earliest studies of the brain, the first insights into colour vision, ground-breaking work on tissues, the initial steps in the study of crystals, the control of animal disease, the forensics of poisons, and the invention of the stethoscope and the sphygmomanometer: all have roots in Paris in the years around the Revolution but are not discussed in these pages. Some of the most important discoveries were in mathematics, and there, like too many biologists, I am obliged to gloss over the topic in the hope that others can do a better job than I. Whatever its limitations, my hope is that this book will provide a taste of the intellectual and social frenzy that ruled in France in the half-century and more that spanned the execution of Louis XVI. As an overture to its contents I append to this preface a list of the major figures involved in the joint political and scientific dramas of Paris in the Revolutionary era.

I thank David Colquhoun, Ian Grojnowski, Iain Hunt, Tegid Jones, Sarah Kendrew, Sandy Knapp, Brian Lapping, Max Leonard, Chris Lintott, Norma Percy, Jane Selley, Valerie Shrimplin, Luciana Sivilotti, John Warren and Tim Whiting for comments; any errors that remain are, of course, my own. I translate many of the longer quotations from French sources, but leave briefer passages in their original form in the expectation that readers will have no difficulty with them; as D'Artagnan says in Alexandre Dumas' *Twenty Years After,* which follows the adventures of the Three Musketeers on an unlikely trip to England, '*L'anglais n'est que du français mal prononcé.*' Anyone unfortunate enough to have to listen to my own spoken French will find that the opposite is also true.

DRAMATIS PERSONAE

Many major French scientific figures are mentioned in the following pages and many more do not find a place. I list here only those alive during the revolutionary period. Together they represent the most glittering assemblage of researchers ever gathered in a single city and although numbers of them were executed or imprisoned in those turbulent years, several of the survivors gained high political position during the Napoleonic era.

Appert, Nicolas 1749–1841 Inventor of tinned food, the stock cube and the pressure cooker. Imprisoned during the Revolution.

Arago, François 1786–1853 Secretary of the Paris Observatory, surveyor of France, Spain and Scotland, discoverer of magnetic eddy currents. Later Prefect of the Pyrénées-Orientales, Minister of Marine Affairs and the Colonies, and Prime Minister of France.

Bailly, Jean-Sylvan 1736–1793 Astronomer and political philosopher. Leader of the breakaway faction that took control and sparked off the Revolution. First Mayor of Paris. Guillotined.

Berthollet, Claude Louis 1748–1822 Chemist, explosives expert and inventor of bleach. Later a Senator.

Biot, Jean-Baptiste 1774–1862 Mathematician, balloonist, first student of atmospheric chemistry and discoverer of extra-terrestrial origin of meteorites.

Borda, Jean–Charles de 1733–1799 Military engineer, mathematician, cartographer, expert on voting systems and inventor of 'repeating circle' theodolite.

Bosc, Louis 1759–1828 Entomologist, naturalist and agricultural researcher. Fled to the United States after the Revolution. Later French consul in New York.

Bougainville, Louis Antoine de 1729–1811 Explorer and plant-collector. First French circumnavigator. Imprisoned during the Terror. Later a Senator.

Carnot, Lazare 1753–1823 Physicist, geometrician, engineer and 'Organiser of Victory' in the Revolution's wars against its neighbours. Later Minister of War.

Cassini, Giovanni Domenico and descendants 1625–1845 First Director of the Paris Observatory; patriarch of the four-generation dynasty who ran the Observatory, organised the Survey of France and the first national map. Cassini IV imprisoned during the Revolution.

Chaptal, Jean-Antoine 1756–1832 Chemist and industrialist; extracted sugar from beet. Later Councillor of State and Minister of the Interior.

Charles, Jacques 1746–1823 Physicist and student of gases. Inventor of the hydrogen balloon.

Condorcet, Nicolas de 1743–1794 Mathematician, expert on electoral systems and fluid dynamics, political philosopher and instigator of the metric system. Delegate for Paris in the first National Assembly. Murdered (or committed suicide) in prison at the time of the Terror.

Coriolis, Gustave 1792–1843 Mathematician, expert on rotating systems. Associated with the Coriolis force, important in weather forecasting, oceanography and long-distance gunnery.

Cotte, Louis 1740–1815 Priest, astronomer and founder of modern meteorology.

Cousin, Jacques Antoine Joseph 1739–1800 Mathematician and astronomer. Imprisoned at the time of the Terror. Later member of the Senate.

Cuvier, Georges 1769–1832 Founder of modern palaeontology, expert on extinction, President of the Bible Society of Paris and later Vice-President of the Council of State.

Dalibard, Thomas-François 1709–1799 Botanist and author of first Flora of Paris, jointly (with Buffon) the engineer of the world's first lightning conductor.

Daubenton, Louis-Jean-Marie 1716–1800 Comparative anatomist, animal breeder and first director of the Paris Museum of Natural History. Later a Senator.

Delambre, Jean-Baptiste 1749–1822 Director of the Paris Observatory, pioneer of the first triangulation of France and of the metric system.

Desmarest, Nicolas 1725–1815 Geologist of the volcanoes of the Auvergne and student of earthquakes. Imprisoned at the time of the Terror.

Dietrich, Philippe-Frederic de 1748–1793 Geologist and mining engineer, and the first to perform '*La Marsellaise*' in public. Mayor of Strasbourg. Guillotined.

Dolomieu, Deodat de 1750–1801 Geologist and mineralogist, after whom the rock dolomite is named. Imprisoned at the time of the Terror.

du Pont de Nemours, Eulethère Irenée 1771–1834 Chemist and expert on explosives. Fled to the United States and set up the world's largest chemical company.

Fourcroy, Antoine 1755–1809 Chemist, physiologist, joint discoverer of iridium, and pharmacologist. Deputy for Paris in the National Convention. Later, Councillor of State.

Fourier, Joseph 1768–1830 Mathematician and discoverer of the greenhouse effect. Later Prefect of the Department of Isère.

Franklin, Benjamin 1706–1790 American inventor of the lightning conductor and bifocal spectacles. Discoverer of the Gulf Stream and the effect of oil on troubled waters. Active in Parisian politics and the first American representative to the French Republic.

Gay-Lussac, Louis Joseph 1778–1850 Physicist, meteorologist, expert on gases and early balloonist. Set world height record of 7000 metres in 1804. Later Prefect of the Department of Haute-Vienne.

Germain, Sophie 1776–1831 Female mathematician with an interest in number theory and an expert on the elasticity of solid bodies.

Guillotin, Joseph-Ignace 1738–1814 Physician, anatomist and opponent of the death penalty, but remembered for his promotion of a decapitation device. Deputy for Paris in the first Revolutionary assembly. Imprisoned during the Terror.

Humboldt, Alexander von 1769–1859 German naturalist, geographer and explorer of South America and Siberia, largely resident in Paris.

Jussieu, Antoine Laurent du 1748–1836 Physician and botanist. Second head of the National Museum of Natural History.

Lacépède, Bernard 1756–1825 Naturalist and expert on reptiles and fish. Member of the first Revolutionary Legislative Assembly. Later, President of the Senate.

Lagrange, Joseph-Louis 1736–1813 Mathematician, statistician and astronomer, founder of the decimal system of measurement. Later, member of the Senate.

Lalande, Jérôme 1732–1807 Surveyor and astronomer. Inventor of an early form of theodolite. Freemason and one of the first to admit his atheism.

Lamarck, Jean-Baptiste de 1744–1829 Inventor of the word 'biology'. Early proponent of evolution and of the notion that the same rules mould both biological and political progress.

Lamoignon de Malesherbes, Chrétien Guillaume de 1721–1794 Botanist and agriculturist. Argued against the death penalty for Louis XVI. Guillotined with other members of his family.

Laplace, Jean Baptiste Meusnier de 1754–1793 Geometer, surveyor and engineer. Killed at the siege of Mayence (Mainz).

Laplace, Pierre-Simon 1749–1827 Mathematician and astronomer, 'the French Newton'. Predicted the existence of black holes. Later Minister of the Interior and Senator.

Latreille, Pierre-André 1762–1833 Zoologist and expert on arthropods. Imprisoned during the Revolution, but found a rare beetle in his cell, an event that led to his release.

Lavoisier, Antoine 1743–1794 Founder of modern chemistry and modern physiology. Munitions expert, agricultural researcher and tax-collector. Guillotined.

Leblanc, Nicolas 1742–1806 Chemist and physician, inventor of the Leblanc Process to manufacture sodium carbonate (soda) from sodium chloride (salt). Committed suicide after his factory was confiscated.

Magendie, François 1783–1855 Physiologist, pharmacologist and brain scientist. Pioneer of vivisection.

Méchain, Pierre 1744–1804 Astronomer, geographer, surveyor and pioneer of the metric system.

Monge, Gaspard 1746–1818 Physicist, mathematician, chemist and geologist. Promoted a revised calendar. Member of the Revolution's Executive Council and Minister of Marine Affairs. Later, President of the Senate.

Parmentier, Antoine-Augustin 1737–1813 Pharmacist and pioneer of nutrition. Introduced the potato into France. Later, Head Pharmacist to the Napoleonic armies.

Ramond, Louis 1755–1827 Geologist and botanist of the Pyrenees. Deputy for Paris in the Revolutionary era. Imprisoned during the Terror. Later, member of the Council of State.

Romme, Charles-Gilbert 1750–1795 Physician and mathematician, architect of the new Revolutionary Calendar and member of the National Convention. Stabbed himself just before execution.

Rosne, Jean-François de 1774–1855 Pharmacist. Extracted 'essence of opium', the first alkaloid drug. In fact not opium itself, but a relative.

Rozier, François 1734–1793 Priest, botanist and agricultural researcher. Killed by revolutionary forces during the siege of Lyon.

Sage, Balthazar 1740–1824 Chemist, mineralogist and mining engineer. Founder of the School of Mines. Imprisoned during the Terror.

Saron, Bochart de 1730–1794 Astronomer and mathematician, expert on the orbit of comets. Guillotined.

Seguin, Armand-Jean-François 1767–1835 Chemist, physiologist and pharmacist. Extracted opium and tested on animals. Developed new methods of tanning and became immensely rich.

Tracy, Destutt de 1754–1836 Physiologist of the senses and philosopher of mind. Imprisoned during the Terror. Later, a Senator.

PRELUDE:

A FLASH OF INSPIRATION

Nay is it not rather the very murkiness, and atmospheric suffocation, that brings the lightning and the light?

THOMAS CARLYLE, *The French Revolution*

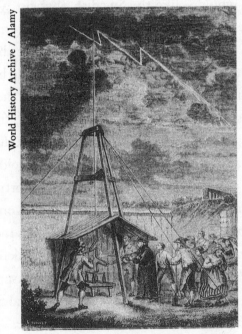

A striking result in the suburbs of Paris

In the spring of 1752, Louis the Well-Beloved of France, as he was known to at least some of his subjects, was much amused by a book entitled *Experiments and Observations on Electricity made at Philadelphia in America*. Louis was so taken by the tricks described that he ordered his own researchers to test one of the work's as yet untried ideas. A man was to be placed in a sentry box. From its roof would protrude a long metal rod that rose into the air and descended into the box itself. As storm clouds passed overhead, the unfortunate experimenter would be instructed to hold an iron baton and to move it closer to the rod. Sparks might then pass between the two as the charge grounded itself through his body (had the box been hit by lightning, he would – like the Swedish physicist who built a similar device in St Petersburg a year or so later – have fried).

The king's investigators were concerned that this scheme might not work, and decided to try it out in private before they dared perform in the presence of royalty. A retired dragoon was hired to act as the subject, and on a stormy May afternoon in Marly, a village a few miles west of Paris, the fateful test was made. It was a success: as predicted, the elderly soldier generated a shower of sparks when he approached the forty-foot rod. In his terror he ran to fetch the local *curé*, who at once offered himself up as a second subject. The cleric, too, was much struck by the experience. The technique was then demonstrated before the royal personage, and news of its success spread across France. Soon it was communicated to the Royal Society in London, which did not take a great deal of notice.

The experiment and the experimenters each cast a long shadow through history. The Philadelphia book was by Benjamin Franklin, a signatory of the United States Declaration of Independence, an active supporter of the radicals of both France and his own nation, and an inventor of global repute. The well-beloved monarch was Louis XV, the penultimate monarch before the bloody episode of 1789. He made real efforts to improve his nation's governance, and was a keen supporter of enquiries into the natural world. In 1774, the crown passed to his grandson, Louis XVI, who nineteen years later met his end on the newly developed guillotine ('So gentle that one would not know what to say if one had not expected to die and one would think that one had felt but a light breeze upon the neck'; a sensation soon experienced by large numbers of his erstwhile subjects). The two masters of the sentry box were the Comte de Buffon and Thomas-François Dalibard. The former was the most eminent naturalist of the day and a devotee of the then widespread belief that life and human affairs were suffused by a mystical force that led to change; the latter his student, who had translated the Franklin book, written (in Latin) a text on the plants of Paris, and who himself made advances in the study of electricity and magnetism. The name of the dragoon is, alas, not recorded.

All these individuals, and many more among the great and good of late-eighteenth-century France – several of whom came to a sticky end on the apparatus that put paid to Louis XVI – were actors in a drama in which major figures in physics, chemistry and other fields played a large part in domestic affairs, while individuals whose main reputation was made in government did work of real value in science. The experiment collapsed in the face of human imperfection, but in its brief existence the revolution of the researchers was, as Dickens put it in *A Tale of Two Cities*, an age of wisdom and of foolishness, of belief and of incredulity, and of hope and of despair. As is true of all such convulsions, the affair was filled with contradictions. To William Wordsworth it was a blissful dawn, to Edmund Burke a drunken delirium, directed by what he described as a 'sect of ambitious and fanatical atheists'. Both were right. For *philosophes* and *politiques* alike, the summer of 1789 was, in several ways, both the best and the worst of times.

The nation's literature and music were then rather in eclipse, for France had no equivalents of the British Romantics such as Wordsworth, Coleridge and de Quincey, or composers of the quality of Beethoven, Mozart and the Bach dynasty. Instead, science, somewhat burdened with philosophy, became the language of intellectual life. As a result, there was an explosion of innovation, with the emergence of the metric system, the first modern maps, new crops, new museums, observatories and academies, novel electoral systems, revised calendars and radical systems of education, together with advanced technologies and industries in which France for a time led the world.

The new regime soon faced attacks from its royalist neighbours, but thanks to its technical prowess was able to beat them off. The first explosive shells, improved gunpowder and high-tensile steel, production lines for weapons, the semaphore telegraph, spy planes in the form of balloons, canned foods for army and navy use and even new ways to tan soldiers' boots helped France to prevail. More peaceful areas of enquiry, from astronomy to botany, made equivalent advances.

The experts who were behind them were deeply entangled

with the nation's economy, its defences and its government. In time, some became senior military men, mayors of large cities, senators, ministers at the heads of various departments and even heads of state, while others accumulated vast fortunes. Their skills helped to mould the society that emerged after the fall of the *Ancien Régime*.

Many have become household names to their intellectual descendants. They include Franklin and Buffon, together with Ampère and Coulomb of electrical fame, the biologists Lamarck and Cuvier, the chemists Lavoisier, Fourcroy and Berthollet, the physicists Coriolis, Gay-Lussac and Carnot, and the astronomers and mathematicians Lagrange and Laplace. In their native city they are honoured with a dozen Métro stations and a rash of street names, including those of no fewer than twenty biologists in a small area around the city's botanical garden, the Jardin des Plantes (the Rue Darwin, in contrast, is a narrow alley in a distant suburb). Their discoveries, rather than their involvement in affairs of state, are what have lasted in the public mind, but almost all of them also played an important part in the events of the years that led to, and followed on from, the downfall of the monarchy.

That period could also boast of several figures remembered for their prominence in politics whose involvement in research has slipped from the pages of history. The economist Jacques Turgot, finance minister to Louis XV and intellectual ancestor of the free-marketer Adam Smith, saved France from fiscal collapse. He was among the earliest to use mathematics to study economic problems; and for him 'the truths of political and moral science are capable of the same certainty as those that form the system of physical science'. Turgot saw the difference between evaporation and vaporisation (a word he invented) for the former involves only the surface while the latter pervades the whole liquid. Long before the emergence of the kinetic theory he speculated that heat is related to the rapid movement of tiny particles and that this explains why objects expand when they are warmed up. Turgot wrote on the nature of crystals, on weights and measures, and on the causes of the *aurora borealis*, and also came up with schemes as various as water purification plants for use at sea, icebreakers on rivers, new techniques for steel manufacture, and the quarantine of infected farm animals.

Under his influence, the venerable *Collège de France* was given a spring clean. Professors of church law were replaced by others charged to investigate the laws of nature. Its chair of Syrian was transmuted into a position in experimental physics, and that in Greek and Latin into an equivalent post in mathematical aspects of the same subject. Soon, almost half the College's nineteen permanent posts were devoted to such topics. Many of those who taught, or were taught, there had illustrious careers and – as the great economist had no doubt hoped – made discoveries that helped to transform the nation's industries.

Turgot was not the only governmental figure with a talent for research. Even in historical terms he is less celebrated than is another prominent player who, before he took up despotism, spent a large portion of his life in the laboratory. The fame of Jean-Paul Marat, who stood at the other end of the ideological spectrum, now turns not on his investigations into light, heat, electricity and sexual disease, but on his central and sanguinary role in the revolt and his own violent death.

Marat had been a radical since his youth. He spent several years in exile in England, some of them in Newcastle upon Tyne, where he sold patent medicines based on the waters of Harrogate. He also found time to agitate against the rulers of his adopted land. The subtitle of his polemic *Chains of Slavery* gives a hint of his views. It was 'A work in which the clandestine and villainous attempts of Princes to ruin Liberty are pointed out, and the dreadful scenes of Despotism disclosed'. Another pamphlet warned his fellow citizens of the danger of 'enemies of the people', and promoted the cure: 'five or six hundred heads cut off would assure your repose, freedom, and happiness', a figure later revised to two hundred thousand. Once back in Paris, Marat put his theories into action and became a notorious enthusiast for the guillotine, before he himself was murdered in revenge; as Carlyle summarises his career, 'All dogs have their day; even rabid dogs.'

Marat's scientific work has left rather less of a mark. In 1775 he was awarded a medical degree by the University of St Andrews for his studies of venereal infections. The honour involved no more than the submission of a request signed by two medical men and payment of the appropriate fee but did recognise his abilities as a physician (Dr Johnson, when told of this practice, claimed that the university's habits meant that it grew 'richer by degrees'). Later, Marat published his *Essay on Gleets*, which recommended the insertion into a patient's urethra of wax tapers soaked in emollient chemicals such as marshmallow extract, turpentine, and olive oil rather than the solid probes coated with lead salts used by others, which did more harm than good (his interest in sexual disease came from 'the deplorable situation of a bosom friend'). In addition, he attacked the use of mercury to cure eye disorders because of the damage it did. Instead he recommended electric shocks to the temples together with inhalation of the essence of marshmallow, followed by copious bleeding, which at least did no harm. He was the first to notice that syphilis caused night-blindness, and to describe the black spots seen by some people after intense exercise which are, we now know, due to blockages of blood-vessels that can lead to blindness.

Soon after his return to his native city, he recorded, with some pride, that his house was often besieged by the carriages of hopeful patients. In a few years he made enough money to retire from practice and to turn full-time to research. Six years before the famous electrical experiments of Galvani on frogs, he described how the creature's leg muscles contracted when a 'strong discharge' was applied. In addition, Marat translated Newton's book on optics and earned the disapproval of the establishment for his criticisms of the great man and for his claim that the spectrum appeared not from refraction as the white light beam passed between glass and air, but from diffraction as it passed through a narrow slit before encountering the prism itself. There were, he said, just three 'primitive colours', yellow, red, and blue, rather than the seven described by Newton. He did thousands of experiments, some based on his own invention, the 'solar microscope'. They involved topics as different as the colours of soap bubbles, electricity, and the nature of combustion as revealed by magnified candle flames illuminated by the Sun. Fire was, he claimed, due to an 'igneous fluid', a companion to his 'electrical fluid', which, he thought, made plants grow. Marat also speculated on the colour of shadows when viewed on different backgrounds and even made the earliest example of a diffraction grating, which used a fine grid to break white light into its constituent hues. In addition, he was the first to note that a needle on a pivot could be deflected by an electric current through a nearby wire, and so anticipated (without realising it) the discovery thirty years later of the link between electricity and magnetism. Like his monarch, he became interested in electrical storms, and claimed to have worked out the speed of light from the time it took for a flash to travel from one cloud to another (his figure is a tenth of the modern estimate, and he could never have measured the tiny interval involved). As a hobby, he collected butterflies.

Marat's results were published in a series of well-received volumes, and on their translation into German were praised by Goethe himself. Even so, to his considerable bitterness he failed to gain entry to the intellectual elite, in part because of his heretical views, but also as a result of his fiery personality, once manifested in a fist fight with the pioneer of the hydrogen balloon, Jacques Charles, who had accused him of fakery.

His great desire was to become a member of the Royal Academy of Sciences. This had a dozen honorary adherents, most of whom were aristocrats who almost never attended its sessions, but it also boasted fifty or so fellows, many of them 'pensioners', who drew a salary (unlike their equivalents in the Royal Society in London, who paid – and still pay quite handsomely – for the privilege).

As the constitutional temperature rose, so did Marat's contempt for the Academy as a representative of the monarchy he so hated. He abused its members as 'A collection of vain men, very proud to meet twice a week to chatter – approvals for 3956 new processes ... ranging from the concoction of rouge, of hair ointments, of body plasters, of treatments for bed-bugs ... to the most advantageous forms for toupées, for wigs and for enema nozzles.' He was sure that in time the corrupt establishment would be overthrown and that his own ideas would triumph. Science was to be guided by public opinion and mathematics should be suppressed because 'a servile devotion to symbols and formulae' made large parts of the enterprise inaccessible to the people. As the disturbances grew further, he wrote that 'At last I began to breathe in the hope that I would see humanity avenged and myself installed in the place which I deserved.' When the chance at last arose, he became leader of a faction that drove many academicians to exile, imprisonment or death and destroyed the Academy itself.

Marat's demise, stabbed in his bath by Charlotte Corday in reprisal for the bloodshed he had fomented, was made heroic by the painter Jacques-Louis David, who transformed the banal murder of a tyrant into a romanticised portrait, now in the Louvre. The image does not show the repulsive symptoms of skin disease picked up while the erstwhile physicist was hiding from the police in the Paris sewers (but to Carlyle the result of a 'malady this History had rather not name'), which forced him to spend hours each day in a bath of emollient liquid.

Even royalty was swept up in the mania for discovery. Louis XV, of electrical sentry box fame, had a wide and genuine interest in the world around him, and his ill-fated grand-son Louis XVI inherited his talents. The last king is often painted as an effete fool, but at school young Louis excelled in both physics and mathematics. When the future monarch was fourteen, a mathematical work entitled *Eléments d'Algèbre* was dedicated to him by the author, his tutor. As he wrote: 'the pleasure you found in the solution of the majority of the problems it contains and the ease with which you grasped the key to their solution are new proofs of your intelligence and the excellence of your judgment', which, even given the hyperbole inevitable in an address to royalty, suggests that the young prince was no dimwit. Once enthroned, Louis XVI set up a laboratory decorated with locks that he designed and built himself and filled with geometrical instruments and telescopes, tools of his lifelong fascination with geography and astronomy.

One of the central figures in the crises of those years was not French, although he spent many years in Paris. Benjamin Franklin, who had finished his own formal education at the age of ten, became much involved in the Royal Academy. He was on the committee that interviewed Marat to investigate his suitability for membership, and offered himself in return as a subject in an experiment that showed that his 'igneous fluid' was emitted by his own bald pate. The application was denied.

In his day, Franklin was the best-known inventor in the world. He wrote the book that led to the Marly experiment and is now most famous for his observation, carried out in Philadelphia a few months later, that a kite flown during a thunderstorm would generate sparks when an earthed key was held close to its line. He did much more in the world of technology, and dabbled in philosophy too, with his poignant aphorism that 'Beer is living proof that God loves us and wants us to be happy.'

Franklin was born in Boston in 1706, but lived for fifteen years in England, in a grand house off the Strand, which he had to flee in 1775. He died less than a year after the fall of the Bastille. The official eulogy delivered to the Academy of Sciences began: 'A man is dead, and two worlds are in mourning.' Those worlds might have been America and France, or science and politics, given Benjamin Franklin's close involvement in each. Swimming flippers, a new kind of stove, bifocal lenses, a map of the Gulf Stream and the demonstration, on a pond in Clapham, that oil can still troubled waters were all benefits to mankind, as was the urinary catheter and the glass armonica, a series of milled bowls of different size and thickness that spin on an axle and with a touch on the rim with a moist finger give a sweet tone. His interests extended to the improvement of navigation, to the possibility of refrigeration with evaporating liquids, and to the demography of the new United States, where he anticipated the ideas of Thomas Malthus by thirty years. In addition, he helped to draft the Declaration of Independence, was a founder of the American Philosophical Society and the University of Pennsylvania, and became the first representative of the United States of America to France.

Benjamin Franklin worked at a period when science had entered the public arena, and when there seemed to be almost no limit to what it could do. In Paris, electricity and its sister magnetism were the talk of the salons and the public fell over itself to accept the powers of the new 'electrical fluid'. In 1774 the German physician Franz Mesmer put forth his theory of 'animal magnetism', the notion that, in a parallel to certain internal tides of the body caused by the moon, diseases could be cured with artificial tides generated by iron filings swallowed and attracted with a magnet. That uncomfortable process was soon replaced by the 'animal magnetism' possessed by a few dominant personalities, Mesmer included, and transmitted by the laying-on of hands. A commission of enquiry into his assertions was appointed, with Franklin as a member. He was accompanied by several other figures who would soon play a large part in the ideological tempest that rocked the nation. They included the chemist Antoine Lavoisier, the physician Joseph-Ignace Guillotin, and the astronomer Jean-Sylvan Bailly. Each underwent the magnetic treatment to no effect, and a blindfolded boy was unable to identify a 'magnetised' tree. The theory was nonsense and its proponent faded from view.

Franklin had long been interested in the real sparks that enliven the atmosphere. His observations led in time to the adoption of a device able to defuse the electrical, if not the ideological, storms of his day and which became an important player in a conflict between physics and politics that came to a blood-soaked end. His most famous achievement was not to debunk the non-existent powers of electricity but to protect humankind against its real threats. He came up with the idea of the lightning conductor: 'Would not these pointed Rods probably draw the Electrical Fire silently out of a Cloud before it came nigh enough to strike, and thereby secure us from that most sudden and terrible Mischief!'

As the experiment performed to entertain the King of France was the first to show, he was right; and his insight has much improved public safety. It is in addition a microcosm of the intellectual ferment of his times.

In homage to Franklin's eminence, in 1776, just after the Declaration of Independence, Turgot himself composed – with the literary flair of those capacious years – an epigram that hailed his works: '*Eripuit caelo fulmen, sceptrumque tyrannis*'; 'He snatched lightning from the heavens, and the sceptre from tyrants' (Louis XVI in contrast became annoyed by the foreigner's popularity, and commissioned a chamber pot in which his image was placed in the bottom of the bowl).

So universal are his rods today that most of us have forgotten the horrors of electrical storms, but before they were invented sparks from the heavens were a real menace. Lightning tended to target the highest point in a town or village, which in many places was the church spire. The theological implications were a serious concern, for as Thomas Aquinas had put it: 'It is a dogma of faith that demons can produce winds, storms, and rain of fire from heaven', and to see God direct his anger not at the sinners but at those who hoped to save them much discommoded the clergy. To scare off the unwelcome visitors, church bells were rung at the height of a tempest, while more rational pastors were sure that the bells interfered with the flash itself, and inscribed them with the words *Fulgura frango*: I break up thunderbolts. Such beliefs often led to disaster. Again and again, the devout came under attack, with the death of thousands. In the Italian city of Brescia the authorities had stored gunpowder in the vaults of the Church of San Nazaro. When the servant of Satan cast his fatal bolt, much of the town was destroyed and three thousand people were killed. Not until 1786 did the Parliament of Paris set forth an edict 'to make the custom of ringing church bells during storms illegal on account of the many deaths it caused to those who pull the ropes'.

Some places were for mysterious reasons spared the wrath of the heavens. In Geneva, the cathedral seemed safe, but the nearby (and lower) bell tower of the Church of St Gervais was hit again and again, in a contrast that led to much ecclesiastical controversy. In truth, the reason was simple: the cathedral's metal roof was connected to the ground by iron drainpipes, while its rival was not so favoured. Such accidental good fortune explains the many claims that safety devices had been invented long before Franklin by, among others, the builders of Solomon's Temple.

We know rather more about the uneasy atmosphere above us than did the American savant and, had he realised the risks, he might never have carried out his kite experiment. A lightning flash is an electrical spark that stretches a kilometre or more from one end to the other. Its motive power is generated as the atmosphere churns on a stormy day. Hail and raindrops accumulate charge in much the same way that someone who walks on a nylon carpet may pick up enough static – up to ten thousand volts' worth – to get a nasty shock when he touches a metal doorknob. In a thunderstorm, hot moist air shoots upwards to generate great clouds, the summits of which may be ten kilometres high. As the air rises, it cools and takes with it billions of tiny ice crystals. Its waters also freeze into larger lumps of hail, heavy enough to fall or to stay at a constant altitude. The two elements rub against each other and generate electrical energy, which in most clouds leads to a huge positive charge at the summit. Lower down there builds up an equivalent negative charge. Lightning makes a flash within the cloud when the imbalance becomes too great. A bolt strikes the ground when the energy stored in the cloud's base is sufficient, and close enough to the surface, to send down a tentative spark known as a 'leader'. That attracts further jolts, to give the forked and branched appearance beloved of artists. Other injections of charge into the atmosphere, such as the mushroom clouds of the atomic bomb and the plumes of a volcano, can also generate a series of flashes.

Sometimes a discharge travels from ground to air, from tall buildings or mountaintops as they build up their own electrical potential. They may emit an ominous hum before the spark itself. Now and again, a leader has a positive, rather than a negative, charge. That generates a 'sprite', a brief outburst of light ten kilometres across that lasts no more than a thousandth of a second and has more in common with a fluorescent light than with a true thunderbolt. As a reminder of the enormous gaps that remain in our knowledge, nobody yet understands quite how charge is transferred between the cloud's small ice crystals and its hail.

Storm clouds appear more often in places with lots of dust, around which water droplets can form, so that in tropical oceans thunder is rarely heard. Over Europe, in contrast, such particles are abundant, and with air pollution have become more so. The Industrial Revolution was in its infancy in the late eighteenth century, and today's smokestacks and diesel fumes pump out billions of particles. Thunderstorms in addition have become more frequent over modern cities because of the heat they generate and the atmospheric disturbance caused by tall office blocks. France now suffers more flashes than Franklin ever saw and will see even more with the increases in humidity and temperature that come with climate change.

We live on a planet tormented by electricity, with fifty strikes a second – five million a day – across the globe. No more than one ground hit in a hundred thousand kills someone; a proportion much smaller than before the invention of Franklin's device but still the cause of death for thousands each year (and men are at several times more risk than are women, not because they attract the attentions of Beelzebub, but because they are more often at work, or at pleasure, outdoors).

Franklin's discovery that lives could be saved with an earthed piece of metal was at once welcomed by freethinkers, to such a degree that for a time umbrellas and hats protected by his *paratonnèrres* became popular in Paris. His invention was in contrast rejected by most believers, who fulminated against attempts to interfere with God's wrath and to 'control the artillery of Heaven' (they included the priests of Brescia, who knew of the heretical apparatus but refused to erect it on their steeple until their flock had paid a terrible price for their stupidity).

Other disputes of the time had a more rational basis. Which was better, a pointed conductor, or one with a rounded end? Franklin preferred them 'made sharp as a Needle and gilt to prevent Rusting' but others disagreed. The quarrel continued for years, and was at times as embittered as that about the correct way to open a boiled egg that sparked off the war between the Big-Endians and the Little-Endians in *Gulliver's Travels*. In North America, the use of one or the other was interpreted as a statement in favour of the rebels or of the Crown. George III, to advertise his displeasure at the colonial revolt, had the sharpened structures on Buckingham Palace replaced with rounded versions, and put pressure on the Royal Society to give its imprimatur to the latter. The president replied that 'I will always do my best to fulfil the wishes of His Majesty, but I am able to change neither the laws of nature nor the effects of its forces.'

The electrical split across the Atlantic continued long after the constitutional climate had cooled, for the British felt that a ball welded to the tip of the metal shaft improved the efficiency of the conductor, while the Americans stuck to Franklin's sharp points. In fact, the mother country was probably right. As a leader sparks down from the skies towards its target, it generates a 'streamer', a torrent of charge that flows up from the rod. When it meets its partner, it completes the circuit. A rounded tip with a diameter of about a centimetre can generate a longer streamer than one that emerges from a sharp point, and hence makes the contact a moment earlier. That claim is disputed by some, while other attempts to improve the effectiveness of such devices, for example by placing radioactive material in the tip, have been abandoned.

Franklin believed that his invention worked because it drained storm clouds of their electrical charge. There he was wrong, for the best any system can do is to direct a tiny portion of their power direct to Earth before it can do too much damage. Because of the massive energy of a strike, no *paratonnèrre* can provide complete protection, for the current may take additional routes to the ground to set fires, blow walls apart, and kill. Ships are at risk, and the replacement of metal yacht hulls with non-conductive fibreglass has increased the danger. A vessel on a lake is more liable to suffer damage than is one on a salty and conductive sea. There have been various attempts to ward off strikes with rocket-powered wires fired into the clouds, but a typical thunderhead can restore the charge so lost within a few seconds.

Some thirty years ago, the idea that the threat could be banished altogether found new life. Across the Atlantic, a new generation of 'lightning elimination' systems was touted as a cure for the problem in airports, radio towers and skyscrapers. They were based on multiple points arranged like an upside-down umbrella, and were in fact similar to a device sketched by Marat himself in his book on electricity. Their promoters went so far as to attempt to change the century-old insurance rules of the United States to insist that all commercial structures be protected by their invention. Had they succeeded, they would have made millions, but in truth their product works no better than that developed two hundred years ago.

The most bitter disagreement about Franklin's invention was based not on theological fantasy or on furtive attempts to manipulate the laws of physics, but on the widespread belief that it was not a shield against electrical hazards but instead attracted them from far away. Those who lived near a rod would hence face disaster. A few saw even greater dangers. The Reverend Thomas Prince of Boston blamed 'the points invented by the sagacious Mr Franklin' for an earthquake that rocked much of North America in 1755: 'In Boston more are erected than anywhere else in New England, and Boston seems to be more dreadfully shaken. O! There is no getting out of the mighty hand of God!'

In 1780, in the small northern French town of Saint-Omer, a retired lawyer and amateur inventor named Charles Dominique de Vissery de Bois-Valé erected one of Franklin's gadgets on the highest point of his house. As if to tempt fate, it was tipped with a sword perched on a globe decorated with an image of fiery rays. The sword was earthed by a tin tube that crossed the wall of a nearby property and terminated in a chain suspended in a deep well. Vissery's aim was, he insisted, to 'serve humanity and the State' and he had already shown his public beneficence with his invention of an underwater breathing apparatus. Whatever motives lay behind the fiery sword, his aged female neighbour (an 'old grumbler') petitioned local aldermen against it on the grounds that the 'machine would attract thunder from all over the city'. They summoned bailiffs to remove the contraption.

The defendant attempted a compromise and replaced the sword with a shorter weapon. That did not pacify his neighbour, or the mob that by then surrounded his house. The city took Vissery to court, and a three-year legal battle began. At last the case arrived at the Superior Provincial Council in Arras, the local court of appeal.

Vissery's main defender, a well-known advocate called Antoine-Joseph Buissart, was chosen because he himself had an interest in technology and had invented an apparatus to measure atmospheric moisture (he was known as 'the Barometer' as a result). The aldermen felt that the dangers of Vissery's rod were so obvious that it should be removed without further ado. The defendant's counsel claimed instead that the law should defer to the judgment of the *philosophes*, and produced an eighty-six-page brief that depended on their technical arguments to make the case.

The affair became enmeshed in intense discussions about the nature of electrical storms. Each side was supported by its own theoreticians, many among them members of the Academy of Sciences in Paris, where the action in Arras had become a matter of great interest not just to physicists but to the educated public as a whole. The whole business was soon bogged down in arcane speculations, the question of round or pointed rods included. The specialists consulted included Nicolas de Condorcet, then Secretary of the Royal Academy, and Jean-Paul Marat, well respected for his work on the 'electrical fluid'. Some were convinced that rods could protect against electrical storms, but others argued that they would attract them, and might do the same not just for earthquakes but for volcanoes as well, a claim that did not quieten the concerns of the burghers of Saint-Omer. The lawsuit ground on and seemed doomed to end in stalemate.

Buissart had, however, hired a youthful assistant to argue his defendant's cause, and the new advocate's radical contribution won the day. The young counsel was himself interested in scientific matters; one of his fellow pupils at school remembered him – in the tradition of many aspirants to that profession – as 'a melancholy boy ... I do not remember ever having seen him laugh'. As an adult, too, he was a less than attractive figure: 'his complexion was livid and bilious, his eyes dull ... he always wore green-tinted glasses'. His health was never good; he had jaundice and constant nosebleeds ('he covered his pillow with fresh blood each night'), while his mouth and eyes twitched without cease, all perhaps the symptoms of a severe allergy. The Saint-Omer dispute was his first major case. It led to a clash between the law and scientific speculation that in the end caused the deaths of some of the greatest minds of the age, and led to his own execution. His name was Maximilien Robespierre.

Robespierre – Carlyle's 'sea-green incorruptible' – took a novel and more forensic view of what lay behind the dispute, for he insisted that the law of the land must take account of the practical observations of sensible men and need not concern itself with obscure and contradictory theories about physics, politics, justice or any other topic. Whatever philosophers might argue on one side or the other, nobody could point to a case in which a strike on a *paratonnère* had caused any damage (or, for that matter, had done any good), or could show that places with such structures were more, or less, at risk than those without. The Saint-Omer case was not a banal disagreement between neighbours, but touched on the powers of the judiciary when faced with technical disputes and, indeed, on the conflict between haughty speculation and simple common sense. What, in the fixed opinion of some – but not all – *philosophes*, ought to be the truth must always defer to the evidence of the eyes. Facts were facts and theories were best left to those who could be bothered with them. The complainant's case hence had no merit.

The brutal simplicity of Robespierre's logic, together with his oratorical powers, won the day. The lawsuit against Vissery was dismissed, although the defendant had, to his annoyance, to pay the costs. In the event, the unfortunate litigant died soon after the Arras verdict, and the next occupier of his house removed the rod.

Robespierre soon published his speech for the defence, in which he claimed that 'the whole of Europe has its eyes on this case', and did not fail to send a copy to Benjamin Franklin, who he hailed in a servile note as 'the most famous man of science in the universe'. The young advocate was, on the merits of his performance, elected to the Academy of Arras, the first step in a career in which triumph was succeeded by hubris and then by disaster when, a decade later, Robespierre became a leading member of the Jacobins, the radical group that had seized control of the National Convention, the governing body of the Revolution.

Many of those involved in the disturbances of 1789 saw the philosophical ideas earlier promoted by Rousseau (a keen botanist) and Voltaire (an enthusiast for the work of Newton) as the main motive force behind its stirring events. Others placed more importance on technology. John Adams, the second President of the United States, went so far as to say that 'It is universally believed in France that the electric wand has accomplished all this revolution.'

Opponents, too, were persuaded that scientists had caused the disaster. The royalist Antoine Rivarol blamed the bloodshed on that profession, whose members occupied 'the savage heart of society'. Most of all, he disapproved of chemistry: 'Its disciples have everywhere employed solvents and decomposition [to obtain] ... the reconstruction of all by revolt against all.' They would 'dissect living men to better understand them'. Edmund Burke, who in his *Reflections on the Revolution in France*, published just a year after the event, predicted the Reign of Terror, the death of Louis XVI, and the probable return of an emperor, agreed. The disorder was due to the insensibility of the 'geometricians and the chemists', who are 'worse than indifferent about those feelings and habitudes which are the support of the moral world ... These philosophers consider men in their experiments no more than they do mice in an air pump ... they would sacrifice the whole human race to the slightest of their experiments.' Scientists were not just involved in the outrage, they were to blame for it.

Robespierre, too, came to hate such people, but for quite different reasons. In spite of the large part they had played in the first days of the great reformation, several academicians had begun to obstruct his bloody attempts to construct an absolutist state. Robespierre made his views clear: 'No race of men is more dangerous to liberty, more an enemy to equality, than the aristocrats of intelligence, whose reputations stand alone and exert an influence partial, dangerous, and contrary to the unity which should rule over everyone.' His satraps used that argument and the logic of the Saint-Omer case to bolster their power. So-called 'experts' with their vague ideas should be dismissed not just from the legal system but from public life. The common sense of the average citizen should rule instead. Soon Robespierre insisted that every intellectual forum be destroyed: 'All academies and literary societies established or endowed by the nation are eliminated ... What do the diverse hypotheses by which certain *philosophes* explain the phenomena of nature matter to legislators?' The radical painter David, too, claimed that such places were 'the last refuge of all aristocracies'. They, together with the nation's universities, were closed down.

After the dissolution of the Royal Academy of Sciences the Jacobins began to attack its individual members. Robespierre had once argued against the death penalty, but he soon changed his mind. The Reign of Terror began ('Legislators, place Terror on the order of the day! ... The blade of the law should hover over all the guilty'). As the months grew bloodier, his views moved closer to those of Marat, as he said: 'The revolutionary government owes to the good citizen all the protection of the nation; it owes nothing to the Enemies of the People but death.' Robespierre joined the twelve-strong Committee of Public Safety, which was in effect the new regime's judge, jury and executioner, a tribunal of instant condemnation, with no need for witnesses or defence. At the height of the Terror, in June 1794, the Paris guillotine was busy for six hours a day, and two thousand people were beheaded in three weeks; in Carlyle's sonorous words: 'The clanking of its huge axe, rising and falling there, in horrid systole-diastole, is portion of the whole enormous Life-movement and pulsation of the Sansculottic System!' As was almost inevitable, the lawyer himself became a victim. His arrest was ordered, and to avoid humiliation he attempted suicide with a pistol, but did no more than shatter his own face. On 28 July 1794, Robespierre was guillotined, with a last and frightful scream when the executioner tore off the bandage that supported his damaged jaw.

Eight weeks earlier, perhaps the greatest French scientist of all had met a similar fate. Antoine Lavoisier was the epitome of that era's marriage of technology and politics. A nobleman with the sense of entitlement of his class, he was much involved in public affairs and did his best to use his knowledge to improve the lot of the hungry masses. A close friend of Benjamin Franklin, he was the discoverer or co-discoverer of oxygen, nitrogen and hydrogen, a pioneer in the study of metabolism, and a contributor to the first geological map of France. In his spare time he was active in the development of the metric system and in the improvement of military explosives.

Lavoisier had a fierce schedule of work. He rose at five and worked in his laboratory until nine. From then until seven in the evening he occupied himself with affairs of state, and returned to his laboratory until ten. Saturdays were what his widow later described as her husband's 'blissful day' when he worked from morning to night with groups of students and colleagues. He spent a good portion of his own considerable wealth on his laboratory and commissioned the construction of many new instruments, including a balance accurate to one part in four hundred thousand.

Antoine Lavoisier is remembered most of all as the founder of modern chemistry. He dismissed the ethereal notions of the alchemists in much the same way as Enlightenment thinkers had rejected the divine right of kings. Such views, he felt, had kept mankind in chains from which he must be released. To his predecessors, what we now call zinc oxide was 'philosophic wool', while calcium acetate was 'shrimp eyes salt', terms designed to confuse. Their textbooks were just as hard to decipher: 'The grey wolf devours the King, after which it is burned on a pyre, consuming the wolf and restoring the King to life' (gold is extracted by skimming off salts of lesser metals generated by antimony sulphide, the 'grey wolf', and roasting the mixture until just gold remains). Lavoisier quashed all that and coined many of the words used by today's chemists, from sulphuric acid to oxygen and to the French term for nitrogen, 'azote' (English-speakers hated this incursion of a foreign tongue and Thomas Jefferson described the new nomenclature as 'premature, insufficient, and false').

He saw order in what had been confusion, and made the first logical arrangement of the elements with his 'Table of Simple Substances', materials that could not be broken down into smaller units by chemical means. They ranged from oxygen to sulphur and from mercury to gold. Every object around us is based on a series of elements ('the last point which analysis can reach'), which – unlike mixtures such as air or water – cannot themselves be further divided. He identified thirty-three candidates, nitrogen among them. They included silver, arsenic, cobalt, copper, lead, magnesium, silicon and more.

The great chemist noted also that the same element could exist in different forms. He built a huge burning glass with two large lenses, which was situated outside the Louvre, close to a popular promenade, and placed a diamond at the focal point. To the alarm of the fashionable ladies who looked on, experiments on a sunny summer's day made the diamonds disappear; the carbon had combined with oxygen to make carbon dioxide, which blew away. When the stones were sealed away from the air before they were heated, they remained untouched.

Master chemist as he was, Lavoisier hated the vague notions of earlier times. For him, they belonged in the realm of mysticism. His particular target was 'phlogiston', a numinous essence that was supposed to pervade all combustible materials and was responsible for fire and for the transmutation of one substance into another. It was, he showed, as much of a myth as was animal magnetism. In the tradition of Robespierre, who himself had insisted on the primacy of fact over speculation when it came to the law, he wrote that the supposed essence was 'a veritable Proteus that changes its form every instant', and that chemistry needed a stricter logic that would allow its practitioners 'to distinguish what is fact and observation from what is system and hypothesis'. Even so, Lavoisier made the eccentric decision to add light and heat, or 'caloric', to his list of elements, perhaps the wraith of phlogiston, which proved harder to exorcise than he was prepared to admit.

Across the Channel, Joseph Priestley had already isolated oxygen and carbon dioxide, but the Englishman argued that air was not a compound but an element in its own right, and that his experiments had shown that by losing some mysterious essence, it could produce new elements. He saw a regular gradation from dephlogisticated air (in fact oxygen), through common air and phlogisticated air (what we now call nitrogen, plus a little carbon dioxide) down to nitrous air (nitric oxide: one nitrogen combined with a single oxygen) and to dephlogisticated nitrous air (which is in modern terms nitrous oxide, two nitrogens and an oxygen, otherwise known as laughing gas). His French equivalent demolished that idea with a simple experiment in which he set fire to a lump of phosphorus inside a sealed vessel. The standard view was that when an object burned, it released phlogiston, which meant that the metal should have lost weight, but in fact the opposite was true, for the white 'calx' or oxide that emerged from the flask was heavier than the original object, while the volume of air decreased by around a fifth. The experiment was repeated with mercury, with the same result. Even better, when the mercuric calx was exposed to much higher temperatures, liquid mercury re-emerged and oxygen gas was driven off. Air was hence not one of the alchemists' four fundamental elements, a partner to earth, water and fire, but was a mixture of several components. Oxygen, Lavoisier had proved, was an element that could combine with others, in a process that could in some circumstances be reversed. Soon the whole of chemistry began to fall into place.

Newton had claimed that he saw further because he stood on the shoulders of giants. His French descendants of a century and a half later often trod on illustrious toes instead, as they stole their rivals' ideas, blocked their appointments, or obstructed the publication of their results (and there not much has changed). Lavoisier was jealous of his reputation and attempted to lay claim to the discovery of oxygen itself. He fell into bitter arguments about priority with Priestley, who had visited his fellow experimenter in Paris and had told him about his own observations. In fact a Swedish chemist had isolated what he called 'fire air' even earlier, but with studied rudeness Lavoisier failed to respond to a letter in which the Swede pointed this out; as he said to a colleague who reproached him for his behaviour: 'My friend, you know that those who start the hare do not always catch it.'

His experiments continued and Lavoisier was among the first to show that water is a compound of oxygen and hydrogen. His *Traité élémentaire de Chimie*, published in the year of the fall of the Bastille, synthesised his own results and those of his fellows in a new and rational world of physical order, just as social disorder broke out around him.

Antoine Lavoisier was an embodiment of Enlightenment philosophy in a context much wider than that of chemistry. To the chemists, physicists, astronomers and biologists of his era, nothing could be more valuable to government than their own profession. Its ideas should inform every affair of state. Many academicians saw it as their civic duty to become involved. Some among them – and a few even in Britain, for Joseph Priestley had to flee to the United States when he greeted the incidents across the Channel as an omen of the Second Coming of Christ – were drawn into the civic turmoil. In France, the years after 1789 began with a collaboration of *philosophes* and *politiques* but ended in a bloody conflict between them that put paid to the great chemist himself.

Like many of his fellows, Lavoisier was affluent enough to pay for his own research. The money came from the French peasantry through his involvement in a tax system based on essential goods such as tobacco and salt, rather than on personal wealth. From it he drew a large income. The institution that collected the cash signed contracts with the state to produce a certain flow of tax. Its members kept any excess for themselves (in Adam Smith's words, 'Those who consider the blood of the people as nothing in comparison with the revenue of a prince may perhaps approve of this method of levying taxes'). The iniquities of the system were a major impetus behind the cataclysm to come. Barriers were built around cities, those who adulterated tobacco were pursued, and the grain market was rigged to maximise what speculators could squeeze out. Marat, embittered as he was, used Lavoisier's involvement in such affairs to take revenge on one of the many who had denied him his rightful honours. As he wrote of the founder of modern chemistry: 'I denounce to you the Coryphaeus of the charlatans ... and the greatest schemer of our times. If you ask me what he has done to be so extolled, I shall reply that he has procured himself a salary of a hundred thousand livres, that he formed the project of turning Paris into a vast prison, and that he changed the name of acid to oxygen ... These are his qualificants for immortality. Proud of these high achievements, he now sleeps upon his laurels.' A fellow extremist joined in: 'Lavoisier became a chemist; he would have become an alchemist if he had followed only his inextinguishable thirst for gold. But he and his associates have found surer means to slake that thirst through the excessive moistening of tobacco and the speculative and monopolistic purchase of grains. France owes them eight or ten famines.'

The guilty party was hauled before the court. Its verdict is remembered for the supposed response of the presiding judge to calls for mercy from those who saw the condemned man as a major intellectual figure: '*La République n'a pas besoin de savants.*' The translation of the term *savant* is not simple in modern context, but given the extraordinary talents of Lavoisier and his colleagues, many of whom would today merit Nobel Prizes, the appropriate twenty-first-century rendition seems to me 'The Republic has no need for geniuses.'

On the day before his execution on 8 May 1794, Lavoisier wrote his last letter, to his cousin: 'I trust that my passing will be remembered with some regret and perhaps some honour. What more could I ask for? I will probably be spared the troubles of old age by the events in which I find myself embroiled. My only regret is that I have not done more for my family ... Evidently it is true that to live according to the highest standards of society, to render important services to one's country, and to devote one's life to the advancement of the arts and human knowledge is not enough to preserve one from evil consequences and dying like a criminal!' Within hours, the fifty-year-old chemist and more than two dozen fellow tax farmers were guillotined. The job took little more than thirty minutes. Their bodies were stacked on a wagon, their heads gathered in a wicker basket and the whole lot thrown into a common grave. The radical journal *L'Orateur du Peuple* gloried in their fate: 'The blood which inundated the square reminds us of the couches of purple upon which in earlier times they slept in languor.' A year or so later, the blood of the judge gushed forth in the same place.

His phrase gives this work a title, but – as so often in history – its accuracy is contested. Some claim that the quotation was invented by enemies of the Jacobins to blacken their reputation, while others insist that the words are a true reflection of the trial itself even if no written record survives. We will never know who is right, but the argument is a reminder that politics is a dirtier business than is chemistry. Lavoisier and many of his fellows met their end because of their involvement in that alien and unsavoury trade, but their discoveries in biology, geology, physics, astronomy and more have become the foundations of today's science. This book tries to show how.

CHAPTER I

THE WALL OF THE
FARMERS-GENERAL

Hope deferred maketh the heart sick.

THOMAS CARLYLE, *The French Revolution*

Jean-Sylvain Bailly, first mayor of revolutionary Paris,
distracted by astronomy

In the Place de Stalingrad stands a three-storey circular edifice fronted by an elegant portico. Within its walls is an expensive restaurant called *La Rotonde*. The structure was built not to feed the rich, but to starve the poor; to collect taxes levied on food and other necessities from the workers of Paris. The *octroi* was an impost payable on all goods that entered the capital. Its headquarters was in the Barrière de la Villette, as the rotunda was first known, part of a wall built in 1788 by the Farmers-General, the tax-gathering arm of the French state. It was the last of seven successive *enceintes* to surround the city since Gaulish times. The barricade, three metres tall and twenty-four kilometres long, was pierced by sixty-one toll gates designed in the classical manner. Through them, in principle at least, all food, fuel, tobacco and other goods had to pass and to pay. The structure was less than popular and became the target of the epigram that '*Le mur murant Paris rend Paris murmurant.*'

The peasantry had been promised tax reform for years, but in spite of flickers of interest by the authorities, it never appeared. For Paris, always on the edge of disaffection, the wall was the last straw. On the eve of the attack on the Bastille an enraged mob stormed its gates and made breaches in the barrier. The toll itself was abolished within a few months, leaving only a nominal levy on entrants to the city to pay for its hospitals and poorhouses. With the return of the monarchy, the penalties were restored and became one of the targets of the many riots that shook Paris in the first half of the nineteenth century. An *octroi* lasted in one form or another until 1943 but the wall itself was demolished as part of the improvements to the city made by Baron Haussmann in the 1860s, and just four gates (La Villette included) survive. Its course is now marked by a ring of traffic-choked boulevards on either side of the river and, below its foundations, by two Métro lines.

The gigantic obstacle was the idea of no less a figure than Antoine Lavoisier. At the age of eleven, he had inherited the equivalent in modern terms of a million pounds sterling or more, and over a decade this sum much increased. In his twenty-fourth year, with the aid of a large loan, he spent twenty times as much in the purchase of a share in the tax farm, France's system of collection of government revenues. The *Fermiers Généraux* dated back to 1681, and their organisation was accompanied by a sister group, the *Régie Générale* (who were paid fixed salaries to collect dues rather than speculating against the state by creaming off profits from any surplus over the agreed return). Its investors made fortunes, while many of those forced to stump up for its demands were driven into penury. The system led to bitter disagreements between rulers and ruled, and helped to spark off the great revolt. Whatever the consequences, the founder of chemistry must have felt that he had made a wise decision when he became a shareholder, for his investment provided an annual income of, in modern terms, three million pounds for the rest of his somewhat truncated life. He spent much of it on his research.

His first involvement was as a member of the tobacco commission in the Marne, Champagne and the Ardennes. Tobacco duty was a major earner, but was – like other parts of the system – under constant attack from fraud. The growers sold snuff on the sly, or adulterated the product with wood ash (which was a mistake, for the new member tested it with acids and looked for the bubbles of gas that then appeared). As his interests in the tax farm grew, he began to realise that not just the duty on tobacco was a victim of false pretences. Sixty thousand people were involved in smuggling salt, essential for food preservation in the days before refrigerators, and even more in other frauds that surrounded the convoluted revenue system.

At that time, France was, as it remains, intensely centralised, with the capital as large, and as rich, as the nation's next six cities combined. Lavoisier estimated that a fifth of the commodities that should have paid a levy entered Paris illegitimately, sometimes with the simple trick of a delivery of material to a house with the front door outside the old and leaky official cordon, and its removal from a back door within the chargeable area (another approach was to leave the city in one's coach accompanied by the hollow image of a footman, and to come back home with the fake servant stuffed full of valuable goods). So outraged were the *Fermiers* about such frauds that they were happy to agree that an impregnable barrier was needed. The wall was born.

Their system of tax collection reaches back to the Romans, and has had a discreet rebirth today. When a new territory was conquered by the legions, it was milked of its wealth not by the state itself, but by *publicani* (the 'publicans' expelled by Jesus from the temple). Competitors bid for the right to collect the cash and made promises about the amount they would pay to the treasury. Any excess went straight into their pockets and any deficiency had to be made up from their own funds (needless to say, when those who tilled the fiscal soil had been too optimistic, means were found to ensure that they did not lose too much, if any, of their investment). Much the same happened two millennia later, when in the 1890s the United States Treasury gave a contract to a John D. Sanborn to collect a large sum of duty owed by distillers and railroad companies in return for a bonus of half of what he obtained. As could have been predicted, fraud again raised its head and, in the debate that led to this practice being outlawed, the representative from Kentucky described such schemes as 'reeking and buoyant with corruption'. The phrase has a perfect fit with the actions of both the *Fermiers Généraux* and today's Private Finance Initiatives, railway and postal sell-offs, bank bailouts and the like, in all of which speculators make grotesque profits from the public at minimal risk, as they are almost always rescued by the state if their gamble goes wrong.

The largest and most stringent tax farm in history was that of France in the final decades of the *Ancien Régime*. Revenue depended on a complex and much-avoided patchwork of laws. Goods were smuggled between high- and low-tariff regions, the poor hid from the officials, and the richest were in any case asked to pay trivial amounts. As the years went by, elements of rationality crept in and more cash flowed towards the seat of government, but most of it was wasted on useful pastimes such as the new Palace of Versailles and on wars against the Spaniards and the Dutch.

However the money was spent, the burden bore far more upon the peasantry than on aristocrats, clergy and military men (and even professors were sometimes exempt). In time, a few anomalies were removed, but for most people there remained an almost opaque set of impositions that made great holes in their tiny incomes. The *gabelle* (the duty on salt) was the largest source of cash, and so keen on it were the *Fermiers* that their officials poisoned the salt used in tanning and the like, which meant that many peasants paid for their poverty with their lives. Other penalties included the *taille* (a property levy), the *taillon* (a military levy), the *capitation* (a poll tax), the *vingtième* (income tax), the *tabac* (tobacco), the *aides* (a forfeit based on the consumption of wine, wood, paper, soap and the like), the *traites* (customs duties), the *timbres* (stamp duty on legal documents), the *dime* (paid by property owners to the Church) and the *entrée* or *octroi* (imposts on goods as they entered Paris and other cities). Other levies were less direct; thus, the *corvée* obliged peasants to work unpaid for several days each year to mend local roads, while in some places special burdens were placed upon Jews and other groups.

The Farmers-General each entered into a contract with the state for a renewable period of six years. The forty principal players employed some twenty-five thousand agents throughout France, most of whom were hired (in spite of their own widespread corruption) to enforce the rules. They imprisoned several thousand people a year, banished plenty of others to forcible service in the armed forces or to the galleys, and flogged women and hanged a respectable number of men to encourage the populace to pay up. The institution was the nation's second largest employer after the army and collected half its income. *Fermiers* were, needless to say, chosen with reference to their wealth, their loyalty, and their place in public life rather than by merit. In a further presage of the trickeries of today, their interests were in their own revenues rather than in the general good. Bureaucracy wasted vast sums, while the profits skimmed off by those in charge added to the already painful levels of taxation paid by those at the bottom of the financial heap.

Whole towns rose up against the representatives of the state, but the revolts were quashed with whatever brutality was necessary. The system was a microcosm of the injustices that in the end led to the collapse of the old regime. French taxes weighed far harder on income, tiny as it often was, than on property, vast as it might be. Like today's Value Added Tax, a great deal was based on the consumption of essential goods rather than on the ownership of castles so that the poor suffered most.

In 1789, France was the largest country in Europe, with around twenty-seven million inhabitants. Six out of every seven lived by farming, the great majority as tenants or share-croppers. Their lives were difficult indeed, and the English novelist Tobias Smollett, who had visited two decades earlier, described the people of the countryside as 'diminutive, meagre, withered, dirty, and half naked'. For them, the Church, the aristocracy and the tax collectors were omnipresent and all-powerful. Their situation was dire. The agriculturalist Arthur Young, who travelled to France just before the fall of the Bastille, wrote: 'The country has a savage aspect: husbandry is not much more advanced than among the Hurons.' He blamed 'a minute and vicious division of the soil' that drove the peasantry into poverty. A peasant woman who at first he took to be sixty or seventy, so bent and wrinkled was she, was in truth no more than twenty-eight.

At the top of the tree were the nobility, some four hundred thousand in all. They alone could attain high Church rank, become ambassadors, or command a regiment. Some were poor and Smollett tells the tale of one such hovel-dweller, who asked his son: '*Chevalier, as-tu donné a manger aux cochons?*' Even so, many attained mighty wealth, as the noble mansions scattered across France still remind us. So important were they to the nation's health that they were exempt from the property tax and from much of the *vingtième* and the *capitation*, and were also allowed to take advantage of their ancient and valuable monopolies in the production of flour and wine. The *noblesse d'épée* – the nobles of the sword – descended from those who had followed the country's ancient monarchs. More numerous, and more vulgar, were the *noblesse de robe*, whose titles were recent (and quite often bought for a considerable premium) and who paid a little more to the authorities. The clergy, too, were allowed to pay a reduced penalty based on an annual lump sum from Church to state.

As the eighteenth century wore on, the financial problems became more acute. In an extension of the endless quarrel with England about transatlantic possessions, the nation became involved in the American War of Independence. The new Congress asked France for uniforms and arms for fifty thousand men. France complied and itself declared war on the British in 1778. The government accumulated huge debts as a result. The revenue system did not help, for in Britain at that time the authorities managed to claw back almost a third of gross domestic product as taxes, while those across the Channel managed less than half that.

France still laboured under the regime established decades earlier by Louis XIV's economic adviser, Jean-Baptiste Colbert. He had set up a system of central control that stifled innovation and led to a huge bureaucracy. The economist and part-time physicist Jacques Turgot began to argue instead that France's financial health did not depend on the ability of the excise system to milk cash from the populace. In the end, what really mattered was how productive the country could be (which in his day meant in the main how much food it was able to grow). As a result, the economy rested on the backs of the peasants. However – as he saw – under the existing rules they could never better their lot, for so much of their income was confiscated that many had too little capital even to enclose their fields. If farm workers and others were allowed to keep more of the fruits of their toil, they would have more incentive to improve their own efficiency and, as an incidental, that of France as a whole. High taxes, forced labour, exclusive guilds and barriers to trade interfered with this and should be done away with.

Turgot was appointed financial regulator of the region of Limoges, and set out to improve the area's economy. Under the direction of Louis XV, the 'Baker King', the trade in grain had been ruled by the police rather than the market, with strict regulations that ensured that Paris, with its excitable inhabitants, should always have supplies whatever the shortages elsewhere. With one stroke Turgot abolished such controls. He also began to reduce the liabilities faced by the poor and increase those of the rich with a property tax. The inefficient system in which peasants were forced to work on the roads was replaced by one that used paid contractors, a move urgently needed across the whole nation, for the transport system was so useless that in terms of the time to travel from Calais to Perpignan, or from Strasbourg to Brest, France was three weeks long and three weeks wide. Within months of Turgot's reforms, his own domain began to right itself. Soon he was appointed as Minister of Finance and Public Works to the whole country, and began to deal with the budgetary crisis.

In spite of some successes, Turgot became more and more unpopular among the affluent as his new taxes began to bite and because of his objections to the American war. The costs of that 'would be so enormous that they would postpone, perhaps forever, any attempt at necessary reform . . . the fate of the monarch might hinge on this fateful decision'. Within a couple of years he was dismissed and returned to his twin hobbies of physics and astronomy, before falling victim to gout.

His successor was a Swiss-born Protestant, Jacques Necker. Soon after his arrival, Necker presented a faked set of accounts to the monarch. A national debt of forty-six million *livres* was disguised as a surplus of ten million. That welcome news meant that he could arrange more loans and cut down the need for revenue, but in fact his dishonesty pushed the economy further towards disaster, and on the eve of the Revolution, half the national income was soaked up by the payment of interest. Nature did not help. In July 1788, an enormous hailstorm destroyed vines and other crops across France. It was followed by a long drought and a winter with temperatures below zero for the whole of December and January; a record that has never since been broken. It was so cold that wolves were seen in the plains of the Languedoc. The price of bread doubled, and in Paris reached a high point in July 1789, when a day's supply took almost nine tenths of the wages of an average worker. Violence broke out across the country as the long-suffering peasants, so long fobbed off with false promises, made their grievances felt.

All this, combined with the spread of the Enlightenment idea of progress, made the constitution rock, and in the end fall. The half-hearted attempts by Louis XVI to remedy his nation's fiscal problems had failed because the local *parlements* of France (regional councils more akin to appeal courts than to parliaments proper) blocked any reform that threatened their power. In 1787, new provincial assemblies were established, with Lavoisier a prominent member of the body elected by Orléans. So grave was the financial situation that later in the same year the king summoned the Assembly of Notables – an *ad hoc* group of grandees, from bishops to judges and princes to plutocrats – to deal with the situation, but they too were more concerned with their own revenues than with the country's problems. The ball was then passed to the Estates-General, another and rather more democratic advisory body to the monarch. It had not met since 1614, but so acute was the crisis that in the first months of 1789 its members were summoned to Paris.

The assemblage reflected the imbalance of both the tax system and of French civic affairs as a whole. It consisted of the First Estate (the clergy), the Second (the nobles), and the Third (everyone else; or, at least, every employed male).

The Catholic Church had ten thousand priests and bishops, the nobility fewer than half a million members, while the commoners and peasants were a mass of many millions. In a distorted form of democracy, each Estate had long been given an equal vote on matters under discussion, which meant that the clergy and the nobles could always defeat a proposal that favoured the common people (Lavoisier saw strengths in the system: 'the rank, the property, the enlightenment of the first two orders should no doubt be counted').

Elections were held at the body's emergency congress, with the Third Estate generously given a double portion of seats. From the start, scientists played a prominent part, with three members of the Royal Academy elected to the Estates-General, all as delegates from Paris, while three more (Lavoisier included) were named as alternates. The new body saw the need for reform. Most of its participants were happy to accept the monarchy in principle, but wanted a limit on its powers, an attack on corruption and the iniquities of tax, and a free press. Without much enthusiasm, Louis agreed to receive the new body, the Third Estate last of all, but in the Hall of Mirrors at Versailles he could bring himself to speak to only one aged member of that group, to whom he said a reluctant '*Bonjour*.' Annoyed by such snubs, and by a continued lack of real progress the representatives of the general public began to assert themselves. After a fractious debate, they demanded that members of the other two sections should join them, and although not many did, those who gathered reinvented themselves as an *Assemblée Nationale* and, in effect, attempted to form a government.

The powers-that-be then locked out that recalcitrant assemblage from a session of the Estates-General. At the suggestion of Dr Joseph Guillotin (a deputy from Paris), the discontented deputies moved into an adjacent tennis court, the Jeu de Paume. There they elected the astronomer Jean-Sylvain Bailly, a Parisian member, as their leader, swore an oath of fealty to their new administration and demanded a revised constitution. The monarchy was, for the first time, under real threat.

The governing body presented a series of documents, the *Cahiers de Doléances*, to the King that pointed at a variety of problems, with the chemist Antoine Fourcroy among those involved in their composition. More than six hundred such papers were submitted, from all classes and creeds. Louis accepted some of their suggestions, but not enough to satisfy either the National Assembly or the unhappy peasantry. Unrest grew in the streets and across the countryside until, on 13 July 1789, the wall of the Farmers-General was attacked and in part destroyed. That convulsion was followed by the celebrated affair at the Bastille on the following day, when the prison was stormed by a mob described in *A Tale of Two Cities* as a 'remorseless sea of turbulently swaying shapes, voices of vengeance, and faces hardened in the furnaces of suffering until the touch of pity could make no mark on them'.

In fact the overthrow of that edifice – a gloomy fortress of the fourteenth century – did no more than anticipate a plan to replace it with a park and a fountain engraved with 'Louis XVI, Restorer of Public Freedom' (a fountain, without the inscription, was indeed built later but was replaced by a monstrous plaster elephant that celebrated Napoleon's victories but soon fell into ruin). At the time of the prison's liberation, it contained just seven prisoners: four forgers, two mentally ill inmates (one of whom thought he was Julius Caesar), and an aristocrat locked up at the request of his family for sexual excess. Even so, there was plenty of bloodshed on the day, with a hundred of the assailants killed, and the prison's commander hacked to death and his head paraded on a pike through the city. A pamphlet circulated soon afterwards summarised the philosophy that had brought down the Bastille: 'Those who rule over us look grand only because we are on our knees: Rise up!' The Revolution had begun.

The city itself has been much sanitised since those bloody times and today's view from the Tour Eiffel makes it hard to imagine the conditions then faced by its inhabitants. The lives of most Parisians (albeit not those of its *philosophes* and *politiques*) were difficult indeed. Population density was three times that of London, with people crammed into noisome blocks that had not been touched for centuries and which faced disease, prostitution and crime. 'How different was my first sight of Paris from what I had expected', wrote Jean-Jacques Rousseau of his own first visit in 1742. 'I had imagined a town as beautiful as it was large. I saw only dirty, stinking alleys, ugly black houses, a stench of filth and poverty.'

The district of Les Halles, which held the ancient central market, is a microcosm of the waves of social and physical turmoil that have swept over the city, and of its constant ability to reinvent itself, with science and technology often the engine of change.

In 1789, the area contained more than a hundred thousand people per square kilometre. Cattle, sheep, fruit, vegetables and bread were sold in filthy streets next to an overcrowded cemetery, the thousand-year old Cimetière des Innocents, whose millions of corpses raised the level of the ground by two metres and whose festering contents now and again burst into adjacent basements. It took the reeking morass just nine days to consume a body, and the mountains of bones that built up were disinterred and stored nearby. Just before the end of the Old Regime, the whole pile collapsed in on itself and the cemetery was closed, with its skeletons spirited away to excavations beneath the city streets that had been dug long before to provide building material. The bones were the first inhabitants of the Paris Catacombs, which now hold the remains of six million of its departed citizens.

The area's residents faced hunger, crime and disease, and lived in hovels that had shown little improvement since the Middle Ages. Across the capital, one in four women aged between fifteen and thirty-five worked as a prostitute, and in a place as desperate as Les Halles the figure must have been even higher. Its people were poised on the edge of revolt. In October 1789 came a grand explosion, almost as important to the progress of the Revolution as had been the fall of the Bastille three months earlier.

The market women, or *poissardes* (fishwives), were a formidable group. They had long seen themselves as interlocutors between the people and the palace. By tradition they would march to Versailles when a new heir to the throne was born, there to be royally entertained and also to exercise what they saw as their right to complain about any particularly outrageous acts by their rulers. Within three months of the fall of the Bastille, Paris was beset by famine. Supplies of bread almost disappeared. After a series of rabble-rousing speeches that denounced a great banquet just held by the King, the market women had had enough. They besieged the Hôtel de Ville, and on a rainy evening in October set from its doors to march to Louis' palace thirty kilometres away. On the way they gathered in more and more women – bourgeois as well as proletarian, and thousands strong – as well as a few members of the opposite sex, and were followed by an armed group of National Guardsmen, themselves in mutinous mood. The marchers had gathered up various weapons, including two cannon stolen from the town hall. Soon they besieged the palace. In Carlyle's less than generous words, they formed 'groups of squalid dripping Women; of lankhaired male Rascality, armed with axes, rusty pikes, old muskets, ironshod clubs (batons ferres, which end in knives or sword-blades, a kind of extempore billhook), looking nothing but hungry revolt'.

Within a few hours they burst into the royal residence itself and besieged Marie-Antoinette in the king's bedroom. To calm the crowd, Louis XVI agreed to meet a delegation of women, one of whom was so overwhelmed by her encounter with the monarch – who saw himself, and was seen by many of his subjects, as almost a demigod – that she fainted in his presence. The crowd's main demand was that the court move to Paris, and with some reluctance, Louis agreed. He and Marie-Antoinette, together with their young son, appeared on the balcony, where in a reversal of mood typical of those febrile times, the spectators began to roar their approval. On 6 October, the royal coach, accompanied by a vast throng, with its leaders carrying pikes decorated with the heads of two of the royal bodyguard who had fallen victim to *batons ferres*, made its way to the capital. There, Louis was greeted by its first Mayor, the astronomer Bailly. The king never saw Versailles again.

In retrospect, the march of the market women can be seen as an inevitable step towards a death sentence for the monarchy, and – some time later – for the monarch himself. He had been revealed not to be inviolate but to be as much subject to the wishes of the people as was anyone else. In two stormy days, those who had long lived with the stench of a cemetery filled with the putrescent remnants of Old France buried that decayed society forever.

A civic convulsion began. The Church's huge estates were offered for sale, and a new paper currency, which at once began to lose its value, was introduced. On the first anniversary of the Fall of the Bastille a vast demonstration took place in Paris, an affair later formalised as an annual holiday and, with the exception of the periods of German occupation, celebrated every year since. Louis was forced to announce that 'I, the King of the French, swear to employ the power delegated to me in maintaining the constitution decreed by the National Assembly and accepted by me.' New elections were held for various communes throughout France. Those chosen for Paris alone included no fewer than eleven physicists, chemists and mathematicians, together with even more physicians, surgeons, pharmacists and engineers.

The most radical faction met in the Convent of the Jacobins (as the Dominican friars were referred to in France). It became known as the Jacobin Club, and Robespierre rose to become its most prominent member. It was accompanied by another extreme group, the Club of the Cordeliers (the French name for the Franciscans, whose monastery they occupied), whose leaders included Marat and the bloodthirsty Danton. The Jacobins demanded a complete break from Rome, but the Pope retaliated by removing his support from any priest who accepted the regime. In revenge, the state ensured that any cleric who followed his orders would lose their pensions. Louis and his family then fled to the northern town of Varennes in an attempt to rally his fellow royalists, but were intercepted and forced to return. He became a prisoner in his own palace. Across France disturbances began to mutate into massacres.

In Paris, too, the mood became uglier. The mob killed several hundred of the ruler's Swiss Guards. They then stormed the city's prisons and murdered anyone they saw as a traitor (in fact most were innocent burglars, thugs and the like). Priests were killed by the sans-culottes, while after one round of bloodshed the head of the murdered friend of the queen, the Princesse de la Lamballe, was paraded through the streets. Soon both the Jacobins and the Cordeliers found themselves threatened by provincial dissidents and by a hostile army of French émigrés, a threat made more serious by the stated intention of the Emperor Leopold of Austria and the King of Prussia, with support from other European monarchies (Britain included), to destroy the upstart regime.

Under the direction of the physicist and engineer Lazare Carnot an urgent decree was issued: 'Young men will go into combat. Married men will forge weapons and transport supplies. Women will make tents and uniforms and serve in hospitals. Children will make bandages of used linen. Old men will have themselves carried into public places to arouse the courage of warriors and to preach hatred of kings and the unity of the Republic.' Thanks to the exhortations of the elderly, a vast army was gathered. When the Prussians at last attacked, as they did three years after the downfall of Louis XVI, the situation seemed desperate, but against all expectations the invaders were destroyed at the Battle of Valmy in 1792, in part – as we shall see – with the help of advances in chemistry and physics made in Paris (Goethe was at the battle and noted that 'At this place, on this day there has begun a new era in the history of the world'). Carnot, the erstwhile engineer, was hailed as the 'Organiser of Victory' (and his son Sadi became, three decades later, one of the founders of modern thermodynamics).

Even so, the brave new world continued to feed upon itself. Civil war broke out in the Vendée on the Atlantic coast, and peasants laid siege to the port of La Rochelle in the vain hope that a British fleet might come to their assistance. Carnot was told to 'exterminate the rebels to the last man', and was also instructed to recapture Lyon with fixed bayonets, and to bombard the naval port of Toulon in the south with a rain of fire to burn the place to the ground. The National Assembly member and chemist Antoine Fourcroy was asked to look into 'mines, gases, or other means to destroy or asphyxiate the enemy' in that distant province, but never did. Even without the help of such technology, two hundred thousand were killed in the Vendée, while a lesser number fell in the many parts of Brittany that rose up. Corsica declared itself independent, cities such as Lyon and Marseille rejected the whole idea of change, and in Toulon the locals flew the Cross of Saint George and handed over two dozen naval vessels to the British (who hatched a plan to transform the port into a new Gibraltar) even as at the opposite end of the country a fleet from across the Channel blockaded Dieppe.

Drastic measures were called for, and used. In Paris, the radicals took full control. A tribunal under the sway of Robespierre was set up to hunt down 'enemies of the people'. A summons to its court was in effect a sentence of death. The Terror began, and large numbers of citizens began to fall before it.

France, like Britain, had a long and chequered history of public execution. In earlier times, and in most places, murderers were burned, but in the south-west they were buried alive with the bodies of their victims. In some regions counterfeiters suffered no more than mutilation, but in others they were boiled to death. Often criminals were hanged from multiple gallows on the top of local hills. Decapitation was reserved for the nobility, and if a murderer died before his execution date, his body was hanged anyway (if he escaped arrest, his portrait sometimes suffered the same fate). The corpses of suicides were hanged as a matter of routine.

Judicial killing was popular entertainment. On special occasions, the monarch himself might join the audience, but Louis XV at the age of eleven refused to accept such an invitation. Thirty-six years later, he was himself attacked and stabbed by a religious maniac, Robert-Francois Damiens. The assassin was seized, tortured and sentenced to death. A huge crowd gathered in the Place de la Grève in Paris (where, later, strikers often assembled). Many waited for days perched on benches erected on rooftops to get a decent view of the torments of the failed regicide. After the victim was dragged into the arena, his flesh was torn with pincers, his hands were cut off, molten lead and wax was poured into his wounds, and his arms and legs were torn off by horses before his torso was incinerated. Casanova, who was present, was forced to stop up his ears to exclude the screams of the victim, and expressed revulsion at the large numbers of women, aristocrats among them, who enjoyed the spectacle.

Damiens' execution led to widespread disgust among liberal members of the establishment. Some even demanded the end of the death penalty. The abolitionists for a time included Robespierre himself, a man who not long afterwards became addicted to the scent of blood. Their views did not prevail until the mid twentieth century, but calls for a less vile means of official murder were soon heeded. The chattering classes of those days were more successful than perhaps they had hoped.

But how to do the job? A citizen called Girardet suggested, in a ghoulish presage of a technique used until recently in a supposedly civilised nation, that an asphyxiation booth – a gas chamber – would work well. Charcoal and sulphur would be burned below it and the victim would suffocate, while a glass panel would enable the audience to relish his distress.

That idea was not taken up, but in 1790, Dr Guillotin persuaded his fellows that technology would solve the problem. An apparatus for decapitation would do the job: 'the mechanism falls like thunder, the head flies off, the blood spurts, the man is no more'. The story then grew that he had also claimed that 'Now, with my machine, I cut off your head in the blink of an eye, and you never feel it!', which wits used as an excuse to name the apparatus after the good doctor, who in fact opposed the death penalty. His relatives changed their surname to show their disapproval.

Such devices had already been used in Britain, with the 'Halifax Gibbet' and the 'Scottish Maiden', but the French turned to their experts for a more rational approach. Dr Louis, secretary of the new Academy of Surgery, tested the efficiency of blades set at different angles on corpses in a local hospital. In April 1792, a Parisian armed robber was the first to have the honour of sampling the new instrument – the 'silence mill', as it was labelled. The ceremony drew a crowd (many of whom were disappointed that the business was over so fast), and its success led the state to order eighty more of the devices, to be dispersed over France. They were, thanks to the activities of the new Committee on Public Safety, soon in great demand.

The expertise of the executioners improved with practice. In September 1793, the National Convention declared that terror should be the order of the day. A Committee of General Security was established, and traitors were dragged before its tribunal, whose sentence was almost always death. On one day of that bloody episode, twenty-one members of the National Assembly were guillotined within little more than half an hour, to the cheers of the mob.

Even so, in some places the demand for death outgrew the supply of machines. When the reactionaries in Lyon were at last defeated, the National Convention decreed that the city should be destroyed and that a column be erected on the ruins, inscribed with the words 'Lyon made war on liberty. Lyon no longer exists.' Two thousand citizens were executed, many tied together with ropes and killed with cannon fire, while at Nantes, even more faced the *noyade* and were drowned in boats sunk on the Loire.

Death in various guises came to many of those involved in the disturbances, on both sides and at the highest level. After a vote for execution with a majority of just one in the six-hundred member Assembly, Louis XVI suffered on the scaffold, as later did his wife, and his mistress, Madame du Barry, while his young son, the Dauphin, was imprisoned and died of tuberculosis at the age of ten (the rumour that he had been spirited away and that his descendants had claims on the throne of France was disproved when the DNA from the Dauphin's preserved heart matched that of his officially recognised modern kin). Danton preceded Robespierre as victim, as did the leaders of the more moderate (or less extreme) parties in the Assembly, and dozens of their followers, together with the main agents of the Reign of Terror itself. Even the printer who came up with the famous motto *Liberté, Egalité, Fraternité* fell victim to the new machine.

Across the nation more than fifteen thousand people were executed, half a million imprisoned, and almost as many placed under house arrest (a proportion of the population greater than in the Soviet Union at the time of the Gulag). Hundreds of thousands more died by the sword or through starvation. The names of the vast majority are lost, or remembered only by historians. Even so, some of the victims are still celebrated among their scientific descendants, albeit for their careers more than for their fate.

The year 1789 was almost as important in the history of science as it was in that of politics. Lavoisier's seminal *Traité elémentaire de Chimie* was published, together with the first journal devoted to a single discipline, the *Annales de Chimie*, while the botanist du Jussieu came up with a huge account of the taxonomy of plants, and the mathematician Pierre-Simon Laplace did the same with a memoir on the solar system that set the foundations of modern astronomy.

The people's revolt was – at least in its first days – itself a celebration of reason over passion. It marked the application of new ways of thought to matters of state. Researchers and technicians began to play a central part in national affairs. Their successes and failures show the power and the limitations of logic in understanding the universe of man rather than that of Nature.

As one of their earliest acts, the *philosophes* set out to produce a rational France. The mathematician Condorcet penned a hefty work entitled *Esquisse d'un tableau historique des progrès de l'esprit humain*. Civilisation, he wrote, was driven by the pursuit of pure knowledge, and its advance would build a more perfect world. As he put it: 'The sole foundation for belief in the natural sciences is the idea that the general laws that direct the phenomena of the universe, known or unknown, are necessary and constant. Why should this principle be any less true for the development of the intellectual and moral faculties of man?' The importance of such rules was manifest in the declaration of 1789, which states that the rights of man are 'natural, inalienable and sacred', and that ignorance of that fact was the 'sole cause of public misfortune and general corruption ... The exercise of the natural rights of man has no limits except those which assure to other members of society enjoyment of the same rights'. The French decree, unlike that of the United States (which blamed its own bid for freedom on the errors of a foreign power), saw the nation's collapse as due to a wanton disregard of inherent human attributes.

Condorcet's idea that civil liberties can be illuminated with mathematics seems odd to his intellectual descendants today, most of whom have a less elevated view of their own importance. Even so, it was behind the logic that gave rise to the Revolution. Prominent figures were entranced by the ability of chemists to reveal the hidden structure of air or water, and by astronomers' equivalent insights into the perfection of the cosmos. Some were blunt in their purity of belief. The physiologist Destutt de Tracy abandoned his interest in the biology of vision and took up philosophy. He summarised his ideas, and those of many of his colleagues, in just one sentence: 'Ideology [a word he invented] is part of zoology.'

The hunger for order reached absurd lengths. Because of its shape, France is often referred to as *l'Hexagone*. Mathematicians took that trigonometric coincidence as the basis of a new scheme of governance, to be based on multiples of the number three (its Masonic relevance may also have been important). There were to be eighty-one administrative regions, each of 324 square leagues, every one divided into nine districts, with each district split into nine communes. The plan was abandoned as impracticable and was replaced by *départements* based on river basins and mountain ranges.

In a new (and equally short-lived) calendar, each month – named Liberty, The Bastille, Equality and the like – was to be divided into three ten-day weeks, with the five days that remained celebrated as festivals of the workers, or *Sansculottides*. The extra day necessary in a leap year or *sextile* was to be referred to as the Françiade, which would provide another excuse for celebration. The idea did not catch on, and the mathematician Jean-Charles de Borda's attempt to reset the clock into a ten-hour day, a hundred-minute hour, and a hundred-second minute ran out of time even sooner. Undeterred, the new regime devised new identities for the years and months, with 1792 to be marked as Year One of the calendar. New Year's Eve would be celebrated on the autumn solstice, and each month was given a name based on climate, with Brumaire (foggy), Pluviose (rainy), Floréal (flowery) and so on (parodied across the Channel as 'Snowy, Flowy, Blowy, Showery, Flowery, Bowery, Hoppy, Croppy, Droppy, Breezy, Sneezy and Freezy'). The scheme lasted for less than a dozen years, and its author was cut off even sooner, for he too was condemned to death.

In spite of such excesses real progress was made. A new system of measurement was developed, based not on an arbitrary standard such as a monarch's foot, but on the size of the Earth. A decimal currency emerged, and there was much discussion of the statistical basis of the electoral system. Great improvements in manufacture and in agriculture transformed the economy. New weapons defended the state, while the first balloons revealed the secrets of the atmosphere even as astronomers discovered the order that seemed to pervade the universe and geology revealed the immense age of our planet. Vast numbers of new plants and animals were discovered. The royal botanic garden, the Jardin de Roi, was renamed the Jardin des Plantes and graced with a new museum, the Muséum d'Histoire Naturelle. Its researchers were as important to physics and biology as Lavoisier had been for chemistry, for as well as discovering radiation, they laid (without realising it) the foundations of the theory of evolution.

Whatever the Revolution's desire for logic, for the logicians themselves brutal reality soon broke in. Many were forced to flee and to hide in the depths of France. The chemist Fourcroy wrote that 'I went without bread for ten months ... I saw almost nobody. I refused invitations, dinners, I was as usual outside every faction.' The botanist and geologist Louis Ramond was elected deputy for Paris in 1791, but fell out with the Jacobins and fled to the Pyrenees. He was caught and imprisoned at Tarbes: 'In that long solitude, in that deep silence, what do you think I did? Think of myself? No, I forgot myself. I left prison without rancour, indeed without anything, dressed in old rags. I walked without shoes and lived on the few sous that had not been stolen from me; I turned my resentment against events and not against men, I conquered fate by patience, and gained consolation from the study of nature.' Louis Bosc, an eminent entomologist, also took to the hills: 'I spent days on natural history or manual labour and in hunting. Unable to obtain the books I lacked, I undertook a description, with sketches, of forest spiders, as the least well-known.' Bernard Lacépède, who worked both on physics and on fish, was another who was forced to hide: 'I forgot the world and saw the universe.'

Even Destutt de Tracy, inventor of the word 'ideology', spent almost a year inside, cogitating on the physiology of the senses. Cassini, too, director of the Paris Observatory, was imprisoned as a royalist, and wrote that his talents had done no more than prolong his captivity, which – he was convinced – depended on simple envy and ignorance. Other fellows and associates of the Academy of Sciences locked up at the time of the Terror included the explorer Louis Antoine de Bougainville, the astronomer Jacques Cousin, the geographer Nicolas Desmarest, the entomologist Pierre-André Latreille, the engineer and geologist Deodat de Dolomieu, and the chemist and colleague of Lavoisier, Balthazar Sage.

Painful as their experiences may have been, those individuals at least survived. Others paid a heavier price. For them, as for Lavoisier, their brush with affairs of state proved fatal. In those years, almost one in four active fellows of the Academy died: executed, killed in battle, murdered, or by suicide.

François Rozier, a pioneer of agricultural research, was shot during the siege of Lyon, while the mathematician and engineer Jean Baptiste Meusnier de Laplace suffered the same fate in the attack on Mayence (now Mainz) by the Prussians.

The astronomer Bochart de Saron, who studied the orbits of comets and was instrumental in the recognition of Uranus as a planet, supported the new regime, but paid with his head for his earlier membership of the despised *parlement* of Paris. He continued to make calculations in his condemned cell until the day he was executed. The distinguished botanist Chrétien Guillaume de Lamoignon de Malesherbes made the mistake of pleading on behalf of Louis XVI at his trial, and was decapitated after being forced to watch the execution of his son-in-law, his daughter and his grandchildren. The geologist and chemist Philippe-Frederic de Dietrich, mayor of Strasbourg at the time of the downfall of Louis XVI (and the first person to perform '*La Marseillaise*' in public), was condemned by the tribunal under Robespierre 'in the interests of the people', while François de Rochefoucauld, geologist, physicist and translator of the works of Benjamin Franklin, was assassinated by a provincial mob. The mathematician Charles-Gilbert Romme, who had developed the new calendar, when condemned to death stabbed himself with a knife on the steps of the courtroom to avoid public humiliation.

Nicolas de Condorcet was more than a philosopher, for he had worked on problems as distinct as electoral systems and the fluid dynamics of canal boats, and had been elected a delegate for Paris in the National Assembly. He had hoped to use his talents to design a new way of life, and wrote in 1790 that he had for thirty years 'rarely passed a single day without thinking about political science'. Condorcet designed a national education system and promoted the rights of women, but made the fatal error of speaking in favour of the king at the time of the vote on his execution. After several months hidden away in Paris, he escaped to the countryside, but he too was identified and imprisoned. Two days later he was found poisoned in his cell, either through suicide or murder.

The career of the astronomer Jean-Sylvain Bailly is a microcosm of how often, and at what a high price, the brilliant minds of that age fell prey to illusions of the power of logic. He took his first step towards the guillotine when he led his followers into the Jeu de Paumes in the first days of the new regime, but before he experienced the 'light breeze upon the neck', rose higher in the firmament than did any of his scientific contemporaries, as first signatory of the Tennis Court Oath, first leader of the National Assembly, and first mayor of Paris.

Bailly's career began with the arts, but he became frustrated by their frivolity and moved instead to the study of the universe. He was inordinately proud of his status as member of all three royal academies, the *Académie Française*, the *Académie des Sciences*, and the *Académie des Inscriptions et Belles-Lettres*, and wrote five hefty works on the history of astronomy, in which he much exaggerated the knowledge possessed by the ancient Egyptians. These were matched by other volumes on the decline of humankind from a golden age, an era he was certain would, thanks to 'the universal language of science', soon return.

As a young man, Bailly had been taken up by Nicolas Louis de Lacaille, an abbot and astronomer who had travelled to the Cape of Good Hope to make a catalogue of the southern stars. His protégé was, the Abbé said, his most talented pupil. Bailly's incursions into the study of the heavens began with his calculation of the arc of Halley's Comet, which reappeared in the skies over Paris in 1759 after an absence of seventy-five years. He set up a small observatory in the Louvre, and two years later, in company with Lacaille and the finance minister Turgot, observed a transit of Venus. He also analysed anomalies in the movements of the Moon as recorded from ancient times, and became a member of the Royal Academy of Sciences at the age of just twenty-six.

He is best remembered for his research on the satellites of Jupiter. Galileo had found that the brightness of the four moons that could then be identified varied with time, for they pass into the shadow of their parent in a regular way. They hence act as a natural clock in the heavens and might perhaps be used to measure longitude, the distance east or west across an ocean. The hope was to find the time difference between the moment when a particular moon passed behind its parent, compare it to that recorded in Paris, and transform this into a measure of distance (the difficulty of observing distant satellites at sea was not entirely solved by the invention of a suspended chair in which the navigator could sway to and fro).

In his first months as mayor, Bailly built up the capital's food reserves, improved its sewage system, its slaughterhouses, burial grounds and hospitals, founded a system of public workhouses, and did his best to control prostitution. His works came to naught when, at the height of the disorder in Paris, he announced martial law and his soldiers shot down dozens of anti-royalist demonstrators as they massed upon the Champ de Mars. He was dragged before the tribunal and sentenced to be executed on the place of massacre. His death was even more cruel than usual, for the mob would not profane the sacred ground and the guillotine had to be reassembled in a ditch, where the populace threw mud at him on a winter's day. When a member of the crowd shouted '*Tu trembles, Bailly?*' he responded, with some stoicism, '*Oui, mais c'est seulement de froid.*'

His fate is perhaps better evidence of the limitations of science in human affairs than of its power. Bailly's career and downfall, together with that of many of his fellows, is a microcosm of the links between that endeavour, statecraft and philosophy in his turbulent era, and a reminder of how in the modern age they have drifted apart. The work of those who suffered imprisonment and worse at that time was fundamental to much of today's biology, chemistry, astronomy and more, but the mystical ideas that accompanied it have left almost no imprint on posterity. In the dismissive words of Thomas Carlyle: 'Poor Bailly, how thy serenely beautiful Philosophising, with its soft moonshiny clearness and thinness, ends in foul thick confusion of Presidency, Mayorship, diplomatic Officiality, rabid Triviality, and the throat of everlasting Darkness!' True as that might be, whatever the beliefs of those who pursue it, science itself persists. The *philosophes* of the Revolution laid the foundation for the advances of the next two centuries and more, and their 'universal language' is still a discourse that connects every modern practitioner of the sciences to those bloody times.

CHAPTER II

ASHES TO ASHES

Men who love law, and will have even an Explosion
explode itself, as far as possible, according to rule . . .

THOMAS CARLYLE, *The French Revolution*

Antoine Lavoisier in his laboratory

Car bombs are easy to make, for their main ingredient is used in huge amounts by farmers. The artificial fertiliser ammonium nitrate, when mixed with fuel oil and provided with a detonator, can have devastating effects. ANFO, as the compound is known, is a simple but effective tool of terror. In 1993, the Provisional IRA detonated a truck filled with a ton of the stuff in Bishopsgate, in the City of London. It killed one person, did £350 million worth of damage and cleared away an inconvenient historical monument called the Baltic Exchange. The site was used to build the office block known as the Gherkin (sold not long ago for £700 million), while the remains of the Exchange are in Estonia, where they still await reconstruction. The New York World Trade Center bomb later that year used the same material, as did the Oslo atrocity of 2011 and many of its equivalents across the globe. That simple technology generates the explosive power and accuracy of a sophisticated missile for just a couple of hundred pounds.

In London, chemistry was turned to violent ends long ago. In 1605 Guido Fawkes stored almost a ton of gunpowder in the vaults of the Houses of Parliament which, had he not been caught, would have made a bang even greater than that set off by his co-religionists four centuries later. Gunpowder is saltpetre – potassium nitrate – mixed with carbon and sulphur. The saltpetre is a source of oxygen, and the two other elements act as fuels. When given a suitable push, the powder explodes, the compounds in the mineral break their bonds, the liberated oxygen ignites the other components and their joint reaction produces a high-powered wave of pressure.

Today's state-sponsored killers use more complex and expensive materials than did yesterday's religious fanatics, but all depend for their murderous success on the unexpected properties of an element that makes up most of the atmosphere. Their big bang began with Antoine Lavoisier.

Nitrogen was first isolated by the Scottish physician Daniel Rutherford in 1772. He was a student of the Glasgow professor Joseph Black, who had earlier done the same for carbon dioxide, which he called 'fixed air'. Fixed air, Black had found, was unable to sustain life, or allow a flame to burn. Rutherford took the matter further, for after allowing a mouse to die when placed in the stuff, and burning a candle and a lump of phosphorus in the vessel, he passed what remained through lime water to soak up the carbon dioxide. That left a smaller volume of gas that would itself maintain neither life nor a flame. Rutherford then made the universal error of the time, for he referred to the residue as 'dephlogisticated air', a substance from which the mythic essence had been removed.

Lavoisier's first contribution was to accept nitrogen as an entity – an element – in its own right. Air, he had found with his burnt phosphorus experiments, was a mixture of distinct elements rather than a single substance whose properties could change with the addition or removal of an imagined power.

Now we know of ninety-one natural elements, with plenty of others made in the laboratory. They can be arranged in a 'periodic table' of rows and columns that unite members with similar properties and hint at the nature of the reactions that can take place between them. The nineteenth-century idea that such units were arranged like a musical scale in 'octaves', with a tendency for substances with similar properties to be eight places apart, has been superseded, but it reflects the logic of modern chemistry, which arranges them by atomic weight, a measure based on the numbers of the elementary particles called protons in the atomic nucleus. Nitrogen comes in at number seven in a table that now has a hundred and eighteen members, with the unstable artificial element called ununoctium the most recent to be synthesised.

Lavoisier's term 'azote' for Black's gas means 'lifeless' (and the word is still used in French). However, as he explored its properties, he realised that with sufficient input of energy, nitrogen, inert as it might appear, could combine with some of its sister elements to make a variety of compounds. They include the raw material of the explosives that have killed two hundred million people since the late eighteenth century, but are also the basis of the artificial fertilisers that keep ten times as many from starvation today. Its extended family includes laughing gas, hydrogen cyanide, heart drugs, rocket fuel, superglue, and the silver salts used in black-and-white photography. The gas is a metaphorical breath of fresh air for both plants and animals, but as the ammoniacal reek of the cemetery at Les Halles reminds us, it is also a herald of mortality.

Beneath what seems a passive personality, nitrogen has many talents. They come from its ability to combine with other substances. The capacity to make such links is determined by an element's 'valency', a measure related to the numbers of electrons that spin around its core. Each link can involve just a single point of attachment, but quite often the tie is made with two or more, to give a double, or even a triple, bond. Hydrogen has a valency of one and oxygen of two, which means that water has the formula of H_2O. Oxygen gas, O_2, has two atoms of the element held together with a double bond. Nitrogen is unusual, because in most compounds it has a valency of three, and as a result makes three links between its paired members as it floats in the atmosphere.

A triple alliance is powerful indeed, but once it has been broken, the element becomes seized by an immediate urge to fall into bed with anything that will have it. Before such a ceremony can be arranged, the strong affinity of its atoms for each other must be fractured. In the atmosphere, electrical storms act as matchmakers and persuade the gas to consecrate a union with oxygen or hydrogen. In laboratories and factories, the job calls for high temperature and pressure, together with chemical catalysts. So successful has been that technology that the nitrogenous productions of nature are now dwarfed by those of man.

Many of the compounds that emerge from the factories are unstable, which is good news for terrorists and farmers alike. Ammonium nitrate is a composite of nitrogen, hydrogen and oxygen, with the formula NH_4NO_3. The material is fairly unreactive under most circumstances, and breaks up in the soil to make a useful fertiliser, but when pushed hard explodes into action. It does no more than burn when lit with a match, but bursts into fury when its links are fractured with a sudden shock. The chemical has locked up the energy invested in its manufacture in the form of the bonds that tie it together. When they are released, ammonium nitrate brings death or life, depending on how rapidly the escape is made.

A 1947 disaster revealed its Janus face. The *Ocean Liberty*, loaded with tons of nitrate fertiliser donated by the United States to a hungry post-war France, was moored in the port of Brest. Also on board was a cargo of motor oil, paint and paraffin. As the vessel was unloaded, a wisp of smoke emerged from the hold. The fire spread. An attempt to tow the ship out to sea failed when it grounded on a sandbank. Five hours after the first hint of a problem, the ship blew up. The explosion destroyed thousands of houses and killed thirty people.

Those who wreak such destruction on purpose need a detonator – an agent able to push the prime ingredient away from its stable state. It may be a flame, a spark or a reactive mixture of chemicals, while for some compounds even a slight tap will do the job. The Bishopsgate bomb was set off with a fuse made of the commercial explosive Semtex, itself based on a salt of nitrogen. When the detonator was activated, a wave of unease passed through the sacks of fuel-soaked fertiliser. At once the ammonium nitrate vaporised and its molecules broke down into steam and nitrous oxide (a combination of two molecules of nitrogen with one of oxygen). The heat ignited the fuel added to the mix, which burned at an enormous rate to make even more gas. As it expanded, the pressure caused millions of pounds' worth of damage with a lorry-load of chemicals that cost little more than a decent meal for two in a City restaurant.

The Chinese discovered the magic power of potassium nitrate in the ninth century and saw it as the essence of life because it flared up when thrown on a fire. Soon they began to use it to make rockets and thunder-flashes to demoralise their enemies and terrify their horses. Four hundred years on, they had guns with a one-inch bore. The fatal powder soon spread across Europe. It was first used in anger in England in 1327 to power primitive cannon that looked rather like an upended bell and were directed at the Scots.

England's first gunpowder mill was founded in 1561 at Waltham Abbey, north of London. For many years it was under the control of the Walton dynasty, of Izaak Walton fame. The proprietors were well aware of the dangers of their trade: 'Everyone is charged with the utmost caution and prudence in the handling of the powder ... [and] are most earnestly beseeched not to let emane from their mouths oaths or swearwords ... whereby the Name of our Lord is dishonoured.' Any worker who ignored that elementary precaution was at once dismissed. Other rules (often disregarded) insisted that the material must pass through London by water rather than by road, and that stores of it were not allowed within the City or Westminster, or within two miles of any royal palace. After much pressure on the owners, in 1787 the Waltham Abbey factory was sold to the government (which means that the production of explosives was Britain's first nationalised industry).

War has always been a catalyst for technology. As the years went on, various *ad hoc* improvements were made to the powder. With not much more than trial and error, a variety of specialised propellants emerged. The charge used for pistols, which accelerate their bullets over a few inches, had more saltpetre than that utilised in rockets, slow burners with plenty of time to gain speed on the way to their target. The version designed for cannons contained less of the explosive component, for their bronze barrels were fragile and burst unless caution was used.

Saltpetre was expensive and hard to find, and there was pressure to reduce the amount used. In the days of the *Ancien Régime*, four grades of powder of decreasing power were on sale in France: the military stuff, or *poudre de guerre*; for hunters a *poudre à giboyer*; for commercial use *poudre royale*; and for mines and quarries *poudre de mine*. In addition, an even weaker *poudre de traite*, or traders' powder, was sold to slave dealers, who used it for currency with which to buy their human cargo. Lavoisier himself almost lost his life when the mob misunderstood a shipment of *poudre de traite* to be not for trade, but for treachery.

In the uneasy years of the late eighteenth century, the demand for armaments grew fast. The nation with the most powerful weaponry was likely to prevail. Soon an arms race was under way, which, thanks to the expertise of its chemists, the French won.

The Seven Years War, which began in 1756, dealt with the ticklish relationship between the royal families of Europe, those of Britain and France included. It raged from the Caribbean to West Africa. In the end, the British triumphed and France lost its Canadian territories. In a belated attempt at revenge, Louis XVI enlisted his nation as a proxy in a conflict that would change its future, and – in time – that of the world. His academicians did a lot to shape the result.

Two years after the American Declaration of Independence, with encouragement from Benjamin Franklin, France recognised the rebels as legitimate and declared war on Britain. It supported Washington with money, with arms and with men.

All this involved enormous expense in an economy already on the edge of collapse. In the first decades of the eighteenth century the Gunpowder Farm – a parallel to the private tax-gatherers who later made Lavoisier rich – had been tasked to control the manufacture and sale of the explosive. It did its job with characteristic greed and ineptitude. The finance minister, Turgot, realised that reform was essential. Like his British equivalents, he saw that the manufacture of explosives should be under national control, and bought out the monopoly's forty factories. In 1775, the organisation was replaced with a *Régie des Poudres*, with Lavoisier himself at its head. The great chemist moved into the Grand Arsenal, near the Bastille, where he began to improve his nation's explosives.

In earlier times, the quality of gunpowder had been tested by seeing how far a cannon ball would travel when fired with a standard charge. That method depended on wind and weather and was replaced by a pendulum system, with the cannon at its bob and its deflection when fired a statement of the powder's strength. The new head of the Gunpowder Commission improved the system with a measure of the nature, and the volume, of the gases generated when a particular blend was used. He found that the optimal proportion was of six parts of saltpetre to two of sulphur and one of charcoal. Structure was also important. He began to add water to the saltpetre, carbon and sulphur as they were ground together, so that the paste dried to form grains rather than a fine dust. The new formulation was more effective than before and further gains were made when the paste was forced through a sieve to form even larger and more solid particles. A denser powder gave a bigger bang, and the raw material was then squeezed in a press before it was allowed to dry and broken into fragments for use in artillery pieces. Lavoisier discovered that whirling the ingredients in a centrifuge packed with copper balls gave an even better product. His research, he said, with some exaggeration, doubled the power of French explosives, and he boasted that 'North America owes its independence to French powder.'

The armaments business still faced plenty of problems. One was the shortage of saltpetre. France had for some time imported the stuff from India, but the nation lost its colonies in the subcontinent to the British at the end of the Seven Years War, while the British assured their own supplies when they overthrew the Nawab of Bengal, in whose territory the compound was abundant. The *Régie des Poudres* faced a great shortage. It was forced to scavenge for raw material on farms and in insalubrious basements. A law known as the *fouille* (the 'excavation') allowed its officials to raid homes in search of the precious substance. The searchers were not popular, and often added to their income with demands for bribes to avoid particular properties.

Saltpetre is formed from the reaction of nitrogenous

compounds such as those found in animal waste with other soil chemicals. In the eighteenth century and earlier it had been gathered from crystals on the walls of manure pits, in the rubble of old buildings and in certain rocks. More came from human and animal excreta. These were piled into beds, mixed with wood ash or straw, and kept moist with nitrogen-rich solids and fluids for a year or so. The reaction generated nitrate salts, and the mixture was transformed into saltpetre when it was filtered through potash, a product made from wood ash that acted to remove other salts, leaving only potassium nitrate behind.

In 1778, the Royal Academy offered a prize for a solution to the saltpetre problem. One difficulty was that most people did not know what the substance actually was. Some argued that it came from a reaction between the air and the earth, others appealed to phlogiston, while yet others believed it was made by plants. Many of the entries were imaginative: rabbits should be kept for their dung, or a law should oblige innkeepers to accumulate vats of their customers' urine, while one entrant felt that saltpetre was alive and could be bred in farms. Such ideas came to naught.

Lavoisier showed that the crucial compound was a relative of nitric acid. He recommended that nitrate works be set up across the nation, and in 1777 wrote a book entitled *Instruction sur l'Établissement des Nitrières et sur la Fabrication du Salpêtre*. That gave advice on how to find soils and rubble that contained the mineral, and how to leach it out with water, evaporate off the liquid, and collect its crystals. In an extension of his earlier work on the geology of France, he also identified places in the Loire valley and elsewhere that would yield suitable raw material. Almost at once, production shot up and prices dropped by half.

Emissaries were dispatched to Paris from across the nation for instruction in how to make the crucial chemical, and in 1793, with invaders on all sides, its manufacture went into high gear. The saltpetre hunters combed the countryside, aided by an army of volunteers who collected the stuff as a patriotic duty. In Carlyle's words: 'The Earth-heap rises at every door; the Citoyennes with hod and bucket carrying it up; the Citoyens, pith in every muscle, shovelling and digging: for life and saltpetre.' As the citizens, male and female, laboured, many of them sang the Saltpetre Song, to the tune of 'La Marseillaise': *'Descendez dans nos souterrains, La Liberté nous y convie . . .'* Within a few months, there were six thousand extraction plants across France, and output went up by five times.

In Paris, what had been the Abbey Church of Saint-Germain-des-Prés was renamed the Atelier de l'Unité and became a refinery that treated a hundred tons of raw saltpetre every day. Its products were shipped to a factory downstream, on the stony plain of Grenelle, on the Left Bank. The ancient abbey next to the church was used to store the raw material, and was quite soon destroyed by an explosion (another blast killed three hundred workers in the factory itself).

On 30 Ventôse (20 March) 1792, a great armaments festival celebrated the triumph of the chemists. A procession of students from the courses on saltpetre and its manufacture, which had attracted young men from all over France, was accompanied by trumpeters and military bands, gun carriages, miners, two mothers and babies from each section of the city, and – as stars of the show – the professors who had educated the patriotic scholars, among them Lavoisier, Fourcroy and Berthollet. The participants carried garlanded baskets of the raw material and of gunpowder, while others bore the machinery used to make it. The new copper centrifuge was raised on high, with a banner inscribed with the motto *Mort aux Tyrans*. The high point was a saltpetre bust of the hero Marat, which was set up on a pyramid of the same stuff.

Not satisfied with such successes, the city's chemists set out to develop new explosives. One was to be based on the unstable chemical potassium chlorate. Quite soon, an accident in the research station killed two of the workers, and the idea that it might be used as a propellant was abandoned. The chemists then had the idea that compounds put inside cannonballs could be used to manufacture the world's first explosive shells. Their prototypes were based on sulphur, tree resins, potassium nitrate, pulverised gunpowder, turpentine, linseed oil and alcohol and, they claimed, 'no ship-rigging could resist the action of these cannonballs', which could also be involved in land warfare 'to burn rations, fodder, uniforms, faggots, barricades, and villages where the enemy might be dug in'. The projectiles were tested with great success on a mock-up of a hull, but were ignored by the authorities. A couple of years later – and as could only happen in France – the idea was revived by the artillery officer Pierre Choderlos de Laclos, who is better remembered for his erotic novel *Les Liaisons Dangereuses*. In spite of its dangers, Laclos used potassium chlorate to fill the missiles and in time they became part of every nation's apparatus of death.

The army also needed better guns and, once again, technology came to the rescue. Many were made from church bells, which were torn down in their thousands for raw material; as the rabble-rousers put it: 'Thus this brazen source of noise, hanging so uselessly in the air for centuries, which served only to fatigue us with the importunity of sound, today becomes one of the most powerful means of our defence.' New methods for the purification of copper and tin emerged, and the bronze alloy produced was poured into moulds to make artillery pieces. At the same time, another group of academicians, the mathematician Gaspard Monge and the chemist Claude Louis Berthollet included, developed new and efficient methods of steel manufacture, again accompanied with an attack on aristocratic fripperies: 'Fellow citizens, let us transport to our forges those prideful balustrades, those grilles that have nothing to preserve, and if we find the qualities of good iron there, let us convert them into steel.' The material was used to build the first functional submarine, demonstrated in front of a huge crowd on the Seine. The plan was to use it to attach explosives to British ships, or lay mines in the Thames, but the scheme came to nothing.

All this activity meant that France soon had guns and ammunition sufficient not just to defend its own borders, but to send quantities to the American rebels. As Lavoisier himself declared: 'It can truthfully be said that it is to these supplies that North America owes its freedom.' As so often in the interaction of chemistry with politics, chemistry won.

That victory has been repeated many times (although, with nuclear weapons, physics now threatens to take the gold medal). The structure of most modern explosives, potent as they may be, is not very different from that of gunpowder. A nitrogenous compound of some kind acts as a reserve of bound oxygen, and is combined with a variety of fuels and with elements such as carbon or sulphur, or reactive metals such as ground aluminium, which interact with the gas on its release.

Death has become a global business. One of Lavoisier's fellows in the armaments trade was Eulethère Irenée du Pont de Nemours. His father Pierre had courted the great chemist's widow after his execution, but she rejected him and had a brief and disastrous second marriage to the physicist Count Rumford. Alarmed by his own close brush with the guillotine, the younger du Pont de Nemours fled to America. There he set up a gunpowder factory, which grew into today's enormous E. I. du Pont de Nemours company, prime provider of ammunition for the American Civil War and the two world wars, a secret site for the production of the Hiroshima bomb, and now the source of a range of products as diverse as Neoprene, Nylon, Teflon, Mylar, Kevlar and Lycra, together with a variety of drugs, insecticides, fertilisers and more.

In comparison to the weaponry that now pours from its factories, Lavoisier's munitions were feeble indeed. Once detonated, gunpowder's wave of energy travels at less than the speed of sound, while those of its modern equivalents move at a supersonic rate. Unless packed into a cartridge (or a barrel), the eighteenth-century propellant is more or less harmless, and a pile lit with a match will do no more than burn, while many modern compounds would macerate anyone foolish enough to set light to them. My father, an industrial chemist, worked on munitions at the time of the Second World War, and accidentally poured some picric acid (a nitrogenous chemical) into a sink where another reactive agent was lingering. It blew up and scarred him for life. Plenty of those involved in such enterprises have paid the same price, or worse.

The new era of explosives began with the invention of nitroglycerin in Italy in 1846. The compound was far more dangerous than the crude mixtures worked on by Lavoisier and his colleagues. Glycerin itself was a simple sugar discovered twenty years earlier by the French academician (and student of Fourcroy) Michel Eugène Chevreul. To make the explosive, it was added drop by drop to a mixture of concentrated nitric and sulphuric acids. The process was a ticklish one, as the liquid that emerged was unstable and could be set off with a slight jolt. The job had to be done with great care and the mixture kept at a low temperature in an ice bath. Sometimes it was shipped in frozen form, but that too was dangerous, for if it melted it became even more liable to spontaneous detonation. When the stuff does go off, whether by accident or on purpose, the shock wave travels at thirty times the speed of sound and the charge expands by a thousand times as it transforms itself into a gas that may, for an instant, reach a temperature of 5000°C.

The fearsome liquid played a large part in the construction

of the first railroad across the United States as engineers blasted a track through the Rocky Mountains. On the way there were frequent, and lethal, accidents, which led the authorities to treat the stuff with suspicion and, for a time, to forbid its transport. It had instead to be synthesised on site.

One such disaster killed a close relative of the man responsible for its European supplies, whose company sold an unstable mixture of nitroglycerin with gunpowder called 'Blasting Oil'. In 1864, an accident blew up Emil Oskar Nobel and several of the workers in their Swedish factory. Devastated by that tragedy, Emil's older brother Alfred set out to find a safer alternative.

What was needed was a way to make the product less susceptible to shock, with no loss of power. Nobel found the key in the fossilised skeletons of tiny marine creatures that had been transformed into a porous soil called kieselguhr. The material soaked up the lethal oil and made it far more stable than before. In 1867, he patented the compound under the name 'dynamite', and soon made a vast fortune. Factories sprang up in many places. The British Parliament had passed an Act to forbid 'the manufacture, import, sale and transport of nitroglycerine and any substance containing it within Great Britain', but Nobel persisted in his efforts, and the remote location of Ardeer on the Clyde coast – which he described as 'a sand desert where the wind always blows' – became the home of the largest explosives factory in the world.

In time, new versions emerged. Gelignite, used in blasting, was an amalgam of nitroglycerin and nitrocellulose (a reactive nitrogen compound), mixed with pulped wood and saltpetre to absorb the active material. It was easy to transport and became a favourite of terrorists. Ballistite was the same stuff blended with camphor, a carbohydrate, to increase its stability. It was useful in gunnery, as it was smokeless and generated a lesser blast that did not destroy gun barrels. Over the years, other propellants such as cordite (a compound of nitroglycerin with nitrocellulose and petroleum jelly) emerged and were used to lethal effect in the many wars of the twentieth century. They include a substance known as RDX (Research Department Explosive), much used in bombs, torpedoes and depth charges. When blended with a soft plastic, it can be moulded into a gel, now sold as Semtex, the raw material of the Bishopsgate detonator and the force behind the 1988 Lockerbie disaster. So urgent was the demand for RDX that the British handed over the secrets of how to make it to the Americans, and a plant was built on the Wabash river. It incorporated the largest nitric acid plant in the world – which in an odd twist of Franco-British history was run by the E. I. du Pont de Nemours Company. Ironically enough, Nobel himself was prescribed nitroglycerin to reduce the symptoms of heart disease, which it does, we now know, when the material is broken down into nitric oxide (one nitrogen linked to one oxygen), a molecule that relaxes blood vessels. He refused to take his medicine and died soon afterwards.

Recent advances in Nobel's dangerous world involve mixtures of quite different classes of chemical, some with massive power but too unstable to be safe for general use, mixed with less sensitive but still potent components. A process of 'co-crystallisation' means that both ingredients are dissolved in the same liquid and cooled until a solid blend with a regular structure of repeats of each emerges. Quite often, the hybrid is better than each element alone.

Such substances still get most of their clout from gases: carbon dioxide, water vapour, or oxides of nitrogen, released when the energy held in their chemical bonds is set free. The newest potential entrants to the munitions wars are different, for they depend on the disruption of salts of nitrogen arranged in complicated cage-like structures held together with dense bonds. These keep the whole system under enormous internal strain. When this is released, a large part of the force comes from the breakdown of the cage itself and the liberation of the energy invested. Octanitrocubane is a cube of carbon atoms, each attached to nitrogen and oxygen. Carbon prefers to make solid structures with an angle of 109 degrees between each atom (as in diamond), rather than the right angle they are forced into in this novel compound. When set off, the energy stored in the strained bonds is released, as are carbon dioxide and nitrogen, which generates a shock wave that travels at ten kilometres a second. At present, the stuff is far too expensive and difficult to make to be practical, but such substances or their descendants may fuel the wars of the future. Under extreme pressure and high temperature, nitrogen itself might even be transformed into a diamond-like structure that would store vast quantities of energy in this way. The material has been speculated about, but never made.

Nitrogen is a two-faced element. First used as an agent

of death, it has become essential to the world of life. Experiments done in Paris two decades after Lavoisier's execution showed why. Dogs fed a diet of gluten, sugar, olive oil or starch, all of which lack nitrogen, sickened and died. In fact, nitrogen is a component of all proteins and of DNA, and makes up about one part in thirty by weight of our own bodies.

Lavoisier himself saw that a shortage of its salts was in part responsible for the dreadful poverty of his nation's peasants. Chemistry had protected France from attack and, he was sure, could also make his nation bloom.

He took his expertise onto the farm. First, he set up a model estate in the Beauce, a region south-west of Paris. It was a substantial enterprise of eleven hundred hectares, which cost him the equivalent of around fifteen million pounds. In 1783 he was elected to the *Societé d'Agriculture de la Generalité de Paris*, and later became a member of the rival *Comité d'Agriculture*. He attended and spoke at dozens of their sessions, and in his book *On Agriculture and Trade in the Orléanais* noted that French farmers were no more than a third as efficient as their fellows across the Channel. One problem was the shortage of fertiliser. Most peasants could afford hardly any animals with which to dung their plots. They had no more than four or five cows, or a few score sheep, which often starved in winter through lack of food and as a result produced little manure. In some places, fallow land was open to anyone who wished to graze their stock on it in the hope that some goodness would return to the soil, but that scarcely touched the problem and much of the land had to be left *en jachère* – in long-term disuse – through lack of nutriment.

To improve the soil, more livestock was called for, and to feed those animals, forage crops would be essential. To test his ideas, the farmer of taxes and of gunpowder penned twenty cows and five hundred sheep into fifteen hectares, and fed them well. They produced twelve cartloads of excreta per hectare. In true analytical style, every input of food and output of manure was weighed and noted, as was the amount of seed planted and crop harvested. There was a dramatic increase in production on the experimental plot, thanks to his favourite element.

Even so, for the nation as a whole, a shortage of available nitrogen remained a considerable problem. In Brittany, the peasants used seaweed as a source, while those near cities preferred soot from chimneys, ash from fireplaces, or the waste from woollen mills. Elsewhere, rivers were dredged for their rich silt.

The obvious source of fertiliser was dung, and in France the most convenient producers of that material were the citizens themselves. As the Abbé Rozier, a pioneer of botany and the founder of a school of agriculture in Lyon, claimed: 'L'engrais tiré des excrémens humaines est, de tous les engrais, l'engrais par excellence.' Such 'night soil' was much used, either in liquid form or as a dried powder called *poussette*, although there were complaints that it made the food taste odd and annoyance at the fact that barrels of faeces were transported in the same carts as open churns of milk. The practice was widespread. In nineteenth-century China, users of public toilets were tipped by the attendant, rather than vice versa, in acknowledgement of the value of their deposit. Human waste was also the source of the Indian saltpetre that became so useful to the British gunpowder trade. At the time of the monsoon, the local peasants fertilised their plots with their own excrement, some of which was transformed into potassium nitrate by soil bacteria. A few months later came the dry season, and the substance crystallised on the surface, ready for collection by employees of the colonial power.

Britain, the proud harvester of Indian evacuations, was reluctant to appeal to the rear ends of its own citizens to improve the nation's farms, and the night soil was thrown (or, later, piped) into rivers: 'Our hordes of population, instead of being enrichers of the island, in an agricultural point of view, are absolute impoverishers. They draw off the corn, the roots, and the flesh from the land; and they send it away into the sea, by means of the Thames, the Severn, the Humber, the Tees, and Tyne, and scores of other great wasters of the elements of human food.' Small quantities of the nation's excreta were sold under bland names such as 'alkine-vegetative powder', but the idea never caught on, perhaps, some claimed, because John Bull's meaty diet made his faeces smell worse than those of the effete French. In Paris, the noxious liquid was used to help pay the rent, while in London, citizens had to pay 'gong farmers' to take it away.

Part of the reason that Britain could afford such *pudeur* was that its soils were better managed than were those across the Channel. Even so, as numbers grew, the search for the crucial element began to stretch across the world (and in time even the British began to use the contents of their water closets to feed themselves).

In distant lands, farmers used not the excrement of sheep, cattle and men, but that of birds, seabirds most of all, to nourish their crops. Their enormous flocks and cramped roosts mean that their wastes built up into great beds fifteen metres thick of a substance called guano. At the time of the Incas in Peru, the stuff was used to nurture the main crop, maize, with a hundred barges a day sent out to offshore islands to mine the beds. The raw material came from the digestive efforts of the Guanay Cormorant, the Peruvian Pelican and the Peruvian Booby. Each was protected by stringent rules, and any trespasser on their native soil was put to death. So successful was the system that the coastal hills maintained a population of thousands, ensconced behind a wall that kept the hungry mountain-dwellers at bay.

The Prussian explorer Alexander von Humboldt, later much involved in the intellectual life of Paris, saw the islands on his journey through South America in the first years of the nineteenth century. He became interested in their malodorous mineral, but believed it to be an ancient rock rather like coal, rather than a resource refreshed by animals. Back in France, he presented a sample to the chemist Fourcroy, who found that as much as one part in six was nitrogenous and noted that it would indeed make an excellent fertiliser. Humphry Davy – Fourcroy's British equivalent – came to the same conclusion and planned to mine the material from the cormorant colonies near his childhood home in Cornwall. Unfortunately, its goodness had been leached away by the constant rain. With his encouragement, the first experiments on the powers of guano were carried out on St Helena in the South Atlantic. The material doubled the yield of the ground upon which it was spread.

A Peruvian associate of Simon Bolivar (the liberator of much of South America, who spent many years in London) had attended Davy's lectures at the Royal Institution. One of them gave an account of that remarkable substance. On his return to his native land, the Peruvian was charged by Bolivar himself to regulate its use. For a time the system worked almost as well as that of the Incas, but was soon defeated by the greed of the Old World. In the 1820s, a young French mining engineer, Jean-Baptiste Joseph Dieudonné Boussingault, was sent to South America to assess the possible use of guano on his own nation's farms. He spent ten years in Peru, and once back home used his large fortune to import the material and to test its effects on plant growth on his estate in Alsace. Its value soon became obvious.

There, Boussingault established the world's first agricultural experimental station. He was elected to the Academy of Sciences, and also found time to become a member of the National Assembly as representative for his native department. Boussingault wrote a popular work on rural economy, in which he promoted the importance of fertilisers, guano included, to his nation's peasants. They took to it with enthusiasm, and inspissated bird manure became a valuable commodity. Soon, an era of 'guano piracy' began, with raids on the coasts of Namibia and Patagonia, and of those of remote islands off the Arabian peninsula. The lust for dung reached its high point when in 1856 the US Congress passed the Guano Islands Act. It allowed the United States to annex suitable islands, at least until their resources had been removed. The nation still retains nine of the sixty-six scraps of land to which this policy was applied. Japan, Mexico, Australia and more joined the scramble for droppings. Britain claimed Christmas Island and the Malden Islands in the central Pacific, while France managed to seize two small islets off the coast of French Guiana.

In some places the land grabs ended in bloodshed. The Chincha Islands War of 1864 broke out when Spain tried to reassert its supremacy over its former colonies, Peru and Chile, with an occupation of the birds' rocky islands. In the end, the invader was forced to withdraw, in part because France had supplied Peru with naval vessels. In time, a Frenchman, Auguste Dreyfus, obtained the sole right to export its product to Europe. He built the largest square-rigged ships ever seen and gained an immense fortune from the millions of tons he shipped back home.

The first cargo arrived on European shores in 1835. A consortium of French, English and German merchants ensured that within five years the initial annual shipment increased a hundred-fold. Petrified avian faeces became the basis of an era of massive productivity that fed the workers who streamed to the new industrial cities from the land.

It could not last. Soon, Peru had exported more than twelve million tons of its most precious resource. It generated a quarter of the nation's income, much of it spent on the highest railways in the world, on new sewers and hospitals for

Lima, and on a World's Fair. Its raw material began to run out, but capitalism had no concern about that. What became a retreat from sustainability soon became a stampede.

It has now developed into a rout. Meat, once a luxury, has become a staple to billions. That change in taste killed off the raw material of the guano trade, for chickens are often raised on fish meal manufactured from anchovies, the food of the Cormorant, the Pelican and the Booby. The Peruvian birds have starved in their millions to give their distant cousins brief lives in crowded sheds across the world. A little thought would have cut out the fish meal factory and husbanded the birds' odoriferous product instead. Conversely, all attempts at control have failed. The fragment of the business that remains survives on sales to organic gardeners. In 1979, the Peruvian authorities made the islands protected zones in an attempt to establish a sustainable harvest. Laudable as that may be, its production will never again match that of the past.

For a time, a replacement source of nitrogen was found in sodium nitrate mined in Chile and elsewhere, but that was expensive and produced far too little for European needs. As geology began to fail, botany was called in to help.

Each year, lightning generates ten million tons of nitrogenous compounds. Three and a half thousand million years ago, that was life's main usable source of the element, and its abundance was limited by a shortage of raw material. As so often, Darwin's machine came up with a clever trick. Around two thousand million years ago, a bacterium evolved an enzyme that was able, with much hard work, to snatch (or 'fix') the gas from the air and combine it with hydrogen to produce an ammonia-like compound. That mutation spread to many other bacteria, and life's ability to soak up aerial nitrogen increased by thousands of times. A billion and a half years later, thanks to the emergence of green plants, the air began to fill with oxygen and, fuelled by those two potent gases, evolution exploded. In time, plants such as peas, beans and vetches – legumes, as they are called – themselves found a way to coax nitrogen from the bacteria. They housed them in their roots and, as a reward for food and shelter, used their products for their own ends.

Farmers have long thought, in the words of the diarist John Evelyn, that 'the Earth, in the years of repose, recovers its vigour by the attraction of the spirits which it receives from the air', but had no idea how it did the job. Lavoisier had noted that leguminous feed crops such as lucerne and clover increased soil fertility and he realised that nitrogen was somehow involved. Boussingault continued the work. He found that clover and its fellows would grow even in sterilised crushed brick without fertiliser – which proved that they must be able to produce the essential compound themselves, perhaps because they 'find in the atmosphere a part of the nitrogen that contributes to their organisation'. He spent thirty years in attempts to work out how they did it, with no success.

Now, every step in that biochemical chain has been unravelled. Huge sums are invested in attempts to persuade crops such as wheat to take up the hitchhikers and even to introduce their crucial genes into the plants themselves.

Success would transform the global economy but still seems far away. In spite of this failure, beans, clover and the like are nowadays planted across vast tracts of land, and thanks to the efforts of the world's farmers generate twice as much nitrogen fertiliser as do thunderstorms.

Noble as their efforts might be, chemistry has now taken over from biology as the engine of the elemental juggernaut. In 1898, Sir William Crookes, president of the British Association for the Advancement of Science, had claimed that 'All England and all civilised nations stand in deadly peril of not having enough to eat', for food was needed as the population expanded, and not enough fertiliser was available to grow it. His challenge was met in Germany in 1912.

There, the chemist Fritz Haber found that hydrogen could be persuaded to link itself with nitrogen, with the help of a catalyst of iron under two hundred atmospheres of pressure and a temperature of 500°C, to make ammonia. That in turn could be used to produce both explosives and fertilisers. In 1919, to some irritation by those who had just faced his nation's artillery, Haber received the Nobel Prize for his work. In his acceptance speech, he explained that 'the demand for fixed nitrogen, which at the start of this century could be satisfied with a few hundred thousand tons a year, must increase to millions of tons'. He was right.

Like his Gallic predecessors, Haber made an intellectual journey from farmyard to battlefield. He went further than had the French chemists for he invented the poisonous gases used in the trenches and developed into the compound Zyklon B, later used to such dreadful ends (his wife killed herself when she found out what he had done). The Haber process has been to blame for almost all the millions of deaths in the conflicts of the twentieth century.

Deplorable as that may be, his technology in truth saved many more people than it destroyed. Since its invention, there has been a fourfold increase in human numbers, more than matched by a huge increase in farm production. The amount of ammonium nitrate synthesised has gone up by two hundred and fifty times since Haber opened his first factory. A human body needs two kilograms of nitrogen a year. For almost the whole of history, nature met that demand. At the time of Christ, about a million tons a year were added to soils by human effort, almost all with the help of legumes. Today, more than a hundred million times as much man-made fertiliser is produced every twelve months. To do so uses half the output of every nuclear power station on the planet.

Half the protein in the body of every reader of this book now finds its raw material in some century-old German technology. The number of people fed per hectare has risen from two at the time of Haber's Nobel Prize to five today. His process keeps a quarter of the world's inhabitants alive and, without it, two billion men and women (a figure equivalent to the entire population of Europe and the New World) would starve. In the last fifty years, the amount of artificial nitrogen fertiliser used has gone up by ten times, and on present trends the figure will double again in the next fifty. Haber's invention gave birth to a world in which the work of nature was first matched, and then overtaken, by that of man.

Once it has done its job in the fields all that extra nitro-gen must find a home. Boussingault realised that there was a constant exchange of the element between the soil, plants, animals, rivers, seas, and the atmosphere. He had identified the nitrogen cycle, a market that circulates chemical capital across the globe. It has begun to spin at record speed.

If all the nitrogen from fertiliser were taken up by plants, the world would need no more than twelve million tons of the stuff a year. In fact it uses ten times as much. A factory delivers almost all its output to the farmer, who loses a little as he spreads it on his land. The rain washes some away and more bleeds off into the atmosphere, so that just half is taken up by crops. Yet more is lost when some of the harvest is discarded as it is processed.

Cattle demand lots of grass or maize, and lots of fertiliser. A vegetarian platter uses about one part in twenty-five of the fertiliser that emerges from the pressure vessels, but a steak uses one part in six. Every American, as a result, needs about a hundred kilograms of available nitrogen a year, while Europeans use no more than half the transatlantic dose and Africans get by on a tenth of that.

The excess has to go somewhere, and thanks to the winds and the rain, it does. As a result, the world has bloomed, but not always in the right places. Fertiliser washed from the soil finds a home in forests, in rivers, and in seas. London's river may seem cleaner than it was in the nineteenth century, but the hidden pollutant has not gone away. Nitrate in the Thames has been measured every month since 1868. Until 1940, levels were stable, but the amount doubled at the time of the Second World War, and did so again in the 1970s. Farmers were to blame, for in wartime the uplands of southern England were stripped of their sheep and ploughed for wheat, while the 1970s saw an enormous increase in fertiliser use.

Brittany faces even more of a problem, for it is a centre of high-intensity agriculture, with the run-off of manure from its fourteen million pigs almost as great as that from the vast enclosures of the United States. Its rivers are full of nitrogen. Blooms of algae appear off its coasts, while seaweed grows wild and then rots. Some beaches have been closed because of the stench. An attempt to control the situation with heavy fines led the locals, in the tradition of their ancestors, to riot. The situation across the Atlantic is even worse, with damage to half of all the United States' rivers. Even the icy lakes of Siberia and Alaska have been overtaken by the algal explosion. The sea bottom off New Orleans is now a 'dead zone' larger than Connecticut, and in China, too, the blooms reach far out to sea. The amount of active nitrogen dumped in the oceans has more than doubled over the past century, and its concentration across the whole eastern half of the north Pacific has rocketed.

The stuff that streams from the farm joins up with oxygen to make nitrous oxide (laughing gas). That reacts with oxygen to give nitric oxide – one atom of oxygen with one of nitrogen. Coal and oil fumes add more, plus a dose of nitrogen dioxide (one nitrogen with two oxygens). Such gases produce ozone, which affects both human health and natural vegetation, while nitrous oxide is a greenhouse gas three hundred times more potent than carbon dioxide. The dangers of the latter are well known, but the natural carbon cycle has been perturbed by no more than one part in ten, while that of nitrogen is eighty per cent off balance.

Alfred Nobel hoped that his invention would put an end to war, as no state would dare to use high explosives in battle because of the dangers of retaliation. He was wrong, and the twentieth century became the bloodiest in history. As physics took over from chemistry, the weapons that emerged were so horrific that his prediction has been more or less correct but the new terrorism may change that equation. And how long can we survive the crises of climate, pollution and hunger? Lavoisier's inert gas binds the worlds of life and death into an inextricable embrace. Its powerful and aggressive split per-sonality is shared, alas, with those who tinker with it.

CHAPTER III

LET THEM EAT CHIPS

The Irish sans-potato, had he not senses then, nay a soul? In his frozen darkness, it was bitter for him to die famishing; bitter to see his children famish.

THOMAS CARLYLE, *The French Revolution*

Parmentier with his favourite vegetable

In April 1793, just six months before the start of the Terror, the gardens of the Palais de Luxembourg were in bloom. Parisians had long strolled through their alleys to admire the riot of colour, but in that year the decorative beds were replaced by serried rows of flowers in an improbable bluish-purple. They were of just one species, planted to replace the parterres and lawns that had long surrounded the grand edifices. The flowers were there to promote a crop much favoured, for reasons both practical and ideological, by the country's rulers. The emergency of 1789 gained much of its impetus from a famine that had spread through France after the summer drought and icy winter of the previous year. The disastrous state of agriculture also played a part. Thomas Carlyle writes of the 'lank scarecrows, that prowl hunger-stricken through all highways and byways of French Existence', and he was not exaggerating.

Starvation was familiar, for there had been a severe food crisis every decade or so for the previous three centuries. Much of Europe shared the problem, and the failure of the Irish oat crop in 1728 led Jonathan Swift to write his polemic *A Modest Proposal for Preventing the Children of Poor People From Being a Burthen to Their Parents or Country, and for Making Them Beneficial to the Publick* (which argued, with a certain irony, that the poor should sell their infants as food for the rich).

Two decades before the Revolution, the pharmacist Antoine-Augustin Parmentier started what became a lengthy campaign to assuage his nation's hunger. His name is not today much celebrated outside his native land, but there it still appears on menus both grand and modest. All the dishes involved – *hachis parmentier, potage parmentier, champignons parmentier* and more – involve an ingredient that before his time was used in France, if it was used at all, only for animal feed. Thanks to his efforts it became a staple. The plant was already eaten in Spain, Germany and elsewhere, but in the land of Louis XIV the Church regarded its underground lifestyle with suspicion, and the authorities prohibited its use on health grounds, as they assumed that it caused leprosy. Its lumpy surface did rather resemble the deformations characteristic of that disease, and the 'doctrine of signatures' which claimed that 'like leads to like' saw that as evidence of causation. Even so, he saw to it that the item was at last declared safe by the medical establishment.

Parmentier was France's proselytiser of the potato. With it he rescued his fellow citizens from starvation, fuelled their radical zeal, and helped to feed the Napoleonic armies as they raced across Europe. His work set the stage for today's abundance, but the problems now faced by his favourite foodstuff are a salutary reminder that the modern world is, behind its façade of plenty, still at constant risk of hunger.

Parmentier had trained as a medical chemist (and later in life returned to that profession when he was appointed chief apothecary to the Napoleonic armies) but as a young man changed direction to become one of the earliest, and greatest, students of nutrition. He became an active supporter of the revolutionary regime and his favourite foodstuff was planted around the Parisian palace as a statement of the new era of equality in all things, food included.

After the emergence of wheat, barley, lentils and the like at the origin of agriculture in the Middle East ten thousand years ago, vegetables from carrots to cauliflowers crept on to the plate. None packed the punch of the potato. The young chemist met his first tuber during his imprisonment in Prussia at the time of the Seven Years War, when he had little else to eat and yet, to his surprise, remained healthy. Released on parole, he collaborated with a German agriculturalist interested in the plant and once back home began to study it in more detail. He found it to be, in many ways, far superior to France's then staple items of wheat, barley, rye and oats. In time, he received a prize offered by the Royal Academy of Sciences for the development of a new food to be used in times of hunger, and with it bought a tract of land upon which to grow his favoured vegetable. With the help of his sister he set up a laboratory in which he analysed its chemistry (and, later in life, extended his interests to sewage, vaccination, and the culinary value of chestnuts). A few months before the collapse of the old regime Parmentier produced a popular work entitled *Traité sur la Culture et les Usages de la Pomme de Terre, de la Patate et du Topinambour,* which gave advice not just on the cultivation of potatoes but on Jerusalem artichokes – *topinambours* – as well. He was in illustrious company, for across the Channel, in *The Wealth of Nations,* Adam Smith had also extolled the vegetable: 'No food can afford a more decisive proof of its nourishing quality.'

Now the high priest of the tuber has a Métro station of his own. It contains a statue of a gentleman in a powdered wig about to hand a sample of his comestible to a burly rustic, who wears a dubious expression. Passengers can ease their bones on what look like tractor seats while they admire the mesh design upon the tiled walls, placed there in honour of the trellises used by Parmentier to support his experimental plants.

Jerusalem artichokes have had less success than has the *patate*, which shapes the lives of millions. Potatoes are tough, and succeeded even on the poor soils of eighteenth-century France, starved of fertiliser as the nation then was. They are much more nutritious than seed crops and, even better, a crop can be squeezed in between two sowings of seeds, to give an extra harvest each year.

The ex-pharmacist promoted his *pommes de terre* in the face of apathy and even hostility. He persuaded the economist Turgot to eat some in public and to order peasants to join him at table as proof that they were safe (a few did, but most remained suspicious). Then he planted rows of them on the sandy and infertile ground of Sablons, on the outskirts of Paris. Guards, so the story goes, were sent to surround the beds in daylight hours as a hint of their value, but were removed when darkness fell in a scheme to tempt the locals to steal the tubers and to cultivate them in their own gardens. With his sights set higher Parmentier hosted a banquet in which the vegetable was present in all twenty courses, from potato soup to a tart made from its flour, and ersatz coffee concocted from the same stuff. The guests, Benjamin Franklin included, found the repast mediocre, but the host himself regretted only that he had been unable to 'prepare a liqueur with potatoes to make my company completely happy' (news of vodka had not yet penetrated into France). And, at the pinnacle of public life, Marie-Antoinette was persuaded to wear a bouquet of their flowers to assure her subjects that the plant had a noble pedigree.

With such assistance, the new delicacy was in time accepted by the masses, even as it was disdained by the upper classes. Didérot in his *Encyclopédie* had earlier noted that 'The potato is rightly reproached as a cause of gas, but what are winds to the vigorous digestions of peasants and labourers?', but in 1794 the new Committee on Subsistence and Provisions disregarded that risk and printed ten thousand pamphlets on the joy of tubers, together with a cookbook, *La Cuisinière Républicaine*, which contained more than thirty *patate*-based recipes, from soup to cake. Soon the item was on every proletarian table.

The Americans were less class-conscious. Thanks to an expatriate Parisian chef, 'Potatoes fried in the French manner' became the national dish of republican France's oldest ally, as recorded in the menu of a White House dinner given by Thomas Jefferson. The delicacy was referred to as 'French Fries' (although some latter-day patriots now preface the dish with the adjective 'Freedom' instead). The average American eats around fifty kilograms of spuds each year while Europeans are even more enthusiastic, with almost twice that dose each twelve months.

Potatoes – like maize, peanuts, pumpkins, squash, peppers, tomatoes, cassava, blueberries, prickly pears, avocados, pine-apples, strawberries, sunflowers and tobacco – are natives of the New World. They were farmed in the Andes of southern Peru ten thousand years ago, but did not cross the Atlantic until well into Renaissance times. Since then, they have become the third in line of the globe's food crops, after rice and wheat, with more than three hundred million tons harvested each season. For one person in five across the planet, the comestible is a staple. It can be grown from sea level almost to snowline, and across vast and varied landscapes that stretch from southern Chile to central Norway, although the plant is not happy in very hot places. In the days of the *Ancien Régime* the crop had the further advantage that it could avoid the iniquitous taxes levied by mill-owners, for it did not need to be ground into flour. Not all the news is good, for the potato differs from its rivals in that its edible parts are bulky and hard to transport and to store, which tends to make it a local product rather than a global commodity. In addition, the vegetable is unduly susceptible to disease.

The native land of the cultivated version stretches across South and Central America and includes the Altiplano of the Andes, while other wild kinds grow from the United States to Tierra del Fuego. In the thin soils and sparse vegetation of the cold, dry Andean landscape the plant flourishes at up to five thousand metres. Its swollen underground parts allow it to survive drought and cold, and it needs much less water than do grains. In the Americas before Columbus the crop kept millions alive, and when at last it escaped its native continent that number went up by a thousand times. The humble tuber was a treasure far more valuable than the gold and silver brought back by the Conquistadores (the Spaniards themselves disliked the 'edible stone' and regarded it as a medicament rather than a meal, an idea they picked up from the Incas, who used it to ward off rheumatism).

Almost all the billions of tubers across the globe descend from just a few plants. DNA from old museum collections shows that Peruvian strains began to spread across mainland Europe in the 1600s. A second introduction of Chilean stock was made in the Napoleonic era and their descendants now make up the vast majority of farmed varieties. Quite why the shift from one to the other took place is not certain, but the plant needs short days in certain seasons to persuade it to invest in swollen roots rather than wasting its efforts on sex, with its expensive displays of flowers. Peruvian stocks live in icy mountains close to the equator, with its equal periods of light and dark, and tended to flourish out of control in the long warm days of a European summer, when they devoted their efforts to seductive blooms rather than underground reserves. The Chilean plants, which evolved in a region where days vary in length from spring to autumn, may have been more productive on this side of the Atlantic.

The first specimens were brought into the Canary Islands little more than thirty years after they were noticed by Europeans. From there they passed to mainland Spain. Their medical importance seemed obvious, and Teresa de Avila, the founder of the Barefoot Carmelites, attributed her recovery from illness to the miraculous vegetable. It had other helpful properties. An enigmatic reference in Shakespeare's *Merry Wives of Windsor* has Falstaff, who hopes that he has persuaded two women to share his bed, come out with a remarkable command: 'Let the sky rain potatoes.' He shared the widespread belief that the plant was an aphrodisiac that, one work of the time claimed, was liable to 'incite to Venus'. A century and a half later, the *Encyclopaedia Britannica* still saw it as a 'demoralising esculent'.

The potato has green berries rather like those of deadly nightshade and mandrake. All three belong to a group called the Solanaceae, a name that derives somewhat ominously from the Latin *solamen*, to put to sleep. Other members include the tomato and the aubergine. Tobacco is in the same botanical tribe, but its addictive component made it welcome to Europeans well before its humble relative found favour. Other reasons to reject the potato included its unnatural habit of growing from what look like roots rather than from seeds, and its failure to gain a mention in the Bible. Even the hungry did not always approve, and a shipload sent to relieve a famine in Naples in 1770 was sent back to its donors.

In Italy and Germany, the delicacy was picked up by reformist sects. Persecuted by the Catholic Church, the Protestant *patate*-eaters were driven northwards and their foodstuff went with them. Peter the Great of Russia became aware of its talents in the seventeenth century while a student of naval architecture in the Netherlands and sent samples back to his native land. In time, the crop began its slow spread across Europe and beyond to become 'the poor man's bread'. Now, China has become the largest producer and India is not far behind. Its native continent has also come up fast, with Peru – its original home – at the head of the South American pack. The Third World now grows more than half the global crop and in India and China the plant took no more than thirty years to become a staple.

Everywhere, the new foodstuff's arrival sparked off a surge in numbers. Between the Norman invasion of England and the end of the nineteenth century, world population rose by five times. The famous tuber was in part responsible, for almost all the increase took place after 1650, when it began its conquest. In Ireland it arrived in the year of the Bastille, and within seventy years the population rose from two to nine million. The diet of many of its citizens consisted of just that item, plus milk or cheese – which, monotonous as it may be, is enough to support life. An acre of land planted with potatoes in raised 'lazy-beds' well provided with manure, or with rotted turf or seaweed, together with enough grazing for one milk cow, would support a family of eight. Thomas Malthus blamed the crop for what he saw as a deplorable development; in his somewhat grudging words, 'more food produces more mouths'. Everywhere there was a dramatic increase in stature after its arrival. In France, the average height of soldiers rose by more than a centimetre in the generation that first experienced it. As *pommes de terre* spread across Europe, mills made bread from their flour while distilleries produced useful new products such as vinegar and cheap spirits.

Parmentier was more right than he knew about the benefits of the potato. Not only is the plant a better source of sugars and starch than are wheat or rice, and not only does it generate more protein per acre than almost any other crop, but it also contains plenty of vitamins. One large tuber provides a fifth or so of the daily needs for the B group (whose absence leads to beri-beri, pellagra and anaemia), and half the necessary dose of vitamin C, with a concentration in its flesh equivalent to that of a lemon. It also contains plenty of trace elements such as iron and zinc, and is in addition a source of fibre as a portion of its starch comes in a form hard to digest.

Not all the news is good, for the potato generate poisons in its leaves and in badly stored tubers. Most varieties do not contain much, but some do have enough to be harmful until just before the crop is mature. Nobody – apart from those foolish enough to make tea from its leaves – seems to have suffered much damage in recent years (Elizabeth I's cook was fired when he served boiled leaves – which the Queen rejected – rather than the more conventional part of the vegetable).

As the flowers in the Luxembourg gardens show, potatoes can be as sexual as other plants, and crosses between lines are often used to transmit genes for disease resistance or speedy growth from one variety to another. The commercial crop itself is, in contrast, almost always propagated from tubers. Those structures are not roots, but underground stems, while the 'eyes' from which new plants develop are in fact a form of leaf. The buds beneath them are the points from which a new stem, identical to its progenitor, emerges when the fragment of tissue is planted. Huge numbers can be generated from a favoured specimen to give a clone specialised for taste, for yield, or for resistance to disease.

The build-up of errors as a clone is copied again and again

poses a challenge for breeders. Farmers once believed in the plant's inherent 'degeneracy', as for many varieties quality does decline over the years, but in fact that is a reminder of the central truth of inheritance: that sex purges lineages of errors and that without it decay is inevitable.

One hundred and seven species of potato are known in the wild. Just four are cultivated in the Andes, and only one has made it to the wider world. The native kinds are very variable at the DNA level and even in the numbers of chromosomes. The main domestic version has four sets (twice as many as we possess), while other species have up to six.

Almost all the billions of farmed plants belong to the species *Solanum tuberosum*. That has, through the efforts of breeders over the years, become divided into large numbers of named sub-types, from Accord to Yukon Gold. Most have not withstood the test of time, of disease, or of the market, and have disappeared, but seed merchants can still tempt enthusiasts with more than a hundred varieties.

In 2011 the plant's DNA was read from end to end. It has some unexpected features. The potato has more genes than we do (which is a statement about how little we understand about genetics rather than of the vegetable's sophistication). Most of the message consists of sequences repeated many thousands of times. Two cultivated varieties may differ in millions of places in their genome and may each possess a host of genes that have been damaged by mutation. Attempts to mate individuals from closely related breeds then face problems when paired and damaged segments of the double helix get together.

Potato DNA contains large numbers of genes that protect against disease, although many are no more than the hulks of defences against now defunct strains of fungus or insect. Those enemies have been replaced by more virulent forms in the endless arms race between parasites and their hosts. Parmentier's vegetable remains a fragile beast.

The most notorious epidemic arrived in Europe in the 1840s. It led to millions of deaths and to political storms whose consequences echo today.

The Breton peasant Jean-Marie Déguignet kept a diary through his long and adventurous life in which he gave an account of the hardship and superstition of the local people. In 1845, he wrote of their explanation of a disaster that had struck their crop: 'The disease began with an attack on the leaves of the plant. It was black as charcoal, therefore it could have come only from the Ruler of the Dark Empire. The stench of the leaves could only be that of hell as it broils ... the tubers' spongy mess the very image of the damned in the fiery furnace.' The peasants blamed the calamity on the devil, who had not long before appeared in the region in the guise of a black cat. Déguignet himself was well aware that the problem was due to 'a simple microscopic black mould'.

The devil had come to Brittany through carelessness. A few years earlier, a different and less destructive contagion emerged in northern Europe, and in 1844 the Belgian government introduced a new and – they hoped – resistant stock from North America. It brought with it the infection that so alarmed the Bretons.

Late blight, as the condition is now known, devastated

the whole of France. The crop had already suffered from the intense drought of the 1840s, when the ice on the summit of Mont Blanc melted for the first time in decades, and the harvest dropped by a quarter. In Ireland, the situation was even worse. Almost every citizen ate fourteen pounds or so of potatoes each day. Crop failure meant famine. The botanical plague that struck in 1845 lasted for five years. More than a million Irish people died and around the same number emigrated.

Other parts of Europe were less dependent on the crop, but the effects of the blight were still dire, with almost as many deaths overall as in Ireland, albeit in a much larger population. In France, the birth rate fell even as the death rate shot up. Hungry people roamed the countryside. Peasants struggled with landowners or abandoned their farms, mills were burned and grain wagons hijacked. Thousands of Frenchmen moved to the cities, while others emigrated to North America, to Mexico, and to Algeria. Trade barriers prevented the import of food from countries less hard hit and soon the whole economy fell into a slump.

Often – in Ireland most of all – the victims were blamed for their own predicament. In an omen of modern times on this side of the Irish Sea, the most deprived were subject to a Poor Law, introduced to control a supposed 'natural passion for idleness'. If a citizen had appealed to 'indoor relief' (the workhouse) for food he faced starvation rations even before the blight arrived. When it did, a scandal soon became a disaster. The workhouse at Kilkenny was built in 1832 to hold thirteen hundred people. By 1851 more than three times as many were crammed in. A mass grave was opened to house the victims of typhus, tuberculosis and simple starvation. When this was excavated not long ago, about half of the thousand skeletons showed signs of scurvy, a disease absent from those buried in earlier years as proof that before the famine their main food-stuff had provided essential vitamins as well as fuel.

In early 1848, in a reflection of the bloody disorders of sixty years earlier – and for much the same reason – the streets of Paris filled with hungry and furious crowds. Déguignet records that this, too, had been predicted by aged Bretons, who saw signs in the sky that warned of a new revolt. The then ruler was Louis Philippe I, the last of the Bourbons, his policies a throwback to the *Ancien Régime* (and his administration the source of the phrase 'they have learned nothing and forgotten nothing'). He was forced to abdicate and fled across the Channel. For a few months a Second Republic, proclaimed by a poet, held sway, and free elections were held. The old guard then fought back, and troops killed five thousand of the insurgents. The disturbance, like its pre-decessor, was sparked off in part by starvation, and fell to the forces of reaction. In another echo of those times, a relative of Napoleon took control, for Louis-Napoléon Bonaparte was elected head of state and, like his uncle, soon proclaimed himself emperor.

As Karl Marx noted in his *Eighteenth Brumaire of Louis-Napoléon*, his coup's success came from the fact that the French citizenry still lacked any sense of internal cohesion. There was no proletariat that might identify itself as a shared class, organise and rise up; instead 'the great mass of the

French nation is formed by the simple addition of like entities, much as a sack of potatoes consist of a lot of potatoes huddled into a sack'. Any attempt at a workers' dictatorship was bound to fail (the book is also noted for the comment that 'all great world-historical facts and personages appear, so to speak, twice ... the first time as tragedy, the second time as farce').

That year's famine led to revolts large and small in Germany, Italy, Poland, Ireland, the Austrian Empire and Denmark. Most were put down, but at least the serfs were freed from their chains in Austro-Hungary, and Denmark too saw a first step towards democracy. Late blight may not have been the sole cause of the Year of Revolutions, but in many places it was the straw that broke the constitutional camel's back.

Plenty of Englishmen were infuriated by such developments. For them, the guilty party was obvious. The reformer Cobbett saw the potato as the root of 'slovenliness, filth, misery and slavery', while his fellow activist Cobden felt that any race that depended on it would never 'lead the way in arts, arms or commerce'. Carlyle – no friend of Ireland, nor of revolt – talks of how the blight had made the Irish peasantry of his day into creatures even more miserable than the French sans-culottes: 'the Irish sans-potato darkens the English towns, lodging in any pig-hutch, and undersells the Saxon native and drives him to emigrate'. He berated the vegetable's role in France, for its abundance had obliged the peasantry to become dependent upon it, and its fragility and frequent failure meant that they were forced 'to die fighting for an immortal Hope and Faith of Deliverance'.

Neither the blight nor the cataclysms that followed were the work of the devil. Instead the infection is due to a mould (not in fact a fungus, but a member of a different group, the water moulds) called *Phytophthora infestans* – 'the infectious plant-destroyer'. Its life cycle was worked out in Paris in the 1860s. Its homeland is in central Mexico, where it copies itself in ways both sexual and asexual. It has relatives that attack tomatoes, soybeans and more, but the scourge of the potato does more damage than any other. The mould multiplies at great speed and generates billions of infectious particles that blow in the wind or float downstream and, on windy days, may travel fifty miles. Once these reach a host, they hatch to give cells that swim towards their target. The plague does best in warm, damp weather towards the end of the season. It can live its life in just four or five days to produce a new generation ready to lay waste to the fields.

To survive from one year to the next, the parasite needs a winter refuge, and on the farms of those days one was easy to find. Some plants were always left in the ground after the harvest, and these were a sanctuary for the water mould, which was poised for another attack when spring arrived. Today, those who cultivate the vegetable make more of an effort to root out the stowaways, or rotate their crop with grains or cabbages from year to year, or grow stock in northern Scotland or Canada, which have cold winters that snuff out their enemy. The plant-destroyer always fights back.

It has had many changes of identity since the grim days of the 1840s. In the Andes, the domestic crop's original home, the pest does not bother with sex and reproduces as a series of clones. Preserved DNA from infected leaves collected across Europe over the past two hundred years shows that one clone (which has disappeared from our own continent but is still present in its native land) dominated that epidemic. Later attacks involved a mixture of different asexual varieties as a hint that the pest had by then invaded several times from the New World. Those pioneers have since then gained many mutations that allow them to infect a wide range of potato lineages. The pressure to succeed was so great that competition among the various asexual strains led to rapid evolution and to the defeat of one host variety after another.

Then matters took a turn for the worse. For most of the pest's European career, just one of its two genders (if they can be so called) had crossed the Atlantic. Celibacy was forced upon it as a result. One day, sex raised its blighted head. In the great European drought of 1976, fresh stocks of potatoes were imported from Mexico. At the time, nobody realised that there the agent of blight had two sexes. When the Mexican potatoes arrived, they brought the second sex with them. The lonely Europeans at last had partners, and celebrated the honeymoon in Scandinavia. Sex provided a potent new weapon, for it produces millions of new mixtures of genes each season. These copy themselves to produce vast numbers of novel strains that have now spread across Europe and beyond, to cause millions of pounds' worth of damage. The 'Euroblight' network every year looks at the DNA fingerprint of the pests across the continent. One clone makes up around a third of the total infections, and in Western Europe a second clone is the cause of almost as many. Eastern

Europe has a wider range of individually rare versions, but they are being replaced by more virulent invaders from the west. Millions are spent on attempts to control the plague, with European fields sprayed twenty times or more in a bad season.

The potato has plenty of other enemies. Early blight flourishes soon after the crop is planted and does almost as much harm as its autumnal relative. Another fungus causes potato wart, while virus Y, transmitted by aphids, can wipe out a whole crop. It became a pest no more than two decades ago and is now a major enemy. A hot summer is described by experts as a 'sprouty year', for the plants mature too fast and become inedible. Too much bright light after harvest also leads to the build-up of poisons. Wet soil causes hollow heart, brown rot and black leg, while its opposite leads to jelly end rot and deep common scab, not to mention dolly-shaped disease, in which the tubers have a constricted waist.

If heat, cold, rain, drought, moulds and viruses spare the poor farmer, more sophisticated foes are ready to take their place. Eelworms love the taste and can stay dormant for twenty years until the next crop is planted, while slugs are waiting in the wings (and the wave of southern European species that has crawled northwards over the past few years has made the problem worse). Then there are the insects. The Colorado potato beetle was not recorded on the crop until quite late, with the first instance in 1859, half a century after the creature was first noticed on wild plants in the United States. By 1874 it had reached the East Coast, and in 1922 the insect appeared in France and has now got as far as China. With strict controls the creatures have more or less been kept out of Britain and the German plan to drop millions of them on England during the Second World War came to naught. They have been accompanied by waves of other beetles, aphids, leaf-hoppers, moths and more. Mice, moles, voles, badgers and feral pigs are also fond of a spud or two when they get a chance. The trade in the European Union alone is worth six billion pounds a year. A billion of that is spent on the war against pests, and the figure is certain to increase. Those who grow the vegetable must sometimes fear that they have strayed into the plot of *Cold Comfort Farm*.

What is to be done? Once, the answer seemed simple: blast the pests with chemicals. In 1846 a Swansea man wrote to the *Gardeners' Chronicle* with the observation that the blight, which had devastated the farms around Copperopolis, as the town was then known, had spared gardens near what was then the world's largest refinery, perhaps because the fumes killed its agent. The letter was ignored, but thirty years later in France, a disease of vines called downy mildew was vanquished with a compound of copper sulphate, quicklime and water known as Bordeaux mixture. It was then used to treat potatoes. In that first skirmish of the chemical battle it worked well, but new mutations appeared in the blight and the compound lost its power (and is now banned on ecological grounds). Dozens of pesticides, many based on the chemistry of poison gases, have since been tried. They work well for a while, but – as always – evolution fights back and the targets become resistant. The Colorado beetle, in particular, has an almost uncanny ability to come up with new strategies. Paris Green, once used to kill sewer rats, was a fearsome compound of copper and arsenic that in time put paid to millions of beetles, but natural selection got round that. In the 1940s DDT was introduced, but was defeated within five years. By the 1980s, the pest could withstand the worst that chemistry could throw at it.

A bacterium called *Bacillus thuringiensis* makes a certain protein toxic to insects, plant pests included. The poison is more specific in its targets than are crude compounds such as DDT, which kill more or less whatever they touch. It has been quite successful against the dread beetle, but signs of resistance have emerged even there.

Another strategy is to breed new varieties that can outwit their foes, at least for a time. Crosses with wild relatives have delivered many resistance genes to where they are needed, although that has its problems because the hybrids may also inherit variants that cause bitterness or poor texture. Breeders can now circumvent the messy business of sex altogether by fusing cells of two different lineages in the laboratory. With that trick, even species that in normal circumstance will not cross can be persuaded to enter into a relationship, which means that genes can be imported from far away. Cells in culture can also be exposed to moulds or to viruses with those that survive chosen to grow into new plants.

Such work goes on without much public concern, but parts of modern biology have been met with positively Gallic obduracy. Thirty years ago it became possible to use a bacillus that invades plant cells to move genes from one species into another. One of the first targets was the potato, which was provided with the short section of double helix that allows it to make the poison secreted by *Bacillus thuringiensis*.

The Green movement has long approved that substance as a 'natural' insecticide. It remains for some reason quite opposed to the notion that the DNA that makes it should be inserted into a crop to allow it to make the stuff itself. The first engineered potatoes were planted in the United States in 1995, and were soon grown on fifty thousand acres. In 2001 they were withdrawn because complaints by Greens in Europe and Japan had destroyed the export market. The plants died a commercial death and that fate may be shared by new strains that make vitamin A or have been provided with genes from amaranth (a staple grain of the Incas rich in amino acids). A new approach is to use the bacterium to insert resistance genes from wild potatoes rather than from a different group of plants, to generate clones that resist the blight and other afflictions. Even so, not one such line has yet managed to overcome Green propaganda.

Deliberate untruths by the 'ecological' movement mean that the cost of obtaining permission to grow such plants now far outweighs that of research. As a result, most companies have given up on the transgenic toxin technology. Now, though, an engineered blight-resistant potato may soon be approved for use in the United States, although it will no doubt face another wave of dishonest propaganda in Europe.

The battle between crops and their pests has parallels with that between bacteria and antibiotics. There, the situation is dire, with almost nothing left in the medical armoury. Health authorities now keep newly developed versions in reserve against epidemics or novel infections, to cut down the chance of resistance caused by overuse. The same might be – but has not yet been – done with potato varieties.

The struggle of farmers with the forces of nature goes on long after the harvest is over. Most crops must be stored before they can be sold. That may be more difficult than it seems. Potatoes are sensitive in storage. Breton and Irish peasants of the mid nineteenth century were condemned to long periods of hunger even in blight-free years. Their varieties could not last more than a few months after the harvest, for the damp climate was just right for rot. For three summer months, when one crop had been exhausted and the next was yet to come, they relied on grains to tide them over, but often those failed and they starved. Parmentier was aware of the problem, but the best he could suggest was that the vegetable be kept dry and sheltered from frost in a shallow hole covered with straw.

Technology has moved on. Tubers – unlike wheat or barley, which are more or less in a state of suspended animation when in storage – generate heat after the harvest and soak up oxygen and give off carbon dioxide as their economy ticks over. In a modern storehouse they are taken through a series of regimes. First they are cooled down to restrain their natural exuberance, then given a couple of weeks at a slightly higher temperature to enable them to dry out and to heal the wounds made when they were snapped off the parent plant. Then they are cooled again so that most of their time behind closed doors is passed at around 5°C. At the last moment they are reanimated to allow them to convert excess sugar into tasty starch. During their hibernation a discreet set of chemical treatments prevents them from sprouting, and helps to kill off enemies that invade their haven and cause – among other conditions – dry rot, soft rot, silver scurf, black dot, pink rot and *Pythium* leak. The natural shocks that stored potatoes are heir to still destroy around one part in twelve of the world crop. Even with the best technology the reserves cannot last for much more than around ten months.

As a result, the sole guaranteed way to retain the crop's value – or that of most other foodstuffs – is to preserve it in some way. The idea is ancient indeed and without it our ancestors would have starved.

Hunter-gatherers had vessels in which they dried meat and fish over a fire or in the sun. Salt allowed food to be stored over the winter (one reason why the salt tax, the *gabelle*, was hated), and the Romans were so hooked on the stuff that they had to add a solid dose to each glass of wine for otherwise the drink seemed insipid. Fermentation began long ago, probably by accident. Cheese appeared well before people began to drink milk, and beer allowed the first farmers to preserve the goodness of barley in liquid form. When beer or wine went sour, it did not take long to find out that the acid liquor would protect other items from decay.

The potato was a pioneer of preservation. The hardy Andeans froze part of their harvest as the temperature fell at night and then soaked the edible parts in an icy stream. They trampled them hard as they melted on a warm day to squeeze out as much water as possible, and dried them in the sun. *Chuño*, as it was called, lasted for years and all that was needed to whip up a tasty dish was to add hot water.

The Andeans had invented freeze-dried food, long before Clarence Birdseye came up with a twentieth-century version. Parmentier himself experimented with dried potatoes: 'after they have been peeled, sliced, and dried in a stove or oven, they acquire the transparency, hardness and dryness of horn; they break clean, and the fracture has a vitreous appearance'. He gave barrels of the stuff to the explorer Lapérouse, who visited Australia in 1788 before he and his crew disappeared forever. Today, those anxious for a simple but tasteless meal · can buy instant mashed potato in any grocery.

The crisp is another Gallic innovation. It was invented by the celebrated chef Alexis Soyer, who fled to England after the disturbances of the 1830s and became *chef de cuisine* at the Reform Club. He democratised his talents with a 'Famine Soup' given away free in Ireland and wrote a work entitled *A Shilling Cookery for the People* which showed that a sliced potato fried in oil and allowed to dry would last for months.

The modern age of food preservation was born in that hotbed of innovation, eighteenth-century Paris. The restaurants of France, the home of *haute cuisine*, themselves began when diners started to sit at individual tables at set times rather than quarrelling about who could grab what at a single *table d'hôte*. The first to open, with a nod to the sophisticated cuisine of its neighbour, was the Grande Taverne de Londres, which set out its wares in the Rue Richelieu in 1782. The new regime then overthrew the guilds that restricted the numbers of chefs, which further encouraged the growth of such places. A generation of culinary artists invented dishes based on exotic ingredients, potatoes included.

One of the most successful was Nicolas Appert. As a young man he had departed to Germany, where he learned the culinary trade. Back in his native city he opened a confectioner's shop, and became caught up in the republican ferment. He even accompanied Louis XVI in the van that took him between his prison and the tribunal and in the end to the guillotine, but had the good sense to retire into private life after a period in jail at the time of the Terror.

Quite soon, Appert became interested in keeping food fresh, and after some experiments with fruit suspended in syrup came up with an idea that was to change the world. He found that food heated up in a bain-marie, poured into a stout vessel until it was full to the brim, and closed with an airtight seal while it was still hot would last for months or even years. Heat, he felt, did the job: 'the action of the fire destroys, or at least neutralises, all the ferment which, of their nature, modify and deteriorate animals and plant material . . . Carrots, cabbage, turnips, parsnips, onions, potatoes, celery, chard, beets, and generally all vegetables also need only to be bleached or prepared in fat or without it and can be used as soon as they are taken out of the container.' With no knowledge of how it worked Appert had invented tinned food. Sixty years later, Louis Pasteur showed that the process killed bacteria that would otherwise make their contents go off.

Appert's first experiments used garden peas held in empty champagne bottles, for he knew that they were strong enough to withstand pressure, but he soon shifted to custom-made glass vessels and then to metal containers. A wide variety of foods, from meat to milk and fruit, could be preserved by 'appertisation' (as the process is still called in France, if nowhere else). His product was tested by the Navy, and well received: 'the meat broth is really good ... the boiled meat is eatable, yellow peas and garden peas possess the freshness and the flavour of recently harvested vegetables'.

Appert set up a shop in a fashionable street. His new delicacies were not cheap, for each item cost as much as a working man's daily wage (in comparison to the ten minutes or so it now takes to earn enough to buy a sachet of dried potatoes) but they were fashionable and the *Almanach des Gourmands* even found the products of the *'conservateur par excellence'* preferable to fresh foods. His products were tested by a panel of experts, Antoine Parmentier included. They were impressed. Appert then established a factory to mass-produce the stuff, selling it across France and in time across Europe. His prices dropped and the range extended to dishes as sophisticated as a fish stew in a wine sauce, not to speak of an entire sheep in a bottle, preserved as a publicity stunt. Even the need, in the absence of tin-openers, to carry a hammer and chisel did not slow demand. The first can-opener was not invented for another half a century, and was deemed so dangerous that its use was restricted to shopkeepers, who opened their customers' containers for them.

Appert's moment came when the Emperor Napoleon summoned him to help solve the problem faced by every army; that it marches on its stomach. He developed vessels that held ten kilograms of meat or vegetables, and their contents fed the hundreds of thousands of French soldiers who invaded Russia. In a further contribution to his nation's culture the *cuisinier* then discovered that both wine and beer could be preserved in the same way, so that troops and travellers would always have their favourite beverage to hand. Appert became a national hero and in 1810 received a grant of twelve thousand francs to persuade him to reveal his secrets. His *Livre de tous les Ménages ou l'Art de Conserver pendant Plusieurs Années toutes les Substances Animales et Végétales* was translated into several languages.

Nicolas Appert then occupied himself by inventing the stock cube and the pressure cooker, but with the defeat at Waterloo his factory was destroyed and he died, almost forgotten, in poverty. The real fortunes were made by the English consortium that patented the tin can in 1812 and profited from its global success (they did not publicise the fact that they had stolen the idea from a Frenchman). In the modern world, a typical European eats around fifty kilograms of tinned food each year, the United States makes more than a hundred billion metal cans each twelve months, and across the world five times more are produced.

The emergence of the potato led to an era not of decay, but of progress in agriculture and nutrition so all-pervasive that famine has been forgotten. Hunger was behind the downfall of Louis XVI, and his nation's agricultural pioneers did a lot to abolish it.

Whether their descendants will continue to do so is less than certain. The world faces a dietary crisis that might become as great as those of earlier times. For many crops, a third of the output may be lost to disease. Yet more rots in storage while alarming amounts of food are simply jettisoned. The average European abandons around a hundred kilograms of comestibles each year, with some people dumping half of what they buy. A quarter of all bread and a third of all salads find a home in the bin (potatoes, on the other hand, have a better record). The amount now wasted in the developed world is equivalent to the entire food production of Sub-Saharan Africa.

A shortage of land is also a problem, as is the addiction of farmers to expensive fertilisers and scarce water, while for the potato, which does not flourish in hot weather, global warming is a further threat. Even worse, many crops have hit a biological brick wall, with little variation left for breeders to utilise. European potato production is in steep decline, and France itself grows just half as many as it did in the 1960s.

Other plants face the same problem. In the sixty years after the Second World War, the global yield of grains went up by three times, but those halcyon days are over. France, Britain and Germany have seen almost no increase in wheat, barley and oat production for the past decade, and other nations are also close to the limit. A few years ago Japan hit a yield barrier for rice at around five tons a hectare, a figure now almost achieved by China. The world may soon find it hard to feed its people.

A search across the wild for genes may help. The idea began with the great Russian geneticist Nikolai Vavilov, who himself collected rare native forms of Old World crops and obtained unusual potato varieties from the Americas. Potato breeders now have access to a gene bank and research station in Peru that contains many wild species, together with some of the thousand and more selected forms cultivated by locals (some of whom use several hundred varieties in the course of a year). Those crops retain far more diversity than do those cultivated elsewhere, while their as yet untamed relatives are able to cope with high grasslands, the edges of deserts, mountain rainforests, and the humid subtropics. They are a valuable but under-utilised resource that might improve today's stocks. Unfortunately, many are now under threat from the spread of commercial farms.

Homogenisation has emerged in another way. Most cultures once had their own staples: potatoes in Europe, rice in the Far East, or maize in South America. That has changed. A British supermarket contains all those items, but so does its equivalent in Kuala Lumpur, Shanghai or Buenos Aires. Thai food may be available almost everywhere, but McDonald's has dozens of restaurants in Thailand. The newly diverse diet in each city conceals a grand simplification across the globe and the loss of many local ingredients.

As if a decrease in crop diversity were not bad enough, a new age of disease may be around the corner. The late twentieth century was an era of botanical extinction. Chestnut and Dutch elm blight laid bare great tracts of Europe and North America as new clones wiped out millions of trees. Rice blast disease is now in a hundred countries and reached the United States just two decades ago. An aggressive race of wheat stem rust has spread across Africa and Asia since it emerged in Uganda in 1999.

Part of the problem comes from the natural movement of fungal spores, the largest living element of the air. They far outweigh the birds and the bees and are so abundant that an average breath sucks up half a dozen. The movement of infected specimens also causes much damage. The destruction of North American chestnuts through the import of Asian trees and the loss of production caused by the sexual potato-blight strains imported four decades ago from Mexico can each be blamed on such carelessness.

The potato is more at risk than is any other crop. The genes of the late blight have been tracked for years. DNA shows that a new and virulent clone is on the move. The first British examples were recorded in 2005. It has now reached India and China, the two biggest producers. It attacks almost all varieties and has evolved into an aggressive enemy.

Modern agriculture is to blame. The wild ancestors of our food plants lived scattered in small and diverse groups among many other species, which limits the ability of parasites to move from place to place or to overcome the defences of vast numbers of identical individuals at one go. Now, half the world's land surface has been transformed into farmland, and a potato field may contain millions of copies of the same clone, raw material for an infection that can spread like a forest fire.

All this has echoes of the eighteenth- and nineteenth-century plagues that led to so much public disorder. If all the diseases that affect the top five food plants – potatoes, rice, wheat, maize and soybeans – were to be eliminated (and there is not much sign of that) farmers could feed half a billion more people than today. If in contrast each was one day to face losses equal to those now found in the worst-hit places, that would leave enough food for no more than one person in three. Such a cataclysm is unlikely but far from impossible.

The world may need to double its agricultural production in the next half-century. The task calls for a new Parmentier. He would face the problem that in the modern world, almost all fruits are forbidden. Of the four hundred thousand known kinds of plant, fewer than three hundred have ever been used as a regular foodstuff, although around half that vast number might, with some help from artificial selection of the kind used long ago on the potato, become edible. Thomas Jefferson, the first ambassador of the United States to Paris, noted that 'the greatest service which can be rendered any country is to add a useful plant to its culture'. Parmentier did just that job for his native land. One day his intellectual descendants may find a replacement for his essential but endangered crop and – perhaps a greater challenge – might also be able to persuade people to eat it.

CHAPTER IV

FIRE AND ICE

Thus, over France, all stirs that has what the
Physiologists call irritability in it: how much more all
wherein irritability has perfected itself into vitality;
into actual vision, and force that can will!

THOMAS CARLYLE, *The French Revolution*

The respiration experiment: Mme Lavoisier takes notes

The riders who survive to the final stage of the Tour de France, three weeks after the start, have covered the distance from London to Cairo and made an ascent equivalent to twice the height of Everest. They do so at an average of more than forty kilometres an hour. Over the course of the race, each burns around 130,000 calories and to replace them takes on board the equivalent of four hundredweight of potatoes or two hundred and twenty bottles of red wine (in practice they choose a more balanced diet). Their tactics are based on the latest research into metabolism, the study of how the body burns its fuel, uses it for work, and generates waste and heat. For the cyclists, as for everyone else, the mechanism whereby 'irritability is perfected into vitality' is finely adjusted to deal with the challenges they face. Most people are, for most of the time, quite unaware of how close to the limits they live, but those in the desperate struggle that culminates on the Champs-Élysées are conscious of little else.

The Tour began in 1903. It emerged as a spin-off from a furious factional disagreement. The editor of a sports newspaper fell out with some of his advertisers over the Dreyfus affair (a bogus claim that a Jewish army officer had been a traitor that led to his imprisonment and at length to a pardon). In revenge, an anti-Dreyfusard businessman set up a rival journal. As a publicity stunt, he came up with the idea of a national bicycle championship, 'the greatest cycling trial in the entire world; a race more than a month long: Paris to Lyon to Marseille to Toulouse to Bordeaux to Nantes to Paris'. The scheme was a huge success. It drove his competitor out of business, and – with the exception of the war years – has been an annual fixture ever since.

In its early days, the Tour was amateurish, with the riders obliged to buy their own meals along the way and with arduous stages, one of which stretched from Paris to Lyon and took the first winner eighteen hours to complete. Over the years, the sections became less extreme but the race itself grew, to reach almost six thousand kilometres – the distance from London to Washington – in 1927. Other challenges included nails spread on the road by supporters of one or another rider and the post-war suppression of the sponsoring newspaper on the grounds that it had supported the Vichy regime. In modern times, *La Grande Boucle*, as the event is sometimes called, has settled down at around three and a half thousand kilometres, with quite a bit of variation from year to year. It now has dozens of commercial sponsors, and cities pay large fees to persuade the organisers to direct the circus to their own streets. In recent years the Tour has sparked off equivalents across Europe, the Americas and the Antipodes.

Popular as it may be, the sport has not yet attained the global reach of its much older twin, the marathon. That 42.2-kilometre road race began two and a half thousand years ago, when Phidippides ran to Athens with news from its sister city Marathon of a victory over the Persians. Today, more than two million people each year take part in an equivalent occasion. The Paris Marathon is the fifth biggest in the world, with fifty thousand runners, and takes place three months before the Tour. The runners start in the Champs-Élysées, pass the Tuileries and the Louvre, and enter the Bois de Vincennes, where the course doubles back to follow the Left Bank along the Seine, with magnificent views of Nôtre-Dame and the Eiffel Tower for those still in a fit state to appreciate them, before they finish in the shadow of the Arc de Triomphe.

There are plenty of reasons to take part in either contest, for the winner of the Tour makes around half a million dollars, with more to gain through sponsorship. The first past the post at the Paris Marathon makes fifty thousand euros in prize money. Other marathons offer even more generous rewards. The Dubai race is worth around two hundred thousand dollars to the winner, while the champion with the best time in the top six global marathons in a particular year is in line for a cheque that matches that offered by the Tour de France. Indeed, many top professional athletes have no particular need to win, for large sums are available just for taking part.

In the great bicycle race, around two hundred competitors qualify to start, and about one in six drops out as the days wear on. Those who make it to the finish must fight their way through twenty-one different stages over three weeks, with just two rest days. They include three distinct kinds of challenge; a series of long chases across a more or less flat landscape, a struggle up the high – and often hot – mountains of the Alps and the Pyrenees, and the purgatory of time trials, a test of maximum speed. On the flat, teams ride as a group, a 'peloton', in which selected riders take turns to be in the lead to cut down wind resistance for those behind them. In the other two stages, the cyclists may ride in teams or battle it out on their own. In the mountains, the specialist climbers tend to break away from the rest of the pack and enter into a private and painful battle with each other. Much the same happens in some professional marathons, in which paid assistants called 'rabbits' pace a star runner for part of the race and cut down wind resistance by keeping just ahead of him.

The Tour is the equivalent of two marathons a day, a challenge close to the limits of endurance. As proof of that, in the last half-century just four riders over the age of thirty-two have taken the yellow jersey given to the overall winner. In addition, the average speed drops in years in which the course is longer than usual, as a further hint that exhaustion curbs the ability to go on.

Professional cyclists and marathon winners have as a result become guinea pigs for those interested in what happens when man's vital machinery is pushed to – and sometimes beyond – the bounds of its capabilities. The athletes who reach that frontier, on wheels or on foot, suffer plenty of wear and tear. Participants in both races may faint from heat exhaustion and some suffer muscle cramps through loss of salt caused by drinking too much in an attempt to stay cool. Often they are simply unable to continue because their energy reserves run out. Both sports also come with threats of worn-out joints, thin and brittle bones, damaged arteries and enlarged hearts. The immune system may begin to lose its power as the numbers of white blood cells drops, with increased risk of infection. Female athletes in endurance sports sometimes cease to menstruate as their oestrogen levels fall. To make up for that, members of the opposite sex who take part in bicycle races face impotence brought on by the narrow saddle's tendency to restrict blood flow to an organ not much used in the event itself, together with low sperm count because of the warm and sticky conditions on the saddle. There are also real dangers of accident; as Mark Twain put it: 'Get a bicycle; you will not regret it, if you live.' Even so, in the Tour de France the participants' years of hard exercise give them a rate of mortality 40 per cent below that of their fellow citizens.

In the final stage of *La Grande Boucle*, in front of a huge crowd, the riders make eight laps around some of the most familiar monuments of the revolutionary era, in the opposite direction from that taken by the city's marathon. They circle the Arc de Triomphe, the Tuileries, the Louvre and the Place de la Concorde before a return to the Champs-Élysées itself. Before that ceremonial ride-past the overall victor – often with a margin of less than an hour over the three-week course – has already been decided but that does not put a stop to the other riders' frenzied efforts to display their abilities (and their sponsors' logos) to the world.

Marathons and bicycle races have each begun to approach the frontiers of physiological possibility. For the former, the world record for women has been unchanged for twelve years as a hint that some biological limit has been reached. The male equivalent still shows slow advance and was last broken in October 2014, with a time of two hours, two minutes and fifty-seven seconds, twenty-six seconds faster than the record set in the previous year, and five minutes better than that recorded by Steve Jones when he took the laurels in Chicago in 1984. In the Tour, average speeds have reached a plateau, with the record set ten years ago. What improvement there has been comes as much from advances in technology as in endurance, and as we shall see, some of the earlier peaks were not quite what they seemed.

In the hundred and more races since the contest began, it has been won by twenty-one Frenchmen, ten Belgians, seven Spaniards and the same number of Italians. The once undisputed overall champion was an American, who took the yellow jersey a remarkable seven times only to be stripped of his title after being found guilty of drug abuse. Cheats had been around since the first race, when some participants wheezed around part of the course and then took the train to speed themselves on their way, but in time dishonesty became the norm.

Almost none of the cyclists who now hurtle down the final lap – even the Frenchmen among them – are aware that both the research in human physiology that allows them to reach such extraordinary levels of aptitude and the earliest enquiries into the chemistry of narcotics that enable some to break the rules began two centuries and more ago in a laboratory just a few minutes' ride from the final straight. Its discoveries are reflected in some of the most positive, and the most negative, aspects of modern sport.

The guinea pig was first used as an experimental animal in 1780 by two researchers remembered more for their work in the physical sciences than in biology. Antoine Lavoisier made the first table of the elements, and Pierre-Simon Laplace was a major figure in the study of the cosmos. As was true for most of the scholars of those days, their interests were eclectic: the former was involved in the study of fermentation and of the geology of France, while his colleague was interested in the speed of sound and the movement of liquids in narrow tubes. The talented duo had already collaborated on the synthesis of water from hydrogen and oxygen. In a further extension of their intellectual empire, they then began to carry out the earliest studies of the biology of metabolism.

In his laboratory at the Arsenal, close to where the Canal Saint-Martin now enters the Seine, Lavoisier had found that when mercury was heated with air, it produced a compound which he called a 'calx'. At higher temperatures, a remarkable gas that caused candles to burn with a brighter flame – oxygen – was driven off. Air was a mixture of the self-same gas mixed with nitrogen and with carbon dioxide. Just one of its components was the breath of life; as he put it after a series of metabolic experiments in which the content of inspired and expired air was analysed: 'Eminently respirable air that enters the lung, leaves it in the form of chalky aeriform acids ... Respiration acts only on the portion of pure air that is eminently respirable ... the excess, that is its mephitic portion is a purely passive medium which enters and leaves the lung ... without change or alteration. The respirable portion of air is able to combine with blood and in its combination gives rise to its red colour.' In modern terms, oxygen enters the lung, reacts with components of the blood, and leaves it as carbon dioxide, with nitrogen a passive partner. Our abilities, athletic or otherwise, are fuelled by a simple chemical reaction.

Then began the collaboration between Lavoiser, Laplace and the guinea pig. The unfortunate animal was put into a closed container. After ten hours the amount of oxygen used, and of carbon dioxide produced, was measured. They were equivalent; as had been the case in the mercury experiment, nothing was added and nothing removed by the passage of the gases through a living creature. Instead there was no more than a change of chemical state. Lavoisier and Laplace then went on to investigate the energetics of the reaction. They placed their subject in what they called a 'calorimeter', an apparatus they invented to measure the production of heat. It consisted of one metal box inserted into a somewhat larger one, with the gap between them filled with ice. That was melted by the warmth of the animal's body, and the volume of water that dripped out gave an estimate of how much had been generated. Over a day and a night a third of a litre was produced, together with a solid dose of 'chalky aeriform acid'. The reason seemed obvious: 'Respiration is thus a phenomenon of very slow combustion, very similar to that of coal. It is conducted inside the lungs, not giving off light, since the fire matter is absorbed by the humidity of the organs of the lungs. Heat developed by this combustion goes into the blood vessels which pass through the lungs and which subsequently flow into the entire animal body ... animals that breathe are in truth combustible substances that burn and consume themselves.'

The two scientists were wrong in the claim that the 'slow combustion' takes place in the lungs with just heat distributed by the blood, for every cell in the body has its own internal furnace, but their ideas were quite correct in other essentials.

Like every fire, the vital blaze needs sustenance: 'If animals did not replace, through nourishing themselves, what they lose through respiration, the lamp would very soon run out of oil and the animal would perish, just as the lamp goes out when it lacks fuel.'

A human guinea pig then joined the team. A young student, Armand-Jean-François Seguin, was instructed by his superiors to don an airtight suit of taffeta soaked in gum. Attached to the collar was a bag that extended over his head. A metal mask sealed with putty and with a tube attached was placed on his face and Monsieur Seguin was asked to breathe oxygen to see how much he consumed under different circumstances.

The subject starved himself for several hours before the first experiment, in which he sat at rest in a warm room while the demand for the vital gas was measured. Then he was placed in the cold and his rate of use increased by about a tenth. After a meal it went up by rather more, and a solid bout of exercise that – in a presage of the Tour de France – used a metal pedal to raise a weight of fifteen pounds through a height of 650 feet doubled his oxygen demand. Lavoisier suggested that with his apparatus it might be possible to measure the consumption of a philosopher, a scholar or a composer as they applied themselves to their trades but never did the experiment. That idea gave rise to the spurious Freudian notion of 'psychic energy' which if blocked led to emotional problems, but in truth the amount of physical effort needed for cogitation, philosophy, composition or writing tedious works about the French Revolution is minuscule.

Seguin went on to try to estimate the amount of food soaked up and water vapour produced under a range of conditions. He weighed himself before and after exercise while wrapped in his taffeta suit and did the same to his food and drink and to his excretions over several days in an attempt to measure what was burned and what emerged as waste. Then he covered himself with oil to prevent loss of water through the skin and measured the vapour in his breath (he also bathed in quinine to see if any of the bitter drug could be tasted as it passed into the body, but the stuff stayed stubbornly on the outside). Seguin's investigations were less of a success than his earlier efforts, but they did show some link between water loss and food intake, temperature and hard work.

In his *Traité Elémentaire de Chimie* of 1789, Lavoisier gives a succinct account of the overall results: 'The animal machine is governed by three types of regulators: respiration, that consumes hydrogen and carbon and furnishes heat, digestion, which replenishes ... that which is lost in the lungs and transpiration, that increases or diminishes in accordance with the necessity to carry away more or less heat.'

The great chemist went on to attempt to use his discoveries to improve the hospitals and prisons of Paris, all of which were in disarray. A study of vital statistics (another of his enthusiasms) had shown that in Edinburgh, one patient in twenty-five died soon after they entered the city's hospital, while in the worst Paris establishment, the Hôtel Dieu, the figure was one in five. Conditions were disgraceful, with several people in a bed and the dead sometimes sharing a mattress with those still alive. A commission was sent across the Channel to find out what should be done, but the disorder on Lavoisier's native streets meant that the project had to wait. In the last days of his life the hopeful reformer found himself in one of the dank cells he had so criticised a decade earlier.

Part of the problem in such places was, he was sure, that the inmates suffered from a shortage of oxygen. He sampled the air in a crowded theatre at its lowest point, the orchestra pit, and in the highest seats, and persuaded himself (wrongly) that there was less of the vital gas at the top. He went on to claim (and every academic will sympathise) that in a stuffy lecture hall 'the attention of the audience cannot be sustained beyond two or three hours' and that the 'lecturer does not receive the tribute of applause and recognition on which he might have counted under more favourable circumstances'.

Armand Seguin's experiences have been extended many times, in many ways. The amount of heat generated when at rest in a warm room is a measure of what is now called the 'basal metabolic rate'. A typical office worker uses around two thirds of his or her energy input to keep the body clock ticking. Even in periods of intense exercise such as the Tour de France or the last sprint in the marathon, that simple task takes up a quarter of the energy needed. The figure is lower in the old and in the obese (which may in part explain why the latter put on weight in the first place). The heart is the hardest worker in the body, the liver makes a decent effort, while fat is lazy stuff for it generates no more than a hundredth of the heart's heat for every ounce.

The young Seguin's need for extra fuel after a meal reflects another cost of running the vital machine, for to chew, swallow, digest and absorb one's daily bread may use as much as a tenth of each day's energy needs. A steak demands more work than does a slice of cake, for proteins are harder to break down than are fats and carbohydrates (which explains why sugar is bad for the waistline). In addition, an older person, whose body furnace runs low, heats up less after dinner than does someone in their prime.

Life is an endless chemical reaction, in which the molecules that emerge from the digestive factory are pumped in and out of cells, broken down, and reassembled into new combinations, while repair and maintenance never cease. The overall level of activity is controlled by the hypothalamus, a structure at the base of the brain, which balances the amount of work called for against the food available and the demands from outside. One of its most important jobs is to keep the body's internal temperature within precise bounds, a task that itself sometimes consumes vast quantities of energy and sets the limit to what the human frame can achieve.

Intense exercise asks a lot of the body. At rest, the heart pumps about five and a half litres of blood a minute, which means that the entire vital fluid passes through it in that brief interval. In crisis moments of the Tour de France that volume may double. As it does, its participants can generate enough power to light up a one-bar electric fire and even at less frantic times pour out plenty of waste heat. Much the same is true in a marathon. A vast body of information is now available on the energy balance of winners and losers and on the thermal and other challenges they must overcome.

As proof of the cost of keeping cool, hot days mean slow races. The big crowds come to marathons – such as those in the Olympics – held in July and August, but they almost never see a record broken. About half of the top hundred speeds over the past decade have been in the temperate months of April and October. Indeed, each of the six men's marathon records since 2003 has been set in Berlin, where the temperature in September, when the race is held, hovers around 15°C, the ideal level for intense activity. Chicago once featured in the lists but has dropped out, in the main because the thermometer rises too high. The Tour de France also shows the negative fit of speed with sun. For commercial reasons it is held in the height of summer, and many of those who drop out, in the mountains most of all, do so through heat exhaustion.

Whatever the weather, long-distance cyclists and runners are gluttons for punishment. The Iditarod bicycle race traverses a thousand snow-covered miles in Alaska, while the Australian Santos Tour hits eight hundred tarmac kilometres in the South Australian summer, with temperatures sometimes above 40°C. Marathons are held in the fiery deserts of Morocco, on the ice of a frozen Lake Baikal and in the even colder conditions of Antarctica.

In all these events, the body must cope, or fail. Its ability to do so is impressive. One enthusiast, or sadist, ran the equivalent of a marathon on a treadmill in a chamber in which the air temperature started at the truly Antarctic temperature of minus 45°C and ended at 55° above zero, well above the thermal challenges faced by participants in the Sahara's

Marathon des Sables. His body temperature was measured every ten seconds through that hundred-degree range – the equivalent of a shift from ice to boiling water. In the first and last stages he found it hard to handle the conditions and had to use a large proportion of his reserves to cope. Even so, the temperature of his body core deviated over the experiment by less than one degree. His struggle to stay cool towards the end of the trial was painful and risky, for the amount of liquid lost in sweat and urine went up by ten times while his blood pressure shot up to dangerous levels as his internal machinery struggled to keep in thermal balance. Had the intrepid subject continued for much longer he would have been in real danger of the fate of Phidippides, who delivered his news of victory to Athens on a summer day with the words 'Rejoice, we conquer!', but then collapsed and died. Many have followed him.

One common cause of death is over-indulgence in water to replenish that lost in sweat. This alters blood chemistry and may bring a heart attack. Others die from inborn heart abnormalities that are normally harmless, but lead to disaster when the organ is pushed to its limits. The risk shoots up with age.

All this means that research on metabolism plays a large part in both sport and medicine. The energy equation of a cyclist on the Champs-Elysées, or of Phidippides himself, is in its essentials the same as that described by the French pioneers of the late eighteenth century, but in its details has become rather more complex.

The mechanism called upon for a sudden burst of activity

is distinct from that needed in a sustained effort. The world record speed for the hundred metres is 36 kilometres an hour, and for the two hundred metres not much less, at 34.8 kilometres an hour. That for a marathon, its course two hundred times longer than the latter, is no more than 19.5 kilometres an hour. Those differences between sprint and slog evolved long ago, in a world of hungry predators and tasty prey. With its time trials, sprint finishes and mountain climbs the Tour de France tests each of them. The marathon, too, demands excellence in both, for its participants must decide on when to make what they call the 'split', the shift between the fastest they can manage in the first section of the race, balanced against the need to conserve their strength for a slower and more painful trudge to the finishing line.

The ability to walk upright emerged four million years before the invention of the bicycle, and within just a couple of million years had advanced enough to allow our ancestors to run long distances at a steady speed. Walking and running (and, for that matter, cycling) are subtle and complicated talents. Each is in effect a constant controlled fall, which means that every step and every turn of the pedals quivers on the edge of disaster. Men and women face thousands of such risks each day, more than a hundred million in a lifetime. Until the invention of the wheel the battle with gravity represented the largest expenditure of energy for every person in history. It involves almost every skeletal muscle, almost every nerve, and large parts of the brain. Bipedalism, as it is called, has restructured the entire skeleton, and exacts a price in back pain, slipped discs, broken limbs and worse.

Whatever the dangers, man's precarious gait provides abilities denied to all other primates. Part of the endless balancing act comes with springs in the legs in the form of tendons, ligaments and muscles, together with a feedback system that makes *Homo sapiens* far more stable when upright, and far nimbler, than his primate relatives. Because upright walking is so efficient, humans can last longer in the chase than can any other creatures. Cheetahs run fast in the final dash but soon get tired and expend most of their energy on slow strolls through the landscape as they search for prey. In steamy conditions, the maximum speed of an untrained man over a kilometre is no more than about two hundred metres a minute, some seven miles an hour. Many quadrupeds can do much better than that when they break into a gallop – but then to cool down, they have to pant. That form of respiration is not at all effective in soaking up oxygen, so after a few minutes they are forced to slow down, while nemesis in the form of a determined human hunter draws ever closer. Kalahari bushmen may spend eight hours in running down an antelope in the desert heat before, at last, their exhausted prey collapses and the hunter can reap his reward.

All mammals, racing or trudging, must lose heat. Men and women cope with hard work in the tropics because they lack hair, have plenty of sweat glands, and stand erect in the breeze, away from the layer of intense heat just above the ground. Even better, only the head and shoulders – rather than much of the body surface, as in four-legged creatures – are exposed directly to the midday sun.

Much of the research on the biology of exercise (heat

production included) is done on cyclists perched on exercise bicycles, or by runners on treadmills. Athletes have offered up their breath, their urine, their blood and even samples of their muscles as they labour onwards. Strap-on instruments measure electrical activity and the circulation of the body's energy currency as the subjects drive themselves to the limit. Their efforts have much refined the science, and the art, of sport.

The biochemical pathways involved depend on how hard and for how long an athlete exercises, and how much food and oxygen is around. For intense activity over a brief period, as called upon weight-lifters or pole-vaulters, a simple one-step reaction expends the capital held in a muscle's energy bank, with no help from outside. The mechanism is efficient and effective, but does not last more than a few seconds. As it runs out of steam, another system that needs little extra oxygen but pumps out a waste product called lactic acid cuts in. That will sustain a sprint or a speeding bicycle over a few minutes, but the unfortunate sportsman will be in real pain as he crosses the line when his muscles protest as the amount of acid goes up by ten times. The call for oxygen then becomes unavoidable and aerobic activity begins. This is no more than half as effective as the previous arrangement and involves twenty-six distinct steps to generate one unit of metabolic currency.

In real tests of endurance, such as the mountain stages of the Tour or the last few miles of a marathon, that system too runs out of fuel as its raw materials, starch and sugar, are drained. Then the body begins to burn almost its last reserve, fat. That needs around a hundred biochemical steps and is even less efficient. A cyclist or runner at the end of his tether may even begin to break down his own muscles in a desperate attempt to drive onwards.

Cold, too, is expensive. When Seguin was placed in an icy room, he used more oxygen than before. That reflects the work needed to keep body temperature at acceptable levels. Some of that went into shivering, for unpleasant as that sensation may be, it warms us up quite well. A more subtle system involves a tissue called, inelegantly, 'brown fat'. It is related to muscle and contains lots of mitochondria, the cell's energy machines. In most cells, they do useful work, but in brown fat their efforts are unhitched from the internal machinery and are released as heat, just as a high-pressure boiler can let off steam rather than driving a turbine.

Such insights have had a huge influence on endurance sports. Participants must tune up every part of their internal machinery. They eat special diets, with lots of fat but not much carbohydrate until a few days before the start, and then a massive dose of rice, pasta, cereal and the like to build up reserves for the race itself. As the struggle goes on runners and cyclists shift between items such as potatoes, which provide sugars at once, and others such as pasta that release their goodness over a longer period. As is true for all machines, biological or otherwise, the need to lose heat is paramount. Some riders or runners take ice-cold baths or wear special cooling jackets before the start and swallow crushed ice as the stages proceed to delay the onset of heat exhaustion.

Training plays a major part. Real enthusiasts do it in

extreme temperatures, and this, too, improves the ability to cope although not many follow the lead of the great Czech marathon champion Emile Zatopek, who set himself up for an event by running long distances on hot days with his wife on his back. Such preparation persuades muscles to grow and to store more fuel than before. Heart rate drops, the ability to soak up oxygen increases, the threshold at which the lactate system runs out of steam shifts forward, and the number of mitochondria increases. Riders in the Tour can, over several years, improve their power output by as much as one part in six as they progress from novice to champion.

One way to boost the amount of oxygen available is to push up the numbers of red cells with a stay at high altitude. Acclimatisation involves other changes, such as an increase in capillaries within the muscles and in mitochondrial activity. The Alpine stages of the Tour reach two and a half thousand metres, where the air has just three quarters as much of the essential gas as at sea level. A month up high works wonders but even a few days make a difference. Those unable to afford such a regime can buy a hypoxic tent for use at home, which filters out the oxygen as they sleep and provides the benefits of a montane holiday with less inconvenience.

Intense physical activity pushes every athlete to his or her limit. Many among them, in cycling most of all, have as a result turned to another eighteenth-century technology in their attempts to drive themselves even further.

After the death of Lavoisier, his experimental subject Armand Seguin carved out a successful career as an entrepreneur and banker. That made him rich enough to run a busy laboratory (and, as an incidental, to build an enormous chateau). Its researchers were among the first to study an interaction between physiology and chemistry that reached its zenith, if that is the word, in the Tour de France.

Ether was first used in surgery in the 1840s, but had been discovered long before. The sixteenth-century alchemist Paracelsus noted that it could send people to sleep, and the substance was so effective that for a time it became a popular substitute for alcohol in Scotland. Lavoisier, too, was interested in its properties. He noted its readiness to evaporate and how it made an explosive mixture with air. In an aside, he suggested that because it became a gas at the temperature of the body, liquid ether might, when swallowed, purge the stomach of the 'mephitic gases' produced after a heavy meal. That, he felt, could be useful for the relief of headaches and migraines. He was executed before he could take his anaesthetic ideas any further.

Opium, too, had long been known for its ability to promote slumber and as the second-century Greek physician Galen had put it, the stuff '*facit ad maximos dolores*'; it works for extreme pain. He invented what he called an 'Olympic Victors' Dark Ointment' to treat aches and pains brought on by intense exercise. An adhesive bandage coated with a variety of minerals, gums and perfumes, saffron and raw egg and loaded with a solid dose of the drug was applied to the appropriate part of the body. A modern reconstitution shows that opium enters the bloodstream much faster from this mixture than when in simple solution, perhaps because one of the other components helps it on its way.

Opium, in the form of liquid laudanum, was in wide-spread use for pain relief (and for pleasure) in the eighteenth and nineteenth centuries. To use it was always risky. Carlyle describes the death of Mirabeau, a fervent Jacobin (but after his death found to be a traitor): 'The moribund giant, passionately, by sign, demands paper and pen; writes his passionate demand for opium, to end these agonies. The sorrowful Doctor shakes his head: Dormir "To sleep", writes the other, passionately pointing at it! So dies a gigantic Heathen and Titan; stumbling blindly, undismayed, down to his rest.'

The challenge for Mirabeau's physician was to get the dose right. The morphine content of the crude poppy extracts used in those days varied enormously and it was difficult to establish the safe amount to use when making up a draught. In 1803, the French pharmacist Jean-François de Rosne began to solve the problem when he crystallised out from the plant what he called the 'essential salt of opium'. He noticed to his surprise that it was, unlike all other botanical extracts then known, alkaline rather than acid. It was, in fact, the first known alkaloid drug, one of many now used in medicine (they include quinine and the anti-cancer drug vincristine). Rosne's chemical was not in truth the painkiller itself, but a related substance. Seguin himself then extracted another component that was indeed the narcotic. It was soluble in alcohol and when dried out was visible as a residue of white and bitter crystals. It was, he said, 'a completely new vegetable-animal material'. His notebooks mention its effects on animals, but he never published his results. The substance was later isolated by the German Frederich Sertüner, who

named it 'morphium' and sparked off yet another priority dispute between French researchers and their foreign
competitors.

Morphine and its derivatives are now much used in medicine and, in the form of heroin (broken down in the body
into morphine itself), are major drugs of abuse. Those who
take such substances to relieve pain may feel sick, sleepy or
jittery and in high doses suffer a reduction in the drive to
breathe. Abusers often find that their body adapts to the
chemical, so that more and more is needed to produce the
desired effect. Inexorably, they are pushed closer to a fatal
dose, or are forced to suffer the anguish of withdrawal.

The opioids, as the group of substances to which morphine belongs is called, activate certain receptors found in
the brain, the nervous system and the intestine (which means
that the drug causes constipation). They are related to a larger
group of receptors that include those responsible for smell,
taste and colour.

In animals at least opioids play a part in the emotions, for
in certain rodents morphine alters the attachment of young
to their mother or changes the degree to which females show
attachment to a particular male. Faults in the cell-surface
receptors for such active chemicals have also been implicated
in autism, and some even claim that men with a particular
variant of the attachment site are more at risk of divorce.

Morphine changes minds as much as bodies. Sport does
the same, with a similar mix of pain and pleasure. The
importance of psychology was shown in an unkind experiment in which elite cyclists were asked to match their best on

a fixed bicycle as shown on a speedometer on the machine. They strained themselves to the limit and most of them managed the job; but in an ingenious twist the experimenter had manipulated the instrument to show a speed slightly slower than in fact had been achieved. Faced with this challenge, almost all managed to beat their previous personal best. Motivation, it seems, is as important as muscle.

In both the Tour and the marathon, muscles, hearts, lungs and minds must be persuaded to work at maximum intensity for long periods. As they do, the body switches on a chemical reward pathway related to that of the opioids. The endorphins, as the messengers are called, lead to a sense of satisfaction and even euphoria. As a result, sportsmen who experience the 'burn', the breakthrough moment in a race when everything seems possible, share the sensations of a drug-user who has just topped up his dose. As further evidence of the tie between the two addictions, athletes who have just finished a tough race are less sensitive to pain than are those tested at rest, while drug abusers trying to escape from the habit do better if they take hard exercise as they fight their demons.

Perhaps because of this overlap, sportsmen have long been enthusiastic consumers of narcotics. None among them can match the heroic indulgence in stimulants indulged in by professional cyclists. In that sport, at some periods and in some events, almost every participant was doped to the eyeballs.

The French critic Roland Barthes includes in his somewhat impenetrable work *Mythologies* a section entitled 'On the Tour de France as Epic', in which he compares *La Grande Boucle* with the Odyssey. He discusses what he calls the *saut*, or jump – perhaps better translated as 'the burn' – the mysterious and almost divine surge of energy that allows some riders to reach superhuman levels of endurance: 'a veritable electric influx which erratically possesses certain racers beloved of the gods and then causes them to accomplish superhuman feats'. The noble sensation had a hideous twin that could be awoken by drugs. Barthes describes that as an insult to God himself, who would be avenged on anyone who dared to indulge.

He was too confident about the role of divine intervention in bicycle races. From its earliest days the Tour has been an uncontrolled experiment in pharmacology. Some of the illegal substances, in the tradition of Galen's Dark Ointment, are used to relieve pain, but most are taken in an attempt to push outwards the metabolic limits and to quieten the mental torments that arise when the body rebels against orders from the brain. The drugs used vary from the useless to the lethal.

In the early years of the race wine was seen as a valuable stimulant, while extract of deadly nightshade was also claimed to improve performance. In 1952, concerned by such abuses, the authorities hired a physician to keep an eye on the participants. He found a world awash with quackery, in which helpers, or '*soigneurs*', whose main job was supposed to be as masseurs, provided riders with a variety of dubious stimulants. Alcohol and atropine were supplemented by bee stings, toad skin and 'magnetised' food in attempts to force the body as far as it could go.

Ineffective as such treatments were (and futile as the expert's complaints turned out to be) quite soon the participants began to appeal to the real world of medicine for help. There were so many scandals that in 1965 the French government passed a law to ban the use of drugs in all branches of athletics.

The legislation infuriated cyclists, much of whose considerable income depended on chemistry. They threatened to strike and to kill the Tour for ever, but in practice the new law was a dead letter. Attention was again drawn to the abuse when in 1967, the English competitor Tom Simpson collapsed and died as he attempted the strenuous ascent of Mont Ventoux; his last words, allegedly, 'Put me back on my bike.' An autopsy showed that he had consumed a mixture of amphetamines and alcohol, and that the toxic cocktail, combined with extreme heat, had pushed him beyond the boundary. A day later another dozen riders dropped out. All blamed a meal of spoiled fish but it was at once revealed to much public mockery that none of their hotels had served fish on the previous night. The Tour survived.

Another chance for reform came in 1998. The team car of the group sponsored by the Festina watch company was stopped for a customs check at the Belgian frontier and found to be loaded with steroids and other hormones. Several of its members were arrested but were loud in their assertions of innocence. Other teams were also found to be users and several riders were thrown into prison. In protest, their fellow contestants stopped the race and walked for part of one stage, while a few threatened libel suits for anyone who dared hint at abuse. As the scandal grew, backers began to pull out. Tests showed that eight of the nine members of the Festina team were drug-takers, and there was a general assumption that many other competitors were also at fault. Some came up with the dubious claim that they thought that their injections contained vitamins rather than narcotics, but the real excuse was that the only way to succeed was to join in. The affair ended with fines and bans.

Once again, public concern ebbed away. Then, at last, the code of *omertà* that had surrounded the habit began to break up. Several cyclists denounced their colleagues to the media and were attacked in return, until at last, the colossus of them all fell from his pedestal and the scandal got back into the headlines, where it has stayed ever since.

Lance Armstrong is the only person to win the Tour seven times. He had become an all-American hero through his perseverance with the race even after treatment for testicular cancer. For years he denied all accusations; as he said: 'If you consider my situation: a guy who comes back from arguably, you know, a death sentence, why would I then enter into a sport and dope myself up and risk my life again? That's crazy. I would never do that.'

It had already become evident to physiologists that some top participants, the mountain climbers most of all, were able to reach levels of performance impossible without chemical help. Two dozen riders were named and shamed as probable abusers, and the whole sorry business ended with the downfall of the seven-fold winner and a blot on the reputation of the sport that has lasted to the present day.

The United States Anti-Doping Agency had long pursued Armstrong, in spite of his repeated attempts to recruit members of Congress to vote against its budget. The organisation published its evidence against him in 2012. Much of it came from his former team-mates on the US Postal Service team (some of whom had themselves been banned for drug use, and not received the impunity granted to their leader). He was stripped of his titles. After an admission of guilt on the Oprah Winfrey show and a ritual humiliation that continues today, he lost tens of millions of dollars paid by sponsors or given as prize money. In 2015 he was fined another ten million for lying to a promoter about his use of drugs and was sued for a hundred times as much by one of his erstwhile team-mates. The sport's governing body, the *Union Cycliste International*, has also been blamed for its 'special relationship' with him, which involved, for example, the acceptance of pre-dated prescriptions for steroids to suggest that he was free of them at the time of a race.

After endless controversy, the Tour itself now claims to be more or less purged of chemical aids. That cannot be said of other competitions. In 2015 a commission of enquiry 'did not hear from anyone credible in the sport who would give cycling a clean bill of health'. That same year, leaked documents from the international anti-doping agency suggested that as many as a third of the world's top long-distance runners and riders were still suspected of abuse, sometimes with chemicals supposed to be confined to research laboratories. The volume of drugs taken may have gone down, and in the Tour 'riders can now at least be competitive when clean', but the plague has spread to the amateurs. Many professionals now refuse to take part in mixed races in case they are beaten by a narcotised but unpaid devotee. The marathon, too, is at fault: in 2015 the Russian winner of the London and Chicago events was stripped of her titles when her blood was proved to contain drugs and there have been recent claims that many other top participants have also turned to chemistry. So embedded had drugs become in Russia's sporting culture that in 2015 the nation was banned from all international athletic events, cycle races included.

The regulations now demand that test samples should be kept for eight years so that any new technology could be used to punish a rider or runner proved with hindsight to have broken the rules. A sense of prerogative and privilege has been replaced by one of paranoia and cynicism, so much so that many cyclists will not allow their blood or urine to be tested anonymously for research purposes, while – to the irritation of their fellows – others loudly proclaim their noble refusal to take even a painkiller.

Quite what had Lance Armstrong and his colleagues done to push themselves beyond the 'burn'? The key lies in Lavoisier's pregnant sentence about the body's need for oxygen, water and energy, without which 'the lamp would very soon run out of oil and the animal would perish'. Riders have tinkered with every part of the metabolic equation to keep the vital flame turned up as high as possible.

Some narcotics act on the body's ability to deliver oxygen, others on the speed at which it processes its raw materials. Another group is taken in the hope that they will increase power or endurance, while yet more modify the mental state of those desperate to win. Quite often, substances assumed to improve the mechanics of the internal machinery have their prime effect on the mind. As a result, as was the case for Tom Simpson, the mind sometimes pushes the body past its limits.

The older aids, toad venom and magnetised food included, were of no more than psychological value. Strychnine, too, once a popular *aide-cyclisme*, also seems to have little power. The drug was at one time used by students as they studied for examinations, and was supposed to have a more direct effect on muscle contraction, a talent much called upon, claimed the colonial authorities in India, by 'the more debauched among the Rajpoots of the province of Guzarat' (an observation that might now be of interest to men who have spent too long on the saddle). Until not long ago, plenty of riders in the Tour claimed to find it valuable in a different way, but in truth that was self-delusion.

The material is, like morphine, an alkaloid. In 1809, the Parisian physiologist François Magendie fed an extract of the tropical nut that makes it to dogs and found that it caused lethal rigidity. He then separated a leg from its body and left it attached by just an artery and a vein. That animal showed the same symptoms, proof that the poison circulated through the blood rather than, as had been assumed, through the lymphatic system (he was castigated by British biologists horrified by such cruelty). The drug itself was isolated a decade later by the French pharmacist Joseph Caventou.

Amphetamines, the drugs that killed Tom Simpson, are often referred to as 'speed', but the word is more metaphorical than literal. Like strychnine, they stimulate the nervous system (and Simpson himself was an enthusiast for the Rajpoot stimulant). They mimic the effects of the natural messenger adrenalin, the 'fight or flight' hormone, as they speed up the heart, increase the rate at which the lungs fill and empty, improve stamina, sharpen perception and strengthen the will to win. The amphetamine Benzedrine was given to soldiers in the Second World War and in Vietnam Dexedrine was handed out like candy. Ecstasy, another drug in the same group, remains a favourite among clubbers. Those who indulge in it feel more energetic (and, some claim, more amorous) and push themselves to what sometimes prove to be lethal limits, with overheating often the cause of death.

In 1931, the German biochemist Adolf Butenandt set out to isolate the essence of maleness. He coaxed Berlin police officers, that masculine body of men, into donating 25,000 litres of urine. His swimming-pool-full of raw material produced just fifteen milligrams of a new hormone, which Butenandt christened androsterone. Four years later, testosterone itself was extracted from bull testes, and was soon synthesised in the laboratory. It now has more than a thousand man-made relatives.

The first attempt to use that precious substance to improve performance was in nineteenth-century Paris, where the physician Charles Brown-Séquard announced that injections of an extract of guinea pig testicles had increased the average length of his urine stream by a quarter and that he could lift several kilograms more than before. In addition he gained, or so he claimed, a strong sense of contentment. His discovery led to a mania for treatment with masculine extracts (those from human testes included). In time most health-seekers abandoned the craze, but many sportsmen became enthusiasts.

Riders and runners have long abused steroids. They do so because such substances stimulate protein synthesis, improve muscle mass and increase the numbers of mitochondria, of small blood vessels and of red blood cells. They also push up levels of aggression to give a sudden hit of helpful rage. Whatever their powers, the chemicals pose real dangers. They lead to high blood pressure and cause heart attacks. In addition they shrink the testes, cause men to grow breasts, and increase the risk of prostate cancer. The drug may bring about attacks of rage, of mania, and of depression, with real threats of suicide, car crashes and murder.

Another illegitimate stage in the race for competiveness came with the ability to interfere with Lavoisier's 'very substance of the animal', the blood. As he had noticed, oxygen changes the colour of the vital fluid. That is because it interacts with haemoglobin, the molecule in red cells that takes the gas from the lungs to the tissues. A shortage of such cells causes anaemia and feebleness, while an excess leads to clots and high blood pressure.

Training helps, but several less legitimate approaches sometimes lend a hand. The oldest is to remove and freeze a solid dose of the precious fluid well before the race and pump it back in just before the start. Even better, the hormone erythropoietin, used to treat anaemia, may lead to a jump in performance, albeit at the risk of thrombosis and heart attacks. Until not long ago, the stuff was undetectable, and even after a test emerged, riders dosed themselves until a week or so before the race so that it did not show up, or used repeated tiny doses, impossible to detect. More recent narcotics, many of dubious value, include xenon gas, ozone, a variety of steroid hormones, and insulin, while plenty of riders use as yet allowable chemicals such as Viagra and Cialis, caffeine and a powerful painkiller called tramadol.

Such attempts to enhance talent by artificial means are abhorred by fans, most of whom applaud the new detection methods. They must now face another and perhaps even more uncomfortable fact: that biology has started to reveal natural differences that match, or even surpass, the effects of narcotics. When it comes to oxygen demand, to heat loss, and to speed or endurance, the chemicals that matter are not those swallowed or injected, but those made by the body itself.

The double helix of DNA now plays a real part in who wins and who loses. As athletes are pushed closer to their physical limits, natural variation has begun to play a part in success or failure. In sport, pharmacology is giving way to genetics.

Some natural talents (and their opposites) are obvious. My school games teacher's sardonic attempts to persuade my skinny teenage self to throw a heavy steel ball on sports day were, as he was well aware, futile. I was, in contrast, quite a good long-distance runner when forced to take part, while my fat fellows had no chance of success.

The first Olympic marathon was in 1896. The gold, silver and bronze medals were taken by Europeans, as they were in the next twelve Games, to 1956. In 1960, for the first time, an Ethiopian won gold. Unknowingly, he had opened the door to a new era, for in the past decade and more, every winner has been of African descent.

Over a thousand marathons take place each year. In the past quarter of a century, half the gold medallists in the major races have been Africans, in the main from Kenya and Ethiopia. That crude figure disguises how recent the triumph of the continent has been. In the top men's races the proportion of African winners in 1990 was one in six, but is now more than nineteen out of every twenty. Every one of the world's top one hundred competitors is of African origin. Even more remarkable, three quarters of the Kenyan champions come from an ethnic minority of around four million people, the Kalenjin, who live in the mountainous west of the country and who represent, in their entirety, just one two-thousandth of the world's population. Almost all the true descendants of Phidippides have black skin, and his sport has moved back to the continent where athletic ability first evolved.

Why has there been this enormous change? Motivation and hard work no doubt have a lot to do with it, and for many competitors the prizes make an important contribution to the household budget. Even so, differences in biology – both inborn and acquired – are also involved.

As well as the shift in skin colour, over the past three decades the average weight of the top one hundred male runners has gone down from sixty kilograms to fifty-six. Today's champions are shorter and thinner, with spindlier legs, than those of earlier years. The Achilles tendon acts as a spring that stores energy at every step and increases the efficiency of walking or running (a simple metal spring between the knee and the heel leads to a further improvement) and some African champions have more resilient tendons than average. Many of that continent's people have denser bones than do Europeans. As long-distance runners suffer from bone loss and fractures, the resulting ability to train for longer without damage, and to avoid injury in the race itself, may help.

Long, tough and resilient legs matched with light bodies give runners from that continent a mechanical advantage over the stiff and stocky northerners, but more subtle differences are also involved.

The close fit between speed and air temperature found in endurance sports means that the ability to lose heat is crucial. A person acclimatised to the tropics increases blood volume, reduces heart rate and sends more blood to the skin. Just two weeks close to the equator makes a difference, but a lifetime does much more.

Evolution also plays a part. Body shape and climate have strong links across the globe. Tropical peoples weigh less than do those from the icy north or south, an effect that remains even when stature, food and health are taken into account. Pygmies from Africa, Asia, Oceania and the Americas live in tropical forests, which are hot, humid and hungry places. There, the need to lose heat may have made them even shorter and thinner, with relatively longer limbs, than their neighbours. Arctic peoples (and to a lesser extent Europeans) are heavily built, with short arms and legs, which reduces body surface and retains heat in the body core (and almost no champion swimmers – a sport in which heat retention rather than loss is important – are of African origin). Lightweight and leggy runners on hot days soon outrun those with heavier frames.

The basal metabolic rate of many Africans is also lower than that of Europeans, which again reduces the thermal load. In addition, members of some tropical groups have rather thin skin, which improves heat loss, while others can tolerate a higher internal temperature. Even dark pigment may help, for although black objects heat up more in the sun, the sunburn suffered by whites cuts down the ability to sweat.

Another important talent found in certain groups, some Africans included, has to do with oxygen consumption. The Kalenjin live at around two thousand metres (and some Ethiopians live even higher), where the air is very thin. This helps build up the capacity to soak up the vital gas. The best runners among them feed much more oxygen to the brain than average when sprinting. This is a crucial advantage, for a shortage of the vital gas to that crucial organ reduces the will to struggle onwards. Some of their ability comes from the need to soak up more oxygen when yet unborn, which as an incidental increases the efficiency of circulation in adult life. In addition, many top Kenyan athletes run several miles to school each day from infancy. That challenge to heart and lungs leads to permanent improvements, with a larger heart matched with extra blood vessels within the brain.

Just the same is true for the people of the Andes. The Incas maintained two armies, one stationed in the mountains for high-altitude wars, and the other on the plains. When the Spaniards first invaded, the natives retreated higher into the mountains, where Europeans could not follow. After the triumph of Spain, in the new (and grim) silver-mining town of Potosí, many children were born to local women forced to slave below ground. Their sisters from across the Atlantic could not reproduce at such low oxygen levels, and had to retreat to sea-level to allow their foetuses and infants to survive. The first child of Spanish blood to live through birth and childhood in the heights was not born for fifty-three years after the city's foundation.

Populations who face low levels of oxygen over many generations can, as they do for heat tolerance, respond in a Darwinian way. One hundred and forty million inhabitants of Tibet, the Andes, Ethiopia and other mountainous regions live above two and a half thousand metres. Natural selection has helped them to cope. Andeans push up the numbers of red cells and have evolved changes in the heart to deal with their thicker blood. They also have larger lungs than Europeans. Tibetans have lived on the high plateau for no more than four thousand years, but in that time they have evolved to deal with a shortage of oxygen with inborn improvements of transport of blood to and from the lungs that come from an enhanced ability to relax arteries and veins. Unlike the inhabitants of the Andes (some of whom do suffer from mountain sickness) they do not push up the number of red cells, as that pushes up the risk of stroke and heart disease. Ethiopian and Kenyan mountain-dwellers have come up with much the same strategy as Tibetans, albeit with a different set of genes. All this plays a part in their athletic triumph.

In 2013, and again in 2015, a relatively inexperienced Colombian rider took second place in the Tour de France, with a superb performance in the mountains (in the intervening year he did not ride in the Tour but won its Italian equivalent instead). Nairo Quintana was born on a farm three thousand metres up in the Andes, and as a boy cycled fifteen kilometres downhill to school, with the return trip a stiff climb. He is small, slim and has the highest ability to soak up oxygen ever measured in a professional cyclist. The population of central Colombia, his birthplace and still his home, has a high proportion of Native American genes. Quintana's features suggest that he too shares that ancestry, and may as a result carry the genes that improve oxygen uptake. No DNA tests have been carried out, and perhaps they should not be.

Whatever lies behind it, the rise of Africa in foot races has not been reflected on two wheels. Spectators at the 2011 Tour de France were surprised to see one rider – a French citizen – who stood out from his fellows because he had dark skin. Yohann Gène, from Guadeloupe (a French overseas territory), was the first Afro-Caribbean rider to compete in the century-old contest. The second, Kevin Réza, who is also of Guadeloupean origin but was born in Versailles, took part in the 2013 Tour. In 2014 there were no participants of sub-Saharan heritage but in 2015 the two Eritreans, Daniel

Teklehaimanot and Merhawi Kudus, took part, with modest success, as members of the South African team MTN-Qhubeka, a group that represents a foundation that hands out thousands of bicycles to aspiring young Africans.

Given the success of that continent's inhabitants in the marathon, their rarity in bicycle races is a surprise. Part of the problem, no doubt, is that to train to the level needed and to buy expensive equipment takes lots of money, which most Kenyans or Ethiopians do not have. Even so, in some parts of the continent the sport is already well rooted. Rwanda, and Eritrea – once an Italian colony and still influenced by that country's craze for bicycles – are both a source of talent. Eritrea has several professional cyclists, and the sport draws crowds (as does the Tour de France, which is shown in full on state television). Since 2006, Gabon in West Africa has had its own race, *La Tropicale*. The thousand-kilometre course attracts top-level Europeans as well as locals. All this may be the forerunner of a change to come in the identity of top cyclists almost as great as in that who wins gold in the marathon. Perhaps the winners of the Tour, like those of the Marathon, will one day emerge in the continent in which humans found their origin.

La Grande Boucle, in its first days a local affair that emerged from a mean-spirited dispute based on racial hatred, is now a focus for the eyes of the world and an icon of how sport can unite its peoples. As evidence of the progress made since the days of Dreyfus, the four Afro-Caribbean and African participants say that they have met with almost no signs of intolerance. The same is true for African runners in the world's marathons. Nicolas de Condorcet, who helped to formulate the philosophy of human rights that lay behind the events of 1789, wrote that the claim that any human group is of its essence less – or more – blessed with particular abilities than others is 'an attempt to make Nature herself an accomplice of political inequality' (he used the argument to urge the need for votes for women, albeit not their right to stand for election). That was wrong, for modern biology shows that inborn differences in various abilities, athletics included, certainly exist and that the call is not to deny their existence but to deal with them.

Whatever the future role of genes in sport, the experience of Yohann Gène, Kevin Réza, Daniel Teklehaimanot and Merhawi Kudus hints that, two centuries after the violent deaths of both Condorcet himself and of the founder of the science of metabolism, the Revolution's founding principle that all citizens, whatever their native talents, deserve equal rights has at least in part, and at least in one small area of endeavour, been achieved.

CHAPTER V

EINSTEIN'S PENDULUM

He soars, he dwindles upwards; has become a mere
gleaming circlet . . . like some new daylight Moon!

THOMAS CARLYLE, *The French Revolution*

Foucault's pendulum in 1851

In the fashionable Fifth Arrondissement of the French capital stands the Panthéon, a superb neoclassical structure erected as a church in the eighteenth century. Its foundations rest on the crypt of what had been the Abbey of Sainte-Geneviève, the patron saint of the city. Geneviève was known for her ability to quell outbreaks of the 'burning sickness' (otherwise called ergotism and caused by a mould whose poisons lead to convulsions, blindness and gangrene) and as a dependable shield against floods. She died in AD 510, and in the years that followed her abbey emerged as the cradle of the new University of Paris. By the eighteenth century its structures had become dilapidated. They were replaced at the behest of Louis XV, who had sworn to build a great religious monument upon their ruins if he recovered from an illness. He survived, and a considerable part of the nation's treasure was directed towards a suitable gesture of gratitude, which – after many delays caused by shortage of cash – opened in 1790. The remains of Geneviève were reinterred elsewhere, with much jubilation.

The jollity did not last. The Revolution was followed by a revolt against the Church. Anti-clericalism reached its height in November 1793 with a Festival of Reason in the Cathedral of Nôtre-Dame. The new faith would have one God alone, the people. An actress was hoisted on to the altar as an emblem of that deity, the words 'To Philosophy' were carved over the cathedral's main portal, and a corybantic celebration filled the streets (Carlyle hints primly at episodes of a 'Paphian' or sexual character, which he prefers to 'heave under the Veil'). Geneviève herself was not spared for her remains were burned in public (an arm and some fingers had been sent to bolster the faithful elsewhere and came back to the capital when the Church regained its grip). Unfortunately for those who organised the festival, Robespierre then came up with a religion of his own, the Cult of the Supreme Being, celebrated upon an artificial mountain erected on what became the site of the Eiffel Tower. The rationalists paid the price for their blasphemy, for all of them went to the guillotine not long after the celebration of their own potent but pitiless force.

Three years before Robespierre's invention of a Supreme Being, the Church of Sainte-Geneviève had itself been deconsecrated, to become a mausoleum for eminent Frenchmen. Upon its portico was engraved the motto *Aux Grands Hommes la Patrie Reconnaissante*. Among its inhabitants are Voltaire, Rousseau, Emile Zola, and the resistance leader Jean Moulin (the bones of Marat have been removed). It contains a smattering of scientists. They include Gaspard Monge, who helped to plan the meridian project, the mathematician Lagrange and the engineer Lazare Carnot. The Panthéon also holds an empty coffin to represent the Marquis de Condorcet, whose corpse disappeared after his murder (or suicide) at the time of the Terror.

The monument has made its own contribution to science and now features in elementary physics lessons across the globe. The physicist Léon Foucault found fame when, in 1851, he provided his fellow citizens with a direct demonstration of the spin of the Earth and a reminder that all motion is relative. He hung a heavy brass-coated leaden bob from a sixty-metre wire attached to the high point of the building's great dome. Every day, it was set to oscillate to and fro. The mass was free to move in any vertical direction. As the Earth's downward attraction interacted with its planetary rotation, the heavy pendulum – which, like a gyroscope (a word invented by Foucault), had a lot of inertia – lagged behind the turning globe. Given time, the shadow traced out by the end points of its sixteen-and-a-half-second oscillation marked out a full circle on the floor. As the bob travelled, it was displaced by about two millimetres for every swing, and with the help of a pointer attached to the bottom that made lines in a bed of sand the spectators could trace out its course. The pendulum takes thirty-three hours to make a complete circle.

Foucault's apparatus caused a sensation: 'All of those present during the experiment remain standing, lost in thought, silent, before finally departing with a vivid conviction of our continuous motion in space.' Their mental frame of reference – a static Earth at the centre of a spinning universe – had been challenged by an object they could reach out and almost touch, and many who had accepted Galileo's ideas without quite realising why they did were at once convinced that the great Italian was right. In Paris, such a mechanism takes just the same time to make its round as it did a century and a half ago. A Foucault pendulum at either pole takes twenty-four hours to make a complete circuit, as the axis of the planet passes straight through its attachment point. On the equator, the weight keeps, like that in a grandfather clock, to a simple plane and does not circle at all.

The astonished Parisians had been introduced to the joys of relative motion. If a modern visitor were to choose to sit on Foucault's sphere as the experiment goes on, the church and its occupants would appear to him to rotate around his own body. No observation he might make could dispel that impression. For the onlookers, in contrast, the ball with its passenger would seem to move in relation to themselves in a neat illustration of how the perception of movement always depends on the point of view of those who observe it (in 2010, someone – perhaps a drunken teenager – tried the experiment, for one morning the wire was found to be broken, with the ball smashed on the flagstones below).

As so often happens in physics (but, alas, so seldom in biology), discoveries made in one frame of reference soon become relevant to those in quite another. Foucault's demonstration of the Earth's rotation has illuminated topics as apparently unrelated as manned flight, the weather forecast, nuclear weapons and the mathematics of chaos.

Reference frames formed the modern world, for they gave birth to the theory of relativity. Einstein's flash of inspiration came when he realised that a person who jumps out of a window feels weightless, at least until he is returned to the brutality of his previous frame when he dashes his brains out on the pavement. Like that of the oscillating teenager in the Panthéon and like every particle in the universe, the suicide's experience hinges on the context in which his observation is made.

As Einstein's observer plummeted to earth he would experience a delightful lightness of being, followed by severe disappointment. The same would be true in an accelerating system, as much as a decelerating one. An astronaut in a space station feels weightless, but should he be in a spaceship that accelerates at ten metres per second every second he would perceive himself to weigh what he did on his home planet. Einstein pointed out that such a gradual increase in velocity cannot go on for ever, and that every object is limited by constraints set by the speed of light and by its own mass. The interaction between them sets the maximum rate at which a planet, a spaceship, a pendulum or a sub-atomic particle can travel and gave rise to his famous equation in which the amount of energy within any object is equal to its mass multiplied by the square of the speed of light. That insight helped form the future.

The analysis of moving reference frames can, like so many of the foundations of modern physics, be traced to the academicians of eighteenth- and nineteenth-century France, as can, for that matter, the first measurement of the speed of light. Gustave Coriolis was born in Paris in Year One of the Republic. Trained in mathematics, he studied the transfer of energy in machines of various kinds, and had an interest in the movements of billiard balls (a more serious topic than it might seem).

One of his projects involved the mechanics of waterwheels, which were still much in use. Marly, to the west of the city, had a remarkable example, built in the 1680s to feed the fountains, gardens and palaces of Marly itself, of the Trianon and of Versailles. A dam across an arm of the Seine drove fourteen wheels, each eleven metres across and one and a half metres wide. They were linked to two hundred pumps that lifted the waters to a reservoir, and from there to a basin a hundred and fifty metres high, from which they poured down aqueducts to their destinations, in a flow equal to that used by the whole of the city of Paris itself. The contraption demanded a staff of sixty, and the mass of machinery was not at all efficient, but – at some expense – it did beautify the monarch's estates.

Such devices had long been of interest to mathematicians. Coriolis was concerned with the relative motion of different parts of the wheel, from its axle to its paddles, as the linear flow of the stream was transformed into circular movement. Newton's laws of motion – action and reaction equal and opposite, and all the rest – apply to a frame of reference that is not itself in motion, or to be more precise is not speeding up or slowing down. If the system is made to rotate, two new elements enter the equation. One is centrifugal force (which is why a ping-pong ball falls off a record turntable) and the other what we now call the Coriolis force. This acts at right angles to the direction in which the disc spins. It depends on how fast the turntable (or the waterwheel) moves, how massive the object placed upon it might be, and where upon the surface it finds itself.

Neither is a true 'force' in the technical sense but is instead a correction that describes the action of physical laws in a rotating system. If the record player is switched off, the size and weight of its metal disc are the same as when it spins round, but the ball stays in place as evidence that both effects are a function of the moving reference frame rather than of the system itself. When it begins to move, from an observer's point of view the ball follows a curved path before it spills over the edge, but – just as in Foucault's apparatus – the ball itself would sense (if it could) that it was following a straight line and that anyone who watched it was being deflected in the direction opposite to its travel.

Everyone uses the logic of the ping-pong ball every day when they refer to the most familiar framework of all, the planet upon which they stand. Flaubert criticised that lax philosophy after a severe storm, interpreted by the faithful as divine retribution against sinners: 'People believe a little too easily that the function of the Sun is to help the cabbages along.' We all know, needless to say, that the solar disc does not rise and fall in the sky as it circles our planet. Even so, we speak of sunrise and sunset as if our own tiny home was a great astral body rather than a minor satellite of an unimpressive star. In much the same way we assume that rain clouds blow over our heads and do not accept the simple truth that our reluctant bodies are dragged beneath the uneasy atmosphere as the globe spins round.

Coriolis himself had little interest in much more than the physics of waterwheels, but his name has, almost by accident, now entered the vocabulary of many other sciences. In fact much of his work on the physics of a rotating system had itself been pre-empted when the mathematician Pierre-Simon Laplace, in his 1799 book *Celestial Mechanics*, moved on from his grand analysis of the solar system to consider the behaviour of projectiles on the Earth itself.

The Italian Giovanni Borelli had already realised that the roof of a tall tower spins faster around the Earth's axis than does its base, as that high point is further from the planet's centre of rotation. He worked out that a ball dropped from a structure eighty metres high should land about two centimetres to the east at ground level. He tried to confirm that prediction when in 1668 he dropped small objects many times from the Torre degli Asinelli in Bologna. He could see no pattern as other influences – wind most of all – were involved (much later, his prediction was proved correct in an experiment in a German mineshaft).

Laplace, too, saw that a shell fired in his home hemisphere would, because of the spin of the Earth, land a little to the east of its straight-line track and began to study the effect. In time, gunnery officers began to incorporate the appropriate corrections into their calculations. For the feeble weapons of his day they were irrelevant, but as machines of destruction improved, they became essential. In 1918, the Germans built the 'Kaiser Wilhelm Gun', an enormous artillery piece that bombarded Paris from a hundred and twenty kilometres away. Its explosive shells took three minutes to reach the city and were the first man-made objects to penetrate the stratosphere. The projectiles sowed terror as there were no signs of troops nearby. Three hundred and fifty missiles struck the capital, killing more than two hundred. The gunners used the appropriate correction, for if they had not, they would have missed their targets. Nowadays, rockets aimed at enemies across half the world always include the Coriolis adjustment, and can strike within an accuracy of a few centimetres.

Laplace did not realise it, but his research on cannonballs and on what he called the *force centrifuge composé* would in time change our ability to understand the world's weather, its oceans and more. It would also lead to the emergence of weapons more fearsome than he could ever have imagined.

Man has long been interested in climate. The Babylonians depended on astrology to predict when it might rain, but Aristotle, in his book *Meteorology*, written in around 350 BC, came up with some rather modern ideas: 'A whirlwind is due to the failure of a hurricane to escape from its cloud: resistance generates an eddy, and makes a spiral which descends to the Earth'; and 'Now the Sun, as it moves, sets up processes of change and decay, and by its agency the finest and sweetest water is every day carried up and is dissolved into vapour and rises to the upper region, where the cold again condenses it and so the rain returns to the Earth.' As so often, the Greek was right.

The first modern weather records were gathered in eighteenth-century France, not by physicists but by physicians, and not to predict when it might rain but to understand disease. The priest Louis Cotte devoted many years to a detailed national record of temperature, rainfall and barometric pressure from his home north of Paris. He published his data in the *Journal de Médicine* from 1776 to 1782 and then wrote two books, the *Traité de Méteorologie* and *Mémoires sur la Méteorologie*, now seen as the twin foundations of the subject. He did so because, like many others, he believed that climate had a direct effect on dropsy, dysentery, depression and other conditions. Cotte established a network of a hundred and fifty medical correspondents and, with the help of the Royal Academy of Sciences, provided them with accurate thermometers, barometers and rain-gauges. He became convinced (without the help of statistics) that he had uncovered a nineteen-year cycle of temperature. There he was wrong, but the periodic changes in global climate that reflect the El Niño shift of warm and cold water across the Pacific do now seem to happen more often than they did in his day.

No real progress was made in understanding such patterns until it was realised that changes in the weather come from the movements of great masses of air that spin across the globe. The scheme was first suggested by the American William Ferrel, who in the mid nineteenth century saw that blocks of warm air as they rise and move towards cooler regions with lower pressure will not take the shortest path, but will swerve and swirl away from it because of the *force centrifuge composé*. Air will be pulled from the equator towards the poles, not in a straight line from warm to cold, but as cells of high pressure that rotate as they move. Ferrel was quite correct, but he published his results in the *Nashville Journal of Medicine and Surgery* and his name remains almost unknown. That of Coriolis became attached to the idea instead.

The great wheels of high pressure known as anticyclones spin clockwise in the northern hemisphere and in the opposite direction south of the equator. They often lead to good weather, while the equivalent regions of cold and moist air caused by depressions move anticlockwise in the north and clockwise in the south as they are squeezed between the high-pressure masses. As the Earth revolves at a slower pace than does a record player, and as air is less massive than is a ping-pong ball, the Coriolis influence on the atmosphere as measured at any point or any moment is feeble, but given enough time, and enough distance, its effects are dramatic.

A vortex is a spinning section of fluid or gas that retains its shape by virtue of the energy embodied within it. Such systems work on many scales. Lifelong non-smoker as I may be, several of my friends, before they gave up, were proud of their ability to blow smoke rings that could be admired for a few seconds before they melted away. Other structures of this kind, such as the cloak of icy air that sits over each pole and is held in place by the planet's rotation, can last for months. They emerge as islands of order in the sea of atmospheric disorder that surrounds them.

To drive the weather takes energy. Some comes from the Sun's rays, which set up gradients of temperature across the globe, while the Earth's rotation pumps in even more. The force is weak close to the equator, and around that line hurricanes hardly ever happen. Its sunny expanse once presented mariners with real problems, for in the doldrums, as the region is called, they were becalmed. A few degrees further towards the poles, the breezes are – again thanks to the power of spin – more favourable, for there the trade winds blow, in the northern hemisphere from north and east to south and west. Closer again to the North Pole comes a stormier belt of westerlies, the 'roaring forties'. The trades and their mirror image are the opposite edges of a great cell of air that rotates over the North Atlantic.

Many of the winter storms that strike Europe spin off the icy cap trapped over the pole to generate a conveyor belt of clouds that may last for months. That pattern led to the extraordinary British rains of 2014 – the wettest year since records began in 1767, with rivers rising to levels that without great barriers would have swallowed London.

Our sister capital across the Channel is blessed with a better climate than our own but has just as big a problem with floods. Paris was once confined to the Île de la Cité, now the site of Nôtre-Dame; as the Emperor Julian wrote after his stay there in AD 360, 'It is a small island lying in the river; a wall entirely surrounds it and wooden bridges lead to it on both sides. The river rarely rises and falls; as it is in summer, so it is in winter; the water is pleasant to drink for it is very pure and agreeable to the eye.' Julian was lucky, for since his day, sudden deluges have been a constant threat.

The city soon began its spread and its battle with its river. Paris is far enough from the sea not to have to worry about high tides, but the Seine drains a much larger area than does the Thames. In ancient times the river was divided into two arms, one in much the same place as at present and the other passing through what are now the Right Bank districts of Bastille, Belleville and lower Montmartre. After severe storms the whole basin became a lake. The northern arm disappeared long ago, but the area was still a swamp when the Romans arrived (as manifest in the name of the Marais – marsh – district, a place now infested by clothes shops). Even the Roman name for the city, Lutetia, derives from *lutum*, mud, and its motto is '*Fluctuat nec mergitur*': 'She is tossed by waves but does not sink.'

The waves have beaten against the walls of Paris again and again. In 1206 the crisis was serious enough to persuade Bishop Eudes de Sully to summon the relics of Sainte

Geneviève to save his flock. So potent were her bones that, after prayers in Nôtre-Dame graced with their presence, the waters at once receded (as further evidence of their power, the bridge that linked the cathedral's island to the Left Bank collapsed after the ceremony but not until Geneviève's casket had been paraded over it on its way home).

Later inundations such as those of 1784 and 1866 caused immense damage, but the most famous flood in recent history was in 1910, when the river rose by six metres and large sections of the city were submerged as water spread through the new sewers and Métro tunnels, poured into the Gare d'Orsay and swamped thousands of houses once assumed to be safe. The deluge reopened part of the northern branch of the Seine and presented some inhabitants with the unexpected problem that their streets had floated away, for the cobbles so useful to rioters had in many places been replaced with wooden blocks. The city called for help not to its saint but to its sinners, and a mass mobilisation saved the day.

Now the Seine has four great reservoirs on its upper tributaries, ready to hold the waters of the next deluge. Passers-by on the Pont de la Tournelle, which links the Île Saint-Louis to the Left Bank, may never again see the levels recorded in the ancient flood gauge that decorates the structure, but a statue of St Geneviève has been erected upon it just to be safe.

The blocks of air that bring storms have sisters below the oceans. These too obey the rules of Monsieur Coriolis and, like the weather, operate on several scales. The claim that bathwater rotates in opposite directions north and south of the equator when the plug is pulled is not true, as a bath is too small to allow the force to exert enough influence (and in any case, the eddies in a tub vacated a few moments earlier have far more effect on the direction of swirl). In the 1960s, however, a pair of experiments in Sydney and in Cambridge, Massachusetts used circular tubs two metres across with fifteen centimetres of water in each. They were allowed to settle for twenty-four hours and the preferred direction of spin in the two hemispheres was indeed different.

The most familiar marine manifestation of the *force centrifuge composé* is the Gulf Stream, which makes Paris, a city on the same latitude as Kiev or Calgary, a temperate place to live, in climatic terms at least. Its waters once frustrated sailors on their way to the Americas, for they sometimes found themselves driven back even when they had a favourable wind. The great torrent moves a million cubic metres of water every second – five times as much as the Amazon in full flood.

The first chart of its flow was made in the 1770s by Benjamin Franklin himself, who consulted mariners about their experiences on transatlantic voyages. The French saw the importance of his discovery, but the British ignored it. Their Gallic rivals were, as a result, able to gain as much as two weeks in each direction when they crossed to their North American colonies, as they could avoid the marine torrent on the trip west, but seek it out on the way back home. Franklin made a good guess when he speculated that the trade winds blew so much seawater into the Caribbean that it had to escape, and that to do so it poured northwards past the Florida coastline and thence back to Europe to complete the circuit.

The Stream is the most noticeable part of a gigantic eddy called the Atlantic Gyre. This makes a clockwise circle that follows the coasts of the New and Old Worlds, with its centre more or less at the level of the Tropic of Cancer and a southern branch that runs west and warms as it goes before it shifts to the north and east to become the Gulf Stream. The Coriolis force heaps up water in the centre of its vortex by as much as two metres above average sea level.

Because the trade winds blow to the west in the tropics, the great current is narrow and fast at the point at which its waters are first diverted northwards by the American coastline. It becomes wider and more diffuse as it crosses the Atlantic, and even more so as it moves south to re-enter the tropical trade winds on the next round of its endless circle. As it goes, the Stream – like the winds above it – swerves to and fro and generates smaller eddies of water. The orphan patches wander off to the north or the south, to take bits of the tropics into the sub-Arctic and parcels of icy water into warmer climes.

Such areas of liquid stability within the oceans are everywhere. The Maelstrom and its fellow whirlpools are cyclones in the sea that come and go with the movements of currents and tides, but every ocean is full of grander islands of water that spin their way across the globe. The Agulhas Current, for example, delivers tropical packages around the stormy southern tip of Africa into the cold Atlantic. Further north, on the West African coast, a zone of dead water starved of oxygen by a bloom of algae may be trapped into a slow eddy that moves across the Atlantic and smothers any creature unfortunate enough to swim into it.

At any moment, ten thousand marine vortices are in transit across Neptune's realm. They may be three hundred kilometres across and can plunge a kilometre below the surface. Their stately gyration at a few hundred metres an hour insulates them from the world outside and they can last as independent entities for months or even years. Their flat masses are so distinct from the choppy oceans around them that they are visible from space. A few are spin-offs from major disturbances like the Atlantic Gyre, but most set out on a more modest scale on their own. Thanks to the planet's rotation, almost all travel more or less due west, wherever they find themselves.

Whales, sharks and container ships do not take much notice of such obstacles, but plankton, small fish and fragments of garbage may be snared within one for a lifetime and more. The millions of tons of plastic waste dumped in the Pacific have formed a raft of shattered fragments hundreds of kilometres across in the centre of the ocean as evidence that even a diffuse patch of self-contained seawater can trap particles within itself. Much of the oil from the 2010 Gulf of Mexico spill became locked into a structure that delivered most of it to a short length of Louisiana coastline, with Florida left untouched behind the walls of another marine whirlpool.

The ocean's vagaries are important in weather forecasting, in fisheries management, and in pollution control. Its floor, too, bows to the power of Coriolis. The abyss is seamed by canyons eroded by the outflow of great rivers such as the Amazon, and the even larger flows through the Bering Strait. Near the poles, where his force has its greatest influence, the channels tend to be broad and straight, with a general tendency to run east and west. Closer to the Equator such canyons meander across the muddy bottom as evidence that they have been released from its grip.

Coriolis's own experience of the seas and the air, like that of all his fellow citizens (apart from the unvisited montane tribes of the Alps and the Pyrenees), was limited to two dimensions. The reference frame of France's scientists, farmers and sailors was on the surface and each of them could do no more than speculate about what drove the air above or the seas below. The Gulf Stream helped or hindered sailors, the water in harbours rose and fell and storms and heatwaves arrived in ways more or less impossible to predict, but nobody knew quite why.

In 1783, just six years before their nation's political collapse, and in its greatest contribution to technology, all that changed. Frenchmen took to the air. Before that day, man could do no more than experience the atmosphere. Afterwards, he became part of it.

The brothers Joseph and Etienne Montgolfier ran a paper mill in the south-east of the country. Anxious to publicise their product, they began to build hot air balloons from paper (legend has it that they got the idea when an empty paper bag put over a boiling coffee pot floated upwards). After some preliminary experiments, they made one ten metres across, powered by a brazier. They exhibited it to the astonished locals and then travelled to Paris to demonstrate what Joseph called 'a cloud in a paper bag'. The brothers believed that smoke, rather than heat, gave the craft its lift, and insisted that certain fuels did a better job than others. At first they used damp straw mixed with chopped-up wool, but soon managed to develop a more advanced source of the mysterious antigravity power: 'They had caused all the old shoes that could be collected to be brought, and threw them into the damp straw as it burned, together with pieces of decomposed meat, for these are the substances which supply their gas.' On 19 September 1783 the king and queen came to see the experiment in progress, but 'the noxious smell ... obliged them to retire at once'.

The first test flight of a larger craft took place at Montreuil, east of Paris. The envelope was lined with alum to keep it safe from sparks, and its segments were held together by two thousand buttons. The aircraft was given its freedom and rose to a thousand metres, travelling for a couple of kilometres before it fell to earth. The next step came at Versailles, where the first domestic animals took to the air, with 'a sheep, a cockerel and a duck in a wickerwork basket suspended from the Aerostatique Machine by a fifteen-foot rope'.

Then came the crucial moment; the first manned flight. Louis XVI felt that this was so risky that condemned prisoners should be sent up, but he was soon persuaded that the honour should go to worthier candidates. Jean-François Pilâtre de Rozier, a young physicist with an interest in gases, was the first choice (he had already proved his courage with a rubber suit and an air pump that allowed him to descend into methane-filled cesspits, the cause of death for many sewer workers). He was accompanied by the Marquis d'Arlandes, an officer of the Royal Guard. The monarch was right about the risks. On the maiden flight, the two passengers took buckets of water with sponges and long sticks and, as the marquis noted in his account of the experience: 'I took my sponge and quietly put out the little fire that was burning some of the holes within my reach.'

After preliminary tests in a tethered balloon, on 21 November the intrepid aeronauts took off from the Bois de Boulogne, to the west of Paris. The wind took them to the east, and after about half an hour in the air, they landed ten kilometres away, at the Butte-aux-Cailles, in the south-east of the city.

The physicist Jacques Alexander César Charles (whose name lives on in Charles's Law, an equation that links the expansion of gases to their temperature) realised that hydrogen – which weighs far less than does air – would generate much more lift than the Montgolfier 'cloud in a paper bag'. It could be made when concentrated sulphuric acid was poured on to iron. A hydrogen balloon needed a gas bag less permeable than that used to hold hot air, and with help from two engineers, the brothers Anne-Jean and Nicolas-Louis Robert, Charles designed a pilot vehicle. A solution of rubber dissolved in turpentine was painted on to sheets of silk stitched together to make a closed sphere able to hold thirty-five cubic metres of hydrogen and to lift a payload of no more than about nine kilograms. It took several days to fill, for the hydrogen that poured off the half a ton of scrap used to generate it cooled and contracted in the envelope, and had constantly to be topped up. On the twenty-seventh of August 1783, Charles's experimental vehicle was released from the Champ de Mars, and flew fast towards the north.

The balloon rose to around a thousand metres before it touched down some twenty kilometres away, near the village of Gonesse. There it was attacked by terrified peasants, who hurled rocks at it and stabbed it with a pitchfork: 'The creature, shaking and bounding, dodged the first blows. At last it received a mortal wound, and collapsed with a long sigh.'

Indifferent to their infant's plight, Charles and the Roberts went on to build a version ten times larger, ballasted with sacks of sand and armed with a gas release valve, a flap at the top. In the gardens of the Tuileries on the first day of December 1783 – just nine days after Pilâtre de Rozier's adventure – Charles and Nicolas-Louis Robert clambered into the basket, which was held down by four of the grandest aristocrats of France. The Montgolfier brothers released a small test balloon to check the direction of the wind, and the *Charlière* (as hydrogen balloons are still called in France) set off on its historic journey.

An immense throng of four hundred thousand, half the population of Paris and perhaps the largest crowd ever seen until then, gasped in amazement. The spectators included Benjamin Franklin, who recorded that: 'Someone asked me – what's the use of a balloon? I replied – *what's the use of a new-born baby?*' Others were just as impressed: 'It is impossible to describe that moment, the women in tears, the common people raising their hands to the sky in deep silence, the passengers leaning out of the gallery, waving and crying out with joy ... the sense of fright gives way to wonder.' The balloon rose to around five hundred and fifty metres and landed two hours later at Nesles-la-Vallée, some thirty-five kilometres away, just before sunset. Robert jumped out, but Charles was anxious to try again, and was released into the air. The craft shot upwards to about three thousand metres and he suffered from severe pains in the ears as the pressure dropped. Even so, he recorded that the sun as it set then 'rose for me alone' as he soared into the air and 'saw all the rest of Nature plunged into shadow'; the first person in history to do so. As he wrote: 'Nothing will ever equal that moment of total hilarity that filled my whole body at the instant of take-off ... It was not mere pleasure, it was perfect bliss ... a sort of physical rapture ... I could *hear myself living*, so to speak.' After he landed, he never flew again (the Robert brothers themselves later experimented with a sausage-shaped aerostat rowed with oars; it was not a success).

Ballomanie soon became all the rage, with the French well in advance of their rivals across the Channel (as the president of the Royal Society, Sir Joseph Banks, put it: 'Practical flying we may leave to our rivals the French. Theoretical flying we may claim for ourselves') George III wrote to him with an offer of financial support for some British test flights, but Banks was adamant: 'No good whatever could result from them'. As the work went on, the French government tried to reduce public alarm: 'We propose to repeat these experiments on a larger scale. Anyone who shall see in the sky such a globe, which resembles a moon in part hidden by clouds, should be aware that this is not a phenomenon at which they should be alarmed, but is no more than a machine, made of taffeta, or light canvas covered with paper, that cannot cause any harm, and which will one day prove serviceable to the wants of society.'

The authorities were right about the future of flight, but balloons, as Joseph Banks had feared, soon proved to be dangerous. Two months after his first expedition, Pilâtre de Rozier was among the crew of a huge hot-air machine, ten times larger than his previous craft and still one of the largest such devices ever constructed. It was launched in Lyon on a blustery day and was much overloaded, for a number of visitors leapt on board and drew swords to insist on their right to join the passengers. As it rose, it was soaked through and suffered a rip in its envelope. After a few minutes it plunged to earth with, to its inmates' surprise, no injuries. Undeterred, de Rozier began to set new speed and height records, but he met his death when his last craft, a hybrid of a Montgolfier design and a *Charlière*, caught fire and crashed in a failed attempt to cross from Boulogne to England. Because hydrogen was so light, he had assumed that any escape from the balloon would vent into the atmosphere before a spark from the fire reached it. Though Marat himself claimed to have warned him about the dangers, de Rozier paid for his confidence with his life. His fate, soon to be followed by that of many others, was marked by an obelisk, which is still in place.

His hybrid design became known as a *Rozière*. The hydrogen gave most of the lift, and the heated air when added provided a little more, which was lost as it cooled so that the navigator could persuade his craft to rise and fall. The system used far less fuel than the Montgolfiers' version, which had constantly to stoke a fire large enough to stay aloft. In today's manned craft, hydrogen has been replaced with the safer helium, although a world shortage of that gas, brought about in part because of the millions of party balloons filled with the stuff, may soon demand a rethink.

A variety of wild schemes as to how to use the new invention soon emerged. Franklin himself suggested that a footman could travel faster if much of his weight was lifted by a bag of gas. Another idea was to set up a balloon postal service. That had to wait for its moment until Paris was besieged by the Prussians in 1870, with letters sent out in their tens of thousands in balloons and the microfilmed responses returned to the capital by homing pigeons. The devices were also much used for display and for mass entertainment, the latter enlivened by the occasional death of an aeronaut.

Balloons also found a place in war. Joseph Montgolfier himself had seen the military potential of his invention. 'I possess a super-human means with which to introduce our soldiers into an impregnable fortress. They may enter through the air ... With a large enough bag it will be possible to introduce into Gibraltar an entire army which, borne by the wind, will enter right above the heads of the English.' That idea never took off, but Benjamin Franklin's speculation that balloons would be invaluable in 'elevating an Engineer to take a view of an Enemy's Army, Works, &c; conveying Intelligence into, or out of, a besieged Town, giving Signals to Distant Places, or the like' soon did.

Impressed by his logic, the French government had set up a *Corps d'Aérostiers* to be used as observers in the struggles that followed the downfall of Louis XVI. At the Battle of Fleurus in 1794, in what is now Belgium, where the republican army faced its royalist invaders, a tethered balloon with messages dropped down a wire to the ground allowed the French to spy on, and to defeat, the enemy.

Valuable as those ideas may have been, the devices found their natural home in the study of the atmosphere. The first manned flight of the *Charlière* was itself a step in that direction, for the aeronauts took with them a barometer and a thermometer. Two decades later, the Corps of Aeronauts was sent to Egypt with Napoleon, but when his fleet was attacked by Nelson, most of their equipment was destroyed. Just one craft made it back to France. It was used in a second meteorological expedition. In 1804, the mathematician Jean-Baptiste Biot and the physicist and expert on gases Louis Joseph Gay-Lussac set off in its basket to measure the proportions of nitrogen and oxygen and the strength of the magnetic field at different altitudes. They found little change with height. Biot passed out on the first flight, but on a second, solitary attempt, Gay-Lussac ascended to just over seven thousand metres – the highest point that mankind had ever reached.

Joseph Banks remained a sceptic: 'I see an inclination in the more respectable part of the Society to guard against the *Ballomania* until some experiment like to prove beneficial either to society or to science is proposed.' There was as a result somewhat of a lacuna in the exploration of the atmosphere until 1862, when the British Association for the

Advancement of Science established a committee to study 'Hygrometric and other Conditions of the Upper Air'. The meteorologist James Glaisher set out to measure air currents, the intensity of sunlight, electrical charge, atmospheric pressure and the structure of clouds in his craft *Mammoth*, powered by town gas. He took with him barometers, thermometers and hygrometers, a compass, a chronometer, a pair of binoculars, a magnet, and a ball of string. Glaisher made more than twenty ascents, most of them from landlocked Wolverhampton to reduce the danger of being swept out to sea. He noted his symptoms when in the hostile heights: 'At 19,435 feet the hands and lips assume a dark bluish colour but not the face. At 21,792 feet I experienced a feeling analogous to sea sickness ...' On one occasion his craft ran out of control and its pilot passed out. He rose to six, or perhaps even seven, miles above sea level, far higher than the summit of Everest. He was lucky to survive, for a few years later two French aeronauts died on a flight from Paris at a level well below his record. Their corpses were found in the basket, with blackened faces and mouths full of blood. They carried oxygen but lost consciousness before they could use it, perhaps because they rose faster than had the more cautious Briton.

Glaisher found that Gay-Lussac's claim that the temperature dropped by one degree Celsius with every hundred metres' gain in altitude was correct, but that it did not apply above about ten kilometres from the surface. That was the first hint that the atmosphere was not a simple cloud of gas but was divided into distinct strata.

Now, thanks to manned and unmanned balloons, helped by planes, rockets and satellites, we know that the ocean of air is, like the sea itself, arranged in both vertical and horizontal layers and is, like the deeps, in constant movement. The lowest segment, the haunt of the aeronauts, is known as the troposphere. Its currents and vortices generate most of the weather. Because of the centrifugal force of the Earth's spin, the troposphere bulges at the equator to around twenty kilometres thick, while at the latitude of France the figure is around half that (which means that a fit Parisian could, given a suitable ladder, climb to the edge of space in a couple of days), and at the poles no more than five or six kilometres. Its temperature drops with height to around minus fifty degrees. Then the trend reverses, as can sometimes be seen in the flat tops of thunderclouds unable to penetrate the thermal ceiling. The stratosphere has begun. It stretches out to around fifty kilometres and, because heat is generated as solar ultraviolet generates ozone, warms to around minus fifteen degrees. The stratosphere is succeeded by the mesosphere. That reaches to eighty-five kilometres and contains enough gas to cause meteorites to burn up, while beyond it lies the upper atmosphere, a sparse five hundred kilometre layer bombarded by the Sun's rays. Above that comes the home of artificial satellites, accompanied by just a few molecules, and then comes space itself, which is almost – but not quite – void.

Balloonists soon found patterns in the medium in which they were suspended. At the time of the American Civil War, an intrepid amateur on the Union side discovered that he could rise above the Southern forces besieging Washington and pass back dispatches on their positions to his own commanders. When his vessel was launched, a westerly breeze pushed him over the enemy's lines. That raised the hopes of the Confederate troops, who pursued him on horseback with the assumption that he would be forced to land when his fuel ran out, but he then dropped ballast and his spy plane rose to three thousand metres, where it found an easterly that took him back to safety.

Such devices are still the workhorses of meteorology. Around eight hundred stations across the globe use them, some sending up several a day. Most are filled with hydrogen (cheaper than helium) and have global positioning system sensors together with instruments that radio data back to base. Some soar to forty kilometres before the envelope disintegrates and the instruments parachute to earth. With their help the secrets of the atmosphere have begun to reveal themselves.

One insight came with the discovery of the jet stream. The first hints of that elevated causeway came when the 1883 eruption of Krakatoa moved dust across the world in just a few weeks. The equatorial smoke stream, as it was initially called, has sisters across the planet. Early pilots were baffled to find that sometimes they had travelled far further over the ground than they expected. They had, in fact, strayed into one of the rivers of air that seam the upper atmosphere. Balloons swallowed up in such a torrent may travel for thousands of miles before they come back to Earth.

Most jet streams blow from west to east, at heights of eight thousand metres and more. They are strongest near the poles, where they are sparked off in places where masses of icy air collide with warmer sections of the atmosphere. Because the Coriolis force is so powerful in that part of the world, the Arctic jet stream (like the Gulf Stream far below) meanders in great arcs on its way across the Atlantic. As it does, the clash between the icy air of the polar vortex and the warmer atmosphere to the south generates areas of high and low pressure in the peaks and troughs of its errant waves, some of which veer south to hit Europe. If the polar jet sits in the far north conditions in Europe stay settled, but if it moves further south it can deliver a queue of storms that lasts for months.

Weather forecasters map its position every hour while airline pilots – like the French sailors who used Franklin's map to ride the Gulf Stream – take advantage of its movements, for a favourable high-altitude gale can cut more than an hour from a New York to London flight. The torrent has also been used for more sinister ends. In the last year of the Second World War the Japanese released thousands of booby-trapped balloons which soared upwards before they found the stream and headed towards enemy territory. A barometer estimated their height and caused ballast to be ejected if the crude weapon dropped too low. It took them about four days to make the trip. Most fell into the sea, but three hundred or so made it to the United States. Just one succeeded in its murderous aim, when a pregnant Oregon woman on a Sunday picnic picked it up. The device killed her and five children with her in the only Second World War deaths from enemy action in the mainland United States. For a time, the authorities suspected that the weapons had been launched from submarines, or even from prisoner-of-war camps, but the sand used for ballast was identical to that found on Japanese beaches, and their origin was proved.

Balloons have returned to peaceful uses. Tens of thousands are scattered across the globe, many used for simple enjoyment. Pleasure has become debased into competition, and records for height, speed and endurance have been broken again and again. Not until 1999 did an aerostat put a girdle around the Earth. The *Breitling Orbiter* was sponsored by a Swiss watch company. Its *Rozière* design used a closed sac of helium to produce a modicum of lift, supplemented by hot air generated by propane cylinders, which were jettisoned as they emptied. The envelope had a cramped gondola just big enough for two passengers. It took off at dawn and swept south and west over the Mediterranean until it reached Mauretania, where the jet stream pushed it eastwards. Almost three weeks later, its passengers landed in Egypt after a trip around the globe that had covered forty thousand kilometres. At times, the balloon had risen to eleven thousand metres.

Such devices are much used by astronomers. They lift a load higher than can any aircraft, and at far less expense than a satellite. A telescope or other device is suspended well below the envelope to reduce the extent to which it blocks the view, and the instrument is mounted on swivels to avoid the craft's tendency to spin. The first such probe was sent up in 1957. It revealed that our local star has a surface far more uneasy than had been assumed, and that the rotation of the electrical storms on its surface (the largest of which can be seen as sunspots) respond, as expected, to the Coriolis force.

The Sun rotates on its axis no more than once every three weeks or so, so that the effect is small. Jupiter – a planet much larger than Earth – takes just ten hours to make a complete circuit, which gives rise to enormous surface stresses, and produces features such as the famous Red Spot, a storm that has lasted for centuries but for some reason has begun to fade away. The sheets of dust known as the rings of Saturn also depend on that force, for they settle in the Coriolis doldrums around their planet's equator.

Foucault himself was much more than a populariser of physics. He is also remembered for the first measurement of the speed of light. In 1850, he shone a powerful beam from a fast-rotating mirror in his laboratory to a fixed mirror some thirty-five kilometres away. In the time it took to make the return journey, his laboratory mirror had moved by a fraction, and a measure of the distance between the outgoing and the incoming beam made it possible to work out the speed at which light travelled. A later estimate with a more compact apparatus gave a measure of 298,000 kilometres a second, which would allow a ray to go round the world eight times in that instant. His measure was within a fraction of a per cent of modern estimates.

Einstein knew of Foucault's figure when he came up with the equation that relates mass to energy and to velocity. The boundaries between space and time as well as those between mass and energy (all of which seemed absolute in Foucault's day) have as a result become blurred. The effect is most noteworthy in frames of reference that most of us find hard to contemplate, from the gigantic, as in the behaviour of light and stars around a black hole, to the unimaginably small, as in the emission of light in tiny quanta that have the properties of both waves and particles.

Most of today's visitors to the Panthéon have the same vague familiarity with relativity and quantum theory as their predecessors had with the Earth's relationship with the Sun. In truth, physicists, if not the public, now know that the behaviour of Foucault's device, like that of all objects when considered on the appropriate scale, is far less straightforward than it appears and that the nineteenth-century spectators had been misled about quite what they had seen.

The suspended mass has had a busy life. It was hauled into place in 1851 but was taken down when the Panthéon was handed back to the Church by Louis Napoleon after his *coup d'état* in that year. After a brief hiatus, it found a new home in the Musée des Arts et Métiers, itself housed within the walls of a suppressed church, and for a time a copy was placed in its original home. In 2010, in the Arts et Métiers, the wire snapped and the original bob was smashed. It has been replaced with a replica. As I write these lines, the Panthéon is under restoration and free of pendula, but across the globe more than three hundred copies of the original give mute witness to the elegant simplicity of the Galilean universe.

The real tale of the pendulum, the planet's spin and the cosmos is more complex than Foucault was ready to admit. Galileo had noted that a church candelabrum as it swung gently to and fro always took just the same time to make its beats. For such minor displacements he was more or less right, but a closer look shows that matters soon become more ambiguous.

The truth about the pendulum is on show in a place that uses its device to celebrate not the stark facts of physics but the mysteries of religion. The Cathedral of Santiago del Compostela in Galicia is built on bones better known than those of St Geneviève, for its crypt is said to hold the relics of St James himself. The church contains a magnificent thurible, the *Botafumeiro*, an ornate silvered-brass object a metre and a half tall that weighs more than fifty kilograms. It hangs twenty metres down from the dome and on feast days is filled with charcoal and incense and set to swing and to breathe flames and clouds of smoke. Its oscillations are pumped hard by a squad of brawny *tiraboleiros*, who pull on a line attached to a roller high in the dome, around which the censer's thick rope is wound. In response to timed commands, they can generate an oscillation of almost ninety degrees. The consecrated receptacle travels at seventy kilometres an hour as it passes through the bottom of its arc, just a few centimetres above the ground. It has broken free on several occasions; once, some say, in 1499 when Catherine of Aragon was on her ill-fated trip to marry her first husband (who soon died and was succeeded in that position by his brother, Henry VIII). Divine providence ensured that nobody was killed.

For such a massive object, with its wide arc and the constant input of energy, the patterns of oscillation are much more complicated than is the simple wave supposed to characterise its calmer sister in the Panthéon. In spite of the ecclesiastical horseplay that surrounds it, the smoking

Spanish pendulum is in truth a better introduction to today's physics than is the elegant device in its neighbour's capital.

Even Foucault's own version has hidden complexities. First, any such contraption needs an input of energy to keep the bob from returning to its stable state, in which it hangs motionless and vertical. Foucault designed a drive, with magnets in the weight and timed pulses of electricity in wires hidden below, to keep his device alive. Modern systems often use a motor that pulls the suspension point up and down and, like the broad-shouldered believers of Santiago, feeds in energy.

Another practical problem came from the need to ensure that the bob travelled in a precise straight line across the centre of its circle, with no deviation to left or to right, for to start even a fraction off the correct track led to complications. That job was harder than it seems. Foucault set his apparatus into motion with a match applied to a thread that held the heavy weight at the appropriate angle, but quite often, several attempts were needed to persuade it to behave in the approved manner.

In fact, any pendulum driven by an external input of energy soon begins to act in an entirely unpredictable way. The problem comes from the diversity of forces involved. Foucault's device is much more than a simple mass suspended in the Earth's gravity. The line from which it hangs is part of the system and is, in effect, a long and flexible pendulum in its own right. That becomes much more obvious when the support is not a thin wire, but a thick, heavy and rather inflexible rope, and when the input of external energy that keeps it in motion is substantial in relation to the weight of the bob. Air resistance further complicates the issue.

The effect is easy to see in a double pendulum. Such devices are simple: take a metre ruler and saw it off at around sixty centimetres, use a pivot to attach the shorter to the longer section, and hang the whole contraption from a swivel. When set into action with a good hard shove, the result is a surprise. Instead of a regular pulse to and fro, within a few seconds the system goes into overdrive and each segment spins round at random. Set up a pair – or more – of identical pendulums, and start them off at the same time in the same direction and with the same motive force, and they will behave in quite different ways. Out of order – the philosophy behind both Foucault's own device and all the physics of his day – has come disorder.

Chaos, that mighty agent, is not confined to cathedrals. In truth, it fills the air, the seas and the universe and every day, in every way, affects us all. Its actions mean that the accuracy of a weather forecast declines fast as meteorologists peer into the future, as do the projections of financial speculators, of statesmen and of surgeons. Even billiards – that apparently rational pastime, studied by Coriolis himself – falls prey to the powers of chaos, for mathematicians (and they like their game simple, with a ball of zero mass, no pockets to swallow it up, a surface with zero friction, and infinitely flexible cushions) have found that a ball tapped into the side at almost any angle will in time, and quite unpredictably, visit every spot on the table.

Many Britons remember the Great Storm of October 1987

and the breezy comment by the weather forecaster Michael Fish that 'Earlier on today, apparently, a woman rang the BBC and said she heard there was a hurricane on the way. Well, if you're watching, don't worry, there isn't.' The winds struck southern England at around midnight, with the highest speeds recorded at Gorleston in Norfolk, at 106 knots. The tempest hit north-west France with even greater power (and there too the forecasters had reassured the population, with talk of no more than *une petite tempête en provenance des Açores*). Gusts of 119 knots hit the town of Quimper in Brittany, with an extraordinary blast of 130 knots at a coastal station near Cherbourg. One fifth of the forests of Brittany were destroyed, and fifteen people were killed in that small and rather empty region, compared to nineteen across the whole of southern Britain.

In spite of the confidence of Mr Fish, forecasts in his day were primitive. Now, with far more powerful computers and much more information on the atmosphere, they are better than they were – but they still quail in the face of chaos. The problem was first realised more than a century ago, when it was found by a French mathematician that a tiny shift in the initial conditions plugged into a theoretical model of a rotating system could build up to give large and unpredictable differences in the end result. The promise of a dependable forecast that stretches ahead for many weeks, the Holy Grail for climatologists, was impossible to fulfil, and the best that could be hoped for even with huge amounts of data was a range of probabilities.

Next winter, or the one after that, may suffer more rain

than even the record deluges of 2014, but the new world of disorder means that we have only the certainty that we cannot be certain about what the weather may bring. Most local forecasts in temperate regions run out of steam less than two weeks into the future. Often that is not enough. Farmers are keen to know months ahead whether the summer will be hotter or colder, or wetter or drier, than usual and to use the information to plan their schedules. Even the great drivers of climate such as El Niño, the oscillation of warm water across the Pacific that influences much of the world's weather, are impossible to forecast for more than two to four years ahead.

One way to test the reliability of any system based on gambling (which is, after all, what weather-forecasting is) is to look not forwards but backwards and to ask how well a prediction made in earlier times in fact succeeded. The results are mixed at best.

In places relatively free of the Coriolis force the historical forecasts do quite well. They were more or less accurate in their predictions of warm winters over the south of the Sahara and their estimates of the chances of wet summers in east Africa. They were much less dependable – and sometimes downright deceptive – when they tried to forecast summer rainfall in northern Europe, a place plagued by the *force centrifuge composé*. Over the world as a whole, predictions were better for temperature than for rainfall, for the latter is more dependent on the erratic movements of areas of high and low pressure. The Meteorological Office in Britain has invested £100 million in a computer that can do 16,000 trillion calculations a second, but so far has been coy about quite how far the machine will peer into the future. It now issues forecasts for six days ahead, two days more than before that investment was made. A tentative look a month ahead is now feasible, but there have been few signs of success in attempts to tease order out of nature's disorder over longer periods.

How could one, in the tradition of Foucault, draw the importance of such random effects to the attention of the public? A chaotic pendulum with a length, like his, of sixty metres would with sufficient input of energy throw itself around in a dramatic demonstration of the limits of classical physics and would no doubt attract the crowds. And where better to hang that homage to the new world of uncertainty than from the now vacant dome of the noble monument to the great men of France? The spectators in the Panthéon would have to be furnished with hard hats and protective apparel against the possibility of accident, but that would add relish to their experience as the mighty flail thrashed above their heads. Their response to the fearsome object would no doubt be much livelier than that of their predecessors, who had remained before Foucault's pendulum 'lost in thought, silent, before finally departing with a vivid conviction of our continuous motion in space'. It might also remind the onlookers that today's scientists are still not much better at predicting and protecting against floods, earthquakes, epidemics and the various shocks that flesh is heir to than was St Geneviève, in whose honour the great edifice in which they stand was built.

CHAPTER VI

THE EMPIRE OF ANARCHY

... instead of a green flowery world, there is a waste
wild-weltering chaos: which has again, with tumult
and struggle, to make itself into a world.

THOMAS CARLYLE, *The French Revolution*

Falkensteinfoto/Alamy

Pierre-Simon Laplace, logician to the universe

The Eiffel Tower was erected, against much opposition, as a temporary entrance for the World's Fair of 1889, itself organised to mark the triumphs of France in the century since the Revolution (one of several other proposals was to build a three hundred-metre tall model of a guillotine, but that did not find favour).

La Tour rises from the Champ de Mars, which played a large part in that era as the launch pad of the world's first hydrogen balloon, the location of the first Bastille Day celebration, and the altar of celebration for Robespierre's Cult of the Supreme Being. In 1791, the open space was for a time renamed the Field of Blood, after the massacre of dozens of protesters by order of the mayor of Paris.

The structure itself was at first derided as a blot on the face of the City of Light. The author Guy de Maupassant often, or so he claimed, ate lunch in the restaurant at its base, on the grounds that it was the one place where he could be guaranteed not to see it. A petition signed by many other grand figures in the arts was florid in its condemnation: 'the grotesque, mercenary invention of a machine builder ... the deflowering of Paris'. The Church, too, was outraged: the tower dwarfed every ecclesiastical edifice in the city and was 'an insult to the Eternal'. Others returned to the logic of Franklin's day to argue that it would attract thunderbolts and endanger the whole city.

The poet François Coppée made his anger public in three dozen verses of doggerel (*J'ai visité la Tour énorme, / Le mât de fer aux durs agrès. / Inachevé, confus, difforme, /Le monstre est hideux, vu de près. / Géante, sans beauté ni style, / C'est bien l'idole de metal,/Symbole de force inutile/ Et triomphe du fait brutal* . . .). Incomplete, confused, deformed, hideous, useless and free of style as the metallic idol might be, Coppée was in one way correct, for the three-hundred-metre mast is indeed, as a monument to science, a triumph of brutal fact. The seventy-two names of the great and good inscribed on its beams include biologists, astronomers, physicists, chemists, geographers and more. All share not just their talents but an attribute once universal among their profession, for every one among them is male (Sophie Germain, the self-taught female mathematician who was just thirteen when the old regime collapsed and whose work on the elasticity of metals was essential to the tower's design, does not get a mention).

Paris's ithyphallic tribute to the talents of the Y chromosome is reflected in another erection a few kilometres to the east. The Panthéon holds seventy-seven sets of illustrious remains, among them the bones of a dozen or so researchers (Foucault, who made the place famous, did not pass the entrance examination). Until not long ago, the monument stayed true to the motto inscribed on its portico, which dedicates it to the *grands hommes* of France. For most of its history it contained the remnants of just one woman, and she had no more than an honorary membership that stemmed from her conjugal virtue as widow of the chemist Claude-Louis Berthollet, inventor of bleach.

In 1995, the good Madame Berthollet was joined by another member of her sex when the remains of Marie Curie, who died in 1934, were interred along with those of her husband Pierre, who predeceased her by almost thirty years (the monument has now been graced by the relics of two more females, both of them anti-Nazi fighters nominated by President Hollande).

Marie Skłodowska, as she had been, was born in Poland, but in 1891, at the age of twenty-four, she moved to Paris to continue her studies in mathematics, physics and chemistry. She was the first woman to win a Nobel Prize and became a figure revered across the world.

The young Pole began her career in a technical workshop that did research on the magnetic properties of steels. There she met Pierre Curie. They married in 1895, Marie dressed in a blue cloak that she later used as a laboratory coat. In the same year, Wilhelm Roentgen discovered X-rays, and soon afterwards, the French physicist Henri Becquerel, who worked at the Muséum Nationale d'Histoire Naturelle, found that certain salts of uranium had the ability to darken photographic paper. At first, he assumed that the chemicals had been energised by sunlight, but in a famous case of serendipity he discovered that they kept their power even when kept in a drawer. Whatever did the job was, it seemed, generated by the compounds themselves. The Curies joined the team set up to study this remarkable effect.

Marie suggested that the phenomenon was due to some form of energy emitted by the spontaneous decay of the element's atoms. With the help of an electrometer, a radiation detection instrument, she then found that pitchblende, a source of uranium, was even more radioactive (a word she invented) and deduced that the mineral must contain another and more potent author of such rays. They purified the material and soon discovered the element polonium, which they named after Marie's native land. On Boxing Day 1898, the Curies and Becquerel announced the detection of an even more powerful source, which they called radium. After three years' work and the purification of a ton of ore they isolated a tenth of a gram of radium chloride.

The 1903 Nobel Prize for Physics was awarded to the three of them. Marie went on to become the first female professor at the University of Paris and the winner of another Nobel Prize, in chemistry this time (but was scorned by the Academy of Sciences, which had to wait until 1979 for its first female member). She became a figure of great dignity, who supervised the X-ray machines set up to help treat casualties of the First World War. Her death from leukaemia no doubt came from the lack of safety precautions in those days, and her notebooks – and even her cookery books – are still so radioactive that they are kept in lead-lined boxes.

Nobody realised this at the time, but the Curies' discovery was a fatal blow for the idea of an ordered cosmos that began with Galileo and had been much refined by French mathematicians of the late eighteenth century. It marked the dawn of the modern era, which sees the universe, as much as the weather, the stock market and the pendulum, as ruled instead by Carlyle's 'loud weltering Chaos, which devours itself'.

The phrase 'treasure your exceptions' comes from a biologist rather than a physicist, but is a touchstone for the whole of science. If an observation does not fit a theory, the theory must give way. It had long been obvious to astronomers that there were anomalies in the movements of the planets and their satellites that were hard to accommodate into a simple scheme of independent pairs of entities that interact through gravity as they circle the Sun. Newton himself saw that his model of attraction between two objects was not enough to explain such behaviour. He tried to analyse the apparent wobble in the orbit of the Moon and realised that to explain it one would have to add the force of the Sun to that of the Earth. He had little success (as one of his contemporaries put it: 'His head never ached but with his study on the moon') and – as a man as much obsessed with the Bible as with the universe – was reduced to speculation about whether divine intervention was needed to explain such incongruities, or even to set the whole system into motion.

The problem was then studied by a generation of French astronomers. The most brilliant among them was Pierre-Simon Laplace, who became Professor of Mathematics at the École Militaire at the age of eighteen. His bones rest not in the Panthéon, but in the cemetery of Père Lachaise (although his name did make it to the Eiffel Tower).

Laplace was a man of extraordinary abilities (and a great deal of common sense, for he fled the capital just before the Terror). As well as his investigations with Lavoisier into respiration, he was involved in the scheme to assess the shape of the Earth, studied the speed of sound, investigated the nature of tides, and discovered that water below zero degrees Celsius remained liquid until a sliver of ice was inserted.

He also did fundamental work in mathematics and statistics. Laplace was the first to come up with a way to combine separate pieces of evidence to test whether a particular result has arisen by chance alone. He used the same logic to work out the optimal size of a jury, given that each juror has a chance of error or bias. The Laplace equation is used in the study of the movement of fluids and the transfer of heat, while the Laplace transform is valuable in the analysis of differential equations for it converts them into a form that can be solved with algebra. Their inventor was not successful in all his endeavours, for he failed in his suggestion that a right angle should be defined to contain a hundred degrees, and his 'social physics', the notion that the laws behind the universe would help to understand crime and disease, had almost as much impact as did Newton's works on theology. His work is dense indeed, but is peppered with provocative phrases such *'il est aisé à voir que . . .'*. In addition, his publications are also rather short of references to the labours of his predecessors, with their results often described as if they are Laplace's own.

Laplace was most celebrated for his work in astronomy. His five-volume *Celestial Mechanics*, published between 1799 and 1825, helped found the discipline in its modern form (Napoleon – once his student at the École Militaire, where he had specialised in mathematics and where the future Emperor had produced new geometrical results of his own – told him that he would read it as soon as he had six months free to do so). As its title hints, Laplace saw the cosmos as a gigantic machine. He was quite explicit in the view that it had a permanent, universal and fundamental pattern; that 'The stability in the system of the world, which assures its duration, is one of the most notable among all phenomena, in that it exhibits in the heavens the same intention to maintain order in the universe that nature has so admirably observed on Earth for the sake of preserving individuals and perpetuating species.' In time he became even more confident: 'An intellect which at a certain moment would know all forces that set nature in motion, and all positions of all items of which nature is composed, if this intellect were also vast enough to submit these data to analysis, it would embrace in a single formula the movements of the greatest bodies of the universe and those of the tiniest atom and for such an intellect nothing would be uncertain and the future, just like the past, would present itself before its eyes.' With enough mathematics it would become possible to predict every episode in the heavens and to work out each step that had led to the patterns seen today. To do so would mark the triumph of rationalism in a logical universe.

Pierre-Simon Laplace is said to have replied to Napoleon's question as to why there was no mention of God in his books that 'I have no need of that hypothesis.' His statement is often taken as a public affirmation of his atheism (a risky admission at the time), but probably refers instead to his rejection of Newton's appeal to divine intervention to keep the astral clock in motion.

His mathematics was formidable, and it was rumoured in Paris that no more than twenty Frenchmen (and half that number of Englishmen) understood it, while an American astronomer who perused his works wrote that 'I never come across one of Laplace's *Thus, it plainly appears* without feeling sure that I have got hours of hard study before me ... to find out and show *how* it plainly appears.' Laplace himself claimed that just one woman in the world could comprehend his treatise. She was Mary Somerville, a self-taught Scots mathematician, whose name lives on in Somerville College, Oxford. She set out to translate his book into English, and did so with a clarity not known to its author. Somerville summarised its central thesis thus: 'The infinite varieties of motion in the heavens, and on the earth, obey a few laws, so universal in their application, that they regulate a curve traced by an atom which seems to be the sport of the winds, with as much certainty as the orbits of the planets.' The most important of those laws ruled gravity, 'the original property of matter, by means of which we ascertain the past and anticipate the future ... the link which connects our planet with remote worlds that might seem to be placed beyond the reach of human facilities'. Unlike electrical charge, which has both a positive and negative face, gravity draws every particle into its power. It acts as an enormous hand able to hold vast numbers of objects in its grip.

Laplace was so convinced of its importance that he came up with the remarkable statement that 'The gravitational attraction of a star with a diameter two hundred and fifty times that of the Sun and comparable in density to the Earth would be so great that no light could escape from its surface. The largest bodies in the universe may thus be invisible by reason of their magnitude.' Those lines could be read as a hint of the existence of black holes (even if they are wrong in detail, for some such structures are not huge but small and extremely dense). The great astronomer had unwittingly predicted the existence of the bodies that, in the end, helped to destroy the idea of a stable, certain and static universe.

He also came up with a theory as to the origin of the solar system that – like his hint of black holes – has at least in part been confirmed by modern astronomy. He saw evidence of order in the arrangement of the planets. First, they all circle the Sun at more or less the same level, the plane of the ecliptic as it is called. Second, they have a pattern in terms of size and density, with the smallest planets close to the Sun and a more or less regular increase in size to the outer reaches of the solar system. Thus, Mercury weighs just a twentieth as much as the Earth but is denser, while the outer planets are huge, with Jupiter more than three hundred times more massive than Earth but with a quarter of its density. As a further hint of a common origin all the planets spin round in the same direction.

The French rationalist felt that such consistency came from gravitational attraction. In its modern form, his theory suggests that a cloud of fiery dust surrounded the early Sun. As it span, rotational force persuaded it to form into a disc, in just the same way as the rings of Saturn emerged around the planet's equator. Remains of the dust trapped inside ancient meteorites hint that the disc began to form just 4567.3 million years ago.

As its dust cooled the system contracted and span faster, as a ballet dancer does when she moves her arms closer to her body in a pirouette. The disc then solidified into individual planets. The process began with tiny grains that stuck together to form objects the size of today's asteroids and grew larger and larger as they pulled in more material and as heavy elements such as iron sank towards the core. That job took less than a million years after the first solids condensed from their gaseous parent. On the outer fringes, less exposed to the power of the solar mass, an adolescent planet could, even with its feeble gravity, persuade material from a wide radius to join its alliance. In time it drew in hydrogen and helium that froze around it. Planets in the inner part of the system were limited in their plans for expansion because the Sun's attraction was more enticing than their own and because the intense heat meant also that only elements that stay solid even at high temperatures – iron, and the raw materials of what became rock – could be gathered in.

Comets did not obey such laws, but the great astronomer dismissed them as scarcely qualified to be members of the solar system, and suggested that most had been sucked up as raw material for planets or swallowed by the Sun. His theory explains many, but by no means all, of the properties of our astral neighbourhood.

Laplace, like Newton, knew that there were anomalies in its behaviour. The Earth as well as the Moon wobbled in an unpredictable fashion. Our local satellite also appeared to have speeded up in its orbit when modern observations were compared with those of the ancients. In addition, Jupiter seemed to be approaching the Sun, while Saturn did the opposite, which is not what the rules might predict. At the same time, the extent to which the Earth's orbit deviates from a perfect circle had decreased when eighteenth-century observations were compared with those from long ago.

The French astronomer realised that many of those irregularities came from the gravitational interactions of objects; not just two, as explored by Isaac Newton, but three or more, as in the case of Moon, Earth and Sun (or, in modern terms, Earth, Moon and artificial satellite). Plenty of others had already struggled to understand that issue. Bailly himself had tried to work out the paths of the moons of Jupiter, taking into account their effects on each other, and those of their parent planet and of other astral objects. He never solved the problem, which – given that Jupiter has more than sixty moons rather than the four he was aware of – remains recalcitrant even when attacked by modern computers.

Laplace remained convinced that the solar system, and by extension the universe, was bound to stay stable because such complexities, tiresome as they might be, were small, periodic and acted as feedback devices that corrected themselves. In some ways he was right.

His equations also persuaded him that it was impossible to give an unambiguous description of the mutual attraction of more than two bodies, whatever they might be. The '*problème des trois corps*', as it was called, had already hinted that three astral objects of about the same size could not stay in a permanent relationship, and that sooner or later, one would be ejected.

A formal proof of that statement has yet to be found, but its author realised that in certain circumstances a more or less stable threesome can emerge. Newton's lunar headache came because he could contemplate no more than a single solution for the interaction of the Earth, the Moon and the Sun. His

French equivalent saw that such equations could be solved if the system involved not an immobile pattern, but constant mutual movement of the participants. He pointed out that if two objects each have their own gravitational field and their own orbit, in certain conditions the positive and negative interactions between them will cancel out to give potential points of stability in space. His suggestion built on the earlier ideas of the mathematician Joseph-Louis Lagrange (a fact not revealed by the author of *Celestial Mechanics*).

In a simple system with two substantial members such as the Sun and the Earth, there are five islands of relative calm called 'libration points' (from the Latin *librare*, to balance) in an otherwise violent gravitational sea, into which a third party might be able to insinuate itself. The first three are on the straight line that connects the local star with our small planet. One is around a million and a half kilometres above the Earth on its sunlit face, and the other at the same altitude but on the dark side. The third lines up with the other two on the far side of the Sun.

The fourth and fifth libration points lie on the orbit of the Earth and form a triangle, with each point at an equal distance from Earth and Sun. The first three points wobble about in rather an unpredictable way, but the last two are more stable.

Laplace's equations had a subtle twist. If a substantial body were to attempt to shelter in one of the five refuges, it could not do so. On the other hand, if the third party is much smaller than the other two (as is the case for moons and for satellites), the arrangement can maintain itself if the smallest partner oscillates or circles near one of the stable points (or, as computers now tell us, moves in a horseshoe fashion or in a figure of eight, switches allegiance to rotate in sequence around each of the other two, or enters into a variety of less probable paths).

Libration points are dead ends in space, for any small object that drives in finds it hard to reverse out. They become as a result hosts to various forms of space rubble. The two Sun–Earth orbital points off the straight line that stretches from one to the other are each circled by a small asteroid. At the outer reaches of the solar system, where planets are far larger, much bigger items fall prey to their charms. The interaction between Jupiter and the Sun has trapped several large asteroids, named after heroes of the Trojan Wars such as Agamemnon, Achilles and Hector. They gain their titles from prominent Greek heroes for one point of libration, and on Trojans for the other (the astronomers' classical history has been weak, for some bear a Greek name while surrounded by Trojans, and vice versa). The Earth–Moon system involves much smaller players, and the two nearby points accumulate little more than dust, although some of the mass of space junk from abandoned satellites may in time find itself trapped in one or the other.

Astronomers now make practical use of Laplace's ideas. Four of the five libration points in the Earth–Sun system have been used as homes for satellites. The most recent is NASA's Deep Space Climate Observatory, launched in 2015 to send a stream of images of the sunlit hemisphere as viewed from the first such point, to help in weather forecasting and to track the 'solar wind' of particles emitted from the Sun. The two closest points to the Earth are not very stable, for they are in effect saddles in a gravitational landscape, with a constant danger that a visitor will roll down one side or another, although a satellite that does so can be nudged back into place by commands from the ground. The third, on the far side of the Sun, is a little inaccessible but is a boon to writers of fantasy fiction, several of whom have imagined a Planet X hidden nearby. Points four and five are in contrast hilltops, and if a resident begins to roll and rotate down the slope, the Coriolis force allows it to circle round the summit in the astral equivalent of dancing round a handbag.

Astronomers have had to import many other elements into their equations. The stream of charged particles from the Sun, the drag exerted by planetary atmospheres and the effects of relativity are all involved. The flattened shape of the Earth causes slow changes in the extent to which its axis tilts, with subtle effects on the movements of the Moon, all of which perturb the harmony of the spheres. Even so, optimists once talked of a solution for the 'million-body problem', which would untangle the gravitational webs that hold not just solar systems but whole galaxies together.

If a complete mechanical (or at least mathematical) simulacrum of a galaxy were ever to be built, it would be cumbersome indeed. Until not long ago, the descendants of Laplace and his fellows assumed nevertheless that such a celestial Heath Robinson device would one day make sense of the universe. They were, alas, too confident. The fatal blow came on the top of the Eiffel Tower.

Soon after the radiation experiments of the Curies and Becquerel it became obvious that such emissions could be picked up almost everywhere on Earth. At first the energy was assumed to come from rocks rich in the relevant elements, but in 1909 a German Jesuit priest and part-time physicist, Theodor Wulf, took an electrometer to the top of the tower to compare radiation levels at three hundred metres with those on the ground. The waves' loss of power with distance on the surface had already been measured and he expected to find an identical drop in activity with height. There was indeed a decrease, but it was rather smaller than at ground level. Wulf made the audacious suggestion that an extra dose of energy was streaming in from space. The idea was ridiculed but soon another German, Victor Hess, ascended in a balloon to five thousand metres and found that far from the radiation fading to zero, there was a threefold increase in its intensity. He had discovered cosmic rays.

The Sun was the obvious source, but Hess took advantage of a total eclipse to show that even when its orb was blocked by the Moon plenty of radiation still streamed in. He had no idea where it came from, but his discovery marked the end of the elegant thesis set out in *Celestial Mechanics*. It revealed that the cosmos is not harmonious, as Laplace had hoped, but is a realm ruled by anarchy, that resonates to the echoes of accidents and explosions far away. On the summit of the Eiffel Tower astronomers saw the first hint that the universe has both a beginning and an end.

The emissions measured high above the Champ de Mars come in many flavours. Some are so powerful that they can pass through the planet, with tiny particles armed with energies equivalent to a cricket ball bowled at test match speed. A few such have been picked up at the South Pole, from their entry point on the opposite end of the Earth. Others are less dynamic but are active enough to cause flashes of light as they pass through the eyes of astronauts. As many as half a dozen of the weaker constituents of the stream hit each square centimetre of the Earth's surface every second. The most powerful, in contrast, arrive at a rate of just one per square kilometre every century or so.

Most of the cosmic noise consists of protons, the nuclei of elements, together with some electrons, which for most of the time spin around that core and reach Earth as gamma rays. The most potent are the nuclei of heavy elements, such as iron. When such radiation bombards the atmosphere, it strikes molecules of nitrogen, oxygen, carbon and other elements to make an 'air shower' of secondary players such as muons (heavier versions of electrons) that spreads out to hit the surface.

Each is an echo of distant and unpredictable disaster, events alien to Laplace's logical theories. In today's astronomy, randomness creeps in on every scale, from particles to suns and to the origins of the cosmos itself. The cold logic of Laplace was based on his own solar system, and had he been aware of the existence of others, he would no doubt have expected his rules to apply there too. Often, they do not.

Given that the sky has ten times as many stars as the Earth has grains of sand, the number of solar systems and planets must run into trillions. That discovery brings joy to those who speculate about life on other worlds, but to the less romantic fraternity that once hoped to develop a stable theory of the universe has proved a source of uncertainty and confusion.

Many of our distant twins lack any sign of regular structure. They are not arranged as flat discs around a central sun in which all members move in similar orbits in the same direction. Instead, some of their planets describe enormous ellipses, their paths close to the fiery centre at some moments, but in the icy furthest reaches at others. Some go round their star in hours, others in years. Instead of spinning around the solar equator, a few make the eccentric decision to move around its poles, while others travel in opposite directions. Odder still, one frequent class in the cosmos, the 'super-Earths', as they are known (with dimensions between that of our own home and Neptune, a planet four times larger), is absent from our local group but makes up almost half the planets across the skies as a whole. In addition, rather than the familiar pattern of increase in size and decrease in density with distance from their parent, gaseous planets ten times the size of Jupiter spin close to their star, sometimes even closer than Mercury does to the Sun. How did they get there?

Today's astronomers accept that all solar systems emerge, like our own, from condensing discs of gas. In some systems they are indeed ordered by size and by density. That scheme, however, is not universal. Planets form and migrate at very different rates, and some of the new worlds show no sign of a neat pattern. For many, a well-behaved infancy develops into an uneasy adolescence and, as senility sets in, to an age of uncertainty. Without notice, a huge planet on the distant edge may spiral towards its star. Other players are then flung into bizarre orbits as the giant passes by, or are thrown out into the wilderness of space. The icy goliaths near the centre cannot hold on to their frozen shrouds and their gaseous clouds burn off to leave rocky cores as super-Earths that may, in time, fuse together to make planets of their own.

Such patterns emerge from the power that rules the double pendulum; the accidents of time. A small shift in initial conditions magnifies itself to generate drastic and unpredictable consequences. The theory behind such behaviour was worked out in the late nineteenth century by the French mathematician Jules Henri Poincaré, the intellectual descendant of Laplace himself. His interests were as wide as those of his predecessor (a first hint about what became the theory of relativity included), but in the end, his work was to destroy many of his predecessor's ideas.

Poincaré became involved in the endless search for a general solution of the three-body problem. Like Laplace, he did not resolve that issue, but he did notice a point that Laplace had missed. He found that minor anomalies in the movements of planets and their satellites could feed upon themselves to end in collapse, so that conditions at the start did not predict how the system would end up. His discovery opened the door to the world of chaos theory, which now plays as large a part in astronomy as it does in the study of climate, of earthquakes, and of stock markets. Tiny perturbations in the skies do not always correct themselves, but can run out of control and tear down the edifice to which they belong. The author of *Celestial Mechanics* was sure that one day ambiguity would be banished from the universe. He was wrong. Now, nothing is certain except uncertainty.

That pernicious agent determines how far ahead it may be possible to forecast the behaviour of any system. For a double pendulum the predictable period is a matter of seconds, for French or British weather about two weeks, for an economy a few decades. In the heavens, the onset of anarchy might take millions of years, but in the context of cosmic time that can seem little more than an instant. The asteroid belt around our own Sun is already so full of random accidents that the movements of its members cannot be forecast with any accuracy beyond a few thousand centuries ahead.

Computer simulations at the Paris Observatory have examined the future of our planetary neighbours in this new world. Under a veneer of stability, they hint that the Earth and many of its fellows may be poised on the edge of disaster. From the City of Light we have heard – it's in the stars – that sometime soon we will collide with Mars (on this side of the Channel, it must be said, a calmer view prevails, with those who gaze at our murky firmament confident that the astral insurrection will be long delayed, if it happens at all).

For the Earth, Venus and Mars, uneasy shifts in their orbits suggest that we can say little for sure beyond about fifty million years in the future. The stolid and icy giants at the edge of the system are more predictable, but collisions between planets – or even expulsions from the solar club – are possible within the life expectancy of the Sun, about five thousand million years from now.

The planet Mercury is the most mercurial of all, for the orbit that takes it closest to its star is not much different in shape from that of the distant giant Jupiter. Should the two coincide too closely, the smaller partner may descend into chaos as their gravitational fields interact. It might then fall into the local inferno or crash into its neighbour Venus. That could then tempt Mars into a course in which it collides with Earth, while others predict that Mercury will be pushed out altogether before it has the chance to do much damage. Mars is already rather odd. The red planet is further from the centre than is the Earth, but has just a tenth of its mass. That anomaly might reflect an ancient accident in which it played leapfrog with its neighbour and moved further out into the hierarchy.

Such disorder means that planets may tip over, with their north poles shifted south, and vice versa. Mars has jittered about over the past few hundred thousand years, but has never undergone a complete flip-flop. Earth itself may have done a partial somersault half a billion years ago, just after the Cambrian explosion of life. Geology shows that there were then great glaciations near the modern equator, but how could that freeze over without the planet becoming a snowball, with every ocean covered in ice a kilometre thick? Earth then teemed with complex creatures, all of which would have been exterminated, with no survivors to repopulate the planet. The ancient glaciations may not have taken place where their scars remain, but at the earth's northern and southern ends, when today's tropics were at the poles. Our home still quivers, but by happy chance the Moon stabilises matters and ensures that the world does not turn upside down too often.

Chaos also rules more distant skies. In the 1920s, the astronomer Edwin Hubble realised that there were vast numbers of galaxies beyond the Milky Way, our own star complex, which was until then supposed to encompass the whole universe. The 1990 space telescope named after him is still hard at work, and has discovered so many new galaxies in the small patches explored so far that there might be two hundred thousand million in the universe as a whole.

Hubble classified his new-found formations either as flat discs, ellipses with a central bulge, or spirals. Such elegance gave hints of order. Now, with the help of modern instruments, randomness has reared its disagreeable head within even the most graceful of his structures.

Galaxies, like solar systems and elephants, have long memories, and many among them retain evidence of desperate struggles long ago. Plenty more are yet to come. The Andromeda system is the immediate neighbour of our own Milky Way and will within five billion years devour it. Its mass of stars races towards us at a hundred kilometres a second. Long before the cosmic crunch the two giant clouds of cold dark gas that surround each party will gain an uneasy sense of each other's presence. Billions of new stars will form as the gravitational dispute is resolved and the clash of personalities rearranges the heavens into a new and unpredictable pattern.

The signals first identified on the Eiffel Tower are echoes of distant outbursts of energy, a side effect of incidents such as these. Their sources are hard to track down, because rays and particles bounce around various cosmic bodies, and sometimes speed up as they veer past before they reach the Earth. The birthplace of the highest energy particles is quite unknown. Most of the rest are born in the Milky Way, but quite where is not certain.

In a few cases, the labour pains can be seen in action. In the first scene of Shakespeare's *Hamlet*, just before the Ghost appears, a guard on the battlements of Elsinore speaks of 'yond same star that's westward from the pole / Has made his course to illumine that part of heaven / Where now it burns'. Those lines were added by the author to his original version of the play in the first few years of the seventeenth century, just after the sudden appearance of a new and bright heavenly body. Comets, 'stars with trains of fire', as Shakespeare called them, were well known to foretell great events, but this was not among them, for it stood fixed in the firmament. Shakespeare himself saw two such new objects. One was in 1572, when he was eight years old, and the other – which burned for more than a year – in 1604. Nobody without a telescope in the northern hemisphere has seen such a display since then but the fortunate inhabitants of Australia were able to view a similar spectacle in the southern sky in 1987.

Galileo wrote of the 1604 star that it was 'bigger than all the stars and all of the planets except Venus ... reddish-brown like Mars ... but with something of the golden brilliance of Saturn'. It 'sparkled, namely it seemed to die out only to flare up at once, such that it had the redness of Mars when it appeared to go out and the splendour of Jupiter when it burst forth again'.

That portentous body was in fact a supernova, a massive star that collapses and bursts into self-destruction, sometimes no more than twenty thousand light years from Earth. Such fireworks in the sky are spectacular exemplars of the constant collisions and explosions that pervade the universe. Supernovae are the source of a good part of the waves – X-rays and gamma rays included – that batter our own planet. They also accelerate other particles nearby as they sweep past. A typical example emits as much energy as the Sun will generate over its entire lifetime but is consumed within a few months. Such objects evolved from the earliest generation of stars, hundreds of times bigger than the Sun and made only of hydrogen, helium and small amounts of lithium. Those ancient structures emerged just a few hundred million years after the Bang, and a few have been glimpsed in the distant reaches of the universe.

Before its spectacular suicide, Hamlet's portent was a 'white dwarf', an object which in the last years of its life was dense and hot, no bigger than the Earth but with as much mass as the Sun. Such systems start as binary pairs, two stars that circle cautiously around each other. If they get too close, and are too unequal in density, the gravitational attraction of the more massive member begins to steal material from its companion. In terms of actual diameter, the intruder may be no more than a mosquito that buzzes around its target, but – just like a mosquito – in the end it can do enormous damage. It sucks a stream of hydrogen from its lighter companion until it has an accumulated an ocean of the stuff on its own surface. When that becomes deep enough it reaches critical mass and becomes a gigantic hydrogen bomb that flares off into space.

In other cases, one large star collapses in on itself with much the same effect, to become a neutron star no bigger than about twenty-five kilometres across, but with twice the mass of the Sun. Some among them spin at great speed and produce regular pulses of radiation. The burnt-out husks of such disasters can be detected with radio telescopes, and even if few of the explosions can be seen with the naked eye, they happen every thirty years or so even within our own modest galaxy. As the skies are scanned with ever more intensity, hundreds more emerge every year.

So much energy is generated in the death throes of a white dwarf that its final dissolution produces new elements through nuclear fusion, in which light elements are brought together under extreme conditions to generate heavier ones. They are the major source of all those higher in the chemical table than hydrogen, helium and lithium, the products of the Big Bang. The new-born elements are broadcast through the universe; in time, some will come together to form a disc around a sun and, at last, a new planet. Our astral home and our very selves are as a result, and like every other object in the universe, built of stardust.

Another substantial dose of radiation comes from a less showy source, one predicted by Laplace himself. Black holes are bodies so dense that neither light nor almost anything else can escape. If the Earth were through Heaven's command to become a black hole and retain its original mass, its diameter would drop from thirteen thousand kilometres to little more than a centimetre. Any object unfortunate enough to be dragged in would leave no evidence of its existence.

The smallest black holes known are no more than ten kilometres across. Tinier versions may exist, while the largest are bigger than our solar system, with a mass equal to that of a minor galaxy. Our own galaxy has a black hole at its heart four million times more massive than the Sun. Such objects grow as they shovel up stars or fuse with their neighbours. The Milky Way alone has as many as a hundred million black holes, with untold billions in the cosmos as a whole. Another and far more distant example, born in the first days of the cosmos, is twelve billion times more massive than our local star.

As such structures spin they drag their reluctant neighbours along. That throws a wide region into chaos and spits out cosmic energy. Great stars may be forced into tiny orbits while dust, rubble, asteroids, planets and stars dragged into the hole reach enormous temperatures and in their demise generate lots of X-rays, gamma rays, ultraviolet rays and radio waves. As it consumes a nearby star or fuses with another black hole, the hungry abyss may emit a million times more energy in the form of X-rays alone than our own Sun does across its entire spectrum. The electronic chatter that bombards the Earth has a history that would have astonished the physicists of Curie's time, and horrified their rational predecessors.

How did such disorder emerge? Until not long ago, the

universe was assumed, in eighteenth-century tradition, to be in a steady state, with new material generated to match the loss of old. That notion has now been abandoned, and the Big Bang has become part of the cultural inheritance of mankind. In some ways its name is deceptive (and indeed was coined by an opponent to mock the theory), for it was not a conventional explosion of the kind that bursts out to fill a space with fragments. There was nothing to occupy, for space itself began at that instant, as did time, matter and energy. The question as to where it took place also makes no sense, although we can work out that the universe was born just under fourteen billion years ago.

The cosmic background radiation is a low hum that pervades the universe. It was discovered in 1964, when it was found that waves came in even from empty parts of the sky (in the days before digital television, that echo of the birth of the universe made its presence felt as the black and white 'snow' on the screen of an untuned set). It was emitted about 380,000 years after the Bang, as the universe ended its first phase of expansion and the temperature had dropped enough for particles to combine to form hydrogen.

The cosmos has been cooling ever since, and now has an average temperature of just 2.75° above absolute zero (the moment when all molecular movement stops). The background radiation – unlike that generated by the explosion of stars – is even, calm and almost unruffled, albeit with occasional ripples that give it an overall variation in temperature of about one part in ten thousand.

The almost smooth background is universal, but in the

foreground, existence is lumpy on every scale, from elements to chemical compounds, from oceans to mountains, and from planets to stars, black holes and galaxies. How did it get from its bland origin to the complex mess of today? At first sight it seems to defy the universal law of entropy: that pattern breaks down into random noise. In fact, just as Poincaré predicted, and just as is true for the pendulum in Santiago del Compostela, a small amount of structure in its earliest moments, plus the input of gravity, sparked off a self-propelled and in the end chaotic process. The tiny ripples in the background are the remnants of minute fluctuations in that force that stretched and battered the ancient tissue of space and time. As it did so, it sowed the seeds of today's universe. The cooler parts of the great blanket became centres where that agent was powerful enough to promote the formation of the first astral bodies, while the warmer sections remained as the void that surrounds them. Tiny fragments attracted others, grew into boulders, into solar systems, and at last into galaxies. All are held together by the helping hand of gravity, but sooner or later, all will fall into self-destruction. Huge as the heavenly bodies may be, together they represent less than one part in twenty of the fabric of the universe. The rest is the invisible (and mysterious) dark matter and dark energy.

The cosmos continues to grow, and the further apart two galaxies might be from one another, the faster they rush apart. Stars and planets are rare exceptions to the overall emptiness. On their tiny scale, Newton's force can fight back against the urge to move outwards – but the overall picture is one of enlargement, with scattered groups of rocks that fly away faster and faster from each other. The universe has no edge in the conventional sense – all we can perceive are objects whose light has had time since the Bang to reach the Earth. There may be a vast amount of material outside that bubble, but no astronomer will ever see it.

Apart from the three lightest elements, hydrogen, helium and lithium, matter itself did not emerge until several hundred thousand years after the initial explosion, by which time the universe was a hundred million light years in diameter. The amount of noise in the system would then have been so high that today's background radiation should be even smaller than it now is. One way to overcome that problem is known as cosmic inflation, the idea that the initial expansion took place at an enormous rate in the first unimaginably small instant – one billion billion billion billionth of a second – of its existence. That was far faster than the speed of light, which seems to break the rules. It does not, for the Einstein law applies only to objects that travel through space, with no such restriction on the expansion of space itself.

What remains is the endless question: what was there before the Big Bang? That is rather like asking what is north of the North Pole, but physicists and theologians have each, in their own way, tried hard to imagine what sparked off that seminal occurrence. So far the former have come up with superstrings and branes (whatever they may be), while the explanations of the latter are even harder to penetrate. George Smoot, the Paris-based astronomer who first explored the unevenness of the cosmic background radiation, announced the discovery with the statement: 'If you are religious, it is like looking at the face of God', but when asked whether he himself was a believer refused to answer.

The great exponent of black holes, Stephen Hawking (or at least his editor), had a brush with the same issue. The last line of *A Brief History of Time* claims that when we understand why the universe exists, 'then we would know the mind of God'. Hawking tells us that he was tempted to remove this from the proofs, but that his publisher insisted that this would cost him half his sales, so he relented. In truth, even as today's disorder has supplanted the order that once seemed to rule the worlds of mice, men and galaxies, Hawking, like Laplace and Madame Curie, now sees divine intervention as a 'fairy tale'. Along with almost all his colleagues, he has no need of such a hypothesis to understand the cosmos.

CHAPTER VII

A DEGREE OF LATITUDE

Old landmarks, in any sense, avail not in a new
France.

THOMAS CARLYLE, *The French Revolution*

Cassini Père and the new Paris Observatory

In 1693, King Louis XIV was alarmed to learn that, behind his back, his realm had shrunk by a fifth. The loss was the fault not of invaders but of geographers. They had taken tentative steps towards making the first accurate map of France – and, indeed, of any country in the world. Comparison of their results with previous efforts showed that estimates of the distance from the nation's eastern border to its Atlantic coast had been hopelessly exaggerated. The port of Brest in Brittany was as a result moved east by a hundred miles from its assumed position, which to Louis meant that 'The cartographers have lost me more territory than have all my wars.'

The national contraction came from the 1667 decision by his Minister of Finance, Jean-Baptiste Colbert, to establish a Royal Observatory. It was enjoined to work on practical and applied problems as much as on lofty theories. One central task was to produce maps and charts and, to that end, its members set out to measure the size and shape of their native land, and in time of the Earth itself. So precise were their observations that just a century after the Revolution, they made it possible to determine the distance between the observatories in Paris and in Greenwich to an accuracy (as measured by today's satellites) of just a few metres. Their initial results disappointed the monarch, but the surveyors' work provided new insights into the planet's size, depths, heights, and inner secrets. In addition it laid the foundations of a system of weights and measures that has been adopted by almost every nation (even if NASA once had to spend $100 million to put right errors on a spacecraft because its physicists used metric units while its engineers stuck to imperial measures).

The French failed in their attempt to have the planet's vertical baseline, the meridian, pass from North Pole to South through the Paris Observatory (or if not there, then through some neutral point such as the Great Pyramid) in the face of Anglophones who promoted Greenwich instead, but Paris retains the status it gained three centuries ago as the world capital of measurement. The Bureau International de Poids et Mésures has its headquarters at Sèvres, in the south-west of the city. From there it issues a stream of directives on the correct quanta of length, mass, time, pressure, gravity and more.

The metric system was intended by the radicals who proposed it to depend not on some arbitrary human construct but on a fundamental property of the Earth itself. As so often, hindsight tells us that the idea was less than perfect. Even so, the attempts to establish the metre as the world's unit of length, the litre that of volume, and the kilogram as that of mass led through unexpected routes to the superbly accurate measures of distance, time and other constants used today, on scales from electron to cosmos.

The earliest known measure of all things was that of the Chinese Emperor Qin, who in 221 BC tried to control traffic jams with an edict on the lengths of carriage axles and the breadths of bridges and gateways. It failed. Two millennia later, the world's systems of length, weight and volume were still in disarray. In 1786, at a session of the Committee of Agriculture, Lavoisier discussed the units used in the district

of Péronne in the Somme, a place with about the same
dimensions as today's Greater Manchester. The region had
seventeen different units of area, most of them multiples of
perches, each *perche* of a different size, while the feet used to
measure them off contained a variable number of inches, and
the inches themselves were of a variety of lengths. Arthur
Young noted that 'In France, the infinite perplexity of the
measures exceeds all comprehension. They differ not only
in every province, but in every district, and almost every
town, and these tormenting variations are found equally in
the denominations and contents of the measures of land and
corn.' Some were based not on physical units but on human
effort. A *journal*, for example, was defined in different places
as the amount of ground that a peasant could seed, or scythe,
or plough, between sunrise and sunset.

Weight and volume faced the same chaos. Wheat had the
béthuze, boisselet, cuisse, picotin, quintal, setier and *tonneau*, while
to add to the general gaiety there was a *queue* of wine, a *mire*
of oil, a *corde* of wood and a *pense* of cheese. The peasants
complained, with good reason, that they were cheated by
merchants and landowners, who manipulated the figures
to their own advantage. As a result, one of the first of the
Cahiers de Doléances presented to the monarch in 1789 asked
for an honest system of measurement. The new administration took up the challenge.

France had seen earlier attempts at uniformity. The *pied
du roi* was one sixth of the *toise de Paris*, a unit that descends
from antiquity and whose name is a corruption of the Latin
tendere, to extend. It was based on the distance between the

fingertips of two arms held out straight from the shoulders. The official *toise* was an iron bar mortised into a wall of the fort of Châtelet in 1668, but that had been bent by builders when they banged it back into place after it came loose. Weights were based on the *pile de Charlemagne,* a series of bronze pots made in the fifteenth century. Some fitted inside each other like Russian dolls to give a mass defined to be twenty-five *livres,* while lesser weights were defined with other combinations.

In England, matters were less of a shambles, but were still far from perfect. An inch was defined as the length of three barleycorns (which is not as arbitrary as it seems, for seeds are known for constancy of size even if numbers vary from year to year). The Royal Society had suggested that a new international unit of length should be established. It was to be based on the length of a pendulum that swung with a period of just one second in the British capital (the new yard, as it was to be called, would have been 39.2 inches long, quite close to the modern metre). Their rivals in Paris rejected this idea. Xenophobia no doubt played a part, but the French had a more substantial reason to dislike the scheme. It emerged from an insight granted to the greatest of all English physicists.

Sir Isaac Newton had established that the mutual attraction of two bodies – the Sun and the Earth or the Earth and an apple – depends on their mass and on the distance between their centres of gravity. Gravity itself (Newton's 'most subtle spirit') is the glue that makes the cosmos stick together. Apples fall and the Earth spins round the Sun because they follow a simple rule. The objects (Earth and apple, or Sun and Earth) attract each other with a force that is equal to the product of their masses, divided by the square of the distance between them, with the whole lot multiplied by a 'gravitational constant', a figure that unites the value of gravity throughout the universe and makes it possible to estimate the mass of a sack of potatoes or of our own planet.

In 1672 the French astronomer Jean Richer went to Cayenne in South America as part of a project to assess the relative position of Mars and the Earth by simultaneous observations of the red planet's movements there and in Paris. To his surprise he found that his expensive pendulum clock, accurate at home, lost two and a half minutes a day near the equator. Richer was at a loss as to how to explain this, but fifteen years later Newton realised that, given that the rate at which a pendulum ticks depends on how far it finds itself from the Earth's gravitational core, his clock must have slowed because the planet bulges at its waist, increasing the distance between the two centres of gravity. The Earth was not, as had been assumed, a perfect sphere, but was flattened at the poles. He calculated from the change in rate of the pendulums' swing that the meridian line that passes through both poles was shorter by a ratio of 229 to 230 than the distance around the equator. That figure, around twenty-seven kilometres, is close to modern estimates. The idea that an oscillating weight could be used as a convenient and universal measure of length would hence not work.

Even so, the diplomat Charles-Maurice de Talleyrand (later Napoleon's foreign minister) revived the idea with a subtle modification that gave it an air of objectivity. He proposed that the gravity clock should be set to tick not in an arbitrary city such as London, but at the latitude of 45°, halfway between the North Pole and the equator (a line that by happy chance passes through Bordeaux). He hoped that this would establish an international code of measurement, but the time was not yet ripe.

Earth's deviation from geometric perfection meant that any new system had to be based on a criterion that could, unlike the pendulum, be assessed anywhere. The academicians of Paris used adventurous and ingenious methods in pursuit of that goal. On the way, they found that the shape, size and structure of their planet were more complex and ambiguous than anyone had expected. Their scheme marked the first step in metrology, the art of measurement, a field now based on standards far more universal than theirs, which depended only on the dimensions of the paltry body upon which we find our home. Today it explores the relationships between measures of length, mass and volume and those of magnetism, light, time, electrical current, sound and more; most (but not yet all) of which it can now define within a shared framework.

The committee set up to design the revolutionaries' scheme included some of the great minds of the age: the navigator and military engineer Jean-Charles de Borda, the expert in solid geometry Gaspard Monge, together with Joseph-Louis Lagrange and Pierre-Simon Laplace. They were guided by Nicolas de Condorcet, who in addition to his interest in philosophy was no mean mathematician. He persuaded his colleagues that the base of the new system, the metre as it would be called, should be one ten-millionth part of the length of the meridian from the North Pole to the equator, measured (needless to say) along a line that passed through Paris. They set out to establish just what that figure might be.

Condorcet claimed that the measure would be 'for all men and for all time', and for a couple of centuries he was almost right. The system was to be based on triangulation, a method established long before. The first country to use it in recent years had been Holland, in a scheme described by the mathematician Willebrord Snellius in his 1615 work *Eratosthenes Batavius*, 'The Dutch Eratosthenes'. His Greek predecessor had made an estimate of the size of the Earth by comparing the angle of the Sun on an Egyptian midsummer noon in the southern city of Aswan with that in the northern port of Alexandria. The tale is that in the former the Sun shone straight down a deep well, to be reflected in the water, while in the northern city it never rose high enough in the sky to allow its beams to reach the bottom (in fact Aswan itself is also not far enough south to allow sunlight to shine vertically into the shaft). The angles of the shadow cast by the noonday Sun in each place together with a simple calculation allowed Eratosthenes to work out how far apart the two wells must be. How accurate he was we do not know, for the result was reported in terms of Greek *stades*, a measure now lost.

Snellius saw that similar estimates could be used on the Earth's surface. All that was needed was to mark out a long baseline and then to check from either end of that the angles made by prominent features such as a church spire or a high peak. A triangle was drawn between the three points and one of its sides used as a new base. In time, a grid of adjacent triangles would spread far across the landscape. The distance from one end to the other could then be estimated with basic geometry. In his survey of his native land Snellius measured the distance between two towns more than a hundred kilometres apart with an error of around one part in thirty.

In 1669 the idea came to Paris. The Italian astronomer Giovanni Domenico Cassini had been invited to direct the new observatory. He, his son, his grandson and his great-grandson set in train a project that mapped Louis' kingdom with greater precision than any other.

The first step was taken the following year by the astronomer Jean Picard. An eleven-kilometre base was laid out with wooden rods on a flat plain south of the capital (where it has since been obliterated by Orly airport). Picard then used a telescope with cross-wires to spy out prominent features from each end of his line and beyond. He assessed the angles involved with a metre-wide quadrant, a quarter-circle fitted with a micrometer gauge, to give an accurate measure. He used the figures to estimate the length of one degree of latitude – one three hundred and sixtieth of the radius of the Earth as it passes through the two poles – with thirteen triangles that extended from south of Paris to a clock tower close to Amiens in the north. His estimate of 111,092 metres is just fifty metres shorter than the modern value.

Soon the mappers became more ambitious. Newton's claim of a flattened planet had become a matter of heated debate within the Royal Academy. The elder Cassini believed the opposite: that the globe was not flattened but egg-shaped and pointed at each pole. To sort out the issue, the academicians hatched an audacious plan. They would send experts to the far north and to the tropics – to Lapland and to Peru. If Newton was right, the length of a degree of latitude as estimated on the surface would be greater in the Arctic than on the equator, while if Cassini was correct the opposite would be true. The figures would later be used to help define the new metre.

The expedition to the far north was led by the mathematician Pierre-Louis Maupertuis. In 1736, his team travelled to the Gulf of Bothnia, to the River Tornea, which now forms the boundary between Norway and Russia to the north and Finland and Sweden to the south. Fortified against the Arctic winter by three hundred bottles of red wine, two hundred flasks of brandy and four barrels of beer, they used a vertical four-metre post with a graduated quarter-circle attached to estimate the altitude of the Pole Star at its zenith at the north and south ends of their baseline, which had been measured to an accuracy of one part in two hundred thousand with sticks laid out on the surface of the frozen river. To Maupertuis' delight, their estimate of a degree of latitude as measured on the surface was rather longer than its equivalent in France, as proof that the Earth is indeed depressed. Cassini continued to disagree, and challenged Maupertuis' case with attacks on his rival's morals (and by extension on his calculations) by virtue of his drunken reputation and a supposed affair with a local woman, who much discomfited the French surveyor when she appeared in his home city. Voltaire, in contrast, was delighted and described Maupertuis as the man who had flattened both the Earth and the director of the observatory.

The trip to Peru was more of a challenge, and rather less fun. It was led by Charles-Marie de la Condamine, who set out for South America in 1735 and did not get home for ten years. He too was a considerable mathematician, who had earlier managed to extract large sums from the French state when he spotted statistical faults in the national lottery that guaranteed a win. His team set out their baseline on a plain near Quito (and in an echo of the fate of Abbé Picard's equivalent its trace has been obliterated by an airport, as has, for that matter, that of the British Ordnance Survey). The work was interrupted by quarrels among the expedition members, who complained that they were kept awake by volcanoes, were plagued by vampire bats and were so short of money that they had to sell some of their equipment. In addition they suffered from the depredations of the locals ('hardly to be distinguished from beasts, half-breeds, a species of man that has only the vices of the nations of which it is the mixture, which furtively seize perches, rope, stakes etc.'), who threatened them with violence and killed the surgeon who accompanied the team. To add to his woes, de la Condamine became profoundly deaf.

Their survey spanned three hundred kilometres, with some observation points five thousand metres above sea level on the volcano Cotopaxi. For each, they had to drag a heavy brass quadrant to the site. The high-altitude task fell to Pierre Bouguer, astronomer and expert on ship design, who had become a professor of mathematics at the age of fifteen. They were the highest geographical measurements ever made up to that time, and Bouguer had severe attacks of altitude sickness.

After further rows about the theft of some of their notebooks (which the locals believed contained clues to hidden gold), the expedition members set off home by separate routes. De la Condamine himself made an intrepid journey down the Amazon. On the way, he discovered the source of quinine in the bark of a local tree and in addition was given a sample of rubber, which he sent to the Academy of Sciences (which found no use for it). The expedition found, in a mirror image of Maupertuis' result, that the length on the ground of a measure of one degree of latitude was shorter than in France. The participants engaged in bitter polemic about who deserved the most glory for the discovery, but whatever their rows, it seemed that the Earth did indeed bulge at the equator, and Newton's brilliant linkage of the beat of a pendulum with its shape was confirmed.

The work on the geography of their home country and its neighbours was extended and refined by Cassini's son, his grandson and his great-grandson, Cassini Two, Three and Four as they are known. Cassini Two persuaded the Abbé Lacaille – the astronomical abbot who encouraged the young Bailly – to spin a web of eight hundred triangles from Dunkirk to Perpignan, while Three and Four extended that work and took the first steps to linking the French survey to Britain and to other parts of Europe.

As so often, technology led the way. In the 1780s, the mathematician and naval engineer Jean-Charles de Borda had invented a 'repeating circle', a pair of small telescopes attached to two independent graduated rings, each with a mirror, which could be rotated to estimate the angle between features such as church steeples or mountain peaks. The British had developed a different device, the Grand Theodolite, which was elegant indeed but took many hours to set up. It weighed two hundred pounds, while the new French machine weighed fifteen. The lighter, cheaper and more tractable instrument allowed measurements to be made with far less effort than before, for Gallic insights into the laws of probability predicted that multiple estimates with a simple machine, as many as twenty for each observation, would be far more effective than a single attempt with a behemoth, precise as it might be.

Borda also realised that the earlier schemes had faced a variety of errors. Many came from the expansion and contraction in heat and cold of the poles used to set out the baseline. He came up with the idea of twelve-foot rods made of platinum (a metal not very responsive to changes in temperature). He placed each in a copper sleeve, with the rod attached at one end, but with the platinum extruding from the copper at the other. The free end was marked with a pair of fine scales. As the rate of expansion of each metal with every rise and fall of the thermometer was known, he could correct for the effects of temperature. The British did the job with glass rods, which were cheaper.

The plan was to repeat the earlier triangulations with more care and to measure the precise distance from Dunkirk to Barcelona on a meridian line that passed through the Paris

Observatory. Once the position of the end points had been determined and the length of a degree of latitude established at several places along the line, the figures could be used to estimate the crucial distance between the North Pole and the equator and a global standard of length could at last be created. The idea was presented to Louis XVI by a committee that included Lavoisier, together with the youngest member of the Cassini clan. It received royal assent in 1791, just one day before the monarch made his failed attempt to flee from Paris. The task was not completed until 1815.

The northern and central sections of the transect, from Dunkirk through Paris to Rodez in the Aveyron, was mapped out by a team led by Jean-Baptiste Delambre, then director of the observatory. The more difficult southern leg through the Pyrenees and the wild landscape of northern Spain was under the direction of Pierre Méchain, an astronomer who had worked on the first maps of Germany and of Italy.

The work was supposed to start in August 1792 with a fire lit on the heights of Montmartre to allow its position to be established in relation to that of the Observatory. By unhappy chance, that was the moment when incensed citizens stormed the Tuileries and set the Palais Royale alight, and it was deemed too dangerous to attract their attention with another blaze close at hand. The project was put off. That delay was the first of many. Some came from the practical problems inevitable in then-unvisited France, while the revolts and wars of those years did not help. One issue was to present the geographers with anomalies in their results that reflected not natural hazards or popular unrest but a much deeper, and at the time impenetrable, problem. Tiresome as that was, its solution was later to emerge as one of the foundations of modern geology.

Delambre and Méchain were soon forced to accept that many of the reference points used by their predecessors had vanished with the passage of time or had been destroyed by the mob. In a village near Bourges, Delambre was coolly informed that the people had 'demolished all those steeples that elevated themselves arrogantly above the humble dwellings of the sans-culottes'. Elsewhere there was hostility towards strangers armed with unfamiliar machines hoisted on to mountain-tops and church towers, perhaps, the locals felt, to extract new taxes; as Delambre later wrote of one such encounter: 'Impatience began to spread and there were murmurs from the crowd. A few voices proposed one of those expeditious means, so often used in those days, which cut through all difficulties and put an end to all doubts.' Through good luck, his life was spared. Fog, rain and snow, and the need to ascend lofty and unclimbed peaks added to their woes, as did inaccuracies caused by expansion and contraction of their instruments as the temperature changed, and others that came from atmospheric refraction as they sighted distant points.

The southern leg was even more difficult, for the wild countryside of the Cevennes and the Pyrenees was full of dissidents and bandits. The Catalans were, then as now, hostile to outsiders and the unfortunate Méchain was for a time confined to the city of Barcelona and banned from one of his main trigonometric points, the nearby mountain Montjuic.

To make matters worse, he broke several ribs and fractured his skull when a pump blew up.

As the work went on, Méchain began to notice to his horror that there had been a series of tiny errors which had mounted up as the triangles moved onwards. In a desperate attempt to make the sums fit together he began to correct his figures, but none of his calculations made sense. Soon he became consumed with guilt, and even threatened suicide: 'After all that has happened I can no longer show myself anywhere and my sole wish is to be annihilated.' As the mistakes became more obvious his mood darkened further and he wrote that 'Hell and all the plagues it spews upon the Earth – storms, wars, pestilence and dark intrigues – have all been unleashed against me. What Demon still awaits me?' He died of malaria soon afterwards. When Delambre went through his colleague's papers he was alarmed to find alterations and emendations that suggested sloppy work, but he too attempted to cover them up.

The project was unfinished and the results known to insiders to be less than perfect, but the figures were presented at an international conference in 1799 (the British were not invited). A standard metre, one ten millionth of the estimated distance from North Pole to equator and made of pure platinum, was presented to the world by a Dutch delegate. The bar was in fact similar in length to the ancient *toise*, but the proponents of the metric system did not make a point of this. The units of volume and mass were also made to depend on the mythic object, for a kilogram was defined as the weight of a cubic decimetre (a litre) of water at the melting point of ice, when the liquid was at its most dense. The standards survive, but some of their names do not. A centimetre was at first called called a *doigt* (or finger) while to keep the original name for the litre, the *pinte*, would have given beer-drinking British holidaymakers pause for thought.

After Méchain's death, the Paris meridian was, as planned, extended southwards through Spain and the Balearic Islands. In 1790, the great triangulation was linked to the British Isles with the help of Bengal lights ignited on either side of the Channel, and from Dover onwards to the Greenwich observatory (an experience that persuaded the British government to set up its own Ordnance Survey).

Much of that extended triangulation was carried out under the direction of François Arago, Secretary of the Paris Observatory. He faced difficulties even greater than those experienced by Méchain. In 1808, while he was in Majorca, the Peninsular War broke out, and to ensure his own safety, he was obliged to give himself up for imprisonment. He managed to escape and make his way to Algeria, whence he set off to Marseilles, but just outside the port his vessel was seized by corsairs and he was imprisoned again until he was freed by the French. Unperturbed by these adventures, Arago completed his geographical work, was elected to the Academy of Sciences, became director of the Paris Observatory, in which he made his home, studied the polarisation of light, became involved in magnetism and discovered what are now known as eddy currents, and made the first suggestion that there might be an unknown planet, later identified as Uranus, in the solar system.

Noble as its aims no doubt were – and the Paris metre survived as a global standard for two centuries – the system envisaged by Condorcet was, in the end, almost as arbitrary as had been the *toise*. The notion that some fraction of the Earth's meridian, or of its equator, or of the longest river or tallest mountain in France, or of any other geographical feature might be used in this way is no more objective than a measure based on the distance between an ancient monarch's outstretched hands. The aim had been to define a unit that could be laid out anywhere, and to achieve this, copies of the Paris metre and its kilogram equivalent were sent across the world, but the realisation soon dawned that the purity of Condorcet's notion had fallen by the wayside. With one crucial exception, the units that emerged from the French geographers' efforts have now been supplanted by others that depend on a universal physical constant rather than on the dimensions of a medium-sized planet in a suburban part of the cosmos.

Some of Méchain's doubts about his results were, as so often in research, a hint of a major discovery just around the corner. His triangulation, like its predecessors, was based on the simple but false premise that the physical structure of the Earth is uniform. It is not. The problem comes – as did the mystery of the clock that ran slow in the tropics – from the all-pervasive power of gravity. Méchain had become entangled in an interaction between the measurements of length and those of mass that much confused his calculations.

The problem was studied by Pierre Bouguer, the bold mountaineer of the Peru expedition. He is best known for an eponymous Law, which refers to the extent to which light is attenuated as it passes through air. Bouguer also has the more dubious distinction of lending his name to an Anomaly. It emerged from the difficulties that he too faced in his triangulations across the Andes.

When a Borda circle or its modern equivalent is set, the device must be perfectly level to ensure that the angles measured between distant points are accurate. In Bouguer's day the job was done with a pendulum, which, when it came to rest, set the plane in which the apparatus was placed. As his work went on, and as he moved on from the seashore to the coastal flats, through narrow valleys and at last to the high peaks, he noticed that the triangles became harder and harder to fit together. After much thought, Bouguer suggested that such difficulties – like those experienced by his fellow citizen in Cayenne a century earlier – arose because local gravitational effects had an influence and must be corrected for. By measuring the period of a pendulum in different places, in a small-scale repeat of Richer's observation, he saw that the simple assumption that the Earth was homogeneous was wrong.

He used a pendulum to measure the force of gravity first at the summit of one of the local peaks, and then down on the plain. Gravity had, he found, less power when measured on the mountaintop than on the coast, for as Newton had realised, his high-altitude device was further from the centre of the Earth. He then estimated the sideways gravitational effects of the mountains themselves when viewed from the plain. Comparison of the two figures convinced

Bouguer that – in contrast to previous claims that our planet was hollow – it had a central core: 'it is necessary to admit that the Earth is much more compact below than above, and in the interior than at the surface ... Those physicists who imagined a great void in the middle of the Earth, and who would have us walk on a kind of very thin crust, can think so no longer.' We now know, of course, that our planet has iron at its heart, although it was not discovered until long after Bouguer's death. He estimated that the Earth's average density throughout its mass was about four times that of the Andes, a figure not far from that accepted today.

To complicate matters further, massive rocks such as granite or basalt have more of a gravitational effect than do lighter sediments like chalk and limestone. A decent-sized granite peak nearby can as a result produce real inaccuracies when distances are calculated by triangulation.

Bouguer's famous anomaly has now been mapped across the globe. Great centres of attraction are found in mountain ranges such as the Himalayas and the Andes. The oceans pull less on a pendulum than does the land so that a triangulation carried out on the coastline can be confused by the attractions of the landscape nearby, low as it might be. Even at sea, gravity has an influence. The ocean surface is sixty metres higher in some places than in others because dense rock below attracts billions of gallons of seawater. As a result, a ship on a voyage from Marseilles to Sydney climbs and falls by a height equivalent to that of the Arc de Triomphe on the way. Satellite measures of gravitational anomalies have now revealed hundreds of new mountains in the deeps.

In France, the power of gravitational attraction is quite low and rather uniform along the route taken by Delambre and Méchain from Dunkirk to Paris and a little further, but as the meridian line enters the mountains of the Massif Central it begins to show peaks and troughs over quite short distances. The Pyrenees and Catalonia have the same problem on a larger scale and this no doubt helps to explain some of the difficulties experienced by the unfortunate Méchain. The metric system, it seems, was built on shaky foundations from the start.

That global edifice has now been reconstructed from the ground up. Under the direction of the Bureau International des Poids et Mésures, the metre and its brethren have moved away from the grand scenery of the Arctic, the Andes and France to enter the tiny world of quantum physics. The Bureau's International System of Units has seven basic categories: the metre, the kilogram and the second, plus the ampere (electrical current), the kelvin (temperature, taken from absolute zero), the mole (a unit of chemical mass) and the candela (a measure of light intensity). Almost all now fit into a rigid and logical framework that applies throughout the universe.

Time is now based not on a pendulum, but on the emission of regular pulses of light by certain atoms exposed to microwaves. For many years, the approved timekeeper was caesium, which drove a clock with a precision of one second in 138 million years. That crude device has been supplanted by an 'optical lattice clock', in which strontium atoms vibrate at a particular rate when exposed to intense pulses of light, and which will be accurate to within less than a second in five billion years (if, that is, the Bureau and even the planet is still in existence then).

Length, too, has left the Revolution far behind, for the metre is now defined with reference to time, as the distance travelled by light in a vacuum in 1/299,792,458th of a second. Such advances mean that electrical current, chemical concentration, light intensity and temperature can all be stated in terms tied to the fundamental constants of physics.

The great exception to the new rationalism is the measure of mass, which interacts with gravity, the force that disturbed the audacious geographers of two centuries ago. The global standard kilogram had been defined by the Academy of Sciences as the mass of a litre of water, measured at the temperature of maximum density. To represent that, in 1799 a metal object – the *Kilogramme des Archives* – was made, and copies sent across the globe. The object and its successor, together with their many offshoots, have become central to the world's commerce and to its science. The standard is still in use, but is not related in any logical way to modern measures of length, pressure, current, brightness and the rest, for it takes no account of the local differences in gravity found by Bouguer. The problem remains unresolved but, in the Paris suburbs, the discussions go on.

Battered but unbowed, the 1799 object is still the global arbiter of weighty matters. The original was replaced in 1875 by an improved version made in London. The International Prototype Kilogram, as the new master was christened, is made of an alloy of nine tenths platinum and one tenth iridium (a metal unknown in the 1790s and in the same chemical group as platinum, but far harder). The material was milled into a cylinder the size of a golf ball, with edges rounded off to reduce wear. It has six sisters. They find a home in a basement in Sèvres, where each is stored under two glass covers behind three locked doors, each with a key controlled by a different member of staff.

A hundred or so duplicates have been sent across the world. Once every few decades, they are checked. To the alarm of physicists, the members of the clan have begun to disagree. One of the American copies, which in 1899 was delivered at seventy-five thousand-millionths of a gram less than the International Prototype, had a century later lost a further forty-one of those minuscule units. In .part that was because as a national standard it was sometimes handled, but even the descendants kept in virginal isolation have moved away from each other. Most have gained about five parts in a hundred million over that period. Such mishaps have no doubt afflicted the master as well, but that is always beyond reproach, as its destiny is to define the kilogram, whatever chemistry, physics and time might do. It may have put on as much as fifty micrograms, the mass of a small grain of sand, since it was made.

The increase arises because the metal, unreactive as it may be, can fall into relationships with outsiders such as carbon, oxygen, or even mercury from the thousands of thermometers and other instruments broken in the world's laboratories over the years. A blast of ultraviolet in an ozone atmosphere gets rid of most of the oxides, while solvents can help to clean up the mercury. In future, a piece of gold foil – more reactive than platinum – placed next to the reference object may reduce the pangs of old age, as it scoops up pollutants that would otherwise have combined with the standard itself.

Such errors might seem tiny to an outsider, but in comparison to the precision achieved in the measures of time, or distance, or electrical resistance, to physicists they are grotesque. The kilogram's inaccuracies still infect much of the international system of measurement and the cure has yet to be found.

The newton is a measure of the force needed to accelerate a mass of one kilogram at one metre per second, per second. That figure is used as part of the definition of the pascal, the measure of pressure, and the joule, that of energy (a force of one newton that acts over one metre). The watt, the measure of power, represents one joule per second, and other electrical units such as the ampere do not escape unscathed. Even the candela, the measure of light intensity, is linked in to the system. The epidemic of error that spreads from the kilogram has travelled a long way from the dubious chunk of metal locked away in the French capital.

All this makes physicists, always a fussy lot, rather uneasy. A scheme is now afoot to rationalise the kilogram and to transform its platinum representation into an antique. If it succeeds, it will at last unite the world of measurement into a logical whole.

The hope is to find a new definition of mass that relates it to a measure known as the Planck constant. That figure was formulated at the birth of quantum mechanics, the study of the world on a tiny scale. In the dawn of the twentieth century it emerged that the radiation energy emitted from an object as it was warmed up did not increase in a regular fashion as the temperature rose, but jumped from one level to another. Radiation, light included, hence must come in packages. That observation was the death knell for what until then had seemed the universal logic of Newtonian physics.

The famous constant is the minimum dose needed to make one of those packages. From the human point of view the figure is extremely small. Even so, at tiny scales, quantum effects rule the world. Its value is known with some precision and the hope is that the Planck constant will one day become the glue that holds the world's measurements together.

An instrument known as a watt balance has the potential to link this tiny value both to the study of the cosmos and to the purchase of fruit and vegetables. A measured electrical current of a precise voltage is passed through a coil and the kilogram is then defined as the metallic mass that can just be supported by the appropriate electrical current. That would express weight in the terms used to measure the passage of electricity, which is itself based on a quantum measure. At last the ponderous anomaly which weighs down the whole system could be melted down, and the unit of mass would join the happy household of metrology.

Unfortunately, such instruments are complicated and expensive, with a troublesome lack of consistency in results from one machine to the next, and even between different experiments on the same one. The authorities in Paris have decided that the time is not yet ripe to abandon their metallic icon, but its days are numbered.

A second and more fundamental weakness in the measurement of mass goes straight back to the gravitational irregularity first identified by Newton. The kilogram is often referred to as a measure of weight, but the lump of metal is in truth a measure of mass, the property of an object that describes its mutual attraction to other bodies. Should the magical golf ball in Sèvres be transported to the Moon, it would weigh less than it did on Earth, while a trip to the enormous planet Uranus would cause it to weigh much more. Wherever it went, its mass would not change. Weight is related to mass, but depends also on the strength of the local gravitational field (which means that one guaranteed way for the obese to lose weight is to move to the tropics or to climb the Andes, where their waistlines are further from the centre of the Earth).

For Newton's laws to be applicable across the universe, a constant known as Big G, the gravitational constant, has to enter the equation. That force holds the solar system together, but on a laboratory scale is minute; the attraction of two copper balls of one kilogram that just touch each other is just one hundred-millionth of the mass of either.

Its value was first estimated in 1798 by Henry Cavendish. Cavendish took two small objects connected by a rod to make a dumb-bell and hung it from a thin thread. Two large lumps of lead were then placed on either side, so that their gravitational attraction made the dumb-bell twist. Since the resistance to twisting by the thread, the distance between the bodies and the weight of each one could all be measured, the extent to which the object rotated could be used to work out the crucial figure and, in effect, to weigh the Earth.

Simple enough, and one might assume, given its importance to physics, that its value must by now be fixed to at least the twentieth decimal place. In fact, G is by far the least well measured of all physical units. Around a dozen separate attempts to calculate it over the past decade have produced results that diverge by about one part in two thousand, which is a scandalous level of imprecision. If the distance around our planet through the poles were known no better than is its weight (which depends on the gravitational constant) we would be able to measure it to an accuracy of no more than about a kilometre – compared to the real precision of the sum, which is correct to a few centimetres.

The problem is that – strange as it might seem to anyone who has tried to lift a sack of cement – the gravitational constant is among the weakest of all forces. As a result, attempts to measure it are plagued by external agents such as tidal movements hundreds of miles away and local changes in temperature and atmospheric pressure.

Many modern experiments that attempt to measure G are related to that of Cavendish. In Colorado a reflective ball off which a laser beam can be bounced was dropped thousands of times through a hole in a half-ton tungsten tube. When the great mass was below the falling ball, the object fell faster because of the gravitational attraction of the metallic lump, but when the heavy object was above the shiny sphere its influence worked in the opposite direction and the rate of descent decreased. The difference could then be used to measure the crucial figure. A more recent experiment on a smaller scale uses a cloud of atoms of the element rubidium pushed away from such a massive cylinder by a laser and, when the laser is switched off, falls back towards it at a measurable rate. For some reason, this gives a rather lower estimate of G. At the other end of the size range, schemes are afoot to fire off two satellites, in orbit on either side of the Earth, to see how much they attract each other; if one is over an area of high attraction, its distance from the other will decrease, and vice versa.

The disagreements remain. A 2014 Royal Society conference in London entitled 'The Newtonian constant of gravitation, a constant too difficult to measure?' decided that the answer is still 'yes'. The force of gravity, it seems, causes almost as many problems to modern physicists as it did to their predecessors.

Even so, when it comes to other measures, technology has triumphed. Today's instruments are so accurate that they can even measure changes in the shape of the Earth's surface as a dam fills up. Geodesy, as their subject is called, has revealed our planet to be a fragile and uncertain place whose size, shape and spin changes from year to year and from day to day. Its lumpy and irregular structure wobbles on its axis. Days vary in length as the liquid core grinds round and as tides, storms and ocean currents interfere with its rotation. In the face of all this, the making of maps has marched on.

Although tourists still delight in standing astride the marked meridian at Greenwich, GPS shows that true zero as defined by satellites lies about a hundred metres to the east of that line. That shift comes from improvements of satellite technology and from recent attempts to rationalise the world's measures of distance. They are based on our planet's centre of mass, which has been located with an accuracy of less than two centimetres, and is the point around which every satellite circles, whatever the details of mountains or ocean trenches on the surface. From that central point there has been generated a smooth sphere flattened at the poles to the same extent as the planet itself and the surveys of the world's nations have now been placed on that shared and precise reference framework. It costs £9.50 to gain entry to the Observatory's courtyard, where the graven image of the historic Greenwich Meridian is located, but a brief stroll to the true meridian – still unmarked – enables visitors to bestride the Eastern and Western hemispheres for free.

Today's measurements also reveal a movement of the two observatories of about two and a half centimetres to the north and east each year through continental drift. Across the globe, whole nations are on the move. In time the Mediterranean will close, to be replaced by mountains, while Australia is on its way towards Asia by as much as a metre a decade.

In some places, the land rises and falls at an even greater rate. Everest, the highest mountain in the world, is growing by a third of a metre every century as the plates grind against each other. Finland has been even more buoyant. Since the end of the last ice age, ten thousand years or so ago, it has emerged from ice three kilometres thick. Relieved of its burden, its rocks now leap upwards by as much as a centimetre a year, which gives a rise of two metres or so even in the brief period since the French explorers quaffed their wine and ogled the local women. As a result, some Finnish places now distant from the sea have names such as 'Sandy Cape', while what are now peninsulas are still referred to as islands. The release of pressure in the far north and south as the ice retreats in the warming world also means that the Earth is less depressed than it was at the time of Newton.

And what of the geography of France itself? Colbert took the first step in making his nation a world leader in cartography, and it retains that status. The Cassini map was published in 181 sheets at a scale of 1:86,400, its scale a relic of the *toise*. It took forty years to complete, with the final version not available until 1815. A complete set cost the equivalent of a teacher's annual salary. Over the next century, it was supplemented by more detailed surveys which set out the boundaries of France's four thousand or so cantons (local units set up soon after the Revolutionary government came to power). Later still the mappers formalised the *plan cadastre,* the tangled pattern of land ownership, often of tiny parcels of ground subdivided again and again to accord with local laws of inheritance, which now records more than a hundred million separate plots.

The Cassini plan is a work of art as much as of technology, with its mountains shown as hairy caterpillars spread across the landscape rather than the familiar contour lines of today, which were invented by an English geographer as he measured the gravitational attraction of a Scottish mountain.

Today's elegant maps of the *Institut Geographique Nationale* are themselves artworks in their own way (and at seven hundred euros for a set that covers the whole country at a scale of 1:100,000 are well within most budgets).

The efforts of the Cassinis have now been reborn for the digital age. The French *Geoportail* online system of cartographic display is far better than that available on this side of the Channel. It is consulted by two million people each day. Type in the name of a place and at once a detailed map, accompanied by large-scale aerial photographs, appears. Click a few more times, and images of geology, land use, street maps, waterways, cultural information, property boundaries, power lines, sites of potential riots in cities and yet more appear. A deeper excavation reveals an electronic version of the Cassini map itself. All these pages can be overlaid on each other, and a mix of the modern plan with the nineteenth-century chart in most places shows a close fit.

The French are, as they have every right to be, proud of their role as pioneers of cartography, and in the millennium year they celebrated the joys of the Paris meridian – geographical relic though it is – with a line of brass discs inserted into the pavements of Paris, each engraved with the name of Arago, the agent of the grand triangulation. Most have now disappeared, for they also appear in the novel *The Da Vinci Code* as markers of the supposed Rose Line followed by its hero in his search for a descendant of Christ (who, in a predictable denouement turns out to be French). They have been stolen by believers, evidence of the continued power of the irrational even in a world of measurement that has – almost – been made rational by the advances of technology.

On *Quatorze Juillet* 2000, the Paris meridian was given a further post-mortem boost with plans for a gigantic picnic along its length. Hundreds of tables were laid out from Prats de Mollo in the Pyrenees through Paris to Dunkirk. The party was, alas, washed out. An ambitious scheme to plant a line of ten thousand trees, the *Meridienne Verte* – oaks in the north, pines in the centre, and olives in the south – was never completed, and no more than a few fragments can now be seen.

The British celebrations were even feebler, for in the millennium year just a single tree was planted on the Greenwich line, and that died. Even so, on a clear night the mythic trace that separates east from west can still be seen by London's anxious watchers, for a green laser now shines northwards from the Observatory to enliven the skies above the East End. Its spectral presence reminds that arrondissement's inhabitants that geography still defines its framework in relation to London SE10, even if that postcode's astronomical instruments slipped away long ago.

In Paris, in contrast, the original observatory is still hard at work as a scientific institution. Not far away, the ruler of the world's weights awaits its inevitable demise as it sits silent and enigmatic under its glass dome behind locked doors, becoming more and more imperfect as the years pass by. Its masters hope that soon it will be able to follow its cousin, the platinum metre, also locked away in the Bureau des Poids et Mésures, into a long retirement.

CHAPTER VIII

PRESIDENT JEFFERSON'S MOOSE

Do not ... all embodiments of Force that work in
this miraculous Complex of Forces, named Universe,
go on growing ... reach their height, reach their
visible decline; finally sink under, vanishing, and
what we call die?

THOMAS CARLYLE, *The French Revolution*

DEA / G. Dagli Orti / Getty Images

Georges Cuvier with a fossil fish

On 24 November 1859 the first sentence of the work that united biology into a single science appeared in print: 'When on board H.M.S. *Beagle*, as naturalist, I was much struck with certain facts in the distribution of the inhabitants of South America ...' Such are the opening words of *The Origin of Species*. On the same day, and from the same publisher, came another memorable line: 'Heaven helps those who help themselves ...', the opening of Samuel Smiles' treatise on self-improvement, *Self Help*, which assured its readers that a positive attitude will be a guarantee of success. In the same week, another celebrated volume found a place on the shelves: 'It was the best of times, the worst of times, it was the age of wisdom, it was the age of foolishness ...', the initial phrases of Charles Dickens' *A Tale of Two Cities*.

All three publications were best-sellers, each was a work of exhortation, and each one has a resonance in the history of both biology and of affairs of state. Dickens warned that without constant vigilance all societies will, like that of the *Ancien Régime*, collapse under the weight of their internal contradictions. Smiles took the opposite line: that life is bound to get better for those who bother to make the effort. The author of *The Origin of Species* came up with a simpler and more testable idea. It did not call on intrinsic improvement or decay but argued instead that slow change as a result of pressure from outside allows plants, animals and humankind to adapt to circumstances. Charles Darwin was not an optimist, a pessimist, or a philosopher but – like every good scientist – a realist.

His French predecessors' ideas about the natural world were closer to the beliefs of Smiles and Dickens than to those of the great English naturalist. They searched for fundamental laws of intrinsic improvement or decay on scales that stretched from atoms to solar systems and took in plants, animals and human affairs on the way. There was a tide in the affairs of men as much as those of beasts. As Jean-Sylvain Bailly, astronomer, mayor of Paris, and victim of the guillotine, put it (rather prematurely from his point of view): 'Politics is a science, and I think I have mastered it.'

Whether its waters were on the ebb or on the flow depended on ideology more than evidence. Bailly, like many of his fellows, felt that life was programmed to improve, and that the future was of its nature bright. That conviction had been behind his nation's Declaration of the Rights of Man, which asserts that *'Les hommes naissent et demeurent libres et égaux en droits'*, and is a statement of their *'droits naturels, inaliénables et sacrés'*. In a feeble incarnation of the same philosophy, Britain's New Labour party won the 1997 general election to the strains of a dirge entitled 'Things Can Only Get Better'.

The utopians of the eighteenth century planned to move the world towards the more equal, open and secular system destined by fate to replace the corruption and sloth of the Old Regime. A *'langue universelle'* – the scientific method – would lead to the sunlit uplands, where man's way of life would reflect the perfection of the universe. Other *philosophes* were just as convinced of the opposite. They felt that decay and disaster were intrinsic to both the human condition and the animal world. Degeneration was inevitable unless men of good will struggled against it, with success not guaranteed.

Their British equivalents were, in general, less buoyant

about the relevance of their ideas to society and tended to leave politics to the politicians (which may explain the relative shortage of revolutions on this side of *La Manche*). Darwin in particular disliked the many attempts to draw partisan conclusions from his work. Even so, his theories were appealed to throughout his life by thinkers of a variety of flavours. In a pained note to a friend he once complained that 'I have received, in a Manchester newspaper, rather a good squib, showing that I have proved "might is right", that Napoleon is right, and every cheating tradesman is right.'

In particular Charles Darwin detested the notion that some internal force, whatever its direction, led animals and plants (and by extension human affairs) to change. That idea was quite contrary to his own pragmatic views. His great contribution was to come up with a scheme that could be tested not against beliefs, but against observations.

The English biologist's books and letters are filled with complaints about the difficulties, obscurities and hesitations he faced as he tried to make sense of the mechanisms of nature; as he wrote to his colleague Thomas Henry Huxley, 'I always give all the facts which I can collect, hostile to my notions.' Such scruples have no place in the works of his Gallic equivalents.

Even so, *The Origin of Species* makes reference to no fewer than twenty-seven Frenchmen – more than those of any other nationality except the British themselves. Most among them are more or less lost from history, but four of the grand figures of the revolutionary period – Georges Buffon, Geoffroy Saint-Hilaire, Georges Cuvier and Jean-Baptiste de Lamarck – are still household names, at least to students of evolution. Darwin describes Buffon, in the historical sketch appended to later editions of his book, as 'the first author who in modern times has treated [evolution] in a scientific spirit'. He also writes with approval of Geoffroy, who had noted that what he had called the 'unity of type' of the anatomy of birds, mammals and fish might hint at shared relatedness, and of 'the illustrious Cuvier' for his pioneering role in palaeontology. Charles Darwin's views of Lamarck were – as we shall see – somewhat more equivocal.

All those naturalists and many more were associated with the Jardin du Roi, the king's botanical garden, established by Louis XIII in the seventeenth century and reinvented as the Jardin des Plantes by the new regime. It was at once graced with a new and well-funded Muséum d'Histoire Naturelle. Soon, the place began to burst at the seams as the nation's armies pillaged the collections of Belgium and the Rhineland after the royalist invaders of France had been beaten back. They sent two and a half thousand crates of specimens back home. From Holland they liberated stuffed hippos and orang-utans, while from Liège came an unusual breed of chickens that laid large eggs. The menagerie of the House of Orange was displaced to Paris. When its two elephants Hans and Parki were released into the Jardin des Plantes, each gave, the records tell us, a resounding trumpet in honour of liberty.

The museum and its garden are still there, bounded by the Rue Buffon, the Rue Cuvier and the Rue Geoffroy Saint-Hilaire (a statue of the fourth member of the famous quatrain does decorate the site, but the Rue Lamarck is in a distant suburb). Its researchers had a breadth of knowledge of plants and animals almost unknown among their modern descendants. Their work has stood the test of time. Even so, the mechanisms of change conjured up by those grand figures, distinct as they might appear, each had a strangely mystical air. Most are now hard to identify as science at all and have been forgotten except as convenient tools with which to mock the French. Fortunately, facts remain even as theories are discarded, and the facts uncovered in their gardens and galleries form part of the narrative of modern biology.

The idea of inbuilt decline is ancient indeed and can be traced to the Christian doctrine of the Fall of Man and its many predecessors. Its entry into biology was due to Buffon, whose *Histoire Naturelle* appeared over the four decades from 1749 and was for a time the best-selling book in Europe. Geoffroy Saint-Hilaire was a pioneer in the study of embryos and of comparative anatomy, and late in his career came up with the Darwinian notion of shared descent, that 'there is, philosophically speaking, only a single animal'. The idea of disaster and extinction was that of Cuvier, the father of modern palaeontology. Lamarck in contrast was an enthusiast for the inevitability of improvement and a proponent of the inheritance of acquired characters – the theory that offspring are influenced by the experiences of their parents. He is the best remembered among those illuminati, and deserves a chapter of his own.

The Comte de Buffon first trained as a lawyer. He then became involved in the mathematics of probability (Buffon's needle estimates the value of the geometrical constant *pi* by measuring how often and by how much a needle dropped on to a series of parallel lines overlaps each of them). From there he moved on to the experiments on electricity that so amused Louis XV, to tests of the strength of naval timber and at last to the study of the animal world. He became the grandest (and most corpulent) naturalist of the eighteenth century, and in 1739 was appointed head of the Jardin du Roi. He held the post for the rest of his long career, and under his direction the garden became in effect the world's first biological research centre.

Buffon speculated that life was no more than a series of chemical reactions in which molecules had come together in different combinations to produce at one blow animals as complex as fish and elephants (or, in a later softening of his view, at least to generate microscopic creatures). The process, he felt, still went on; and given that the rules of chemistry were universal, amoebae and even elephants should abound on other planets: 'One may believe that all these vast bodies are like the terrestrial globe, covered with plants, and even peopled with sentient beings, somewhat similar to the animals on earth.'

He also set out to catalogue the animal world, but dismissed the work of his contemporary, the Swede Carl Linnaeus, who had organised it in terms of physical affinity. Indeed, he disliked the whole notion that life could be classified on some objective basis: 'It is to impose on the reality of the Creator's work the abstractions of our mind.' There were, he felt, no distinct categories, and all that could be identified without ambiguity were individuals of one kind or another. He hence grouped his enormous directory in much the same way as chemists of his day sorted out their compounds: in terms of familiarity and of practical value. 'Those which are the most necessary and useful will take the first rank ... Then those which ... inhabit the same locales and the same climates, like the deer and the rabbit.' The horse, the dog and the cow were in the lead, followed by creatures found in France, with the inhabitants of the rest of the world as also-rans (Linnaeus retaliated by christening a foul-smelling plant *Buffonia*). Two centuries later, the Zoothèque, a partial reinvention of the Muséum d'Histoire Naturelle, which once set out its collections in stark obedience to the Swede's laws of taxonomy, has been arranged as a series of spectacles. One gallery, in homage to its ancestor, is of animals useful to man. It contains a goose and a camel, snuggled up not far from a bee.

Buffon, like his colleagues, was happy to draw conclusions about matters of state from his discoveries. He was convinced that the tendency towards decay found in many chemicals was built in to both life and society and would, if not resisted, prevail. Existence had an inbuilt direction: downhill. In time he incorporated the idea into his classification scheme, and made a table of similarities based on shared degeneration from a common stock. Even man faced that risk. A contemporary anatomist made plaster moulds of the handsomest young men he could find in the Paris morgue and tried to recreate Greek sculptures by putting together the most favoured limbs and torsos. He failed to match the beauty of the Hellenic relics, as proof of human decline since its golden age.

Some unexpected figures took such notions in all seriousness. In June 1786, the prime mover of the United States Constitution sent an urgent letter to the author of the Declaration of Independence. For both James Madison, who penned the missive, and its addressee Thomas Jefferson, those were difficult times, for their new nation was in the midst of a financial crisis and was embroiled in bitter arguments about a planned Constitutional Convention. The two men often corresponded about such matters, but this document had to do with weasels. After some initial notes about the animal's smell as 'rankish musk, but not so strong as to be offensive', Madison's pages contain a table of measurements, of 'the width of the ears', of 'the distance between the anus and the vulva', of 'heart round and long' and more.

The figures related to an issue that much concerned each of them, Buffon's claim that the inhabitants of the New World, from weasels to people, had fallen into degeneration. They could never, as a result, compete with the more vigorous natives of the Old, and by implication, the United States was bound to fail.

To Buffon, the problem of decay was at its worst in the Americas because in that part of the world, unlike in France, there had been no attempt by the most perfect creature of all, *Homo sapiens*, subspecies *gallicus*, to arrest the process. The American equivalent of the African elephant was no more than the unimpressive tapir, of the lion just the smaller lynx. The cold and wet climate of the new continent, its marshes unimproved by human effort, was to blame. The damp enfeebled all creatures unfortunate enough to live there, even as it allowed the decadent to flourish (the thirty-five-pound frogs found in Louisiana were quoted as evidence). The director of the Jardin du Roi was also dismissive of Native Americans, for they were lazy, ignorant and dim, with withered genitals and little interest in sex ('no hair, no beard, no ardour for the female ... no vivacity, no activity of mind'). The same fate awaited anyone foolish enough to emigrate to the New World.

The idea had powerful supporters, on Buffon's side of the ocean at least. They included, among others, Hegel, who wrote that 'America has always been and still shows itself physically and spiritually impotent', and that it 'resounded with the almost inarticulate tones of degenerate men'. Such notions became embedded in European culture. In his best-seller Buffon asserted that even the birds of America were dull in colour and could do no more than croak. Across the Channel, the poets listened. Oliver Goldsmith's 1769 poem *The Deserted Village* tells of the fate of its displaced inhabitants, forced by poverty to emigrate westwards across the Atlantic, to a place where they see little but silent bats, dark scorpions, vengeful snakes, savage men and 'those matted woods where birds forget to sing', while Keats bemoans the absence of his brother in the same continent with claims that 'There bad flowers have no scent, birds no sweet song, and great unerring Nature once seems wrong.'

President Jefferson, a naturalist as much as a statesman, was incensed by such claims. He saw them as a slur upon his own idealistic republic, and was insulted by what he saw as their attack on God himself, on the 'fabricator of all things ... their preserver and their regulator'. Any suggestion of degeneracy in His creation spurned the hand of the deity.

Jefferson dismissed the idea. His sole publication in book form, the 1787 *Notes on the State of Virginia*, devotes many pages to a comparison of the dimensions of creatures on each side of the Atlantic. He had already established, thanks to the work of James Madison, that his local weasels were larger than those of

France. Weasels, he admitted, might not be the best guides to excellence, and when he was in Paris in an attempt to drum up support for his new nation, he came up with a remarkable plan: to present Buffon with a stuffed moose. This, he felt, would prove that the Americas could outdo any member of the Old World, at least where horned quadrupeds were concerned. He went to much trouble and expense to obtain a suitable specimen, which after many misadventures and a certain amount of rearrangement of body parts to produce a particularly magnificent example, arrived in France and was bestowed upon the great man. The Comte de Buffon is said to have agreed in his acceptance speech to put right the claim of transatlantic degeneracy in his next volume, but within a few months, in April 1788, he was dead. The promised correction never appeared.

Buffon's ideas had lasting influence. Charles Darwin, on his voyage around the world on HMS *Beagle* in the 1830s, was himself imbued with the notion of American decline. In his explorations around Cape Horn he noted that 'the zoology of Patagonia is as limited as its flora', which is more or less what the theory of transatlantic degeneration predicted. Darwin had also found fossils of gigantic creatures such as the giant sloth, and in his diary he wrote of the region that '*Formerly* it must have swarmed with great monsters: now we find mere pigmies, compared with the antecedent, allied races ... If Buffon had known of the giant sloth and the armadillo-like animals, and of the lost Pachydermata, he might have said with a greater semblance of truth that the creative force in America had lost its power, rather than it had never possessed great vigour.'

On his return to London, however, the young Darwin

began to develop his own and quite different theory about the origin of plants and animals (sloths, armadillos and elephants included). He had noted that the inhabitants of the Galapagos were similar but not identical to those of the South American mainland, while the creatures of the Cape Verde islands in the Atlantic (a group of oceanic volcanoes with a geological history much like that of the Galapagos) instead resembled the plants and animals of nearby Africa. He began to speculate that descent with modification from a common ancestor – change in response to the world outside rather than to some internal urge – was responsible.

In time he came up with a simple mechanism that could drive the process. Its engine was natural selection, the accumulation of successful mistakes, in which random errors allow some individuals to survive and to reproduce while others end in failure. Over the years the successful variants become more common and in time new forms of life appear. Darwin's theory is now widely accepted, even in France.

Every creature, Man included, evolved with no inbuilt direction in the hierarchy of excellence, be it upwards or downwards. *The Origin* sets out an array of evidence, from the domestication of plants and animals, from fossils, from patterns of population growth, from the biology of islands, from comparative anatomy, from animal behaviour, and from much more, to make what its author called his 'long argument'. Several of the ideas discussed in its pages can be found in the writings of each of the talented quatrain of the Jardin des Plantes. Buffon and Lamarck, as Darwin acknowledged, each at least accepted the idea of biological change. In 1833, Geoffroy

Saint-Hilaire came up with an idea close to natural selection itself: 'The external world is all-powerful in alteration of the form of organized bodies ... [modifications] are inherited, and they influence all the rest of the organization of the animal, because if these modifications lead to injurious effects, the animals which exhibit them perish and are replaced by others of a somewhat different form, a form changed so as to be adapted to the new environment.' Cuvier was the first to use fossils to develop a narrative of the past. However, neither he nor any of his colleagues developed their hints into a coherent theory.

Ironically enough, part of Darwin's own case is based, in the tradition of the Comte de Buffon, on biological decay; not as evidence for programmed degeneration, but as proof of the constant vigilance of natural selection. Darwin turned the count's logic on its head when he discusses cases in which structures fall into decline when circumstances change and they no longer play a useful role.

Relict organs are diminished versions of body parts – 'rudimentary, atrophied or aborted' structures – in one species that in their relatives retain their original job: 'Organs or parts in this strange condition, bearing the stamp of inutility, are extremely common throughout nature.' They are evidence both of the constant input of inherited error through mutation and of evolution's ability to police it; to promote the useful and remove the injurious. Relict characters build up when selection relaxes its scrutiny. Male nipples, flightless birds on small islands in which to take to the air risks being swept out to sea, teeth in the foetuses of whales that when adult filter food from the water; for all such attributes once an external challenge has been removed, natural selection, the editor of the imperfect, looks away. To Darwin, decline, as much as advance, showed its machinery at work, with no need to call on mystical forces.

One system has become a microcosm of the process. His book discusses the 'several animals which inhabit caves of Carniola and Kentucky' and have lost their sight. The olm, or *Proteus*, is a blind pink amphibian that lives in limestone caverns in the Balkans (and in an impressive double error in taxonomy is referred to in the local language as the 'human fish'). He also describes the fate of a fish of a more conventional kind.

About a hundred and fifty species of underground fish are known. Most have lost their eyes since they became troglodytes. Their relatives on the surface face the same input of error through mutation, but for them any damage to the ability to see would be fatal. Only in a darkened world can such mistakes build up.

A New World cave fish, the Mexican Tetra (the surface form of which was first described by Cuvier himself), is now a classic of evolutionary regression. The creature is one of the few troglodytes that can be crossed in the laboratory with relatives who have stayed in the sunlit world outside, and has become an experiment in the genetics of decline.

Its homeland is in thirty or so limestone caverns of northeast Mexico. Its habits have emerged at least five times, over several million years, from separate ancestors. The cavedwellers have given up more than eyes. Each has no more than decayed remains of the genes for the visual pigments themselves. They also lose their dark skin colour and the internal clock that allows them to track day and night.

To reduce investment in eyes, clocks and skin pigment allows resources to be directed towards talents more useful in the gloom. The underground fish have more taste buds on their body surface than do their relatives in the open, which helps them find prey. In addition they store more fat, which makes sense for in the depths food is always short. They have tuned up the pressure system that picks up disturbance in the water caused by a potential food item, or by a mate. This allows them to keep their ancestors' complex courtship dances because they can detect the watery waves of passion that emanate from a hopeful partner.

The blind fish also have personalities that fit the empty world in which they live. The animals are calmer than their surface kin, are less gregarious, and never sleep. Damage to a gene that makes an enzyme involved in nerve transmission is responsible.

Populations in separate caves have, as expected from the random nature of mutation, lost their attributes through damage to different parts of the double helix. As a result, the progeny of experimental crosses between them sometimes develop eyes more complete than those of either parent, because the production line has been interrupted in different places. The hybrids are provided with one undamaged copy from one parent, matched with a broken one from the other. They can, as a result, make a better eye than either.

Darwin's 'wrecks of ancient life' gained new interest when it emerged that great sections of DNA have been also been stranded on the reefs of evolutionary neglect. Once again, eyes tell the story.

The retina has pigments called opsins that convert light

energy into nerve signals. Humans have four, one of which comes into play only in dim light. The others are sensitive to the long, medium and short waves that we identify as red, green and blue. Such hues emerge from brain processes and not from physics, for as Newton himself said of his prism experiment, 'The rays themselves have no colour.'

We inhabit a richer visual world than do most mammals, for they have just two such receptors and cannot tell red from green (a problem shared by millions of colour-blind men). Our sensory universe is in contrast less vivid than is that of birds and reptiles, for those creatures have four rather than three bright-light pigments. Our distant ancestors, shared as they were with the precursors of those groups, must also once have had an additional sensor. It may have decayed in the long years in which the mammal-like reptiles of the dinosaur era, most of them not much bigger than rats, spent the day underground, where they had no need to distinguish colours.

The story of vision is not entirely one of decline. Many Old World apes and monkeys, our own ancestors included, clawed back a third receptor by doubling up a length of DNA, which then evolved a new function. It may have been favoured because for an animal that eats ripe fruit the ability to tell red from green is a real help. Most New World monkeys, in contrast, are stuck with just two, perhaps because the useful error never happened.

To lose a talent in the world of sight is as nothing compared to the damage suffered by the senses of taste and smell. There, the stench of decay is everywhere.

Scent is subtle. Caraway and spearmint have the same

chemical formula, but in shape one is the mirror image of the other. Another compound smells of flowers when dilute, but of faeces when concentrated, while some substances with different structures smell the same. Each scent receptor picks up a specific section of the target molecule, but because there are so many of them and because on the cell surface they can combine in many ways, they identify a multitude of signals.

One person in ten is blind to the smell of hydrogen cyanide (which resembles that of almonds) and one in a thousand cannot even respond to the secretions of a skunk (which is more important than it seems as the stuff is added to gas to warn against leaks). Everyone lives in their own aromatic universe and some are more diverse than others. Even so, we are all no more than sensory shadows of our ancestors.

The gene family involved is the largest in the genome, with around eight hundred members. Some make their presence felt not just in the nose, but in sperm, where they help to seek out the egg. Many animals have more sensors than we do, with a thousand in mice and rats with even more. Chimpanzees, too, do better than us, as a hint that *Homo sapiens* lost some of its odoriferous talents not long ago.

Pseudogenes, as the non-functional sections of DNA such as those found in their hundreds in the human taste and smell systems are called, are the corpses of genes that have gone before. The genome is packed with them. In addition, great tracts of the double helix consist of short messages that came in as viral invaders, and other sequences that seem to have spread because of the intrinsic instability of the molecule itself and have since degenerated. It was once the fashion to dismiss all such DNA as junk, but that was premature. Some control the activity of other genes, while pseudogenes themselves may make a faint effort to leap into action. Even so, their presence is proof that much of our anatomy is built upon the wreckage of earlier failures. Buffon would, no doubt, approve.

Geoffroy, too, would find comfort in some of today's discoveries. As Darwin showed, natural selection cares not at all for the fate of organs of no use, but is always alert to any variant that might increase the reproductive success of those who bear it. *The Origin* points at its ability to pick up whatever is on offer and to utilise it in different ways: 'What can be more curious than that the hand of a man, formed for grasping, that of a mole for digging, the leg of the horse, the paddle of the porpoise, and the wing of the bat, should all be constructed on the same pattern, and should include the same bones, in the same relative positions? Geoffroy St Hilaire has insisted strongly on the high importance of relative connexion in homologous organs: the parts may change to almost any extent in form and size, and yet they always remain connected together in the same order.' In Geoffroy's own words: 'It seems that nature has enclosed herself within and has formed all living beings on only one unique plan, essentially the same in its principle, but which she has varied in a thousand ways in its accessory parts ... all the most essential differences come ... from a complication, in a word from a modification, of those same organs.'

Wings, hooves and paddles demonstrate that selection is a pragmatist, ready to seize whatever becomes available. The apparent perfection of organs that look like masterpieces of design comes instead from the accumulation of error, in different ways in different lineages. Birds, bats, flying squirrels and even a gliding snake have all taken to the air, but have evolved the means to do so in quite different ways. As Darwin put it: 'I am inclined to believe that in nearly the same way as two men have sometimes independently hit on the very same invention, so natural selection working for the good of each being and taking advantage of analogous variations, has sometimes modified in very nearly the same manner two parts in two organic beings.'

One remarkable example of such convergence was studied by Geoffroy Saint-Hilaire himself. Napoleon's invasion of Egypt was a campaign of discovery as much as of aggression, with both soldiers and scientists in search of new lands. Geoffroy was among them and, on the banks of the Nile, he became very interested in fish.

Stun guns were invented four decades ago. Fish have had them for rather longer. An electric eel is an enormous cattle prod in which most functions are restricted to the first few centimetres of its two-metre body, while the rest is a lethal weapon. Our own ancestors must have been aware of its power, for African catfish can be a metre long and can generate pulses of four hundred volts to knock out their prey. Ancient Egyptian inscriptions also acknowledge the 'angry fish', while Alexander Volta based his first battery on the structure of the stingray's electric organ.

Many fish generate weak pulses of electricity to help them find their way about, but no more than half a dozen produce a strong discharge. Darwin himself noted that the talent had appeared in lineages that must have diverged 'at an immensely remote period & therefore can hardly owe this similar anomalous organ to community of descent'. They include bony fish such as the African catfish and elephant fish, a pair of distant relatives that separated around a hundred million years ago from the eel-like electric knife-fish that swims in flooded Amazon forests. That trio's own ancestors diverged from other fish two hundred million years earlier. Biological stun guns are even found in two marine rays, members of the other great branch of fishes, the sharks and their kin, from which the bony fish diverged almost five hundred million years before the present.

Geoffroy became so engrossed by such creatures in the years he spent in Alexandria that he ignored 'the bombs, the local fires, the surprises of the besiegers and the plaintive cries of the victims' that accompanied the British siege to carry on with his studies. In a letter to Cuvier, he wrote that his work had convinced him that with electricity, 'One can explain all galvanic, electric, and magnetic phenomena, the nervous fluid, germination, development, nutrition, generation, the intellectual function . . .'

He had breathed too deeply of the heady Napoleonic air in making that claim, but the fish do bear a real message. They tell a tale of a series of stumbles towards an unknown destination, reached in different ways, with different raw material, in separate lineages. In the first edition of *The Origin*, Darwin wrote that 'it is impossible to conceive by what steps these wondrous organs have been produced', but later he became more confident: 'when we look closer to the subject we find in the several fishes provided with electric organs that these are situated in different part of the body, that they differ in construction, as in the arrangement of the plates, and ... lastly, in the requisite nervous power (and is perhaps the most important of all the differences) being supplied through different nerves from widely different sources'.

In addition those organs have cells of quite different shape: long and thin in some species, flattened in others, and square boxes in another. Every species has converted muscle fibres into batteries. Such fibres are based on a rack-and-pinion pair of proteins. Every time they slide past each other, a tiny voltage is generated. The energy is used not to contract muscles but to push electrical charge across a membrane. Just like a series of torch batteries connected to each other, every repeat adds a small amount of power to the system, but instead of two or three units, a fish has millions. Each species takes advantage of the same cellular pathways but with changes in different places. On five separate occasions evolution has seized the raw material provided by mutation to generate structures which, to the lazy mind, are evidence for programmed improvement.

Geoffroy pre-empted Darwin in other ways. He was the first to realise that relatedness is often better revealed in embryonic forms than in adults. Some of his claims seem absurd, for he saw parallels between the anatomy of a squid and that of a dog. He claimed that all that would be needed to transform one into the other would be to fold the dog over in the middle of its back. That would provide it, like the squid, with a hollow interior, together with a brain and anus in close proximity at the front. He was perhaps a little over-imaginative there, but the embryo does hint at some truth in the idea.

The animal world has a shared system of the control of development. A set of genes, 'homeoboxes', as they are called, arrange organs in order, from front to back, as the embryo forms. Squid and dogs have different numbers of such genes, but their basic plan is the same and must descend from a common ancestor. Once again, Geoffroy looked forward towards today's biology.

He was also the first to make biochemical tests of similarity in different creatures, for he found that the ribs of mammals and the shells of crabs share the same chemistry, based on salts of calcium and magnesium. This led him to the radical proposal, now at the heart of evolutionary biology: that all animals are related. His descendants at the Muséum d'Histoire Naturelle and across the world identify what he called 'unity of plan' not with simple salts but with DNA. A trickle of information on kinship has become a torrent, and his claim of a universal tie across the world of life that comes from shared descent even between its most remote subdivisions has been vindicated.

Geoffroy fell into bitter disagreement with Cuvier on that issue, for his colleague insisted on the independent creation of separate groups of creatures. Their quarrel echoed through the intellectual life of Europe. In the summer of 1830, disorders in Paris led to the downfall of the monarch and to the end of the Bourbon line. In Geneva soon afterwards, Goethe said to a visitor: 'Now, what do you think of this great event? The volcano has erupted, everything is in flames!' His interlocutor assumed that the philosopher was referring to the fate of the French royal family, but he was wrong. 'I am not speaking of these people at all, but of something entirely different. I am speaking of the contest, of the highest importance for science, between Cuvier and Geoffroy Saint-Hilaire, which has come to an open rupture in the Academy.'

Goethe was right, for the deposed monarch is now almost forgotten, while the rift between the naturalists marked the beginning of the end for the theory of separate creation. Geoffroy's speculation helped to form Darwin's evolutionary ideas, which have become the organising principle – the grammar – of the whole of biology. Cuvier had insisted that the similarities between the teeth of sharks and of tigers came because those blessed through heavenly intervention with such savage instruments would choose to use them in the same way. His opponent held the opposite view – that the predators had emerged in response to environmental pressures on many separate occasions and that all, in the end, shared ancestry with each other, as they did with herbivores and everything else.

Whatever their views on how life had emerged, the biologists of the Jardin des Plantes were keen to catalogue it. Buffon's idea that animals should be classified on the grounds of usefulness alone was abandoned. His successors divided the classes 'insects' and 'worms' used in earlier times into molluscs, crustaceans, insects, worms, echinoderms (sea urchins and the like) and zoophytes (a mixed bag that included sea anemones and sponges), in an arrangement not far from that of today.

Thanks to molecular biology, life's grand family is coming into shape. Some ties are obvious. Men and chimpanzees share around 95 per cent of their DNA and, the fossils show, diverged from their common ancestor some seven and a half million years ago. The gorilla lineage split off two million years before that, while the great apes found an identity of their own twenty million years before the present. The earliest primates, now long gone, were mouse-like creatures that scuttled around the feet of the dinosaurs, more than seventy million years ago.

The earliest ancestors of kangaroos and the like split from those of mammals around a hundred million years earlier. The mammals themselves emerged about ninety million years before the present, and most groups, from cats to whales, burst into life in the twenty million years after the death of the dinosaurs (which means that men and monkeys have a longer shared pedigree than do deer, rabbits or bats). Animals that evolved in what is now Africa, from elephants to aardvarks, still share some identity, as do sloths, anteaters and armadillos, whose first home was in what became South America.

As the molecular anatomists venture further into obscure corners of the animal kingdom there remain arguments about quite who fits in where. Some of the links are unexpected – insects and nematode worms (many of which are gut parasites) are united into one group on the grounds that they shed their skin as they grow, but earthworms and snails, which at first sight are so different, go together because their embryos look similar. Whatever the disagreements about the details, and there are many, Geoffroy's image of plants, animals and everything else as an extended family has survived. Unity of type, as Darwin called it, has allowed biologists to reconstruct much of the past.

Their science has also begun to say quite a lot about the future. Its message should bring joy to Cuvier if to nobody else. His own model of existence was stark, simple and almost nihilistic in its denial of change. It was based on the power of repeated extinction. For him, the whole idea of biological transformation, whatever its cause, was wrong. Every species had a fixed form that could never alter. Its habits and its habitat were each defined by its God-given identity (Cuvier was president of the Bible Society of Paris). Animals did not adapt their way of life to deal with the challenges of the environment but chose the way of life for which they had been designed.

His ideas about the fixity of existence emerged when he noted that the embalmed cats and ibises collected by the Egypt expedition looked just like modern cats and birds, and that the mummies were identical to modern humans. There had been no modifications in form over what then seemed an immense period and hence no reason to assume that change was built into nature.

In 1796, the young naturalist stood up to give his first public lecture. He spoke of elephants, alive and long gone. He had found that the teeth of modern skulls from Ceylon and from southern Africa were quite different. They must, he suggested, be two species, each as distinct from the other as 'the horse from the ass or the goat from the sheep'. Fossil bones from Ohio and from Siberia differed 'as much as, or more than, the dog differs from the jackal' and both were unlike modern elephants. He named the Siberian species as a mammoth and the American as a mastodon (which translates as 'breast tooth', after the nipple-like protuberances on its molars).

He concluded that 'All of these facts, consistent among themselves, and not opposed by any report, seem to me to prove the existence of a world previous to ours, destroyed by some kind of catastrophe.' Such 'revolutions on the surface of the Earth' had formed the past. Its history was not one of gradual decline or slow advance, but of repeated disaster. Cuvier had discovered extinction.

The notion further discomfited believers, who saw God's creation as both flawless and permanent. As Thomas Jefferson put it: 'Such is the economy of nature, that no instance can be produced of her having permitted any one race of her animals to become extinct; of her having formed any link in her great work so weak as to be broken.' He was soon forced to reconsider his views.

A century before the Declaration of Independence, the remains of gigantic creatures had begun to emerge from Jefferson's native soil. At first they were hailed as proof of the Biblical account of the Great Flood. In fact, they were relics of the mastodon. That had been a solid creature, around three metres high and six tons in weight. Jefferson felt that the bones may have been those of an elephant, or perhaps of an as yet undiscovered pachyderm that roamed in some remote part of the Americas. He was so certain that the gigantic beasts were still around that he asked the explorers Meriwether Lewis and William Clark to keep an eye out for them as they travelled through the far West. They failed to spot a single specimen, and in spite of extensive searches, none have yet been found. Death, as Cuvier had insisted, was a natural part of life, for species as much as for individuals.

The French palaeontologist moved on to look at his local fossils, present in vast numbers in the calcareous hills to the north of Paris. Much had changed in the Hexagon since the distant past, for there he found creatures that ranged from pygmy hip-popotami to large bears. As he extended his searches, Cuvier found a consistent set of seven strata, each well separated from the next, and each with its own unique mix of inhabitants.

To explain this he appealed to gigantic floods that had wiped the world clean again and again. After each, relatives of those who had perished returned from refuges elsewhere. This gave rise to the series of similar but distinct forms that he found in successive layers, with no need for biological change and no sign of any intermediates. His theory had no hint of progress or of decay. Snails and men were different, needless to say, but it made no sense to say that one was supe-rior or inferior to the other. Once again, President Jefferson objected.

One page in six of *The Origin of Species* is devoted to fos-sils. Darwin was much exercised by the apparent shortage of intermediate forms which, on his own theory of slow change, must have existed but which were almost never found. To solve the problem he pointed at the patchiness of the record of the rocks; it was 'a history of the world imperfectly kept, and written in a changing dialect', and gaps were to be expected.

The fossil record is no doubt incomplete. Even so, Charles Darwin's contention that extinction almost always involves the slow disappearance of less adapted creatures in the face of their successors has not held up. As Cuvier claimed, such events often happen suddenly, with no reference to the qual-ities of those who disappeared. The dinosaurs went because of a gigantic meteorite sixty-five million years ago; talented grazers or hunters as they may have been, none survived.

That disaster was just one of five ancient shipwrecks in which whole ecosystems were wiped out, to be replaced by a simpler world that persisted for aeons before complexity built up once more. Had the 'terrible lizards' not been killed off, they might have stayed in charge. The small reptiles that became mammals and led to the evolution of humans may then have gone nowhere. By accident, they did.

The tale of extinction, like that of evolution as a whole, is not simple. Cuvier's elephants tell part of the story. A hundred and seventy species of extinct elephants are known. The earliest lived in Africa some sixty million years ago, and were much smaller than their modern descendants. The mastodon line took up an identity of its own ten million years before the present, while fossils of the elephant and mammoth appear two million years later. Some species became giants, four metres tall, while others, marooned on small islands, were no bigger than large dogs. Just two, the African and the Indian elephant, have survived (although some biologists do classify the forest form found in Africa as a separate species).

The woolly mammoth, the last of its line, was about the same size as a modern African elephant. Its closest modern relative is in fact the Indian elephant, with the last common ancestor alive around six million years before the present, while the African elephant set off on its own a million years before that. Both extinct kinds were adapted to cold, with smaller ears and dumpier legs than their modern kin. Fossil DNA reveals differences in more than a thousand genes between the extinct and the extant. Ancient red blood pigment gave up more oxygen to the tissues at low temperatures than does that of today, with other changes in skin and hair, fat storage, cold sensitivity, and the ability to respond to shifts in day length as the Arctic seasons move on.

At their peak, mammoths and mastodons thrived in numbers even greater than those of the huge herds of wildebeest that flourished until not long ago in Africa. The 'mammoth steppe', as their homeland was called, spread across much of Europe and Asia, and was the largest continuous stretch of habitat that the world has ever seen. Chilly as it may have been, it was even more productive than today's African savannah. At its height, each square kilometre supported, on average, one mammoth, five bison, seven horses and fifteen reindeer. So much methane – a powerful greenhouse gas – poured out of their rear ends that their own abundance may have led to the increase in temperature that led to their demise.

Their activities, like those of the great grazers of the Serengeti, determined the fate of their habitat and of all who lived within it. Since their disappearance the steppe has as a result seen great changes. A few years ago a Russian enthusiast fenced off a solid section of Siberian tundra and filled it with wild horses, bison and deer. The effect has been dramatic, with an increase in rich grassland as the animals trample the soil and recycle nutriments, and less snow cover in winter as their hooves sweep it away. As a result, the permafrost gets colder than before, and in an unexpected bonus releases less carbon dioxide.

Remains of the ancient pachyderms have been found as far south as Honduras. They were the most abundant large mammals that have ever lived. Why did they disappear?

Climate change was largely to blame. The elephants were

picky eaters, and for much of the time the icy landscape in which they lived gave them just what they needed. In Siberia, the steppe was covered with sparse grass, with a few shrubs and even fewer stunted trees, while Europe and North America had rather more generous vegetation. Mammoths lived on the tundra and preferred to eat ground plants, while mastodons were fond of spruce and pine but had the odd nibble at willows, elms and poplars. The young were in addition happy to consume the dung produced by their parents, filled with goodness as it was.

The last ice age began a hundred and ten thousand years ago and ended eleven and a half thousand years before the present. For much of that time, episodes of moderate cold were interrupted by severe chills and by moments of warmth. The elephants' fortunes and those of the other great beasts of the time waxed and waned to match. In general, their range shrank at times of high temperature and grew when the thermometer dropped. When thick ice covered Alaska seventy thousand years ago, the animals were forced to retreat but none of the extinctions of the arctic pachyderms and their companions coincide with cold periods for they were able to move to the south. In contrast, at the times when parts of the far north were almost as warm as today the animals suffered a collapse as their habitat shrank. Ancient DNA collected from Arctic soils contains fragments of double helix from bacteria, from pollen and even – in the form of faeces, remnants of hair and of saliva – of the great beasts themselves, making it easier to track their movements. Whenever the temperature really went up, their favourite plants died off. Mammoths were for a time restricted to three small refuges, in Europe, Siberia and the New World, and mastodons also went into decline. As the climate cooled again, the two flourished once more, but mass graves from around fourteen thousand years ago show that another warm period led to disaster before a brief reprieve when the cold returned. Then, with the end of the last ice age, the thermometer shot up, the vegetation of the northern wilderness was transformed, and the great beasts were lost for ever.

They went fast. The animals were gone from most of the world by ten thousand years ago. The last lonesome mammoth lived three and a half thousand years ago on Wrangel Island, in the Arctic Ocean.

Tools and weapons from that era hint that hunters were also at work. Bones with embedded stone points have been found in Siberia. The hunters were after ivory, used to make spears and knives, rather than meat. Mastodons, too, faced the depredations of hunters, but in most places men did no more than strike the final blow, for they were gone from northern South America and from Alaska well before humans arrived.

Their modern relatives now face the same fate. Ivory is to blame, but for reasons less noble than in ancient times. A large male elephant can generate a hundred kilograms of the stuff, worth well over a hundred thousand pounds, while the trade as a whole is worth almost a billion a year. The real problem began a decade ago, when Islamic terrorists and Somali gangs began to take over what had been no more than a local criminal enterprise. Their actions are concentrated in southern Tanzania and nearby northern Mozambique. The African elephant population has plunged from a million and a half in the 1970s to around a quarter of a million today. Twenty-five thousand animals are killed each year, and at the present rate soon almost none will be left.

The elephant is just one of the many animals under threat. Today's 'sixth extinction', as it has been called, is the latest in a series of grand revisions. More than three hundred land animals with backbones have disappeared since the days of Louis XIV, and for those that remain, the average number of survivors is down by a quarter.

There may be ten million kinds of animal, the majority unknown to biologists. The extinction rate for many has risen by a hundred times in the past century alone. At a guess, some thirty thousand disappear every year. The biggest do worst. When man left Africa, there were more than forty land mammals that weighed more than a ton: from the giant rhinoceroses that roamed what is now Russia to the huge armadillo-like creatures whose bones Darwin found in South America. Now, just eight are left: the two elephants, five species of rhinoceros, and one of the two kinds of hippopotamus. Man did a lot to kill off the others. Almost all the survivors are under serious threat: between 2007 and 2014, the number of rhinos killed rose from thirteen to more than a thousand. Even in the less impressive range of creatures that weigh more than a hundred kilograms but less than an elephant – wildebeest, deer, gorillas, wild horses and more – the situation is dire, with more than half on the edge of extinction. Man and his domestics now represent 95 per cent of the weight of the mammals of the world, a figure certain to increase.

Birds, too, have had a hard time, with at least fifty species lost in the past century, and great declines even in common varieties such as sparrows. At that rate, one kind in five in the western hemisphere may be lost by the end of the century. Frogs and toads have been battered by climate change, by loss of habitat, and by fungal disease, with almost half at imminent risk of disappearance. Certain places face real catastrophe. Half a century ago the great freshwater lakes of the Rift Valley in east Africa sheltered more than two hundred unique fish. They are now being eaten by introduced predators and will soon be gone. The tale of mass extinction may be banal, but the facts are grim indeed.

The problem was noticed even in earlier times. Lamarck wrote of *Homo sapiens* that 'one could say that he is destined to exterminate himself after having rendered the globe uninhabitable'. Buffon, too, planned to provide the Jardin des Plantes with a menagerie, in which one could study the 'relations of animals with the plants of their native country ... At the sight of the vegetation among which they were born, they will give themselves over to love-making under the illusion that they are at home'. His aphrodisiac experiment in conservation biology had to wait, but a zoo was indeed founded on the site. It soon accumulated a vast array of species (among them the giraffe, a gift from Méhémet Ali, Pasha of Egypt, that Geoffroy Saint-Hilaire accompanied on foot in a seventeen-day journey from Marseilles to Paris). In time, they found a place in his huge work on animal diversity and in the collections that still fill the Museum of Natural History. Evolutionary biology began with a catalogue, and the job is still far from done.

The Paris Museum of Natural History now includes the Menagerie, the Gallery of Evolution, the Gallery of Palaeontology, the Gallery of Mineralogy, a series of greenhouses, and a variety of laboratories. They harbour some two thousand researchers. The Garden has the largest collection of plants in the world and an image of each species has been digitised and is open to view to all. The zoo is still involved in conservation. The zebra-like quaggas it held in Cuvier's day have gone for ever, but its experts are involved in the preservation of rare tortoises, frogs, and many more endangered creatures.

The birth of classification, paleontology, and the idea of evolution itself can be traced to the years around the French Revolution. The spectres of Buffon, Cuvier and Geoffroy Saint-Hilaire have good reason to be content as they haunt the galleries of the Muséum d'Histoire Naturelle. Even that of Lamarck, derided as he has been by many of his successors, should manage a wry smile as he looks at some of today's biology. Darwin praised each of the first three great figures for their contributions, and was right to do so, but in private, if not in public, he was scornful about the last-named. Quite why is the province of the next chapter.

CHAPTER IX

HANDING IT ON

How swift is the progress of things and men!

THOMAS CARLYLE, *The French Revolution*

Bibliothèque nationale de France / Bridgeman Images

Jean-Baptiste Lamarck, France's greatest optimist

The third verse of Philip Larkin's best-known poem has a somewhat genetical air: 'Man hands on misery to man / It deepens like a coastal shelf / Get off as quickly as you can, / And don't have any kids yourself' (the first stanza also discusses inheritance but is perhaps a little coarse for a work of popular science).

His view of patrimony, as of life in general, was gloomy, but it is hard to quarrel with the claim that children inherit a great deal from their parents, misery perhaps included. Larkin was blind to Wordsworth's sensations when he learned of the events in Paris that 'Bliss was it in that dawn to be alive/But to be young was very heaven!' To the librarian from Hull, as to the count from Buffon, decline was built in to the human condition.

Buffon's best-remembered successor at the Jardin des Plantes was in contrast a passionate supporter of the lake poet's views, for he was sure that life was programmed to improve. His name remains familiar to all biologists – and indeed he invented the word 'biology' – but not for that reason. Jean-Baptiste Lamarck is notorious for his support of a model of inheritance that has been, at least in the English-speaking world, and at least until not long ago, universally mocked.

In public, Charles Darwin was generous about his French predecessor. Lamarck, he said, 'upholds the doctrine that all species, including man, are descended from other species. He first did the eminent service of arousing attention to the probability of all changes in the organic, as well as in the inorganic world, being the result of law, and not of miraculous interposition.' Lamarck's fellow citizens agreed, for the plinth of his statue in the Jardin des Plantes bears the unambiguous phrase: '*Fondateur de la Doctrine de l'Evolution*'. In private, the author of *The Origin* was less generous.

Lamarck's interests, like those of his fellows, were eclectic. He started out in medicine, moved to the army and then became a bank teller, but after a trip to collect plants with Jean-Jacques Rousseau, decided to switch to botany. For a time he planned a career as a cellist, but in the end biology won, and he published an enormous work on the flora of France. That gave him a place at the Jardin du Roi. In its new museum Lamarck was appointed Professor of Insects and Worms, and in his spare time produced weather forecasts that stretched a year ahead. In addition he attacked the new chemistry of his day (he preferred to stick to Earth, Air, Fire and Water).

He set forth many more ideas in his somewhat neglected book *Researches on the Causes of the Principal Phenomena of Physical Nature; particularly those of Combustion; Evaporation and Vaporisation of Water; Heat produced by Friction between Solid Bodies; Heat which manifests itself in sudden Decomposition, in Effervescence and in the Bodies of many Species of Animals throughout their Lives; Causticity; the Odour and taste of certain Composites; Colours of Bodies; the Origin of Composites and of all Minerals; and finally the Maintenance of Life in organic Beings, their Growth, their Vigour in their Prime, their Decline and Death.*

Valuable as Lamarck's ideas about effervescence may have been, his theories of biological change are what is remembered. Like those of Buffon, they depended on an internal impulse, but the Professor of Insects and Worms saw inevitable improvement rather than programmed decay at the wheel of the biological juggernaut. The driver was '*le pouvoir de la vie*', which he also saw, to quote the words of Carlyle, as the 'Celestial invisible Force' that lay behind the Revolution. Such ideas pervaded much of nineteenth-century biological and social thought.

Darwin despised them. Of the French sage's *Philosophie Zoologique* of 1809 (the year of his own birth), he wrote that there was nothing 'in common between the Origin & Lamarck. I believe this way of putting the case is very injurious to its acceptance; as it implies necessary progression & closely connects Wallace's & my views with what I consider, after two deliberate readings, as a wretched book ... it appeared to me extremely poor; I got not a fact or idea from it ... Heaven forfend me from Lamarck nonsense of a "tendency to progression" [or] "adaptations from the slow willing of animals".' Disagree as he might with such notions, Lamarck's English critic accepted, in a rather grudging sentence, that 'the conclusions I am drawn to are not widely different from his; though the means of change are wholly so'.

In spite of such cross-Channel scorn, in Lamarck's native land his ideas continued to thrive. The first French translation of *The Origin* appeared in 1862. It was made by a schoolteacher called Clemence Royer, who had written to its author with a request that she be allowed to undertake the task. Darwin agreed, but to his dismay Royer added a sixty-page foreword insisting that the theory of evolution negated the claims of the Church and also made the case for what we now know as eugenics. Even worse, his French translator was a passionate advocate of the view that life had a long-term goal and went so far as to add a subtitle, '*Des Lois du Progres Chez les Êtres Organisées*', to the work.

In an exasperated note, Darwin wrote: 'I received 2 or 3 days ago a French translation of the Origin by a Madelle Royer, who must be one of the cleverest & oddest women in Europe: is ardent deist & hates Christianity, & declares that natural selection & the struggle for life will explain all morality, nature of man, politicks &c &c!!! She makes some very curious & good hits, & says she shall publish a book on these subjects, & a strange production it will be.' To the botanist Joseph Hooker he was more frank: 'Almost everywhere in Origin, when I express great doubt, she appends a note explaining the difficulty or saying that there is none whatever!! It is really curious to know what conceited people there are in the world.'

Royer's translation, combined with a certain native chauvinism, may help to explain why *The Origin of Species* had little immediate impact in France. There, the notion that optimism, biology and civic affairs were bedfellows lingered on long after it had died elsewhere. The palaeontologist and philosopher Teilhard de Chardin put it with as much clarity as he could in his 1959 book *The Phenomenon of Man*, published to mark *The Origin*'s centennial. In the spirit of Mlle Royer, he appealed to a 'Law of Complexity-Consciousness': 'from one zoological layer to another, *something is carried over: it grows, jerkily, but ceaselessly and in a constant direction*' (he does allow for a certain amount of what he called 'groping' along the way). For Freud, too, unhappiness and even Jewishness were the memories of ancestors passed on to subsequent generations; as he put it: 'Lamarck's theory of evolution coincided with the final outcome of psychoanalytic thinking.'

Teilhard's bizarre claim that life moves inexorably towards what he called an 'Omega Point', when true perfection will arrive, is close to that of Lamarck, who felt that all creatures were involved in an endless procession to improve the lot of their descendants. Nothing in modern science calls for such a hypothesis. Even so, it has proved hard to strangle the serpent of positivism, which now and again still raises its dubious head, at least among non-biologists.

Darwin wrote in his notebooks, 'never say higher or lower', and in a letter that 'I do not think that any one has a definite idea as to what is meant by higher except in classes that can loosely be compared with man.' *The Origin* also makes the point that while humans may consider themselves superior in the scale of nature to a bee, the bee might disagree. Even so, it also suggests that if it were possible to put extinct groups of creatures into competition with their modern descendants, the former would almost always be exterminated, which hints at forward movement, albeit not of inevitability, while the same might be said of the invasion of New Zealand by European creatures, unmatched by migration in the opposite direction, although nobody who examined the inhabitants of each place before they came into contact could have predicted this.

Today's biology casts further doubt on the idea of a ladder of ascent. Tomatoes have more genes than we do, while a certain Japanese flower has a genome fifty times larger than our own. Men have fewer chromosomes than chimpanzees, and even if we are blessed with larger brains than our cousins, chimps have genes that give them stronger (and hairier) bodies, larger testicles, spines on the penis, and the ability to survive on raw food alone, all talents that we lack. Anatomy, it seems, says rather little about 'higher or lower'.

Even so, some still claim to see progress in the history of life. Popular texts once took it for granted that evidence from extinct creatures revealed a direction to evolution, a notion that lives on in the familiar cartoon of the rise of Western man from the apes. The idea is a caricature of the truth, but in about half of all American natural history museums it is presented as an established fact, largely through a failure to keep their displays up to date.

Horses are a prime example. The glass cases of their fossil bones often show a gradual and consistent increase in size of each named form over the years, with a strong hint of some equine drive to fulfil a manifest destiny as a noble beast of the prairie. The fossils in fact reveal not a conveyor belt of advance but a ragged tree with many branches, most of which came to a dead end. The earliest forms browsed leaves from bushes. Fifty-five million years ago, the ancestors of today's horses were no bigger than dogs. About thirty million years ago half a dozen distinct lines emerged, some of which stayed as browsers, while others preferred to feed from the ground. Quite often, animals on one line of descent were in fact smaller than earlier members of a different line, and even if the modern horse, the sole survivor, is the largest ever, there is no sign of consistent increase in size over the years.

In the light of such evidence, Lamarck's ideas about necessary progress have more or less faded from view. Modern biologists know his name for a different reason, which is (or was) derided as another grand and foolish blunder.

How man hands on misery or any other attribute to his children once seemed obvious. Biologists in Lamarck's day and long afterwards believed in the inheritance of acquired characters, the notion that the qualities of progeny emerge from the experiences of their parents, passed on via what Lamarck had called a 'nervous fluid'. In today's public mind (or at least the version of that mythic beast on this side of the Channel), there he went badly astray. The idea was indeed wrong, but Lamarck was not alone in his beliefs, and in recent times elements of what once seemed absurd have begun to verge on the conventional.

His theory is often discussed in the context of the desire of the giraffe to reach higher leaves, and the longer necks of its progeny that appear as a result, but Lamarck mentions those creatures only in passing. He has a better example: 'The bird that goes on the water because of the need to find its life-sustaining prey spreads the fingers of its feet when it wants to hit the water and move on its surface. The skin connecting these fingers to their base eventually acquires the habit of stretching. This explains the formation, over time, of the large membranes we see today that link together the fingers of ducks, geese, etc. But the bird whose mode of life makes it accustomed to perching on trees inevitably acquires longer, differently-shaped toes. Its nails become longer, sharper, and hooked, so as to grasp the branches on which it so often lands.'

Over the years, nails became sharper and toes became more webbed because such structures were useful. The choice of a particular place to settle down enabled the body to adapt itself to living there; it was the link between inheritance and the outside world: 'It is not the form, either of the body or of its parts, that gives rise to habits and way of life of animals, but it is to the contrary; to the habits, the way of life, and all the other influential circumstances that have with time constituted the form of the body and the parts of animals'. Any organ that was not used would degenerate of its own accord: 'If one masked the left eyes of two newborn babies of opposite sexes for their entire lives; if one then mated them and did the same thing to their offspring ... I have no doubt that after a considerable number of generations their left eyes would naturally be obliterated and imperceptibly tend to disappear.' His ideas reflected the political philosophy of his times: that a healthy and well-educated generation would pass on their advantages until, in time, a more perfect form of government, and of humankind, would emerge.

Lamarck's ideas were mocked even in his own lifetime. Cuvier, a bitter enemy, lampooned them: 'ducks by dint of diving became pike; pike by dint of happening upon dry land changed into ducks; hens while searching for their food at the water's edge and striving not to get their thighs wet, succeeded so well in elongating their legs that they became herons or storks'. In his eulogy on Lamarck's death (a singular custom among French academicians that allowed them to speak ill of their fellows under a cloak of grief) he described his predecessor's theories as absurd: 'nothing is wanting but time and circumstances to enable a monad or a polypus gradually and indifferently to transform themselves into a frog, a stork, or an elephant ... that may amuse the imagination of a poet; a metaphysician may derive from it an entirely new series of systems; but it cannot for a moment bear the examination of anyone who has dissected a hand, an internal organ, or even a feather'.

Such notions were abandoned, so the tale often goes, because of the work of Charles Darwin himself. He showed that the idea that ducks become proud owners of webbed feet by virtue of the habits of their aquatic ancestors and that the children of poets gain angst from their unhappy fathers was foolish. *The Origin of Species* demolished that notion for ever.

That neat story is plausible but wrong. Darwin's views on inheritance were in fact close to those of his French counterpart. In *The Origin* he writes that 'I think there can be little doubt that use in our domestic animals strengthens and enlarges certain parts, and disuse diminishes them; and that such modifications are inherited.' He also believed that organs that were no longer needed withered away of their own volition; thus, the small eyes of moles are 'probably due to gradual reduction from disuse'.

Biology has moved on from such claims, and Darwin's descendants have inserted genetics into his theory with no difficulty. Lamarck's name was, as a result, for many years mentioned in the first lecture of all university courses on that science, but only to dismiss his ideas. Things have changed, and to the dismay of those who teach the subject, the notion that the experiences of a parent can mould the attributes of its children has, in modified form, been reborn. In my own introductory lectures on the topic I am forced, with some reluctance, to be more polite than before about the *Fondateur de la Doctrine de l'Evolution*.

The notion of the inheritance of acquired characters was, or so it seemed, overthrown by a celebrated Augustinian monk. Gregor Mendel's 1866 work on peas, and his successors' research on the double helix, destroyed the idea for ever. Biologists became entirely confident that the machinery of inheritance was insulated from the influence of the environment. The foundation stone of that idea had been cemented into place by the German biologist August Weismann, who identified an impermeable barrier between the 'germ line' (sperm and egg) and the 'soma' (all other cells). He cut off the tails of hundreds of mice for five generations, to no effect. As he wrote: 'Nature has carefully enclosed the germ-plasm of all germ-cells in a capsule, and it is only yielded up for the formation of daughter-cells, under most complicated precautionary conditions.'

Nobody doubts the importance of Mendel's ideas when it comes to inherited diseases, to crop improvement or to insecticide resistance in the Colorado Beetle. Their simplicity and elegance were compromised as biologists learned more, but almost all of the discoveries of today have become incorporated into his framework.

Until not long ago, the ability to transmit acquired characters remained entirely outside the mainstream of that science. Now, ideas close to those of Lamarck have returned, to give geneticists a considerable surprise.

Many people have tried to break through Weissmann's barrier. Almost without exception their assertions have been shouted down because of poor design, self-delusion and simple fraud. Flatfish were placed on surfaces of different colours to see whether the next generation took up their parents' camouflage, and rats in mazes tested to see whether their progeny became better pupils when their parents had learned to run through the labyrinth. Such claims, and many more, were quickly debunked.

Even so, the idea was hard to kill. The Austrian expert on frogs and lizards Paul Kammerer had such faith in it that he insisted that the introduction of Prohibition into the United States would be followed by the birth of a cohort of tee-totallers. In the 1920s and earlier he had claimed that animals could respond to the conditions in which their parents were placed. The olm, the blind Balkan amphibian, was proof; for he had, so he said, persuaded the young to grow eyes when their parents were exposed to light. A *Daily Express* report, in a harbinger of today's journalism, headlined his report: 'Brilliant Scientific Discovery! Eyeless Animals Grow Eyes! Scientist Claims to have Discovered Transference of Good Traits! Genius is Hereditary! Transformation of Mankind!' Others could not repeat the result.

Kammerer then forced laboratory stocks of midwife toads (which in the wild mate on land) to have sex in water instead, and claimed that in just a couple of generations the males developed black pads on their feet that gave them a better hold on the females. The pads were, he asserted, passed on to the next generation.

Kammerer was for a time hailed as the 'New Darwin'. He was then accused of fraud when it was found that the pads of one of the toads had been injected with Indian ink. Shattered by the accusation, he wrote a farewell note, published, unusually, in the journal *Science*: 'it would be a matter of deception that presumably will be laid to me only. Who besides myself had any interest in perpetrating such falsifications can only be very dimly suspected ... I hope that I shall gather together enough courage and strength to put an end to my wrecked life to-morrow.' True to his word, in 1926 Paul Kammerer shot himself on an Austrian hillside.

Half a century later, his cause was taken up by the contrarian author Arthur Koestler in his book *The Case of the Midwife Toad*. Koestler argued (with almost no evidence) that Kammerer's liberal views had made him a target of fanatical Nazis at the University of Vienna who had set out to ruin his career. It seems more probable that his fault was, at best, self-delusion. That has always been rife in biology. Even Pavlov believed for a time that the speed at which a conditioned response was learned increased in the dogs whose parents had been trained to salivate at the sound of a bell. He retracted the claim when he could not confirm his results.

The insistence on a complete separation of genes from the environment became even more embedded as a result of the disastrous attempt in the Soviet Union to rebuild agriculture on Lamarckian foundations. The episode led to starvation for millions.

Trofim Denisovich Lysenko was born to peasant stock and rose to gain entry into a college of agriculture. His supposed discoveries and the transformation of Soviet farming that followed made him famous in his native land, so much so that in the 1930s he was appointed to the Supreme Soviet, the country's highest legislative body.

Outside it he became notorious. His reputation in the West remains that of a simple charlatan, but that is less than fair, for he was involved in some minor advances in crop production. They have been eclipsed by his disastrous readiness to allow dogma to rule discovery. His view was Lamarckian: 'Changes in heredity, acquisition of new characters and their augmentation and accumulation in successive generations are always determined by the organism's conditions of life. Heredity changes and increases in complexity as the result of the accumulation of new characters and properties acquired by organisms in successive generations.' The radical biologist even disliked the idea of chromosomes, shown by the American Thomas Hunt Morgan to bear the genes, and claimed that 'Mendelism-Morganism and Weismannian neo-Darwinism is a bourgeois metaphysical science of living bodies, of living nature, developed in Western capitalist countries not for agricultural purposes but for reactionary eugenics, racism and other purposes.' Those who believed in such ideas were 'fly-lovers and people-haters'. In those desperate days, Nikolai Vavilov, the expert on the origin of crop plants, starved to death in a prison cell and several of his colleagues were executed as enemies of the state.

Lysenko had a particular interest in the differences between what farmers knew as spring crops, which are sown as the soil warms at the end of an icy winter and flower almost at once, and autumn varieties, whose seeds have to be planted in autumn before they can burst into life several months later. The divergence between the two is due to the need of the autumnal group for a dose of cold before it is safe for the plant to emerge from its slumber. The process protects the young shoot from flowering on a warm September or October day, just before the snows come. Lysenko found that the yield of some wheat varieties traditionally planted in April or May straight from the sack could indeed be improved by a burst of chill by being scattered in winter snow before they were planted. He called the effect 'vernalisation' and asserted that it increased the output of grain by as much as four times. Even better, he claimed, varieties that once could grow only in the south would after such treatment succeed in harder conditions in the far north. A brief shock of heat, cold, drought or seawater, Lysenko then claimed, allowed wheat to flourish in places that before had been too torrid, too icy, too dry or too salty to allow the crop to survive.

Vernalisation is now much studied by biologists, but Lysenko took the idea well beyond the limits of science. His discoveries fitted with the Lamarckian (and Marxist) insistence on the inevitability of improvement and in that context he recommended that trees should be planted in clumps because – in true communist style – the strong would support the weak. He also made the remarkable statement that once a line of wheat had been vernalised, or bathed in salt water, its descendants could be sown in the spring, or on salty soil, with no need to waste time on further treatment. Some of his acolytes even asserted that cabbages had been transformed into turnips or pines into fir trees by appropriate cultivation, while one enthusiast said that he had transformed a chicken into a rabbit with the help of the correct diet. At the 1948 session of the Lenin Academy of Agriculture, at which Stalin was himself present, Lysenko's ideas triumphed and his opponents fell silent or fled. The new policy led to disaster.

Even so, his doctrines persisted behind the Iron Curtain until as late as the 1960s. Khrushchev was a supporter, even if by then some furtive conventional genetics was under way, but not until 1964 was its inventor packed off to where he could do no harm. The eccentric Lamarckian spent his retirement feeding cows with butter in the hope that they would generate a breed that produced high-fat milk, and died in 1976.

After that dismal episode most biologists refused even to entertain the possibility of the inheritance of acquired characters. They forgot the central tenet of all science, which is to expect the unexpected. Most of the experiments that had claimed to demonstrate such effects were rubbish, but a few were not.

C. H. Waddington – one of my own professors when I was a student in Edinburgh – was interested in fruit fly development. In the 1930s and 1940s, when Lysenkoism was at its height, he showed that damage to just a few cells in the first few days of larval life led to a cascade of abnormalities in the adult. This, he suggested, came because the embryo travelled down set biological pathways as it grew. Because the track towards adulthood was narrow, with steep sides, it was hard to persuade the growing fly to deviate from it. A minor environmental stress hence had no effect, and faced with the trials of everyday life, almost all the larvae emerged as normal adults. Not until an insect was presented with a real challenge by an experimenter, by a sudden ecological shock, or by an error in an important gene would it be forced away from the ordained route.

Nature, in other words, was able to deal with most problems of nurture, and would yield to the outside world only under severe pressure. Waddington invented the term 'epigenetics' to describe the interaction between the two. DNA is a simple chemical, while a cell, a tissue, an organ or a body is complex indeed. Epigenetics sets out to bridge the gap between chemistry and biology. The word is now much used, but so far its main contribution has been to show that the chasm that separates them is far wider than most biologists had imagined.

Waddington's ideas were at first dismissed, perhaps because his research was published under the title 'Canalization of development and the inheritance of acquired characters'. The paper describes an ingenious experiment. If a culture of fruit flies is exposed to a sudden burst of heat soon after the pupa is formed, a few of the adults that emerge lack one of the 'veins', the support struts, on the wing, because development has been disrupted. By breeding from such aberrant flies for several generations, with the same heat shock each time, more and more individuals in each culture lack a vein.

So far, so predictable; but after about fifteen generations flies without veins began to appear in his experimental lines even when no heat was applied. Several more rounds of selection on such individuals led to stocks in which all the flies showed the abnormality, with no need at all for a heat stress. In one sense, at least, what had started as an acquired character was now inherited.

At first sight this might appear to be simple Lamarckism. In fact, the experiment shows how gene and environment work together. The initial population contained within itself a few small genetic changes that predispose to errors in development. Under normal circumstances they do no damage as the larvae stick to the correct path towards adulthood. A heat shock disrupts the road surface to such a degree that the occasional fly unlucky enough to inherit several of the faulty genes is unable to make a vein. As such individuals are chosen as parents, the inherited errors build up. In time they become so abundant that flies who inherit a particularly toxic mix show the abnormality with no external stress at all. Breeding from those animals then produces a population so loaded with damaged DNA that every individual has aberrant wings even at normal temperatures. A change in the environment has revealed a store of hidden genetic variation.

Cave fish show how the system might work in nature. Surface fish put into water taken from underground (which has its own unique chemistry) find the experience stressful. In some individuals, developmental pathways are overwhelmed and they grow up with small eyes. By breeding from such animals, a small-eyed stock appears in a few generations. Perhaps that is how the eyeless state first arose. Rather than the earliest animals to venture into the depths having to wait for new mutations to adapt them to the dark, the stressful conditions of their new home released hidden variation that could be exploited at once.

Genes, we now know, respond to the environment in unexpected ways. That is often explained (or explained away) as being due to epigenetics, although that statement is frequently more a convenient description than a real insight. Internal and external processes work together and – as in Waddington's experiment – the boundaries between effects within a lifetime and those that pass from one generation to the next become blurred.

The demon drink tells part of the story. An inherited variant that gives the ability to break down alcohol is common in Europe but rare in China. Perhaps natural selection in ancient times favoured Europeans who could cope with the stuff because beer killed off cholera bacteria, while the Chinese took up tea so that boiling water did the job instead. A young Chinese who pours whisky down his throat is hence, because of his genetic heritage, at greater risk of liver failure than is a Scot, but most Chinese prefer not to repeat the experience more than once because they find the stuff so unpleasant.

However, a Scot who comes into contact with whisky for the first time also finds the experience disagreeable, because his genes have not been fired up to deal with it (my own introduction to the importance of epigenetics came an hour after a disastrous race with school friends along a shelf of bottles in a Fort William pub). Undeterred by the repulsive effects of that adventure, I – like millions of British teenagers, then and now – persisted with smaller doses of the narcotic until my liver woke up to the problem, switched on the enzyme, and all of a sudden alcohol (but never again as whisky) became a source of pleasure rather than of pain. Tolerance involves both the evolution of genes for resistance and a shift in their activity when challenged by an external stress.

The body is always on the alert for such encounters. All cells maintain an emergency squad poised to take arms against the metaphorical slings and arrows of the world outside. Some of its members – the 'chaperones', as they are called – cluster round other molecules and protect them when life gets hard. One group allows insects and plants to withstand a heat shock better if they have already been exposed to a burst of high temperature. Others respond in much the same way to threats from disease, starvation, poisons, and even social pressure.

A whole series of sensors, switches and internal regulators summon up the defences. Some alter the activity of sections of DNA when they add a small molecule to it, while others do the same to a target gene with a shift in the proteins that help it to fold. Another system controls gene activity with short versions of the nucleic acids that transfer information from the double helix to the cell. Hormones are also involved. Some such effects last a lifetime. Human embryos blessed with a Y chromosome attain their manhood, and all it implies, with a brief burst in the activity of just one gene. That increases the amount of testosterone made early in embryonic life and switches on an array of other segments of DNA all over the genome that force those who bear the fatal chromosome down the rocky road to manhood.

In almost all such cases the double helix is scrubbed clean when sperm and egg are made and the next generation enters the world as a Mendelian blank slate. Scots babies are born with unprimed livers even when the genes of their parents have been ratcheted up to deal with their nation's favourite narcotic, as proof that the experiences of one generation are not passed on to the next.

Vernalisation in plants, notorious for its role in the Soviet fraud, shows how such systems function at the molecular level. In wheat, the crop studied by Vavilov, both day-length and temperature are involved. As the autumn daylight shortens and nights get cool, a repressor molecule binds round a small group of genes and shuts down the machinery of development. When spring gets under way and the days grow longer and warmer, the repressor gene flicks the appropriate switches in the genome to allow the seed to germinate. When the plant makes pollen and egg, the molecular block on the DNA is removed, direct proof that Lysenko's claim that the effects of external conditions are passed to the next generation is false.

All this fits well into conventional biology, but the Russian charlatan might gain some post-mortem consolation from recent discoveries about how plants, at least, can sometimes hand on information about their own experiences to their progeny.

Plants respond to attack by insects in various ways. They reduce the number of tasty young leaves or grow more spines, or make an extra dose of poison to fight off their enemies. Some even send out scents that attract carnivorous insects in the hope that they will eat the aphids sucking their juices. Such tactics are expensive and the genes involved are not switched on until they are needed.

Simple enough but, against all expectations, the marks

placed on the double helix by a parent to summon up its defences are sometimes passed to the next generation. The first hint of this apparent insult to the memory of Mendel came when it emerged that the progeny of certain plants chewed by insects mount a better response to their enemies than do those whose parents were free from attack. The same is true of those whose progenitors were damaged by infection, by starvation, or by poor light. In each case the next generation is better able to cope than are those with a less battered patrimony. The order of the letters in the DNA remains the same in parents and offspring, but a message added to the double helix has been passed on. It alters the ability of the progeny to respond to a particular stress, and the effect may persist even unto the third generation.

Plants, more than animals, tend to stay in the same place and to face the same enemies for several seasons in a row, so that it pays parents to hand on instructions on how to cope. More important, plants make their germ cells late in life, well after they have suffered the challenges of the world outside. This gives them a chance to prime pollen and egg with information about the dangers to come.

Could the same be true of animals? Some patterns can be interpreted in this way. If aphids become too abundant, the flightless adults produce young with wings that allow them to migrate to a new home. Water flea parents exposed to the chemicals made by predators produce armoured offspring. Once again, chemical marks on the DNA influence the next generation.

In mammals the tale is much less clear. The fate of a foetus can, needless to say, be altered by a mother's experiences to give at least the appearance of the inheritance of acquired characters. Pregnant women who drink too much may have a child with foetal alcohol syndrome, while mothers who are obese, who smoke or have a poor diet may also give birth to a sickly infant. However, mammals begin to make their sperm and eggs when they themselves are still embryos, well before an individual male or female has the chance to abuse drink, tobacco, or cheeseburgers. A hard life after birth hence seems to have little chance of altering the molecular fate of the next generation.

Such is the conventional wisdom, but it is now being questioned. Hunger damages unborn babies, and there, perhaps, the effect can to some extent be passed from parents to children. In 1944, occupied Holland faced a great famine because of a food blockade accompanied by an icy winter that froze the canals and stopped the movement of supplies. More than twenty thousand died and many more had their health ruined. With the return of peace, the children of mothers pregnant at the time of the 'Hunger Winter' were less healthy than those from well-fed families, even if they themselves had plenty to eat. In middle age, they tended to have high blood pressure and to suffer from diabetes and obesity. There were more cases of schizophrenia and depression, too.

All that fits well into a simple narrative of difficult pregnancies, but more remarkable, the children of the next generation – the grandchildren of the days of starvation – themselves seem to be at higher risk of such conditions. That might be due, as in plants and water fleas, to some inherited message left on the double helix that persists for a second generation, but could also be no more than the carry-over effect of a difficult childhood on their own pregnancies once they became adults.

Some effects of this kind are harder to dismiss, for they appear to pass not through mothers, but through fathers. Överkalix is a small community in northern Sweden, more or less at the northern limit of human occupation. A cold summer leads to crop failure and in earlier times often brought famine. In the nineteenth century, fifteen of its seasons were unsuccessful, while in other years people ate well.

In true Scandinavian style, records were kept both of pedigrees and of food production. The descendants of those who lived through those times showed some unexpected patterns. Men who had experienced a season of abundance just before they entered puberty had grandsons who died around six years younger than did those whose grandfathers had been adolescents in a starvation year. Diabetes, in particular, was more common in grandsons with well-fed male ancestors, perhaps because they had inherited a tendency to eat, or to absorb, more food than had their fellows.

Inheritance from a grandmother who had lived through a hunger year had just the opposite effect, for their granddaughters died younger, not older, than average. That may seem odd, but it reflects another quirk of epigenetics, that the effects of certain genes differ when they pass through fathers rather than mothers. The mechanism once again may involve a 'mark' added to the double helix by one or the other parent.

Quite often, the genes involved alter a child's demands

on its mother. In one rare inborn condition, transmission of damaged DNA from the father gives rise to an infant who is hungry and active, while infants who receive it from the mother are passive, quiet and calm. The double helix itself has not changed as it passes through either parent. Instead a parental switch has altered the extent to which it is expressed. The same is true for other genes, for which paternal transmission gives a child who sucks harder at the breast, cries more when hungry, and enters puberty later, while the same variant inherited through the mother does just the opposite. The father wants a child who can extract as much as possible from its mother (whose later pregnancies might be by another man), while the mother wants to put the minimum needed into every infant to save her own resources for later. As so often in biology, selfishness rules.

The medical profession is easily excited by such discoveries, and many stresses have been claimed to have a similar effect. Diet, drugs, tobacco and family pressures have all been blamed for symptoms that persist from parents to children and even to grandchildren thanks, perhaps, to a shift in the activity of DNA. The offspring of men who worked with reactive chemicals, or were exposed to certain drugs, or smoked, might, some say, have a higher risk of cancer, perhaps because their fathers' sperm was marked by their experiences. In rats at least, the effect of a certain pesticide on fertility persists for as many as four generations.

Caution is needed when dealing with people rather than with plants (or for that matter rats). Changes at the genetic level are hard to separate from the simple effects of shared circumstances. An additional question arises because in the case of a female foetus of a hungry mother, or one who drinks or smokes, her own cells have been exposed to stress not just in her mother's womb, but in her grandmother's as well, because her own mother's eggs were generated before she herself was born. Such complications could give a false impression of real inheritance.

The search for epigenetic effects upon human disease often gives ambiguous results. Many Native Americans have problems with adult obesity and diabetes. Their difficulties were once blamed on a 'hungry gene', common because it was adapted to a boom-and-bust economy that, like that of Överkalix, faced feasts and famines. Nothing was found. Then came the notion of an epigenetic effect passed on to programme an infant to lay down fat in good times against a hard season to come. Again, no evidence has emerged. Adult diabetes is better blamed on the fact that among that deprived group, every generation for years has suffered the same disastrous diet. A shared culture, rather than a common biological heritage, is to blame. There, as in many other supposed cases, the genetical jury is still out on the new Lamarckism.

When it comes to its author's ideas about optimism, in contrast, the verdict is clear. We have no reason, in the tradition of that great naturalist, to be cheerful about inevitable progress; but also no call to follow Buffon into a gloomy and inescapable future. As always in evolution, and in science itself, the inheritance of acquired characters included, we have no idea what will happen next and philosophy only gets in the way.

AFTER THE DELUGE

France, since the Reign of Terror hushed itself, has
been a new France, awakened like a giant out of
torpor.

THOMAS CARLYLE, *The French Revolution*

This book began with the Eiffel Tower, erected to celebrate
the centennial of the French Revolution and now the universal
symbol of France itself. Its elegance, and that of its native
city, disguises the disasters – and triumphs – that the people
of Paris suffered in the ten decades between the massacre on
the Champ de Mars, the patch of parkland upon which the
monument stands, and the tower's own birth. That troubled
era emerged in large part from what Gustave Eiffel called
'the great scientific movement of the end of the eighteenth
century'. Many of the most celebrated participants in that
enterprise were active in the Revolution, and several died
for their beliefs, but as the tide of revolutionary bloodshed
receded, others were able to return to their research. In time,
a solid portion of the survivors (some among them once fiery
radicals) became senior figures in succeeding governments of

a variety of flavours, often based on principles very distant from those of 1789.

The discoveries of those days are the foundation of much of modern physics, chemistry and biology. More important to the lives of the people of Paris they gave rise to an economic boom that transformed the French capital, for the labours of its researchers led to technologies that made the city for a time the most productive, and most polluted, industrial centre in the world.

The fuse of that economic explosion had been lit by Louis XIV's finance minister Jean-Baptiste Colbert, who set up the system of central control that long pervaded French society, and French science. In 1666, the monarch, at Colbert's suggestion, established the *Académie Royale des Sciences*. Unlike the Royal Society in London, the *Académie* was firmly defined to be an arm of government. It had a substantial income and was given a home in the Louvre.

From its earliest days its members were asked to deal with practical problems and its charter enjoined them not to waste their time only on 'curious researches' or 'chemists' amusements' but instead to ensure that they acted in 'relation to service of the king and the State'. As the years went by, more and more of their efforts were directed towards applied work. Its surveyors made the first accurate map of France, while its astronomers published the first dependable list of the positions of various celestial objects, a document essential for navigation. Its chemists discovered dozens of new compounds, many of practical value, and its physicists took the first steps towards today's electrical machinery.

Academicians were also commanded to test new machines such as an apparatus to roll lead plate (some schemes, such as those for windmill-powered ploughs, and ships with springs to help them bounce off rocks, failed the examination). The Academy's efforts to apply its members' talents to commercial ends reached a peak in the half-century around the Revolution. In the 1760s, René Antoine de Réaumur, whose name is remembered for his temperature scale and who was also a metallurgist and an expert on insects, was ordered to produce an account of the useful arts. His own contribution was a document entitled *The Art of Hatching and Bringing up Domestic Fowls by means of Artificial Heat*, and he went on to edit an enormous multi-author work, the *Descriptions des Arts et Métiers*, which ran to a hundred and thirteen folio volumes and took twenty-five years to complete. It remains the most extensive single publication on technology ever produced.

Its sections include an eleven-page pamphlet on how to make starch and a thousand-page tome on coal-mining. On the way, it deals with glue, carpets, lamps, soap, locks, charcoal, bricks, noodles, felt, sugar, ironware and fish. Many eminent figures offered their expertise, often on unexpected topics. The astronomer Jérôme Lalande, better remembered for his work on the transit of Venus, wrote nine of the treatises, those on cardboard, parchment and leather included, while the huge volume on mining was penned by Jean-François-Clément Morand, an expert on the thymus gland.

The revolutionary government fostered technology in many other ways. First, it modernised the patent system. Every invention should be the property of its originator and could be protected for fifteen years on payment of the appropriate fee. The guilds that had controlled the numbers allowed into each trade were abolished, on the grounds that every citizen had equal rights to practise any profession. Innovation was stimulated with an expanded system of prizes offered for useful ideas (and Lavoisier himself had launched his career with an award for his plan for improved street lighting). The first message sent by semaphore telegraph by its French inventor, who had done the job with the help of such a subvention, was 'The National Assembly will reward experiments which are useful to the public' (a rival scheme, which involved a cannonball armed with a message and fired from one artillery battery to the next until it reached its destination did not, like the spring-loaded ships, find favour). Almost three hundred such grants were made, for schemes as various as a method for filling hydrogen balloons and a new dye for hats. Under Napoleon the system expanded and became the *Société d'Encouragement pour l'Industrie Nationale*, itself provided with a substantial subsidy and run by a consortium of scientists and bankers.

France's researchers, unlike their more fastidious British equivalents, were happy to become involved in industry. They joined with enthusiasm in their rulers' attempts to direct the course of economic progress, and became keen instruments of the *dirigisme* (tellingly, a word that has no precise English translation) that marked the nation.

The republican administration in its first days lit the bonfire of the vanities of the *Ancien Régime*, many of whose laws and regulations were swept away. Whatever the faults (and there were plenty) of the royalist establishment it had at least imposed some planning rules on its capital: factories that produced lead-based paints and pigments were banned from the centre, as were the smoky furnaces used to make plaster of Paris, while the manufacture of tripe was confined to the Île des Cygnes, well downstream. After the collapse of that regime, and in part because of the urgent demands for military supplies, all such controls were removed. The populace paid the price.

The chemist Jean-Antoine Chaptal had discovered that wine sweetened with beet sugar was stronger and more palatable than the unadulterated stuff. He set up a network of factories to extract sugar from beets, and established others that made white lead (used in paint), together with acids of various kinds. Under Napoleon, Chaptal became Minister of the Interior. He soon saw to it that all remaining restrictions on industry in residential areas were struck off the books.

Within a couple of decades of the Revolution, the City of Light was besmirched. It became, like many lesser places, a centre of the chemical industry: 'a sordid, ugly town. The sky is a low-hanging roof of smeary smoke and the atmosphere is a blend of railway tunnel, hospital ward, gasworks and open sewer. The "features" of the place are chimneys, furnaces, steam jets, smoke clouds. The products are pills, coals, glass, chemicals, cripples, millionaires and paupers.' That is in fact a nineteenth-century description of St Helens in Lancashire, but just the same, if not worse, could be said of contemporary Paris.

By 1801, the French capital contained three thousand factories, many among them based on the discoveries of Lavoisier and his followers. They poisoned the air and the water, and contaminated the streets. Household waste was boiled down for its fat, gelatin and starch, the raw materials of various chemical processes. Tan yards, soap-boiling plants, and vinegar distilleries with their vile stench sprang up next to schools and hospitals. Such enterprises were matched by many others.

Thousands of rancid hides were stored on the open spaces of what had been desirable suburbs with no concern about *exhalations fétides*. The drains ran with the dyes of textile manufacturers. Saltpetre, soda and bleach plants poured out smoke while hat-makers, mirror-makers, gilders and paint manufacturers used compounds of lead and mercury whose waste got into the water and the air. To add to the pollution, heating and baking were fuelled by firewood from forests far to the south, floated down the Seine in huge manned rafts that took weeks to make the journey. Soon, more than a million cubic metres were burned each year.

In a further contribution to the capital's atmosphere, Lavoisier's huge saltpetre operation in the deconsecrated (and soon to be destroyed) Abbey of Saint-Germain-des-Prés was joined by a lead foundry established in what had been the Convent of Sainte-Marie in the Marais. That of the Barnabites, close to the cathedral of Nôtre-Dame, became an enterprise that smelted copper (much of it from church bells), a process that belched fumes of nitric, sulphuric and hydrochloric acid. Within a few years it employed twelve thousand workers.

Many academicians took advantage of the financial opportunities on offer. The chemist Antoine Fourcroy set up a company in the Faubourg Saint-Germain, which had been a fashionable suburb but became a melting pot of the pharmaceutical trade. His factory produced medicines, some useful but others less so (with one based on the dried flesh of vipers). Other products included the antiseptic silver nitrate, together with cochineal, pure alcohol, ammonia and phosphorus. The place evolved to become a distillery for industrial chemicals. It stayed in business for decades until it was closed on safety grounds.

Fourcroy's student Michel Chevreul, the discoverer of glycerin, found that a related chemical called stearic acid made excellent candles, and established a plant to manufacture them, close to where the Arc de Triomphe now stands. The state porcelain factory at Sèvres experimented with new techniques to make hard porcelain, and also developed beautiful (albeit highly poisonous) glazes. The same combination of chemistry and cupidity ruled at the Gobelins carpet factory on the Left Bank, where new dyes were invented and for the first time it was found that chlorine with its noxious stench could be used to bleach fabrics.

All this activity meant that some scientists made fortunes (a phenomenon almost unheard of across the Channel). Jean-Antoine Chaptal, with some help from his political career, himself became rich. Du Pont de Nemours fled the Terror for the United States to found one of the world's largest chemical firms. His collaborator Claude Berthollet worked on chlorine, invented bleach (which is still known as *Eau de Javel* after the site downstream from the Champ de Mars where he had his laboratory) and made large profits from his venture. The physician Nicolas Leblanc patented a technique to synthesise sodium carbonate, a chemical essential to the manufacture of glass, paper and soap. Supplies had depended on wood ash or burnt seaweed. Leblanc's process mixed salt with sulphuric acid, and roasted it with limestone on a coal fire. It was the foundation of a profitable but filthy business, but the enterprise was confiscated by the Republic and Leblanc shot himself. Other players included Nicolas-Jacques Conté, who developed artificial pencils to replace those from England, whose supplies of graphite had been blockaded. He replaced it with clay baked with small amounts of graphite and soot and, quite soon, sold hundreds of thousands a year.

The greatest fortune of all was made by Armand Seguin, who had collaborated with Lavoisier and Laplace in their metabolic experiments and had later worked on narcotics. The French army needed something to march on, and the manufacture of the raw material of boots and saddles was still in a state not much advanced from that of the Sumerians, who had used leather for armour. To tan a hide took two years. First the flayed skin was cleaned of hair and fat and set aside to rot, sometimes with the help of human urine or dung. Once that unpleasant process was over came the tanning itself, based on an acid found in oak and fir trees. The hides were stacked in a ditch between layers of bark and left to mature for a year or more. Nobody had the slightest idea of, or interest in, how the process worked.

Seguin changed all that. He got rid of the hairs with a weak solution of sulphuric acid that penetrated into the skin and congealed its proteins. He then extracted the tannin from shredded bark in a water bath and soaked his hides in the solution, which could be re-used several times. The naked skin was bathed in the extract for a week or so for calf leather, or for twice that for leather made from adult cattle. The whole process could be done in two weeks rather than two years. Seguin was awarded a large grant to set up a factory on the Île de Sève in the Seine. Within a few months it was in full production and was so successful that the island was renamed Île Seguin. Carlyle, in a rather second-hand account, tried to make his readers' flesh creep: 'there was a Tannery of Human Skins; such of the Guillotined as seemed worth flaying: of which perfectly good wash-leather was made: for breeches, and other uses. The skin of the men, he remarks, was superior in toughness (consistance) and quality to shamoy; that of women was good for almost nothing, being so soft in texture!'

Whatever the truth of that claim, Seguin became wealthy as he supplied the French army with boots, saddles and coats. His factory tanned fifty thousand hides a year and generated vast profits; so much so that he could afford to defy Napoleon himself, for when the emperor made repeated demands that the entrepreneur sell him four Arabian horses, their owner shot them dead with his own hand and told Bonaparte's emissaries that their master could have the corpses.

The technologists' willingness to dirty their hands – and their city – with commerce was matched by an equally unashamed desire to dabble in the murky waters of politics. Since Colbert, many of France's finest had made careers as state-funded chemists, physicists, astronomers or naturalists, positions of a kind then almost unknown in England. For some, success led to an ascent into the governmental firmament. In Britain such a career was – and is – almost unheard of; from its leaders' point of view, as Winston Churchill put it somewhat later, scientists should be on tap, and not on top.

As this book has shown, several major figures ended up as martyrs to the Terror because they supported the wrong side. Others were happy to swing with the winds of change in order to advance their careers, even if they were mocked in the *Dictionnaire des Girouettes* – the 'Dictionary of Weathervanes' – for so doing. The roll-call is impressive indeed, and entirely unmatched on this side of the Channel. The mathematician Gaspard Monge, the astronomer Joseph-Louis Lagrange, the chemist Claude Berthollet and the naturalist Bernard Lacépède all joined the Senate, the last-named becoming its president. In the same way, Antoine Fourcroy became a Councillor of State, as did Georges Cuvier and the millionaire chemist Jean-Antoine Chaptal. After his stint as Minister of the Interior, Chaptal was replaced by Pierre-Simon Laplace, who himself rose to become chancellor of the Senate. The physicist Joseph Fourier (remembered for his discovery of the greenhouse effect) became prefect of the department of the Isère, the expert on gases Gay-Lussac the representative for Haute-Vienne, Boussingault of fertiliser fame sat as delegate for Alsace, while the surveyor and physicist François Arago – for a time the representative of the Pyrénées-Orientales – was later appointed as Minister of Marine Affairs and the Colonies and abolished slavery in all French overseas possessions. Towards the end of his career he even gloried for a time in the post of head of state. Seguin himself spurned public service and became a banker, arms dealer and billionaire.

Official recognition came with considerable advantages: a seat in the Senate paid six times as much as a professorship, while a more elevated post provided an income twenty times that of any researcher. Their Anglophone equivalents could do no more than gaze from the cliffs of Dover, sea-green with envy.

In spite of the efforts of the administrator-scientists and their successors, the civic weather in the century after the Revolution was often stormy. The republic was succeeded by a Napoleonic empire, by a restoration of the Bourbon line and then by a rather more liberal monarchy. That fell in 1848 to give a short-lived Second Republic, followed by a Second Empire ruled over by Napoleon's nephew. The Third Republic came to power after the Prussian invasion of 1870 and lasted until the erection of the Eiffel Tower and beyond (and France has had no shortage of political difficulties since then). The era of natural harmony that was supposed to follow the fall of the Bastille seems to have taken a long time to arrive.

Whatever the upheavals, in the past two centuries and more, Paris, its people and its sciences have reinvented them-selves in many ways. Nowhere has the metamorphosis been more obvious than in Les Halles, the home of the market women who sealed the fate of Louis XVI.

In the last days of the monarchy, the putrid cemetery that adjoined the market's decaying sheds was closed. Under the guidance of the astronomical new mayor and his successors, the authorities did much more. They called for an approach that would provide the place with '*de la solidité, de la salubrité, de l'aération, de l'éclairage, de la circulation, du nettoyage, de la sur-veillance, de la commodité des acheteurs et vendeurs*'. In the 1850s, its ramshackle structures were replaced by a series of grand structures in cast iron and glass modelled on the Crystal Palace in London.

They in turn were destroyed in the architecturally dis-astrous decade of the 1970s. As in its twin capital, the wholesale food business moved away from the centre, but Paris's equivalent of Covent Garden was, in the face of public fury, vandalised by the planners. Now, just two fragments of its great halls remain, one in the outer suburbs and the other, for some reason, in Japan. For ten years the site was no more than a vast excavation, the infamous Trou des Halles, as argument went on about what to do with it. It ended up as a litter of feeble parodies of the nineteenth-century market, interspersed with staircases to the biggest underground station in the world, and decorated with a large steel and glass mushroom. The then mayor called it 'a soulless, architec-turally bombastic concrete jungle', and the neighbourhood exuded as much of a sense of Parisian history and of place as did Milton Keynes. It was, however, popular with drug addicts.

That twentieth-century slum has itself now been removed in favour of a bland scheme that mixes parkland with a ren-ovated transport hub and an elegant curvilinear building, together with a music conservatory and a hip-hop centre. Almost all that remains of the area around the ancient market itself is the Church of Saint-Eustache. Even the Croix des

Invalides, once dedicated to the spirits of the departed as their bodies mouldered nearby, has gone. The area's population is a fraction of what it was two centuries ago and – just like those of the generations who had lived there – much of its soul has somehow been spirited away.

The same is true of large parts of the city as a whole. Halfway through Eiffel's 'century of Industry and Science' it became obvious that change was inevitable. The ravages of industry meant that existence for many who lived in what are now desirable *arrondissements* had become almost intolerable: 'Paris is an immense workshop of putrefaction, where misery, pestilence and sickness work in concert, where sunlight and air rarely penetrate ... where plants shrivel and perish, and where, of seven small infants, four die during the course of the year.' An energetic civic renewal began, and has continued to the present day. Almost all the chemical plants in the centre of the capital were banished, a huge development programme was organised, and most of what survived was scrubbed clean of both filth and mystique.

Most of inner London would still be recognisable at least in outline to a visitor from Robespierre's days, but central Paris has been transformed. In the 1850s, Napoleon III, alarmed by the penury, disease, and repeated revolts that marred his capital, ordered the prefect of the Seine department, George Eugene Haussmann, to demolish great tracts of its rotting medieval centre and to 'aerate, unify and embellish' his capital. Three thousand workers tore into the city's heart, and built straight streets lined with tall apartment blocks and embellished by grand squares and monuments. Parks large and small meant that no Parisian was more than ten minutes' walk from a green space.

In spite of complaints by aesthetes about their 'triumphant vulgarity', within a few years Paris had two hundred kilometres of new boulevards, with thirty-four thousand buildings containing more than two hundred thousand apartments, a shift that much improved the lives of those fortunate enough to move in to them. Before the great project, cholera had killed thousands. Haussmann modernised the sewers as much as the streets; before his day, just one house in five in the city had piped water, while in the new neighbourhoods, all did.

Another great improvement was, needless to say, to exclude most of the poor, with their unfortunate tendency to riot. Such economic cleansing is still at work today, with the proletariat banished to grim tower blocks in distant suburbs, where they retain their taste for rebellion. The affluent residents of the centre now speak of living *intra muros*, and they are right, for the boundary of the city proper is set by the line of the defensive wall built by Louis-Philippe in 1844 to avoid a repeat of the Prussian invasion of thirty years earlier. It lasted in places until 1929 and has been replaced by the *boulevard périphérique*, which follows its track and is for most of its length almost as impenetrable as had been its predecessor. London lost its last fortifications in 1760, and the British capital long remained a patchwork of mixed neighbourhoods, but it too has begun to suffer the same process of civic homogenisation for the benefit of a small minority.

Whatever the future for the physical, social, and

intellectual fabric of Paris, and whatever the future role, if any, of research or technology in French society, the years around the fall of the Bastille deserve celebration in their own right. *No Need for Geniuses* was written at the time of the two hundredth anniversary of Napoleon's exile on the island of St. Helena, where he died after five unhappy years. I hope that I have persuaded its readers that the period was one of much more than domestic turbulence. In France, it became perhaps the most productive episode in the history of science and led to an era of unprecedented social change.

This book gains its title from an apocryphal comment by one of the judges of the Terror as he sentenced his nation's greatest scientist to the guillotine. The essence of the revolutionary years and their aftermath is contained in an equally mythic remark, that of Napoleon himself – who at the École Militaire had trained with the astronomer Laplace – to the mathematician Lagrange. Bonaparte is supposed to have said, in response to the latter's observation that there would never be another physicist greater than Newton, that he himself would have achieved that honour had he not been otherwise engaged; that 'If I had not had to conquer the world, I would have become a scientist and discovered it.' With hindsight, the great warrior made the wrong decision, for the legacy of his nation's mathematicians, physicists, chemists, geologists and biologists has survived rather better than has that of its emperors.

INDEX

JUNE 1997

To _____
in _____
compl _____
junior year of
high school and your
wonderful accomplishments
in science and writing.
with all our love,

Papa & Mama

THE
SEASHELL
ANTHOLOGY
OF GREAT
POETRY

THE SEASHELL ANTHOLOGY OF GREAT POETRY

EDITED BY
CHRISTOPHER BURNS

PARK LANE PRESS
New York • Avenel

For Julia, Chris, Morgan,
Maggie and Bronwyn

Since this page cannot legally accommodate all copyright notices,
pages 340–349 constitute an extension of this copyright page.

Copyright © 1996 by Christopher Burns
All rights reserved under International
and Pan–American Copyright Conventions.

A Glorya Hale Book
This 1996 edition is published by Park Lane Press,
a division of Random House Value Publishing, Inc.,
40 Engelhard Avenue, Avenel, New Jersey 07001.

Park Lane Press and its colophon are registered
trademarks of Random House Value Publishing, Inc.

Random House
New York • Toronto • London • Sydney • Auckland

Designed by Liz Trovato

Printed and bound in the United States of America

Library of Congress Cataloging–in–Publication Data
The Seashell anthology of great poetry /
edited by Christopher Burns.
p. cm.
Includes bibliographical references and index.
ISBN 0–517–20011–2
1. Poetry—Collections. I. Burns, Christopher.
PN6101.S44 1996
821'.9108—dc20   95–45461
CIP

8 7 6 5 4 3 2 1

TABLE OF CONTENTS

THE WAY THROUGH THE WOODS

MY PAPA'S WALTZ

INTRODUCTION

Great poetry is personal. Like a seashell held to your ear, a poem resonates to the beating of your heart. The poet brings the words, you bring your life, and together you make the song.

The stories told by great poems are familiar. Constructed from the culture and the symbols the writer and reader have in common, a poem can present a personal experience so truthfully that, as Robert Frost said, it is not read so much as it is "recognized." The account of life it offers can be so accurate that it becomes the reader's own, informing memory, extending vision, and clarifying thoughts. Emotions are given voice.

The language of great poetry, too, is familiar and inviting. All poems capture thought in a rhythmic narrative that is easy to remember, and to that extent poetry is little more than a device—a chant, a mantra, a prayer. But the rhythms employed in great poetry are more intimate; the studied stride of formal speech, the monotones of madness, the quiet sighing of despair, the blurting out of love. And through image, irony, and symbolism the message is structured to turn on the reader in suprise—like life itself. While the syntax may be as difficult to parse as a midnight thought, great poetry breaks through to a higher grammar of ideas and feelings. Let go of the rhyme and listen. Modern verse in particular speaks as we do, using the power of plain words, searing and unadorned.

Too often, though, critics try to understand a poem by holding it at arms' length as if it were a cultural specimen or a puzzle to be solved: Here the poet reveals her neurosis, they say. There the stain of his times shows through. They shine a light into the poet's eye: Exactly what did you *mean* by that? It does deepen the reader's understanding to know a little about the circumstances in which the poem was written. Friends often expect that kind of knowledge of each other. And it is sometimes necessary to enter into a poem's strangeness, however discomforting and difficult the lesson may be. Good friends, too, can be demanding and obscure. But great poetry should be held close. It is often your life and not the poet's that gives the language meaning. The great poems are usually about you.

My goal has been to create an anthology that reemphasizes the personal aspect of poetry, to gather poems that are relevant today, to organize them in a meaningful and

15

provocative way, and to present them in a small format so the book can be carried in a briefcase or chucked into the car's glove compartment.

Not included here are such long, great works as T. S. Eliot's "The Wasteland" and Samuel Taylor Coleridge's "The Rime of the Ancient Mariner." Other masterpieces, like Walt Whitman's "Song of Myself," are represented only by excerpts. A few poems have been chosen to serve as foils for others, and one selection by Dylan Thomas is not a poem at all, but an excerpt from a poetic short story. Included are many fine poems by Edna St. Vincent Millay and by Carl Sandburg, who have been inexplicably neglected in these post-modern times. But with such eccentricities acknowledged, the great poems are here.

Great poetry transcends the boundaries of time, gender, race, and ethnicity. Although there was no intention to be representative, half the poems were written by Americans and half by English, Irish, Welsh, Scottish, and Canadian poets. There are, too, translations from Middle English, Sanskrit, Russian, and Japanese. And this anthology is modern: a third of the poems were written in the last fifty years and a third were written between 1900 and 1945. The date given at the end of each poem is the date of first publication, unless an earlier date of composition is known.

The poems are arranged by subject. Great poems can be read this way. They transcend style; they speak beyond their time; given half a chance they sing together and in counterpoint. Mitchell Goodman and Denise Levertov, for example, were husband and wife, and their poems about the ache of marriage appear here side by side. Robert Frost and Edward Thomas were friends while Frost was living in England; their poems about the dark forest are here together. (Thomas died in the First World War, and Frost continued to be obsessed by this theme throughout his life.) Poets as diverse as Alfred, Lord Tennyson, Sara Teasdale, and Gary Snyder echo the themes and images of "Western Wind" hundred of years apart, as if it were a universal subtext to which everyone returns. Maya Angelou, Jane Flanders, and D. H. Lawrence, like talk-show guests sitting on stools, describe their mothers. Separated by more than a century, Robert Browning and Richard Wilbur talk about the way men look at women. Walt Whitman and Allen Ginsberg call back and forth to each other about the America they have found. And between the surreal rage of W. D. Snodgrass's "Examination" and W. H. Auden's "Unknown Citizen," Lewis Carroll's "The Walrus and the Carpenter" can be seen for the sad, cynical tale it is.

The poems follow the contours of life, the loneliness of the artist, the uses of war, the role of nature, the constancy of love, and the coming on of death. They are the singing of our tribe, called out from the heart across the noisy business of daily life. Read them in a generous spirit, prepared to hear your own heart roaring in your ear.

CHRISTOPHER BURNS

Edgartown, Massachusetts
1996

TO THE READER

As you read, a white bear leisurely
pees, dyeing the snow
saffron,

and as you read, many gods
lie among the lianas: eyes of obsidian
are watching the generations of leaves,

and as you read
the sea is turning its dark pages,
turning
its dark pages.

Denise Leverton   1961

THE
CREATION

THE CREATION

And God stepped out on space,
And he looked around and said:
I'm lonely—
I'll make me a world.

And far as the eye of God could see
Darkness covered everything,
Blacker than a hundred midnights
Down in a cypress swamp.

Then God smiled,
And the light broke,
And the darkness rolled up on one side,
And the light stood shining on the other,
And God said: That's good!

Then God reached out and took the light in his hand
And God rolled the light around in his hands
Until he made the sun;
And he set that sun a-blazing in the heavens.

And the light that was left from making the sun
God gathered it up in a shining ball
And flung it against the darkness,
Spangling the night with the moon and stars.
Then down between
The darkness and the light
He hurled the world;
And God said: That's good!

Then God himself stepped down—
And the sun was on his right hand,
And the moon was on his left;
The stars were clustered about his head,
And the earth was under his feet.
And God walked, and where he trod
His footsteps hollowed the valleys out
And bulged the mountains up.

Then he stopped and looked and saw
That the earth was hot and barren.
So God stepped over to the edge of the world
And he spat out the seven seas—

He batted his eyes, and the lightnings flashed—
He clapped his hands, and the thunders rolled—
And the waters above the earth came down,
The cooling waters came down.

Then the green grass
sprouted,
And the little red flowers blossomed,
The pine tree pointed his finger to the sky,
And the oak spread out his arms,
The lakes cuddled down in the hollows of the ground,
And the rivers ran down to the sea;
And God smiled again,
And the rainbow appeared,
And curled itself around his shoulder.

Then God raised his arm and he waved his hand
Over the sea and over the land,
And he said: Bring forth! Bring forth!

And quicker than God could drop his hand,
Fishes and fowls
And beasts and birds
Swam the rivers and the seas,
Roamed the forests and the woods,
And split the air with their wings.
And God said: That's good!
Then God walked around,
And God looked around
On all that he had made.
He looked at his sun,
And he looked at his moon,
And he looked at his little stars;
He looked on his world
With all its living things,
And God said: I'm lonely still.

Then God sat down—
On the side of a hill where he could think;
By a deep, wide river he sat down;
With his head in his hands,
God thought and thought,
Till he thought: I'll make me a man!

Up from the bed of the river
God scooped the clay;
And by the bank of the river
He kneeled him down;
And there the great God Almighty
Who lit the sun and fixed it in the sky,
Who flung the stars to the most far corner of the night,
Who rounded the earth in the middle of his hand;
This Great God,
Like a mammy bending over her baby,
Kneeled down in the dust
Toiling over a lump of clay
Till he shaped it in his own image;

Then into it he blew the breath of life,
And man became a living soul.
Amen. Amen.

James Weldon Johnson 1927

THEY ASK: IS GOD, TOO, LONELY?

When God scooped up a handful of dust,
And spit on it, and molded the shape of man,
And blew a breath into it and told it to walk—
That was a great day.

And did God do this because He was lonely?
Did God say to Himself he must have company
And therefore He would make man to walk the earth
And set apart churches for speech and song with God?

These are questions.
They are scrawled in old caves.
They are painted in tall cathedrals.
There are men and women so lonely they believe
    God, too, is lonely.

                              Carl Sandburg   1928

THE EARTH

God loafs around heaven,
without a shape
but He would like to smoke His cigar
or bite His fingernails
and so forth.

God owns heaven
but He craves the earth,
the earth with its little sleepy caves,
its bird resting at the kitchen window,
even its murders lined up like broken chairs,
even its writers digging into their souls
with jackhammers,
even its hucksters selling their animals
for gold,
even its babies sniffing for their music,
the farm house, white as a bone,
sitting in the lap of its corn,
even the statue holding up its widowed life,
even the ocean with its cupful of students,

but most of all He envies the bodies,
He who has no body.
The eyes, opening and shutting like keyholes
and never forgetting, recording by thousands,
the skull with its brains like eels—
the tablet of the world—
the bones and their joints
that build and the break for any trick,
the genitals,
the ballast of the eternal,
and the heart, of course,
that swallows the tides
and spits them out cleansed.

He does not envy the soul so much.
He is all soul
but He would like to house it in a body
and come down
and give it a bath
now and then.

Anne Sexton 1975

I DWELL IN POSSIBILITY

I dwell in possibility,
A fairer house than prose,
More numerous of windows—
Superior for doors.

Of chambers as the cedars,
Impregnable of eye
And for an everlasting roof
The gambrels of the sky.

Of visitors, the fairest
For occupation, this—
The spreading wide my narrow hands
To gather paradise.

Emily Dickinson 1862

SONG MAKING

My heart cried like a beaten child
   Ceaselessly all night long;
I had to take my own cries
   And thread them into a song.

One was a cry at black midnight
   And one when the first cock crew—
My heart was like a beaten child,
   But no one ever knew.

Life, you have put me in your debt
   And I must serve you long—
But oh, the debt is terrible
   That must be paid in song.

Sara Teasdale   1916

ONE'S-SELF I SING

One's-Self I sing, a simple separate person,
Yet utter the word Democratic, the word En-Masse.

Of physiology from top to toe I sing,
Not physiognomy alone nor brain alone is worthy for the Muse,
   I say the Form complete is worthier far,
The Female equally with the Male I sing.

Of Life immense in passion, pulse, and power,
Cheerful, for freest action formed under the laws divine,
The Modern Man I sing.

Walt Whitman   1871

GOD IS INDEED A JEALOUS GOD

God is indeed a jealous God
He cannot bear to see
That we had rather not with Him
But with each other play.

Emily Dickinson   c. 1864

YET DO I MARVEL

I doubt not God is good, well-meaning, kind,
And did He stoop to quibble could tell why
The little buried mole continues blind,
Why flesh that mirrors Him must some day die,
Make plain the reason tortured Tantalus
Is baited by the fickle fruit, declare
If merely brute caprice dooms Sisyphus
To struggle up a never-ending stair.
Inscrutable His ways are, and immune
To catechism by a mind too strewn
With petty cares to slightly understand
What awful brain compels His awful hand.
Yet do I marvel at this curious thing:
To make a poet black, and bid him sing!

Countee Cullen 1923

FOR BLACK POETS WHO THINK OF SUICIDE

Black Poets should live—not leap
From steel bridges (like the white boys do).

Black poets should *live*—not lay
Their necks on railroad tracks (like the white boys do).
Black poets should seek, but not search
Too much in sweet dark caves
Or hunt for snipes down psychic trails—
(Like the white boys do).

For Black Poets belong to Black People.
Are the flutes of Black Lovers—Are
The organs of Black Sorrows—Are
The trumpets of Black Warriors.
Let all Black Poets die as trumpets,
And be buried in the dust of marching feet.

Etheridge Knight 1966

CONSTANTLY RISKING ABSURDITY

Constantly risking absurdity
            and death
      whenever he performs
            above the heads
                  of his audience
      the poet like an acrobat
            climbs on rime
                  to a high wire of his own making
and balancing on eyebeams
                  above a sea of faces
            paces his way
                  to the other side of day
      performing *entrechats*
                  and slight-of-foot tricks
      and other high theatrics
                  and all without mistaking
            any thing
                  for what it may not be
      For he's the super realist
                  who must perforce perceive
         taut truth
                  before the taking of each stance or step
      in his supposed advance
                  toward that still higher perch
woman Beauty stands and waits
            with gravity
                  to start her death-defying leap
      And he
         a little charleychaplin man
                  who may or may not catch
      her fair eternal form
                  spreadeagled in the empty air
            of existence

Lawrence Ferlinghetti   1958

THE ARTIST

Mr. T.
    bareheaded
        in a soiled undershirt
his hair standing out
    on all sides
        stood on his toes
heels together
    arms gracefully
        for the moment
curled above his head.
    Then he whirled about
        bounded
into the air
    and with an *entrechat*
        perfectly achieved
completed the figure.
    My mother
        taken by surprise
where she sat
    in her invalid's chair
        was left speechless.
Bravo! she cried at last
    and clapped her hands.
        The man's wife
came from the kitchen:
    What goes on here? she said.
        But the show was over.

William Carlos Williams   1954

ARS POETICA

A poem should be palpable and mute
As a globed fruit,

Dumb
As old medallions to the thumb,

Silent as the sleeve-worn stone
Of casement ledges where the moss has grown—

A poem should be wordless
As the flight of birds.

           •

A poem should be motionless in time
As the moon climbs,

Leaving, as the moon releases
Twig by twig the night-entangled trees,

Leaving, as the moon behind the winter leaves,
Memory by memory the mind—

A poem should be motionless in time
As the moon climbs.

           •

A poem should be equal to:
Not true.

For all the history of grief
An empty doorway and a maple leaf.

For love
The leaning grasses and two lights above the sea—

A poem should not mean
But be.

Archibald MacLeish   1926

POETRY

Poetry is any page from a sketchbook of outlines of a
  doorknob with thumb prints of dust, blood, dreams.

Poetry is the establishment of a metaphorical link between
  white butterfly wings and the scraps of torn-up love letters.

Poetry is the achievement of the synthesis of hyacinths and
  biscuits.

Carl Sandburg   1928

PRAYERS OF STEEL

Lay me on an anvil, O God.
Beat me and hammer me into a crowbar.
Let me pry loose old walls.
Let me lift and loosen old foundations.

Lay me on an anvil, O God.
Beat me and hammer me into a steel spike.
Drive me into the girders that hold a skyscraper together.
Take red-hot rivets and fasten me into the central girders.
Let me be the great nail holding a skyscraper through blue
  nights into white stars.

Carl Sandburg   1918

HOW POETRY COMES TO ME

It comes blundering over the
Boulders at night, it stays
Frightened outside the
Range of my campfire
I go to meet it at the
Edge of the light

Gary Snyder   1992

DIGGING

Between my finger and my thumb
The squat pen rests; snug as a gun.

Under my windows, a clean rasping sound
When the spade sinks into the gravelly ground:
My father, digging. I look down

Till his straining rump among the flowerbeds
Bends low, comes up twenty years away
Stooping in rhythm through potato drills
Where he was digging.

The coarse boot nestled on the lug, the shaft
Against the inside knee was levered firmly.
He rooted out tall tops, buried the bright edge deep
To scatter new potatoes that we picked
Loving their cool hardness in our hands.

By God, the old man could handle a spade.
Just like his old man.

My grandfather cut more turf in a day
Than any other man on Toner's bog.
Once I carried him milk in a bottle
Corked sloppily with paper. He straightened up
To drink it, then fell to right away

Nicking and slicing neatly, heaving sods
Over his shoulder, going down and down
For the good turf. Digging.

The cold smell of potato mold, the squelch and slap
Of soggy peat, the curt cuts of an edge
Through living roots awaken in my head.
But I've no spade to follow men like them.

Between my finger and my thumb
The squat pen rests.
I'll dig with it.

Seamus Heaney   1966

PARADOXES AND OXYMORONS

This poem is concerned with language on a very plain level.
Look at it talking to you. You look out a window
Or pretend to fidget. You have it but you don't have it.
You miss it, it misses you. You miss each other.

The poem is sad because it wants to be yours, and cannot.
What's a plain level? It is that and other things,
Bringing a system of them into play. Play?
Well, actually, yes, but I consider play to be

A deeper outside thing, a dreamed role-pattern,
As in the division of grace these long August days
Without proof. Open-ended. And before you know
It gets lost in the steam and chatter of typewriters.

It has been played once more. I think you exist only
To tease me into doing it, on your level, and then you
    aren't there
Or have adopted a different attitude. And the poem
Has set me softly down beside you. The poem is you.

John Ashbery 1981

CODA

O my songs,
Why do you look so eagerly and so curiously into
    people's faces,
Will you find your lost dead among them?

Ezra Pound 1915

EPILOGUE

Those blessèd structures, plot and rhyme—
why are they no help to me now
I want to make
something imagined, not recalled?
I hear the noise of my own voice:
The painter's vision is not a lens,
it trembles to caress the light.
But sometimes everything I write
with the threadbare art of my eye
seems a snapshot,
lurid, rapid, garish, grouped,
heightened from life,
yet paralyzed by fact.
All's misalliance.
Yet why not say what happened?
Pray for the grace of accuracy
Vermeer gave to the sun's illumination
stealing like the tide across a map
to his girl solid with yearning.
We are poor passing facts,
warned by that to give
each figure in the photograph
his living name.

Robert Lowell   1977

FOR MY PEOPLE

I HEAR AMERICA SINGING

I hear America singing, the varied carols I hear,
Those of the mechanics, each one singing his as it should
    be blithe and strong,
The carpenter singing his as he measures his plank or beam,
The mason singing his as he makes ready for work,
    or leaves off work,
The boatman singing what belongs to him in his boat, the
    deck hand singing on the steamboat deck,
The shoemaker singing as he sits on his bench, the hatter
    singing as he stands,
The wood-cutter's song, the ploughboy's on his way in the
    morning, or at noon intermission or at sundown,
The delicious singing of the mother, or the young wife at work,
    or the girl sewing or washing,
Each singing what belongs to him or her and to none else,
The day what belongs to the day—at night the party of young
    fellows, robust, friendly,
Singing with open mouths their strong melodious songs.

Walt Whitman   1860

FROM "SONG OF MYSELF"

I celebrate myself, and sing myself,
And what I assume you shall assume,
For every atom belonging to me as good belongs to you.

I loaf and invite my soul,
I lean and loaf at my ease observing a spear of summer grass.

My tongue, every atom of my blood, formed from this soil,
     this air,
Born here of parents born here from parents the same, and
     their parents the same,
I, now thirty-seven years old in perfect health, begin,
Hoping to cease not till death . . .

Have you felt so proud to get at the meaning of poems?
Stop this day and night with me and you shall possess the
     origin of all poems,
You shall possess the good of the earth and sun (there are
     millions of suns left)
You shall no longer take things at second or third hand, nor
     look through the eyes of the dead, nor feed on the specters
     in books.
You shall not look through my eyes either, nor take things
from me:
You shall listen to all sides and filter them from your self . . .

Undrape! you are not guilty to me, nor stale nor discarded,
I see through the broadcloth and gingham whether or no,
And am around, tenacious, acquisitive, tireless, and cannot be
     shaken away . . .

Walt Whitman, a kosmos, of Manhattan the son,
Turbulent, fleshy, sensual, eating, drinking and breeding,
No sentimentalist, no stander above men and women or apart
     from them,
No more modest than immodest . . .

Whoever degrades another degrades me,
And whatever is done or said returns at last to me.

Through me the afflatus surging and surging, through me the
     current and index.

I speak the password primeval, I give the sign of democracy,
By God! I will accept nothing which all cannot have their
    counterpart of on the same terms.

Through me many long dumb voices,
Voices of the interminable generations of prisoners and slaves,
Voices of the diseased and despairing and of thieves
    and dwarfs,
Voices of cycles and preparation and accretion,
And of the threads that connect the stars, and of wombs and
    of the father-stuff,
And of the rights of them the others are down upon,
Of the deformed, trivial, flat, foolish, despised,
Fog in the air, beetles rolling balls of dung.

Through me forbidden voices,
Voices of sexes and lusts, voices veiled and I remove the veil,
Voices indecent by me clarified and transfigured.

I do not press my fingers across my mouth,
I keep as delicate around the bowels as around the head
    and heart,
Copulation is no more rank to me than death is.

I believe in the flesh and the appetites,
Seeing, hearing, feeling, are miracles, and each part and tag of
    me is a miracle.

Divine I am inside and out, and I make holy whatever I touch
    or am touched from,
The scent of these armpits—aroma finer than prayer,
This head more than churches, bibles and all the creeds . . .

I dote on myself, there is a lot of me and all so luscious,
Each moment and whatever happens thrills me with joy,
I cannot tell how my ankles bend, nor whence the cause of my
    faintest wish,
Nor the cause of the friendship I emit, nor the cause of the
    friendship I take again.
That I walk up my stoop, I pause to consider if it really be,
A morning-glory at my window satisfies more than the
    metaphysics of books . . .

I understand the large hearts of heroes,
The courage of present times and all times,
How the skipper saw the crowded and rudderless wreck of the
    steamship, and Death chasing it up and down the storm,
How he knuckled tight and gave not back an inch and was
    faithful of days and faithful of nights,
And chalked in large letters on a board, *"Be of good cheer,
    we will not desert you."*

How he followed with them and tacked with them three days
    and would not give it up,
How he saved the drifting company at last,
How the lanked loose-gowned women leeked when boated
    from the side of their prepared graves,
How the silent old-faced infants and the lifted sick, and the
    sharp-lipped unshaven men;
All this I swallow, it tastes good, I like it well, it becomes mine.
I am the man, I suffered, I was there.

The disdain and calmness of martyrs,
The mother of old, condemned for a witch, burnt with dry
    wood, her children gazing on,
The hounded slave that flags in the race, leans by the fence,
    blowing, covered with sweat,
The twinges that sting like needles his legs and neck, the
    murderous buckshot and the bullets,
All these I feel or am . . .

Behold, I do not give lectures or a little charity,
When I give I give myself.

You there, impotent, loose in the knees,
Open your scarfed chops till I blow grit within you,
Spread your palms and lift the flaps of your pockets,
I am not to be denied, I compel, I have stores plenty
    and to spare,
And any thing I have I bestow.

I do not ask who you are, that is not important to me,
You can do nothing and be nothing but what I will infold you.

The spotted hawk swoops by and accuses me, he
    complains of my gab and my loitering.

I too am not a bit tamed, I too am untranslatable:
I sound my barbaric yawp over the roofs of the world.
The last scud of day holds back for me,
It flings my likeness over the rest and true as any on the
    shadowed wilds,
It coaxes me to the vapor and the dusk.

I depart as air, I shake my white locks at the runaway sun,
I effuse my flesh in eddies, and drift it in lacy jags.

I bequeath myself to the dirt to grow from the grass I love,
If you want me again look for me under your boot-soles.

You will hardly know who I am or what I mean,
But I shall be good health to you nevertheless,
And filter and fiber your blood.

Failing to fetch me at first keep encouraged,
Missing me one place search another,
I stop somewhere waiting for you.

Walt Whitman 1855

NEXT TO OF COURSE GOD AMERICA I

"next to of course god america i
love you land of the pilgrims' and so forth oh
say can you see by the dawn's early my
country 'tis of centuries come and go
and are no more what of it we should worry
in every language even deafanddumb
thy sons acclaim your glorious name by gorry
by jingo by gee by gosh by gum
why talk of beauty what could be more beautiful than these heroic happy dead
who rushed like lions to the roaring slaughter
they did not stop to think they died instead
then shall the voice of liberty be mute?"

He spoke. And drank rapidly a glass of water

e. e. cummings 1926

A SUPERMARKET IN CALIFORNIA

What thoughts I have of you tonight, Walt Whitman, for I
    walked down the sidestreets under the trees with
    a headache self-conscious looking at the full moon.
In my hungry fatigue, and shopping for images, I went into
    the neon fruit supermarket, dreaming of your enumerations!
What peaches and what penumbras! Whole families shopping
    at night! Aisles full of husbands! Wives in the avocados,
    babies in the tomatoes!—and you, Garciá Lorca, what were
    you doing down by the watermelons?

I saw you, Walt Whitman, childless, lonely old grubber, poking
    among the meats in the refrigerator and eyeing the grocery
    boys.
I heard you asking questions of each: Who killed the pork
    chops? What price bananas? Are you my Angel?

I wandered in and out of the brilliant stacks of cans following you,
    and followed in my imagination by the store detective.
We strode down the open corridors together in our solitary fancy
    tasting artichokes, possessing every frozen delicacy, and never
    passing the cashier.

Where are we going, Walt Whitman? The doors close in an hour.
    Which way does your beard point tonight?
(I touch your book and dream of our odyssey in the supermarket
    and feel absurd.)
Will we walk all night through solitary streets? The trees add
    shade to shade, lights out in the houses, we'll both be lonely.
Will we stroll dreaming of the lost America of love past blue
    automobiles in driveways, home to our silent cottage?
Ah, dear father, graybeard, lonely old courage-teacher, what America
    did you have when Charon quit poling his ferry and you got out on
    a smoking bank and stood watching the boat disappear on the
    black waters of Lethe?

Allen Ginsberg   1955

THE NEW COLOSSUS

Not like the brazen giant of Greek fame,
With conquering limbs astride from land to land;
Here at our sea-washed, sunset gates shall stand
A mighty woman with a torch, whose flame
Is the imprisoned lightning, and her name
Mother of Exiles. From her beacon-hand
Glows world-wide welcome; her mild eyes command
The air-bridged harbor that twin cities frame.
"Keep, ancient lands, your storied pomp!" cries she
With silent lips. "Give me your tired, your poor,
Your huddled masses yearning to breathe free,
The wretched refuse of your teeming shore.
Send these, the homeless, tempest-tost to me,
I lift my lamp beside the golden door!"

Emma Lazarus   1886

LET OTHER PEOPLE COME AS STREAMS

Let other people come as streams
that overflow a valley
and leave dead bodies, uprooted trees and fields of sand;
we Jews are as the dew,
on every blade of grass,
trodden under foot today
and here tomorrow morning.

Charles Reznikoff   1936

I WILL WRITE SONGS AGAINST YOU

I will write songs against you,
enemies of my people; I will pelt you
with the winged seeds of the dandelion;
I will marshall against you
the fireflies of the dusk.

Charles Reznikoff   1936

FROM "THE PEOPLE, YES"

The people will live on.
The learning and blundering people will live on.
They will be tricked and sold and again sold
And go back to the nourishing earth for rootholds,
The people so peculiar in renewal and comeback,
You can't laugh off their capacity to take it.
The mammoth rests between his cyclonic dramas.

The people so often sleepy, weary, enigmatic,
is a vast huddle with many units saying:
"I earn my living.
I make enough to get by
and it takes all my time.
If I had more time
I could do more for myself
and maybe for others.
I could read and study
and talk things over
and find out about things.
It takes time.
I wish I had the time."
The people is a tragic and comic two-face:
hero and hoodlum: phantom and gorilla twisting to moan with a gargoyle mouth: "They
buy me and sell me . . . it's a game . . .
sometime I'll break loose . . ."

Between the finite limitations of the five senses
and the endless yearnings of man for the beyond
the people hold to the humdrum bidding of work and food
while reaching out when it comes their way
for lights beyond the prisms of the five senses,
for keepsakes lasting beyond any hunger or death.
This reaching is alive.
The panderers and liars have violated and smutted it.
Yet this reaching is alive yet
for lights and keepsakes.
The people know the salt of the sea
and the strength of the winds

lashing the corners of the earth.
The people take the earth
as a tomb of rest and a cradle of hope.
Who else speaks for the Family of Man?
They are in tune and step
with constellations of universal law.

The people is a polychrome,
a spectrum and a prism
held in a moving monolith,
a console organ of changing themes,
a clavilux of color poems
wherein the sea offers fog
and the fog moves off in rain
and the labrador sunset shortens
to a nocturne of clear stars
serene over the shot spray
of northern lights.

The steel mill sky is alive.
The fire breaks white and zigzag
shot on a gun-metal gloaming.
Man is a long time coming.
Man will yet win.
Brother may yet line up with brother:

This old anvil laughs at many broken hammers.
    There are men who can't be bought.
    The fireborn are at home in fire.
    The stars make no noise.
    You can't hinder the wind from blowing.
    Time is a great teacher.
    Who can live without hope?

In the darkness with a great bundle of grief
    the people march.
In the night, and overhead a shovel of stars for keeps,
    the people march:
        "Where to? what next?"

Carl Sandburg   1936

FOR MY PEOPLE

For my people everywhere singing their slave songs
    repeatedly: their dirges and their ditties and their
    blues and
    jubilees, praying their prayers nightly to an unknown god,
    bending their knees humbly to an unseen power;
For my people lending their strength to the years:
    to the gone
    years and the now years and the maybe years, washing
    ironing cooking scrubbing sewing mending hoeing plowing
    digging planting pruning patching dragging along never
    gaining never reaping never knowing and never
    understanding;
For my playmates in the clay and dust and sand of Alabama
    backyards playing baptizing and preaching, and doctor
    and
    jail and soldier and school and mama and cooking and
    playhouse and concert and store and hair and Miss Choomby
    and company;
For the cramped bewildered years we went to school to learn to
    know the reasons why and the answers to and the people
    who and the places where and the days when, in memory of
    the bitter hours when we discovered we were black and poor
    and small and different and nobody wondered and nobody
    understood;
For the boys and girls who grew in spite of these things to be
    Man and Woman, to laugh and dance and sing and play and
    drink their wine and religion and success, to marry their
    playmates and bear children and then die of consumption
    and anemia and lynching;
For my people thronging 47th Street in Chicago and
    Lenox Avenue in New York and Rampart Street
    in New Orleans,
    lost disinherited dispossessed and HAPPY people filling the
    cabarets and taverns and other people's pockets needing
    bread and shoes and milk and land and money and
    Something—
    Something all our own;
For my people walking blindly spreading joy, losing
    time being
    lazy, sleeping when hungry, shouting when burdened,
    drinking when hopeless, tied and shackled and tangled
    among ourselves by the unseen creatures who tower over us
    omnisciently and laugh;

For my people blundering and groping and floundering in the
dark of churches and schools and clubs and societies,
associations and councils and committees and conventions,
distressed and disturbed and deceived and devoured by
money-hungry glory-craving leeches, preyed on by facile
force of state and fad and novelty by false prophet and holy
believer;
For my people standing staring trying to fashion a better way
from confusion from hypocrisy and misunderstanding, trying
to fashion a world that will hold all the people, all the faces
all the adams and eves and their countless generations;
Let a new earth rise. Let another world be born. Let a bloody
peace be written in the sky. Let a second generation full of
courage issue forth; let a people loving freedom come to
growth. Let a beauty full of healing and a strength of final
clenching be the pulsing in our spirits and our blood.
Let the
martial songs be written, let the dirges disappear. Let a race
of men now rise and take control!

Margaret Walker 1942

I, TOO, SING AMERICA

I, too, sing America.

I am the darker brother.
They send me to eat in the kitchen
When company comes,
But I laugh,
And eat well,
And grow strong.

Tomorrow,
I'll sit at the table
When company comes.
Nobody'll dare
Say to me,
"Eat in the kitchen,"
Then.

Besides,
They'll see how beautiful I am
And be ashamed—

I, too, am America.

Langston Hughes 1926

NIGHT FUNERAL IN HARLEM

Night funeral
in Harlem:

Where did they get
Them two fine cars?

Insurance man, he did not pay—
His insurance lapsed the other day—
Yet they got a satin box
For his head to lay.

Night funeral
in Harlem:

Who was it sent
That wreath of flowers?

Them flowers came
from that poor boy's friends—
They'll want flowers, too,
When they meet their ends.

Night funeral
in Harlem:

Who preached that
Black boy to his grave?

Old preacher-man
Preached that boy away—
Charged Five Dollars
His girl friend had to pay.

Night funeral
in Harlem:

When it was all over
And the lid shut on his head
and the organ had done played
and the last prayers been said
and six pallbearers
Carried him out for dead

And off down Lenox Avenue
That long black hearse done sped,
     The street light
     At his corner
     Shined just like a tear—
That boy that they was mournin'
Was so dear, so dear
To them folks that brought the flowers,
To that girl who paid the preacher-man—
It was all their tears that made
     That poor boy's
     Funeral grand.

     Night funeral
     in Harlem.

Langston Hughes   1951

THE FIREBOMBERS

     We are America.
     We are the coffin fillers.
     We are the grocers of death.
     We pack them in crates like cauliflowers.

     The bomb opens like a shoebox.
     And the child?
     The child is certainly not yawning.
     And the woman?
     The woman is bathing her heart.
     It has been torn out of her
     and because it is burnt
     and as a last act
     she is rinsing it off in the river.
     This is the death market.

     America,
     where are your credentials?

Anne Sexton   1972

FROM "HOWL"

I saw the best minds of my generation destroyed by madness, starving
   hysterical naked,

dragging themselves through the negro streets at dawn looking for an
   angry fix,

angelheaded hipsters burning for the ancient heavenly connection to
   the starry dynamo in the machinery of night,

who poverty and tatters and hollow-eyed and high sat up smoking in
   the supernatural darkness of cold-water flats floating across the tops
   of cities contemplating jazz,

who bared their brains to Heaven under the El and saw Mohammedan
   angels staggering to tenement roofs illuminated,

who passed through universities with radiant cool eyes hallucinating
   Arkansas and Blake-light tragedy among the scholars of war,

who were expelled from the academies for crazy & publishing obscene
   odes on the windows of the skull,

who cowered in unshaven rooms in underwear, burning their money in
   wastebaskets and listening to the Terror through the wall . . .

who cut their wrists three times successively unsuccessfully, gave up
   and were forced to open antique stores where they thought they
   were growing old and cried,

who were burned alive in their innocent flannel suits on Madison
   Avenue amid blasts of leaden verse & the tanked-up clatter of the
   iron regiments of fashion & the nitroglycerine shrieks of the fairies of
   advertising & the mustard gas of sinister intelligent editors, or were
   run down by the drunken taxicabs of Absolute Reality,

who jumped off the Brooklyn Bridge   this actually happened   and
   walked away unknown and forgotten into the ghostly daze of
   Chinatown soup alleyways & firetrucks, not even one free beer,

who sang out their windows in despair, fell out of the subway window,
   jumped in the filthy Passaic, leaped on negroes, cried all over the
   street, danced on broken wineglasses barefoot smashed phonograph
   records of nostalgic European 1930's German jazz finished the
   whiskey and threw up groaning into the bloody toilet, moans in
   their ears and the blast of colossal steamwhistles,

who barreled down the highways of the past journeying to each other's
   hotrod Golgotha jail-solitude watch or Birmingham jazz incarnation,

who drove crosscountry seventy two hours to find out if I had a vision
   or you had a vision or he had a vision to find out Eternity,

who journeyed to Denver, who died in Denver, who came back to
    Denver & waited in vain, who watched over Denver & brooded &
    loned in Denver and finally went away to find out the Time, & now
    Denver is lonesome for her heroes,
who fell on their knees in hopeless cathedrals praying for each other's
    salvation and light and breasts, until the soul illuminated its hair for
    a second,
who crashed through their minds in jail waiting for impossible criminals
    with golden heads and the charm of reality in their hearts who sang
    sweet blues to Alcatraz,
who retired to Mexico to cultivate a habit, or Rocky Mount to tender
    Buddha or Tangiers to boys or Southern Pacific to the black
    locomotive or Harvard to Narcissus to Woodlawn to the daisychain
    or grave,
who demanded sanity trials accusing the radio of hypnotism & were left
    with their insanity & their hands & a hung jury,
who threw potato salad at CCNY lecturers on Dadaism and
    subsequently presented themselves on the granite steps of the
    madhouse with shaven heads and harlequin speech of suicide,
    demanding instantaneous lobotomy,
and who were given instead the concrete void of insulin metrasol
    electricity hydrotherapy psychotherapy occupational therapy
    pingpong & amnesia . . .
who dreamt and made incarnate gaps in Time & Space through images
    juxtaposed, and trapped the archangel of the soul between 2 visual
    images and joined the elemental verbs and set the noun and dash of
    consciousness together jumping with sensation of Pater Omnipotens
    Aeterna Deus
to recreate the syntax and poor measure of human prose and stand
    before you speechless and intelligent and shaking with shame,
    rejected yet confessing out the soul to conform to the rhythm of
    thought in his naked and endless head,
the madman bum and angel beat in Time, unknown, yet putting down
    here what might be left to say in time come after death,
and rose reincarnate in the ghostly clothes of jazz in the goldhorn
    shadow of the band and blew the suffering of America's naked mind
    for love into an eli eli lamma lamma sabacthani saxophone cry that
    shivered the cities down to the last radio
with the absolute heart of the poem of life butchered out of their own
    bodies good to eat a thousand years.

Allen Ginsberg   1955

AUTUMN BEGINS IN MARTINS FERRY, OHIO

In the Shreve High football stadium,
I think of Polacks nursing long beers in Tiltonsville,
And gray faces of Negroes in the blast furnace at Benwood,
And the ruptured night watchman of Wheeling Steel,
Dreaming of heroes.

All the proud fathers are ashamed to go home.
Their women cluck like starved pullets,
Dying for love.

Therefore,
Their sons grow suicidally beautiful
At the beginning of October,
And gallop terribly against each other's bodies.

James Wright   1962

LIMITED

I am riding on a limited express, one of the crack trains
    of the nation.
Hurtling across the prairie into blue haze and dark air go fifteen
    all-steel coaches holding a thousand people.
All the coaches shall be scrap and rust and all the men and
    women laughing in the diners and sleepers shall pass
    to ashes.
I ask a man in the smoker where he is going and he answers:
    "Omaha."

Carl Sandburg   1916

CHICAGO

Hog Butcher for the World,
Tool Maker, Stacker of Wheat,
Player with Railroads and the Nation's Freight Handler;
Stormy, husky, brawling,
City of the Big Shoulders:

They tell me you are wicked and I believe them, for I have seen your
painted women under the gas lamps luring the farm boys.
And they tell me you are crooked and I answer: Yes, it is true I have
seen the gunman kill and go free to kill again.
And they tell me you are brutal and my reply is: On the faces of
women and children I have seen the marks of wanton hunger.
And having answered so I turn once more to those who sneer at this
my city, and I give them back the sneer and say to them:
Come and show me another city with lifted head singing so proud to
be alive and coarse and strong and cunning.
Flinging magnetic curses amid the toil of piling job on job, here is a
tall bold slugger set vivid against the little soft cities;
Fierce as a dog with tongue lapping for action, cunning as a savage
pitted against the wilderness,
Bareheaded,
Shoveling,
Wrecking,
Planning,
Building, breaking, rebuilding,
Under the smoke, dust all over his mouth, laughing with white teeth,
Under the terrible burden of destiny laughing as a young man laughs,
Laughing even as an ignorant fighter laughs who has never lost a battle,
Bragging and laughing that under his wrist is the pulse, and under his ribs
the heart of the people,
Laughing!
Laughing the stormy, husky, brawling laughter of Youth, half-naked,
sweating, proud to be Hog Butcher, Tool Maker, Stacker of Wheat,
Player with Railroads and Freight Handler to the Nation.

Carl Sandburg   1916

JAZZ FANTASIA

Drum on your drums, batter on your banjoes,
sob on the long cool winding saxophones.
Go to it, O jazzmen.

Sling your knuckles on the bottoms of the happy
tin pans, let your trombones ooze, and go husha-
husha-hush with the slippery sand-paper.

Moan like an autumn wind high in the lonesome treetops,
    moan soft like you wanted somebody terrible, cry like a
    racing car slipping away from a motorcycle cop, bang-bang!
    you jazzmen, bang altogether drums, traps, banjoes, horns,
    tin cans—make two people fight on the top of a stairway
    and scratch each other's eyes in a clinch tumbling
    down the stairs.

Can the rough stuff . . . now a Mississippi steamboat pushes
    up the night river with a hoo-hoo-hoo-oo . . . and the green
    lanterns calling to the high soft stars . . . a red moon rides
    on the humps of the low river hills . . . go to it, O jazzmen.

Carl Sandburg   1920

THE DANCE

In Breughel's great picture, The Kermess,
the dancers go round, they go round and
around, the squeal and the blare and the
tweedle of bagpipes, a bugle and fiddles
tipping their bellies (round as the thick-
sided glasses whose wash they impound)
their hips and their bellies off balance
to turn them. Kicking and rolling about
the Fair Grounds, swinging their butts, those
shanks must be sound to bear up under such
rollicking measures, prance as they dance
in Breughel's great picture, The Kermess.

William Carlos Williams   1944

NIGHT JOURNEY

Now as the train bears west,
Its rhythm rocks the earth,
And from my Pullman berth
I stare into the night
While others take their rest.
Bridges of iron lace,
A suddenness of trees,
A lap of mountain mist
All cross my line of sight,
Then a bleak wasted place,
And a lake below my knees.
Full on my neck I feel
The straining at a curve;
My muscles move with steel,
I wake in every nerve.
I watch a beacon swing
From dark to blazing bright;
We thunder through ravines
And gullies washed with light.
Beyond the mountain pass
Mist deepens on the pane;
We rush into a rain
That rattles double glass.
Wheels shake the roadbed stone,
The pistons jerk and shove,
I stay up half the night
To see the land I love.

Theodore Roethke   1940

NEW MEXICAN MOUNTAIN

I watch the Indians dancing to help the young corn at Taos
    pueblo. The old men squat in a ring
And make the song, the young women with fat bare arms,
    and a few shame-faced young men, shuffle the dance.

The lean-muscled young men are naked to the narrow loins,
    their breasts and backs daubed with white clay,
Two eagle-feathers plume the black heads. They dance with
    reluctance, they are growing civilized; the old men
    persuade them.

Only the drum is confident, it thinks the world has not
    changed; the beating heart, the simplest of rhythms,
It thinks the world has not changed at all; it is only a dreamer,
    a brainless heart, the drum has no eyes.

These tourists have eyes, the hundred watching the dance,
    white Americans, hungrily too, with reverence, not laughter;
Pilgrims from civilization, anxiously seeking beauty, religion,
    poetry; pilgrims from the vacuum.

People from cities, anxious to be human again. Poor show how
    they suck you empty! The Indians are emptied,
And certainly there was never religion enough, nor beauty nor
    poetry here . . . to fill Americans.

Only the drum is confident, it thinks the world has not
    changed. Apparently only myself and the strong
Tribal drum, and the rockhead of Taos mountain, remember
    that civilization is a transient sickness.

Robinson Jeffers   1932

MILTON BY FIRELIGHT

"O Hell, what do mine eyes
     with grief behold?"
Working with an old
Singlejack miner, who can sense
The vein and cleavage
In the very guts of rock, can
Blast granite, build
Switchbacks that last for years
Under the beat of snow, thaw, mule-hooves.
What use, Milton, a silly story
Of our lost general parents,
          eaters of fruit?

The Indian, the chainsaw boy,
And a string of six mules
Came riding down to camp
Hungry for tomatoes and green apples.
Sleeping in saddle-blankets
Under a bright night-sky
Han River slantwise by morning.
Jays squall
Coffee boils

In ten thousand years the Sierras
Will be dry and dead, home of the scorpion.
Ice-scratched slabs and bent trees.
No paradise, no fall,
Only the weathering land
The wheeling sky,
Man, with his Satan
Scouring the chaos of the mind.
Oh Hell!

Fire down
Too dark to read, miles from a road
The bell-mare clangs in the meadow
That packed dirt for a fill-in
Scrambling through loose rocks
On an old trail
All of a summer's day.

Gary Snyder   1966

HIGH FLIGHT

Oh! I have slipped the surly bonds of earth
And danced the skies on laughter-silvered wings;
Sunward I've climbed, and joined the tumbling mirth
Of sun-split clouds—and done a hundred things
You have not dreamed of—wheeled and soared and swung
High in the sunlit silence. Hov'ring there
I've chased the shouting wind along, and flung
My eager craft through footless halls of air.

Up, up the long delirious, burning blue
I've topped the wind-swept heights with easy grace,
Where never lark, nor even eagle flew—
And, while with silent lifting mind I've trod
The high, untrespassed sanctity of space,
Put out my hand and touched the face of God.

John Gillespie Magee   1941

THE
HIGHWAYMAN

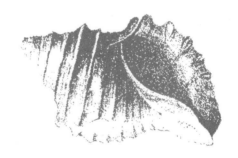

JACK

Jack was a swarthy, swaggering son-of-a-gun.
He worked thirty years on the railroad, ten hours a day,
    and his hands were tougher than sole leather.
He married a tough woman and they had eight children and
    the woman died and the children grew up and went away
    and wrote the old man every two years.
He died in the poorhouse sitting on a bench in the sun telling
    reminiscences to other old men whose women were dead
    and children scattered.
There was joy on his face when he died as there was joy on his
    face when he lived—he was a swarthy, swaggering
    son-of-a-gun.

Carl Sandburg   1916

THE CANTERBURY TALES

GENERAL PROLOGUE

Whan that Aprill with his shoures soote
The droghte of March hath perced to the roote,
And bathed every veyne in swich licour
Of which vertu engendred is the flour;
Whan Zephirus eek with his sweete breeth
Inspired hath in every holt and heeth
The tendre croppes, and the yonge sonne
Hath in the Ram his half cours yronne,
And smale foweles maken melodye,
That slepen al the nyght with open ye
(So priketh hem nature in hir corages),
Thanne longen folk to goon on pilgrimages,
And palmeres for to seken straunge strondes,
To ferne halwes, kowthe in sondry londes;
And specially from every shires ende
Of Engelond to Caunterbury they wende,
The hooly blisful martir for to seke,
That hem hath holpen whan that they were seeke.

When April with its showers sweet
The drought of March hath pierced unto the root
And bathed every vein in such liquor
Of which engendered is the flower;
When Zephyr too hath with his own sweet breath
Inspired in every farm and heath
The tender crops, and the young sun
Hath in the Ram his half course run,
And small birds are making melody
That slept all night with open eye
(So does nature prick their courage up),
Folks then long to go on pilgrimages,
And palmers to seek strange shores,
To distant shrines, known in sundry lands;
And specially from every shire's end
Of England, to Canterbury they wend,
The holy blissful Martyr for to seek,
Who helped them once when they were weak.

THE WIFE OF BATH

A good wife there was from Bath.
Who suffered a slight deafness, which was sad.
At weaving, though, she had a skill
Surpassing those in Ypres and in Ghent.
Nor in all the parish was there a wife
Who to the Offering ahead of her dared go
And if one did, her certain wrath was enough
To cancel any thought of charity.
Her scarves were of the finest weave around,
I dare say they weighed a full ten pound,
That on a Sunday were upon her head.
Her stockings were fine scarlet red,
And shoes, well laced, were soft and new.
Bold was her face, and fair, and red of hue.
She was a worthy woman all her life:
Of husbands married in the church she owned to five,
Not counting the companions of her youth—
But that's another story.
Three times had she been to Jerusalem
And passed over many a strange stream.
To Rome she'd gone, and to Boulogne,
To Spain, to Santiago, and Cologne.
And she knew much of wandering on the way.
Gap-toothed she was, to tell the truth.
Upon an ambler easily she sat,
Well wimpled, aye, and on her head a hat
Broad as is a buckler or a jouster's shield;
With a great rug wrapped round her large hips,
And on her feet a pair of sharp spurs.
Ready to laugh with friends, and gossip, too.
She understood the remedies of love,
And knew its ancient dance.

THE MONK

A Monk there was, fair masterly,
An overseer who loved venery,
A manly man, to be an abbot able.
With many a fine horse in his own stable
And when he rode, men could his bridle hear
Jingling in the whistling wind as clear
And, aye, as loud as the chapel bell
Where the Monk was lord and keeper of the cell.
The rule of St. Maurus or St. Benedict—
Because it was old and somewhat strict
This Monk let, with other old things, pass
Following instead the new world ways.
He cared for that text not a plucked hen
Which said that hunters could not be holy men,
Or that a monk without rules
Is like a fish without water—
Or one might say, a monk out of his cloister.
But for all this text he cared not an oyster;
As I said, his opinions were strong.
Why should he study and make himself sore
Over a book in a cloister, always to pour
Or work with his hands, and labor
As St. Augustine bid? How would the world be served?
Let Augustine have his sweaty way preserved!
Instead, he would rather be a hunter bright:
Greyhounds he had, swift as birds in flight;
Tracking and hunting for the hare
Was all his pleasure, and no cost would he spare.
I saw his sleeves were purfled at the hand
With gray fur, the finest in the land.
To fasten the hood beneath his chin,
He had of well-wrought gold a curious pin,
And at the end of the chord there was a love-knot.
His head was bald, and shone like any glass,
And smooth was his face, as bright as polished brass.
He was a fine fat lord and in good prime;

His eyes bulged out, rolling in his head
And blazing like a fire in the furnace.
His boots were supple, his horse of great estate.
Now certainly he was a fair prelate.
He was not pale like some poor tormented ghost.
A fat swan loved he best of any roast.
His palfrey was as brown as a berry.

THE CLERK

A clerk there was of Oxford, too,
Who hearkened unto logic long ago.
His horse was as lean as a rake,
And he was not too fat, I undertake,
But had a solemn and a hollow look.
Full threadbare, too, was his best coat,
For he had not yet gotten any benefice,
Not worldly enough to gain church office.
He would rather have at the head of his bed
Twenty volumes, bound in black or red,
Of Aristotle and his philosophy,
Than rich robes, a fiddle or gay psaltery.
But for all that, he was a philosopher,
With naught but little gold within his coffer.
All that he could borrow from his friends
He spent on books and learning.
And deeply for their souls he prayed
Who gave him the wherewithal for school.
His studies were all he cared for, or would heed,
Not a word spoke he more than was needed
And that he said in formal reverence.
Short and quick and full of high good sense;
Resounding in moral virtue was his speech,
And gladly would he learn and gladly teach.

Geoffrey Chaucer   1390
translated by Christopher Burns

CINDERELLA

You always read about it:
the plumber with twelve children
who wins the Irish Sweepstakes.
from toilets to riches.
That story.

Or the nursemaid,
some luscious sweet from Denmark
who captures the oldest son's heart.
From diapers to Dior.
That story.

Or a milkman who serves the wealthy,
eggs, cream, butter, yogurt, milk,
the white truck like an ambulance
who goes into real estate
and makes a pile.
From homogenized to martinis at lunch.

Or the charwoman
who is on the bus when it cracks up
and collects enough from the insurance.
From mops to Bonwit Teller.
That story.

Once
the wife of a rich man was on her deathbed
and she said to her daughter Cinderella:
Be devout. Be good. Then I will smile
down from heaven in the seam of a cloud.
The man took another wife who had
two daughters, pretty enough
but with hearts like blackjacks.
Cinderella was their maid.
She slept in the sooty hearth each night
and walked around looking like Al Jolsen.
Her father brought presents home from town,
jewels and gowns for the other women
but the twig of a tree for Cinderella.

She planted that twig on her mother's grave
and it grew to a tree where a white dove sat.
Whenever she wished for anything the dove
would drop it like an egg upon the ground.
The bird is important, my dears, so heed him.

Next came the ball, as you all know.
It was a marriage market.
The prince was looking for a wife.
All but Cinderella were preparing
and gussying up for the big event.
Cinderella begged to go too.
Her stepmother threw a dish of lentils
into the cinders and said: Pick them
up in an hour and you shall go.
The white dove brought all his friends;
all the warm wings of the fatherland came,
and picked up the lentils in a jiffy.
No, Cinderella, said the stepmother,
you have no clothes and cannot dance.
That's the way with stepmothers.

Cinderella went to the tree at the grave
and cried forth like a gospel singer:
Mama! Mama! My turtledove,
send me to the prince's ball!
The bird dropped down a golden dress
and delicate little gold slippers.
Rather a large package for a simple bird.
So she went. Which is no surprise.
Her stepmother and sisters didn't
recognize her without her cinder face
and the prince took her hand on the spot
and danced with no other the whole day.

As nightfall came she thought she'd better
get home. The prince walked her home
and she disappeared into the pigeon house
and although the prince took an axe and broke
it open she was gone. Back to her cinders.

These events repeated themselves for three days.
However on the third day the prince
covered the palace steps with cobbler's wax
and Cinderella's gold shoe stuck upon it.
Now he would find whom the shoe fit
and find his strange dancing girl for keeps.
He went to their house and the two sisters
were delighted because they had lovely feet.
The eldest went into a room to try the slipper on
but her big toe got in the way so she simply
sliced it off and put on the slipper.
The prince rode away with her until the white dove
told him to look at the blood pouring forth.
That is the way with amputations.
They don't just heal up like a wish.
The other sister cut off her heel
but the blood told as blood will.
The prince was getting tired.
He began to feel like a shoe salesman.
But he gave it one last try.
This time Cinderella fit into the shoe
like a love letter into its envelope.

At the wedding ceremony
the two sisters came to curry favor
and the white dove pecked their eyes out.
Two hollow spots were left
like soup spoons.

Cinderella and the prince
lived, they say, happily ever after,
like two dolls in a museum case
never bothered by diapers or dust,
never arguing over the timing of an egg,
never telling the same story twice,
never getting a middle-aged spread,
their darling smiles pasted on for eternity.
Regular Bobbsey Twins.
That story.

Anne Sexton   1971

JABBERWOCKY

'Twas brillig, and the slithy toves
    Did gyre and gimble in the wabe:
All mimsy were the borogoves,
    And the mome raths outgrabe.

"Beware the Jabberwock, my son!
    The jaws that bite, the claws that catch!
Beware the Jubjub bird, and shun
    The frumious Bandersnatch!"

He took his vorpal sword in hand:
    Long time the manxome foe he sought—
So rested he by the Tumtum tree,
    And stood awhile in thought.

And, as in uffish thought he stood,
    The Jabberwock, with eyes of flame,
Came whiffling through the tulgey wood,
    And burbled as it came!

One, two! One, two! And through and through
    The vorpal blade went snicker-snack!
He left it dead, and with its head
    He went galumphing back.

"And hast thou slain the Jabberwock!
    Come to my arms, my beamish boy!
O frabjous day! Callooh! Callay!"
    He chortled in his joy.

'Twas brillig, and the slithy toves
    Did gyre and gimble in the wabe:
All mimsy were the borogoves,
    And the mome raths outgrabe.

Lewis Carroll   1871

FELIX RANDAL

Felix Randal the farrier, O is he dead then? my duty all ended
Who have watched his mold of man, big-boned and hardy-
    handsome
Pining, pining, till time when reason rambled in it and some
Fatal four disorders, fleshed there, all contended?

Sickness broke him. Impatient, he cursed at first, but mended
Being anointed and all; though a heavenlier heart began some
Months earlier, since I had our sweet reprieve and ransom
Tendered to him. Ah well, God rest him all road ever he
    offended!

This seeing the sick endears them to us, us too it endears.
My tongue had taught thee comfort, touch had quenched
    thy tears,
Thy tears that touched my heart, child, Felix, poor Felix Randal;

How far from then forethought of, all thy more boisterous
    years,
When thou at the random grim, forge, powerful amidst peers,
Didst fettle for the great gray drayhorse his bright and
         battering sandal!

                    Gerard Manley Hopkins   1880

PAUL REVERE'S RIDE

Listen my children, and you shall hear
Of the midnight ride of Paul Revere,
On the eighteenth of April, in Seventy-five;
Hardly a man is now alive
Who remembers that famous day and year.

He said to his friend, "If the British march
By land or sea from the town tonight,
Hang a lantern aloft in the belfry arch
Of the North Church tower as a signal light—
One, if by land, and two, if by sea;
And I on the opposite shore will be,
Ready to ride and spread the alarm
Through every Middlesex village and farm
For the country folk to be up and to arm."

Then he said, "Good night!" and with muffled oar
Silently rowed to the Charlestown shore,
Just as the moon rose over the bay,
Where swinging wide at her moorings lay
The *Somerset,* British man-of-war;
A phantom ship, with each mast and spar
Across the moon like a prison bar,

And a huge black hulk, that was magnified
By its own reflection in the tide.
Meanwhile, his friend through alley and street
Wanders and watches, with eager ears,
Till in the silence around him he hears
The muster of men at the barrack door,
The sound of arms, and the tramp of feet,
And the measured tread of the grenadiers,
Marching down to their boats on the shore.

Then he climbed the tower of the Old North Church,
By the wooden stairs with a stealthy tread,
To the belfry-chamber overhead,
And startled the pigeons from their perch
On the somber rafters, that round him made
Masses and moving shapes of shade—
By the trembling ladder, steep and tall
To the highest window in the wall,
Where he paused to listen and look down
A moment on the roofs of the town
And the moonlight flowing over all.

Beneath, in the churchyard, lay the dead,
In their night-encampment on the hill,
Wrapped in silence so deep and still
That he could hear, like a sentinel's tread,
The watchful night wind, as it went
Creeping along from tent to tent,
And seeming to whisper, "All is well!"
A moment only he feels the spell
Of the place and the hour, and the secret dread
Of the lonely belfry and the dead;
For suddenly all his thoughts are bent
On a shadowy something far away,
Where the river widens to meet the bay—

A line of black that bends and floats
On the rising tide, like a bridge of boats.
Meanwhile, impatient to mount and ride,
Booted and spurred, with a heavy stride
On the opposite shore walked Paul Revere.

Now he patted his horse's side,
Now gazed at the landscape far and near,
Then, impetuous, stamped the earth,
And turned and tightened his saddle girth;
But mostly he watched with eager search
The belfry tower of the Old North Church,
As it rose above the graves on the hill,
Lonely and spectral and somber and still.
And lo! as he looks, on the belfry's height
A glimmer, and then a gleam of light!
He springs to the saddle, the bridle he turns,
But lingers and gazes, till full on his sight
A second lamp in the belfry burns!

A hurry of hoofs in a village street,
A shape in the moonlight, a bulk in the dark,
And beneath, from the pebbles, in passing, a spark
Struck out by a steed flying fearless and fleet;
That was all! And yet, through the doom and the light,
The fate of a nation was riding that night;
And the spark struck out by the steed in his flight,
Kindled the land into flame with its heat.

He has left the village and mounted the steep,
And beneath him, tranquil and broad and deep,
Is the Mystic, meeting the ocean tides;
And under the alders that skirt its edge,
Now soft on the sand, now loud on the ledge,
Is heard the tramp of his steed as he rides.

It was twelve by the village clock,
When he crossed the bridge into Medford town.
He heard the crowing of the cock,
And the barking of the farmer's dog,
And he felt the damp of the river fog,
That rises after the sun goes down.

It was one by the village clock,
When he galloped into Lexington.
He saw the gilded weathercock
Swim in the moonlight as he passed,
And the meeting-house windows, blank and bare,
Gaze at him with a spectral glare,
As if they already stood aghast
At the bloody work they would look upon.

It was two by the village clock,
When he came to the bridge in Concord town.
He heard the bleating of the flock,
And the twitter of birds among the trees,
And felt the breath of the morning breeze
Blowing over the meadows brown.
And one was safe and asleep in his bed
Who at the bridge would be first to fall,
Who that day would be lying dead,
Pierced by a British musket ball.

You know the rest. In books you have read,
How the British Regulars fired and fled—
How the farmers gave them ball for ball,
From behind each fence and farmyard wall,
Chasing the redcoats down the lane,
Then crossing the fields to emerge again
Under the trees at the turn of the road,
And only pausing to fire and load.

So through the night rode Paul Revere;
And so through the night went his cry of alarm
To every Middlesex village and farm—
A cry of defiance, and not of fear,
A voice in the darkness, a knock at the door,
And a word that shall echo for evermore!
For, borne on the night wind of the Past,
Through all our history, to the last,
In the hour of darkness and peril and need,
The people will waken and listen to hear
The hurrying hoof-beats of that steed,
And the midnight message of Paul Revere.

Henry Wadsworth Longfellow 1860

THE HIGHWAYMAN

The wind was a torrent of darkness among the gusty trees,
The moon was a ghostly galleon tossed upon cloudy seas,
The road was a ribbon of moonlight over the purple moor,
And the highwayman came riding—
    Riding—riding—
The highwayman came riding, up to the old inn-door.

He'd a French cocked-hat on his forehead, a bunch of lace
            at his chin,
A coat of the claret velvet, and breeches of brown doe-skin;
They fitted with never a wrinkle: his boots were up to the thigh.
And he rode with a jeweled twinkle,
    His pistol butts a-twinkle,
His rapier hilt a-twinkle, under the jeweled sky.

Over the cobbles he clattered and clashed in the dark inn-yard,
He tapped with his whip on the shutters, but all was locked
            and barred;
He whistled a tune to the window, and who should be waiting
            there
But the landlord's black-eyed daughter,
    Bess, the landlord's daughter,
Plaiting a dark red love-knot into her long black hair.

And dark in the dark old inn-yard a stable-wicket creaked
Where Tim the ostler listened; his face was white and peaked;
His eyes were hollows of madness, his hair like moldy hay,
But he loved the landlord's daughter,
    The landlord's red-lipped daughter,
Dumb as a dog he listened, and he heard the robber say—

"One kiss, my bonny sweetheart, I'm after a prize tonight,
But I shall be back with the yellow gold before the morning
            light;
Yet, if they press me sharply, and harry me through the day,
Then look for me by moonlight,
    Watch for me by moonlight,
I'll come to thee by moonlight, though hell should bar the way."

He rose upright in the stirrups; he scarce could reach her hand,
But she loosened her hair in the casement. His face burnt like
            a brand

As the black cascade of perfume came tumbling over his
        breast;
And he kissed its waves in the moonlight,
    (Oh, sweet black waves in the moonlight!)
Then he tugged at his rein in the moonlight, and galloped
        away to the West.

He did not come in the dawning; he did not come at noon;
And out of the tawny sunset, before the rise of the moon,
When the road was a gypsy's ribbon, looping the purple moor,
A red-coat troop came marching—
    Marching—marching—
King George's men came marching, up to the old inn-door.

They said no word to the landlord, they drank his ale instead,
But they gagged his daughter and bound her to the foot of her
        narrow bed;
Two of them knelt at her casement, with muskets at their side.
There was death at every window;
    And hell at one dark window;
For Bess could see, through her casement, the road that he
    would ride.

They had tied her up to attention, with many a sniggering jest.
They had bound a musket beside her, with the barrel beneath
        her breast.
"Now keep good watch!" and they kissed her. She heard the
        doomed man say—
Look for me by moonlight;
    Watch for me by moonlight;
I'll come to thee by moonlight, though hell should bar the way!

She twisted her hands behind her; but all the knots held good.
She writhed her hands till her fingers were wet with sweat or
        blood.
They stretched and strained in the darkness, and the hours
        crawled by like years,
Till, now, on the stroke of midnight,
    Cold, on the stroke of midnight,
The tip of one finger touched it! The trigger at least was hers!

The tip of one finger touched it. She strove no more for the rest.
Up, she stood up to attention, with the muzzle beneath
        her breast.

She would not risk their hearing; she would not strive again;
For the road lay bare in the moonlight;
   Blank and bare in the moonlight;
And the blood of her veins, in the moonlight, throbbed to her
     love's refrain.
Tlot-tlot; tlot-tlot! Had they heard it? The horse-hoofs ringing
     clear;
Tlot-tlot, tlot-tlot, in the distance? Were they deaf that they did
     not hear?
Down the ribbon of moonlight, over the brow of the hill,
The highwayman came riding,
   Riding, riding!
The red-coats looked to their priming! She stood up, straight
     and still!

Tlot-tlot, in the frosty silence! *Tlot-tlot,* in the echoing night!
Nearer he came and nearer! Her face was like a light!
Her eyes grew wide for a moment; she drew one last deep
     breath,
Then her finger moved in the moonlight,
   Her musket shattered the moonlight,
Shattered her breast in the moonlight and warned him—with
     her death.

He turned; he spurred to the west; he did not know who stood
Bowed, with her head o'er the musket, drenched with her own
     red blood.
Not till the dawn he heard it, his face grew gray to hear
How Bess, the landlord's daughter,
   The landlord's black-eyed daughter,
Had watched for her love in the moonlight, and died in the
     darkness there.

Back, he spurred like a madman, shouting a curse to the sky,
With the white road smoking behind him and his rapier
     brandished high!
Blood-red were his spurs in the golden noon; wine-red was
     his velvet coat,
When they shot him down on the highway,
   Down like a dog on the highway,
And he lay in his blood on the highway, with the bunch of
     lace at his throat.

And still of a winter's night, they say, when the wind is in the trees,
When the moon is a ghostly galleon tossed upon cloudy seas,
When the road is a ribbon of moonlight over the purple moor,
A highwayman comes riding—
    Riding—riding—
A highwayman comes riding, up to the old inn-door.
Over the cobbles he clatters and clangs in the dark inn-yard;
He taps with his whip on the shutters, but all is locked and barred;
He whistles a tune to the window, and who should be waiting there
But the landlord's black-eyed daughter,
    Bess, the landlord's daughter,
Plaiting a dark red love-knot into her long black hair.

Alfred Noyes   1906

THE BALLAD OF WILLIAM SYCAMORE
(1790–1871)

My father, he was a mountaineer,
His fist was a knotty hammer;
He was quick on his feet as a running deer,
And he spoke with a Yankee stammer.

My mother, she was merry and brave,
And so she came to her labor,
With a tall green fir for her doctor grave
And a stream for her comforting neighbor.

And some are wrapped in the linen fine,
And some like a godling's scion;
But I was cradled on twigs of pine
In the skin of a mountain lion.

And some remember a white, starched lap
And a ewer with silver handles;
But I remember a coonskin cap
And the smell of bayberry candles,

The cabin logs, with the bark still rough,
And my mother, who laughed at trifles,
And the tall, lank visitors, brown as snuff,
With their long, straight squirrel-rifles.

I can hear them dance, like a foggy song,
Through the deepest one of my slumbers,
The fiddle squeaking the boots along
And my father calling the numbers.

The quick feet shaking the puncheon-floor,
And the fiddle squeaking and squealing,
Till the dried herbs rattled above the door
And the dust went up to the ceiling.

There are children lucky from dawn to dusk,
But never a child so lucky!
For I cut my teeth on "Money Musk"
In the Bloody Ground of Kentucky!

When I grew tall as the Indian corn,
My father had little to lend me,
But he gave me his great old powder-horn
And his woodsman's skill to befriend me.

With a leather shirt to cover my back,
And a redskin nose to unravel
Each forest sign, I carried my pack
As far as a scout could travel.

Till I lost my boyhood and found my wife,
A girl like a Salem clipper!
A woman straight as a hunting-knife
With eyes as bright as the Dipper!

We cleared our camp where the buffalo feed,
Unheard-of streams were our flagons;
And I sowed my sons like the apple-seed
On the trail of the Western wagons.

They were right, tight boys, never sulky or slow,
A fruitful, a goodly muster.
The eldest died at the Alamo;
The youngest fell with Custer.

The letter that told it burned my hand.
Yet we smiled and said, "So be it!"
But I could not live when they fenced the land,
For it broke my heart to see it.

I saddled a red, unbroken colt
And rode him into the day there;
And he threw me down like a thunderbolt
And rolled on me as I lay there.

The hunter's whistle hummed in my ear
As the city men tried to move me,
And I died in my boots like a pioneer
With the whole wide sky above me.

Now I lie in the heart of the fat, black soil,
Like the seed of a prairie-thistle;
It has washed my bones with honey and oil
And picked them clean as a whistle.

And my youth returns, like the rains of Spring,
And my sons, like the wild-geese flying;
And I lie and hear the meadow-lark sing
And I have much content in my dying.

Go play with the towns you have built of blocks,
The towns where you would have bound me!
I sleep in the earth like a tired fox,
And my buffalo have found me.

Stephen Vincent Benét   1922

THE CARPENTER'S SON

"Here the hangman stops his cart:
Now the best of friends must part
Fare you well, for ill fare I:
Live, lads, and I will die.

"Oh, at home had I but stayed
Prenticed to my father's trade,
Had I stuck to plane and adze,
I had not been lost, my lads.

"Then I might have built perhaps
Gallows-trees for other chaps,
Never dangled on my own,
Had I but left ill alone.

"Now, you see, they hang me high,
And the people passing by
Stop to shake their fists and curse;
So 'tis come from ill to worse.

"Here hang I, and right and left
Two poor fellows hang for theft:
All the same's the luck we prove,
Though the midmost hangs for love.
"Comrades, all, that stand and gaze,
Walk henceforth in other ways;
See my neck and save your own:
Comrades all, leave ill alone.

"Make some day a decent end,
Shrewder fellows than your friend.
Fare you well, for ill fare I:
Live, lads, and I will die."

A. E. Housman 1896

THE CREMATION OF SAM MCGEE

There are strange things done in the midnight sun
By the men who moil for gold;
The Arctic trails have their secret tales
That would make your blood run cold;
The Northern Lights have seen queer sights,
But the queerest they ever did see
Was that night on the marge of Lake Lebarge
I cremated Sam McGee.

Now Sam McGee was from Tennessee,
where the cotton blooms and blows.
Why he left his home in the South to roam
'round the Pole, God only knows.
He was always cold, but the land of gold
seemed to hold him like a spell;
Though he'd often say in his homely way
that "he'd sooner live in hell."

On a Christmas Day we were mushing our way
over the Dawson trail.
Talk of your cold! through the parka's fold
it stabbed like a driven nail.
If our eyes we'd close, then the lashes froze
till sometimes we couldn't see;
It wasn't much fun, but the only one
to whimper was Sam McGee.

And that very night, as we lay packed tight
in our robes beneath the snow,
And the dogs were fed, and the stars o'erhead
were dancing heel and toe,
He turned to me, and "Cap," says he,
"I'll cash in this trip, I guess;
And if I do, I'm asking that you
won't refuse my last request."

Well, he seemed so low that I couldn't say no;
then he says with a sort of moan:
"It's the cursèd cold, and it's got right hold
till I'm chilled clean through to the bone.

Yet 'tain't being dead—it's my awful dread
    of the icy grave that pains;
So I want you to swear that, foul or fair,
    you'll cremate my last remains."

A pal's last need is a thing to heed,
    so I swore I would not fail;
And we started on at the streak of dawn;
    but God! he looked ghastly pale.

He crouched on the sleigh, and he raved all day
    of his home in Tennessee;
And before nightfall a corpse was all
    that was left of Sam McGee.

There wasn't a breath in that land of death,
    and I hurried, horror-driven,
With a corpse half hid that I couldn't get rid,
    because of a promise given;
It was lashed to the sleigh, and it seemed to say:
    "You may tax your brawn and brains,
But you promised true, and it's up to you
    to cremate those last remains."

Now a promise made is a debt unpaid,
    and the trail has its own stern code.
In the days to come, though my lips were dumb,
    in my heart how I cursed that load.
In the long, long night, by the lone firelight,
    while the huskies, round in a ring,
Howled out their woes to the homeless snows—
    O God! how
    I loathed the thing.

And every day that quiet clay
    seemed to heavy and heavier grow;
And on I went, though the dogs were spent
    and the grub was getting low;
The trail was bad, and I felt half mad,
    but I swore I would not give in;
And I'd often sing to the hateful thing,
    and it hearkened with a grin.

Till I came to the marge of Lake Lebarge,
and a derelict there lay;
It was jammed in the ice, but I saw in a trice
it was called the "Alice May."
And I looked at it, and I thought a bit,
and I looked at my frozen chum;

Then "Here," said I, with a sudden cry,
"is my cre-ma-tor-eum."
Some planks I tore from the cabin floor,
and I lit the boiler fire;
Some coal I found that was lying around,
and I heaped the fuel higher;
The flames just soared, and the furnace roared—
such a blaze you seldom see;
And I burrowed a hole in the glowing coal,
and I stuffed in Sam McGee.

Then I made a hike, for I didn't like
to hear him sizzle so;
And the heavens scowled, and the huskies howled,
and the wind began to blow.

It was icy cold, but the hot sweat rolled
down my cheeks, and I don't know why;
And the greasy smoke in an inky cloak
went streaking down the sky.
I do not know how long in the snow
I wrestled with grisly fear;
But the stars came out and they danced about
ere again I ventured near;
I was sick with dread, but I bravely said:
"I'll just take a peep inside.
I guess he's cooked, and it's time I looked";
. . . then the door I opened wide.

And there sat Sam, looking cool and calm,
in the heart of the furnace roar;
And he wore a smile you could see a mile,
and he said: "Please close that door.
It's fine in here, but I greatly fear
you'll let in the cold and storm—
Since I left Plumtree, down in Tennessee,
it's the first time I've been warm."

There are strange things done in the midnight sun
By the men who moil for gold;
*   The Arctic trails have their secret tales*
That would make your blood run cold;
*   The Northern Lights have seen queer sights,*
But the queerest they ever did see
*   Was that night on the marge of Lake Lebarge*
I cremated Sam McGee.

                            Robert Service   1907

THE SHOOTING OF DAN MCGREW

A bunch of the boys were whooping it up
    in the Malamute saloon:
The kid that handles the music-box
    was hitting a jag-time tune;
Back of the bar, in a solo game,
    sat Dangerous Dan McGrew,
And watching his luck was his light-o'-love,
    the lady that's known as Lou.

When out of the night, which was fifty below,
    and into the din and the glare,
There stumbled a miner fresh from the creeks,
    dog-dirty, and loaded for bear.
He looked like a man with a foot in the grave
    and scarcely the strength of a louse,
Yet he tilted a poke of dust on the bar,
    and he called for drinks for the house.
There was none could place the stranger's face,
    though we searched ourselves for a clue;
But we drank his health, and the last to drink
    was Dangerous Dan McGrew.

There's men that somehow just grip your eyes,
    and hold them hard like a spell;
And such was he, and he looked to me
    like a man who had lived in hell;
With a face most hair, and the dreary stare
    of a dog whose day is done,
As he watered the green stuff in his glass,
    and the drops fell one by one.

Then I got to figgering who he was,
    and wondering what he'd do,
And I turned my head—and there watching him
    was the lady that's known as Lou.

His eyes went rubbering round the room,
    and he seemed in a kind of daze,
Till at last that old piano fell
    in the way of his wandering gaze.
The rag-time kid was having a drink;
    there was no one else on the stool,
So the stranger stumbles across the room,
    and flops down there like a fool.
In the buckskin shirt that was glazed with dirt
    he sat, and I saw him sway;
Then he clutched the keys with his talon hands—
    my God! but that man could play.

Were you ever out in the Great Alone,
    when the moon was awful clear,
And the icy mountains hemmed you in
    with a silence you most could *hear*;
With only the howl of a timber wolf,
    and you camped there in the cold,
A half-dead thing in a stark, dead world,
    clear mad for the muck called gold;
While high overhead, green, yellow and red,
    the North Lights swept in bars?
Then you've a hunch what the music meant . . .
    hunger and night and the stars.

And hunger not of the belly kind,
    that's banished with bacon and beans,
But the gnawing hunger of lonely men
    for a home and all that it means;
For a fireside far from the cares that are,
    four walls and a roof above;
But oh so cramful of cozy joy,
    and crowned with a woman's love—
A woman dearer than all the world,
    and true as Heaven is true—
(God! how ghastly she looks through her rouge—
    the lady that's known as Lou.)

Then on a sudden the music changed,
   so soft that you scarce could hear;
But you felt that your life had been looted clean
   of all that it once held dear;
That someone had stolen the woman you loved;
   that her love was a devil's lie;
That your guts were gone, and the best for you
   was to crawl away and die.
Twas the crowning cry of a heart's despair,
   and it thrilled you through and through—
"I guess I'll make it a spread misere,"
   said Dangerous Dan McGrew.

The music almost died away . . .
   then it burst like a pent-up flood;
And it seemed to say, "Repay, repay,"
   and my eyes were blind with blood.
The thought came back of an ancient wrong,
   and it stung like a frozen lash,
And the lust awoke to kill, to kill . . .
   then the music stopped with a crash,
And the stranger turned, and his eyes they burned
   in a most peculiar way;
In a buckskin shirt that was glazed with dirt
   he sat, and I saw him sway;
Then his lips went in in a kind of grin,
   and spoke, and his voice was calm,
And "Boys," says he, "you don't know me,
   and none of you care a damn;
But I want to state, and my words are straight,
   and I'll bet my poke they're true,
That one of you is a hound of hell . . .
   and that one is Dan McGrew."

Then I ducked my head, and the lights went out,
   and two guns blazed in the dark,
And a woman screamed, and the lights went up,
   and two men lay stiff and stark.
Pitched on his head, and pumped full of lead,
   was Dangerous Dan McGrew,
While the man from the creeks lay clutched to the breast
   of the lady that's known as Lou.

These are the simple facts of the case,
    and I guess I ought to know.
They say that the stranger was crazed with hooch,
    and I'm not denying it's so.
I'm not so wise as the lawyer guys,
    but strictly between us two—
The woman that kissed him—and pinched his poke—
    was the lady that's known as Lou.

                    Robert Service   1907

RICHARD CORY

Whenever Richard Cory went downtown,
We people on the pavement looked at him:
He was a gentleman from sole to crown,
Clean favored, and imperially slim.

And he was always quietly arrayed,
And he was always human when he talked;
But still he fluttered pulses when he said,
"Good-morning," and he glittered when he walked.

And he was rich—yes, richer than a king—
And admirably schooled in every grace:
In fine, we thought that he was everything
To make us wish that we were in his place.

So on we worked, and waited for the light,
And went without the meat, and cursed the bread;
And Richard Cory, one calm summer night,
Went home and put a bullet through his head.

              Edward Arlington Robinson   1896

THE DEATH OF THE HIRED MAN

Mary sat musing on the lamp flame at the table,
Waiting for Warren. When she heard his step,
She ran on tiptoe down the darkened passage
To meet him in the doorway with the news
And put him on his guard. "Silas is back."
She pushed him outward with her through the door
And shut it after her. "Be Kind," she said.
She took the market things from Warren's arms
And set them on the porch, then drew him down
To sit beside her on the wooden steps.

"When was I anything but kind to him?
But I'll not have the fellow back," he said.
"I told him so last haying, didn't I?
If he left then, I said, that ended it.
What good is he? Who else will harbor him
At his age for the little he can do?
What help he is there's no depending on.
Off he goes always when I need him most.
He thinks he ought to earn a little pay,
Enough at least to buy tobacco with,
So he won't have to beg and be beholden.
'All right,' I say, 'I can't afford to pay
Any fixed wages, though I wish I could.'
'Someone else can.' 'Then someone else will have to.'
I shouldn't mind his bettering himself
If that was what it was. You can be certain,
When he begins like that, there's someone at him
Trying to coax him off with pocket money—
In haying time, when any help is scarce.
In winter he comes back to us. I'm done."

"Sh! not so loud: he'll hear you," Mary said.

"I want him to: he'll have to soon or late."

"He's worn out. He's asleep beside the stove.
When I came up from Rowe's I found him here,
Huddled against the barn door fast asleep,
A miserable sight, and frightening, too—

You needn't smile—I didn't recognize him—
I wasn't looking for him—and he's changed.
Wait till you see."

      "Where did you say he'd been?"

"He didn't say. I dragged him to the house,
And gave him tea and tried to make him smoke.
I tried to make him talk about his travels.
Nothing would do: he just kept nodding off."

"What did he say? Did he say anything?"
"But little."

      "Anything? Mary, confess
He said he'd come to ditch the meadow for me."
"Warren!"

      "But did he? I just want to know."

"Of course he did. What would you have him say?
Surely you wouldn't grudge the poor old man
Some humble way to save his self-respect.
He added, if you really care to know,
He meant to clear the upper pasture, too.
That sounds like something you have heard before?
Warren, I wish you could have heard the way
He jumbled everything. I stopped to look
Two or three times—he made me feel so queer—
To see if he was talking in his sleep.
He ran on Harold Wilson—you remember—
The boy you had in haying four years since.
He's finished school, and teaching in his college.
Silas declares you'll have to get him back.
He says they two will make a team for work:
Between them they will lay this farm as smooth!
The way he mixed that in with other things.
He thinks young Wilson a likely lad, though daft
On education—you know how they fought
All through July under the blazing sun,
Silas up on the cart to build the load,
Harold along beside to pitch it on."

"Yes, I took care to keep well out of earshot."

"Well, those days trouble Silas like a dream.
You wouldn't think they would. How some things linger!
Harold's young college-boy's assurance piqued him.
After so many years he still keeps finding
Good arguments he sees he might have used.
I sympathize. I know just how it feels
To think of the right thing to say too late.
Harold's associated in his mind with Latin.
He asked me what I thought of Harold's saying
He studied Latin, like the violin,
Because he liked it—that an argument!
He said he couldn't make the boy believe
He could find water with a hazel prong—
Which showed how much good school had ever done him.
He wanted to go over that. But most of all
He thinks if he could have another chance
To teach him how to build a load of hay——"

"I know, that's Silas' one accomplishment.
He bundles every forkful in its place,
And tags and numbers it for future reference,
So he can find and easily dislodge it
In the unloading. Silas does that well.
He takes it out in bunches like big birds' nests.
You never see him standing on the hay
He's trying to lift, straining to lift himself."

"He thinks if he could teach him that, he'd be
Some good perhaps to someone in the world.
He hates to see a boy the fool of books.
Poor Silas, so concerned for other folk,
And nothing to look backward to with pride,
And nothing to look forward to with hope,
So now and never any different."

Part of a moon was falling down the west,
Dragging the whole sky with it to the hills.
Its light poured softly in her lap. She saw it
And spread her apron to it. She put out her hand
Among the harplike morning-glory strings,

Taut with the dew from garden bed to eaves,
As if she played unheard some tenderness
That wrought on him beside her in the night.
"Warren," she said, "he has come home to die:
You needn't be afraid he'll leave you this time."

"Home," he mocked gently.
                    "Yes, what else but home?
It all depends on what you mean by home.
Of course he's nothing to us, any more
Than was the hound that came a stranger to us
Out of the woods, worn out upon the trail."

"Home is the place where, when you have to go there,
They have to take you in."
                    "I should have called it
Something you somehow haven't to deserve."

Warren leaned out and took a step or two,
Picked up a little stick, and brought it back
And broke it in his hand and tossed it by.
"Silas has better claim on us you think
Than on his brother? Thirteen little miles
As the road winds would bring him to his door.
Silas has walked that far no doubt today.
Why doesn't he go there? His brother's rich,
A somebody—director in the bank."

"He never told us that."
                    "We know it, though."

"I think his brother ought to help, of course.
I'll see to that if there is need. He ought of right
To take him in, and might be willing to—
He may be better than appearances.
But have some pity on Silas. Do you think
If he had any pride in claiming kin
Or anything he looked for from his brother,
He'd keep so still about it all this time?"

"I wonder what's between them."

                    "I can't tell you.
Silas is what he is—we wouldn't mind him—

But just the kind that kinsfolk can't abide.
He never did a thing so very bad.
He don't know why he isn't quite as good
As anybody. Worthless though he is,
He won't be made ashamed to please his brother."

"I can't think Si ever hurt anyone."

"No, but he hurt my heart the way he lay
And rolled his old head on that sharp-edged chair-back.
He wouldn't let me put him on the lounge.
You must go in and see what you can do.
I made the bed up for him there tonight.
You'll be surprised at him—how much he's broken.
His working days are done; I'm sure of it."

"I'd not be in a hurry to say that."

"I haven't been. Go, look, see for yourself.
But, Warren, please remember how it is:
He's come to help you ditch the meadow.
He has a plan. You mustn't laugh at him.
He may not speak of it, and then he may.
I'll sit and see if that small sailing cloud
Will hit or miss the moon."
                              It hit the moon.
Then there were three there, making a dim row,
The moon, the little silver cloud, and she.

Warren returned—too soon, it seemed to her—
Slipped to her side, caught up her hand and waited.

"Warren?" she questioned.
                    "Dead," was all he answered.
                                        Robert Frost   1914

THE PERFORMANCE

The last time I saw Donald Armstrong
He was staggering oddly off into the sun,
Going down, of the Philippine Islands.
I let my shovel fall, and put that hand
Above my eyes, and moved some way to one side
That his body might pass through the sun,

And I saw how well he was not
Standing there on his hands,
On his spindle-shanked forearms balanced,
Unbalanced, with his big feet looming and waving
In the great, untrustworthy air
He flew in each night, when it darkened.

Dust fanned in scraped puffs from the earth
Between his arms, and blood turned his face inside out,
To demonstrate its suppleness
Of veins, as he perfected his role.
Next day, he toppled his head off
On an island beach to the south,

And the enemy's two-handed sword
Did not fall from anyone's hands
At that miraculous sight,
As the head rolled over upon
Its wide-eyed face, and fell
Into the inadequate grave

He had dug for himself, under pressure.
Yet I put my flat hand to my eyebrows
Months later, to see him again
In the sun, when I learned how he died,
And imagined him, there,
Come, judged, before his small captors,

Doing all his lean tricks to amaze them—
The back somersault, the kip-up—
And at last, the stand on his hands,
Perfect, with his feet together,
His head down, evenly breathing,
As the sun poured up from the sea

And the headsman broke down
In a blaze of tears, in that light
Of the thin, long human frame
Upside down in its own strange joy,
And, if some other one had not told him,
Would have cut off the feet

Instead of the head,
And if Armstrong had not presently risen
In kingly, round-shouldered attendance,
And then knelt down in himself
Beside his hacked, glittering grave, having done
All things in this life that he could.

James Dickey   1959

REUBEN BRIGHT

Because he was a butcher and thereby
Did earn an honest living (and did right),
I would not have you think that Reuben Bright
Was any more a brute than you or I;
For when they told him that his wife must die,
He stared at them, and shook with grief and fright,
And cried like a great baby half that night,
And made the women cry to see him cry.

And after she was dead, and he had paid
The singers and the sexton and the rest,
He packed a lot of things that she had made
Most mournfully away in an old chest
Of hers, and put some chopped-up cedar boughs
In with them, and tore down the slaughter house.

Edward Arlington Robinson   1897

HARD ROCK RETURNS TO PRISON FROM THE HOSPITAL FOR THE CRIMINAL INSANE

Hard Rock was 'known not to take no shit
From nobody,' and he had the scars to prove it:
Split purple lips, lumped ears, welts above
His yellow eyes, and one long scar that cut
Across his temple and plowed through a thick
Canopy of kinky hair.

The WORD was that Hard Rock wasn't a mean nigger
Anymore, that the doctors had bored a hole in his head,
Cut out part of his brain, and shot electricity
Through the rest. When they brought Hard Rock back,
Handcuffed and chained, he was turned loose,
Like a freshly gelded stallion, to try his new status.
And we all waited and watched, like indians at a corral,
To see if the WORD was true.

As we waited we wrapped ourselves in the cloak
Of his exploits: 'Man, the last time, it took eight
Screws to put him in the Hole.' 'Yeah, remember when he
Smacked the captain with his dinner tray?' 'He set
The record for time in the Hole—67 straight days!'
'O! Hard Rock! man, that's one crazy nigger.'
And then the jewel of a myth that Hard Rock had once bit
A screw on the thumb and poisoned him with syphilitic spit.

The testing came, to see if Hard Rock was really tame.
A hillbilly called him a black son of a bitch
And didn't lose his teeth, a screw who knew Hard Rock
From before shook him down and barked in his face.
And Hard Rock did *nothing*. Just grinned and looked silly,
His eyes empty like knot holes in a fence.

And even after we discovered that it took Hard Rock
Exactly 3 minutes to tell you his first name,
We told ourselves that he had just wised up,
Was being cool; but we could not fool ourselves for long,
And we turned away, our eyes on the ground. Crushed.

He had been our Destroyer, the doer of things
We dreamed of doing but could not bring ourselves to do,
The fears of years, like a biting whip,
Had cut grooves too deeply across our backs.

Etheridge Knight   1968

THE EXAMINATION

Under the thick beams of that swirly smoking light,
    The black robes are clustering, huddled in together.
Hunching their shoulders, they spread short, broad sleeves
        like night-
    Black grackles' wings and reach out bone-yellow leather-

y fingers, each to each. They are prepared. Each turns
    His single eye—or since one can't discern their eyes,
That reflective, single, moon-pale disc which burns
    Over each brow—to watch this uncouth shape that lies

Strapped to their table. One probes with his ragged nails
    The slate-sharp calf, explores the thigh and the lean thews
Of the groin. Others raise, red as piratic sails,
    His wing, stretching, trying the pectoral sinews.

One runs his finger down the whet of that cruel
    Golden beak, lifts back the horny lids from the eyes,
Peers down in one bright eye, malign as a jewel,
    And steps back suddenly, "He is anesthetized?"

"He is. He is. Yes. Yes." The tallest of them, bent
    Down by the head, rises, "This drug possesses powers
Sufficient to still all gods in this firmament.
    This is Garuda who was fierce. He's yours for hours."

"We shall continue, please." Now, once again, he bends
    To the skull, and its clamped tissues. Into the cran-
ial cavity, he plunges both of his hands
    Like obstetric forceps and lifts out the great brain,

Holds it aloft, then gives it to the next who stands
   Beside him. Each, in turn, accepts it, although loath,
Turns it this way, that way, feels it between his hands
   Like a wasp's nest or some sickening outsized growth.

They must decide what thoughts each part of it must think;
   They tap at, then listen beside, each suspect lobe;
Next, with a crow's quill dipped into India ink,
   Mark on its surface, as if on a map or globe,
Those dangerous areas which need to be excised.
   They rinse it, then apply antiseptics to it.
Now silver saws appear which, inch by inch, slice
   Through its ancient folds and ridges, like thick suet.

It's rinsed, dried, and daubed with thick salves. The smoky
        saws
   Are scrubbed, resterilized, and polished till they gleam.
The brain is repacked in its case. Pinched in their claws,
   Glimmering needles stitch it up, that leave no seam.

Meantime, one of them has set blinders to the eyes,
   Inserted light packing beneath each of the ears
And caulked the nostrils in. One, with thin twine, ties
   The genitals off. With long wooden-handled shears,

Another chops pinions out of the scarlet wings.
   It's hoped that with disuse he will forget the sky
Or, at least, in time, learn, among other things,
   To fly no higher than his superiors fly.

Well; that's a beginning. The next time, they can split
   His tongue and teach him to talk correctly, can give
Him opinions on fine books and choose clothing fit
   For the integrated area where he'll live.

Their candidate may live to give them thanks one day.
   He will recover and may hope for such success
He might return to join their ranks. Bowing away,
   They nod, whispering, "One of ours; one of ours. Yes.
        Yes."

            W. D. Snodgrass 1961

THE WALRUS AND THE CARPENTER

The sun was shining on the sea,
    Shining with all his might:
He did his very best to make
    The billows smooth and bright—
And this was odd, because it was
    The middle of the night.

The moon was shining sulkily,
    Because she thought the sun
Had got no business to be there
    After the day was done—
"It's very rude of him," she said,
    "To come and spoil the fun!"

The sea was wet as wet could be,
    The sands were dry as dry.
You could not see a cloud, because
    No cloud was in the sky:
No birds were flying overhead—
    There were no birds to fly.

The Walrus and the Carpenter
    Were walking close at hand:
They wept like anything to see
    Such quantities of sand.
"If this were only cleared away,"
    They said, "it would be grand!"

"If seven maids with seven mops
    Swept it for half a year,
Do you suppose," the Walrus said,
    "That they could get it clear?"
"I doubt it," said the Carpenter,
    And shed a bitter tear.

"O Oysters, come and walk with us!"
    The Walrus did beseech.
"A pleasant walk, a pleasant talk,
    Along the briny beach:
We cannot do with more than four,
    To give a hand to each."

The eldest Oyster looked at him,
But never a word he said:
The eldest Oyster winked his eye,
And shook his heavy head—
Meaning to say he did not choose
To leave the oyster bed.

But four young Oysters hurried up,
All eager for the treat:
Their coats were brushed, their faces washed,
Their shoes were clean and neat—
And this was odd, because, you know,
They hadn't any feet.

Four other Oysters followed them,
And yet another four;
And thick and fast they came at last,
And more, and more, and more—
All hopping through the frothy waves,
And scrambling to the shore.

The Walrus and the Carpenter
Walked on a mile or so,
And then they rested on a rock
Conveniently low:
And all the little Oysters stood
And waited in a row.

"The time has come," the Walrus said,
"To talk of many things:
Of shoes—and ships—and sealing wax—
Of cabbages—and kings—
And why the sea is boiling hot—
And whether pigs have wings."

"But wait a bit," the Oysters cried,
"Before we have our chat;
For some of us are out of breath,
And all of us are fat!"
"No hurry!" said the Carpenter.
They thanked him much for that.

"A loaf of bread," the Walrus said,
    "Is what we chiefly need:
Pepper and vinegar besides
    Are very good indeed—
Now, if you're ready, Oysters dear,
    We can begin to feed."

"But not on us!" the Oysters cried,
    Turning a little blue.
"After such kindness, that would be
    A dismal thing to do!"
"The night is fine," the Walrus said.
    "Do you admire the view?"

"It was so kind of you to come!
    And you are very nice!"
The Carpenter said nothing but
    "Cut us another slice.
I wish you were not quite so deaf—
    I've had to ask you twice!"

"It seems a shame," the Walrus said,
    "To play them such a trick,
After we've brought them out so far,
    And made them trot so quick!"
The Carpenter said nothing but
    "The butter's spread too thick!"

"I weep for you," the Walrus said:
    "I deeply sympathize."
With sobs and tears he sorted out
    Those of the largest size,
Holding his pocket handkerchief
    Before his streaming eyes.

"O Oysters," said the Carpenter,
    "You've had a pleasant run!
Shall we be trotting home again?"
    But answer came there none—
And this was scarcely odd, because
    They'd eaten every one.

                    Lewis Carroll   1872

MRS. SEVERIN

Mrs. Severin came home from the Methodist Encampment,
Climbed naked to the diningroom table and lay down.
She was alone at the time but naturally told of it afterward.
"Lord! Lord!" she had called out. "Thou seest me. Wherein is
    my fault?"

When she heard of it, secondhand, Mrs. Birchfield laughed till
    she cried.
"My God! she said, "I'd like to've seen her getting up there!"
For Mrs. Severin, you see, was a very stout old lady,
A spilling mass by buttons, shawls, pins and ribboned
    eyeglasses held together.

The eyeglasses were a shift of drama: hoisted for reading aloud,
    lowered for talking;
They were not interruption. Mrs. Severin's soft incessant sibilance
Through all the days she visited and rocked by the window
Braided inextricably Bible and autobiography. Jesus was near.

"The morning Encampment began the Lord suddenly told me to go.
Ran all the way downstreet to the cars for Canobie Lake,
Didn't fasten my dress or tie my shoes. Left the house open.
    Young ones at the neighbors.
'Lord,' I said, 'I am thy servant'—and stayed the whole
    beautiful, blessed week."

On the listening child her showers of quotation pattered a
    drugged dream.
"'Thought becomes word. Word becomes act. Act becomes
    character. Character becomes destiny,'
Remember that. And praise the Lord," she said, giving off also
Odor of camphor, old rose jars and muttonleg sleeves. "Amen!"

The husband long gone who wasted her inheritance; the
    irritable children
Who hated to have to have her now; the friends who took her
    in now and again: gone.
Here in her false hair and hand-me-downs, patiently talking
    —talking:
Old Mrs. Severin who once, brave on a diningroom table,
    naked confronted her unanswering Lord.

        Winfield Townley Scott   1951

THE UNKNOWN CITIZEN

To JS/07/M/378

This Marble Monument Is Erected by the State

He was found by the Bureau of Statistics to be
One against whom there was no official complaint,
And all the reports on his conduct agree
That, in the modern sense of an old-fashioned word,
 he was a saint,
For in everything he did he served the Greater Community.
Except for the War till the day he retired
He worked in a factory and never got fired,
But satisfied his employers, Fudge Motors Inc.
Yet he wasn't a scab or odd in his views,
For his Union reports that he paid his dues,
(Our report on his Union shows it was sound)
And our Social Psychology workers found
That he was popular with his mates and liked a drink.
The Press are convinced that he bought a paper every day
And that his reactions to advertisements were normal
 in every way.
Policies taken out in his name prove that he was fully insured,
And his Health-card shows he was once in hospital
 but left it cured.
Both Producers Research and High-Grade Living declare
He was fully sensible to the advantages of the Installment Plan
And had everything necessary to the Modern Man,
A phonograph, a radio, a car and a Frigidaire.
Our researchers into Public Opinion are content
That he held the proper opinions for the time of year;
When there was peace, he was for peace; when there was war,
 he went.
He was married and added five children to the population.
Which our Eugenist says was the right number for a parent
 of his generation,
And our teachers report that he never interfered with
 their education.
Was he free? Was he happy? The question is absurd:
Had anything been wrong, we should certainly have heard.

W. H. Auden   1939

Arms and the Boy

Anthem for Doomed Youth

What passing bells for these who die as cattle?
    Only the monstrous anger of the guns.
    Only the stuttering rifles' rapid rattle
Can patter out their hasty orisons.
No mockeries now for them; no prayers nor bells,
    Nor any voice of mourning save the choirs—
The shrill, demented choirs of wailing shells;
    And bugles calling for them from sad shires.

What candles may be held to speed them all?
    Not in the hands of boys but in their eyes
Shall shine the holy glimmers of goodbyes.
    The pallor of girls' brows shall be their pall;
Their flowers the tenderness of patient minds,
And each slow dusk a drawing down of blinds.

Wilfred Owen   1917

97

THE SEND-OFF

Down the close, darkening lanes they sang their way
To the siding shed,
And lined the train with faces grimly gay.
Their breasts were stuck all white with wreath and spray
As men's are, dead.

Dull porters watched them, and a casual tramp
Stood staring hard,
Sorry to miss them from the upland camp.
Then, unmoved, signals nodded, and a lamp
Winked to the guard.
So secretly, like wrongs hushed-up, they went.
They were not ours:
We never heard to which front these were sent.

Nor there if they yet mock what women meant
Who gave them flowers.

Shall they return to beatings of great bells
In wild trainloads?
A few, a few, too few for drums and yells,
May creep back, silent, to still village wells
Up half-known roads.

Wilfred Owen   1918

BASE DETAILS

If I were fierce and bald and short of breath,
   I'd live with scarlet Majors at the Base,
And speed glum heroes up the line to death.
   You'd see me with my puffy petulant face,
Guzzling and gulping in the best hotel,
   Reading the Roll of Honor. "Poor young chap,"
I'd say—"I used to know his father well;
   Yes, we've lost heavily in this last scrap."
And when the war is done and youth stone dead,
I'd toddle safely home and die—in bed.

Siegfried Sassoon   1918

NAMING OF PARTS

Today we have naming of parts. Yesterday,
We had daily cleaning. And tomorrow morning,
We shall have what to do after firing. But today,
Today we have naming of parts. Japonica
Glistens like coral in all of the neighboring gardens,
    And today we have naming of parts.

This is the lower sling swivel. And this
Is the upper sling swivel, whose use you will see,
When you are given your slings. And this is the piling swivel,
Which in your case you have not got. The branches
Hold in the gardens their silent, eloquent gestures,
    Which in our case we have not got.

This is the safety catch, which is always released
With an easy flick of the thumb. And please do not let me
See anyone using his finger. You can do it quite easy
If you have any strength in your thumb. The blossoms
Are fragile and motionless, never letting anyone see
    Any of them using their finger.

And this you can see is the bolt. The purpose of this
Is to open the breech, as you see. We can slide it
Rapidly backwards and forwards; we call this
Easing the spring. And rapidly backwards and forwards
The early bees are assaulting and fumbling the flowers:
    They call it easing the Spring.

They call it easing the Spring. It is perfectly easy
If you have any strength in your thumb: like the bolt,
And the breech, and the cocking piece, and the point of balance,
Which in our case we have not got; and the almond blossom
Silent in all of the gardens and the bees going backwards
       and forwards,
    For today we have naming of parts.

Henry Reed 1946

THE BATTLE HYMN OF THE REPUBLIC

Mine eyes have seen the glory of the coming of the Lord:
He is trampling out the vintage where the grapes of wrath
      are stored;
He hath loosed the fatal lightning of His terrible swift sword:
His truth is marching on.

I have seen Him in the watch-fires of a hundred circling camps,
They have builded Him an altar in the evening dews and damps;
I can read His righteous sentence by the dim and flaring lamps:
His day is marching on.

I have read a fiery gospel writ in burnished rows of steel:
"As ye deal with my contemners, so with you my grace
      shall deal;
Let the Hero, born of woman, crush the serpent with his heel,
Since God is marching on."

He has sounded forth the trumpet that shall never call retreat;
He is sifting out the hearts of men before His judgment seat:
Oh, be swift, my soul, to answer Him! Be jubilant, my feet!
Our God is marching on.

In the beauty of the lilies Christ was born across the sea,
With a glory in his bosom that transfigures you and me:
As he died to make men holy, let us die to make men free,
While God is marching on.

Julia Ward Howe   1862

IF WE ARE MARKED TO DIE

KING HENRY: If we are marked to die, we are enough
To do our country loss; and if to live,
The fewer men, the greater share of honor.
God's will! I pray thee, wish not one man more.
By Jove, I am not covetous for gold,
Nor care I who doth feed upon my cost;
It yearns me not if men my garments wear;
Such outward things dwell not in my desires:
But if it be a sin to covet honor,
I am the most offending soul alive.

No, faith, my coz, wish not a man from England:
God's peace! I would not lose so great an honor
As one man more, methinks, would share from me
For the best hope I have. O, do not wish one more!
Rather proclaim it, Westmoreland, through my host,
That he which hath no stomach to this fight,
Let him depart; his passport shall be made
And crowns for convoy put into his purse:
We would not die in that man's company
That fears his fellowship to die with us.
This day is called the feast of Crispian:
He that outlives this day, and comes safe home,
Will stand a tiptoe when this day is named,
And rouse him at the name of Crispian.
He that shall live this day, and see old age,
Will yearly on the vigil feast his neighbors,
And say "Tomorrow is Saint Crispian:"
Then will he strip his sleeve and show his scars,
And say "These wounds I had on Crispin's day."
Old men forget; yet all shall be forgot,
But he'll remember with advantages
What feats he did that day: then shall our names,
Familiar in his mouth as household words,
Harry the king, Bedford and Exeter,
Warwick and Talbot, Salisbury and Gloucester,
Be in their flowing cups freshly remembered.
This story shall the good man teach his son.
And Crispin Crispian shall ne'er go by,
From this day to the ending of the world
But we in it shall be remembered;
We few, we happy few, we band of brothers
For he today that sheds his blood with me
Shall be my brother; be he ne'er so vile,
This day shall gentle his condition:
And gentlemen in England now a-bed
Shall think themselves accursed they were not here,
And hold their manhoods cheap whiles he speaks
That fought with us upon Saint Crispian's day.

William Shakespeare 1599
King Henry V, Act IV, Scene 2

IF WE MUST DIE

If we must die, let it not be like hogs
Hunted and penned in an inglorious spot,
While round us bark the mad and hungry dogs,
Making their mock at our accursed lot.
If we must die, O let us nobly die,
So that our precious blood may not be shed
In vain; then even the monsters we defy
Shall be constrained to honor us though dead!
O kinsmen! we must meet the common foe!
Though far outnumbered let us show us brave,
And for their thousand blows deal one deathblow!
What though before us lies the open grave?
Like men we'll face the murderous, cowardly pack,
Pressed to the wall, dying, but fighting back!

Claude McKay   1919

AN ARMY CORPS ON THE MARCH

With its cloud of skirmishers in advance,
With now the sound of a single shot snapping like a whip,
      and now an irregular volley,
The swarming ranks press on and on, the dense brigades
      press on,
Glittering dimly, toiling under the sun—the dust-covered men,
In columns rise and fall to the undulations of the ground,
With artillery interspersed—the wheels rumble, the
      horses sweat,
As the army corps advances.

Walt Whitman   1865

COUNTERATTACK

We'd gained our first objective hours before
While dawn broke like a face with blinking eyes,
Pallid, unshaved and thirsty, blind with smoke.
Things seemed all right at first. We held their line,
With bombers posted, Lewis guns well-placed,
And clink of shovels deepening the shallow trench.

The place was rotten with dead; green clumsy legs
High-booted, sprawled and grovelled along the saps
And trunks, face downward, in the sucking mud,
Wallowed like trodden sandbags loosely filled;
And naked sodden buttocks, mats of hair,
Bulged, clotted heads slept in the plastering slime.
And then the rain began—the jolly old rain!

A yawning soldier knelt against the bank,
Staring across the morning blear with fog;
He wondered when the Allemands would get busy;
And then, of course, they started with five-nines
Traversing, sure as fate, and never a dud.
Mute in the clamor of shells he watched them burst
Spouting dark earth and wire with gusts from hell,
While posturing giants dissolved in drifts of smoke.
He crouched and flinched, dizzy with galloping fear,
Sick for escape—loathing the strangled horror
And butchered, frantic gestures of the dead.

An officer came blundering down the trench:
"Stand-to and man the fire-step!" On he went . . .
Gasping and bawling, "Fire-step . . . counterattack!"
Then the haze lifted. Bombing on the right
Down the old sap: machine guns on the left;
And stumbling figures looming out in front.
"O Christ, they're coming at us!" Bullets spat,
And he remembered his rifle . . . rapid fire . . .
And started blazing wildly . . . then a bang
Crumpled and spun him sideways, knocked him out
To grunt and wriggle: none heeded him; he choked
And fought the flapping veils of smothering gloom,
Lost in a blurred confusion of yells and groans . . .
Down, and down, and down, he sank and drowned,
Bleeding to death. The counterattack had failed.

Siegfried Sassoon   1918

DULCE ET DECORUM EST

Bent double, like old beggars under sacks,
Knock-kneed, coughing like hags, we cursed through sludge,
Till on the haunting flares we turned our backs
And toward our distant rest began to trudge.
Men marched asleep. Many had lost their boots
But limped on, blood-shod. All went lame; all blind;
Drunk with fatigue; deaf even to the hoots
Of tired, outstripped Five-Nines that dropped behind.

Gas! GAS! Quick, boys!—An ecstasy of fumbling
Fitting the clumsy helmets just in time;
But someone still was yelling out and stumbling
And flound'ring like a man in fire or lime . . .
Dim, through the misty panes and thick green light,
As under a green sea, I saw him drowning.

In all my dreams, before my helpless sight,
He plunges at me, guttering, choking, drowning.

If in some smothering dreams you too could pace
Behind the wagon that we flung him in,
And watch the white eyes writhing in his face,
His hanging face, like a devil's sick of sin;
If you could hear, at every jolt, the blood
Come gargling from the froth-corrupted lungs,
Obscene as cancer, bitter as the cud
Of vile, incurable sores on innocent tongues,
My friend, you would not tell with such high zest
To children ardent for some desperate glory,
The old Lie: Dulce et decorum est
Pro patria mori.

Wilfred Owen 1920

ULTIMA RATIO REGUM

The guns spell money's ultimate reason
In letters of lead on the Spring hillside.
But the boy lying dead under the olive trees
Was too young and too silly
To have been notable to their important eye.
He was a better target for a kiss.

When he lived, tall factory hooters never summoned him.
Nor did restaurant plate-glass doors revolve to wave him in.
His name never appeared in the papers.
The world maintained its traditional wall
Round the dead with their gold sunk deep as a well
Whilst his life, intangible as a Stock Exchange rumor,
        drifted outside.

O too lightly he threw down his cap
One day when the breeze threw petals from the trees.
The unflowering wall sprouted with guns,
Machine gun anger quickly scythed the grasses;
Flags and leaves fell from hands and branches;
The tweed cap rotted in the nettles.

Consider his life which was valueless
In terms of employment, hotel ledgers, news files.
Consider. One bullet in ten thousand kills a man.
Ask. Was so much expenditure justified
On the death of one so young and so silly
Lying under the olive tree, O world, O death?

Stephen Spender 1942

THE DEATH OF THE BALL TURRET GUNNER

From my mother's sleep I fell into the State,
And I hunched in its belly till my wet fur froze.
Six miles from earth, loosed from its dream of life,
I woke to black flak and the nightmare fighters.
When I died they washed me out of the turret with a hose.

Randall Jarrell 1945

ARMS AND THE BOY

Let the boy try along this bayonet blade
How cold steel is, and keen with hunger of blood;
Blue with all malice, like a madman's flash;
And thinly drawn with famishing for flesh.

Lend him to stroke these blind, blunt bullet heads
Which long to nuzzle in the hearts of lads,
Or give him cartridges of fine zinc teeth,
Sharp with the sharpness of grief and death.

For his teeth seem for laughing round an apple.
There lurk no claws behind his fingers supple;
And God will grow no talons at his heels,
Nor antlers through the thickness of his curls.

Wilfred Owen   1918

ANTRIM

No spot of earth where men have so fiercely for ages of time
Fought and survived and cancelled each other,
Pict and Gael and Dane, McQuillan, Clandonnel, O'Neill,
Savages, the Scot, the Norman, the English,
Here in the narrow passage and the pitiless north, perpetual
Betrayals, relentless resultless fighting.
A random fury of dirks in the dark: a struggle for survival
Of hungry blind cells of life in the womb.
But now the womb has grown old, her strength has gone forth;
      a few red carts in a fog creak flax to the dubs,
And sheep in the high heather cry hungrily that life is hard;
      a plaintive peace; shepherds and peasants.

We have felt the blades meet in the flesh in a hundred
      ambushes
And the groaning blood bubble in the throat;
In a hundred battles the heavy axes bite the deep bone,
The mountain suddenly stagger and be darkened.
Generation on generation we have seen the blood of boys
And heard the moaning of women massacred,

The passionate flesh and nerves have flamed like pitch-pine
        and fallen
And lain in the earth softly dissolving.
I have lain and been humbled in all these graves, and mixed new
        flesh with the old and filled the hollow of my mouth
With maggots and rotten dust and ages of repose. I lie here and
        plot the agony of resurrection.

Robinson Jeffers 1931

THE REAR GUARD

Groping along the tunnel, step by step,
He winked his prying torch with patching glare
From side to side, and sniffed the unwholesome air.

Tins, boxes, bottles, shapes too vague to know,
A mirror smashed, the mattress from a bed;
And he, exploring fifty feet below
The rosy gloom of battle overhead.
Tripping, he grabbed the wall; saw someone lie
Humped at his feet, half-hidden by a rug,
And stooped to give the sleeper's arm a tug.
"I'm looking for headquarters." No reply.
"God blast your neck!" (For days he'd had no sleep).
"Get up and guide me through this stinking place."
Savage, he kicked a soft, unanswering heap,
And flashed his beam across the livid face
Terribly glaring up, whose eyes yet wore
Agony dying hard ten days before;
And fists of fingers clutched a blackening wound.
Alone, he staggered on until he found
Dawn's ghost that filtered down a shafted stair
To the dazed, muttering creatures underground
Who hear the boom of shells in muffled sound.
At last, with sweat of horror in his hair,
He climbed through darkness to the twilight air,
Unloading hell behind him step by step.

Siegfried Sassoon 1918

LOSSES

It was not dying: everybody died.
It was not dying: we had died before
In the routine crashes—and our fields
Called up the papers, wrote home to our folks,
And the rates rose, all because of us.
We died on the wrong page of the almanac,
Scattered on mountains fifty miles away;
Diving on haystacks, fighting with a friend,
We blazed up on the lines we never saw.
We died like aunts or pets or foreigners.
(When we left high school nothing else had died
For us to figure we had died like.)

In our new planes, with our new crews, we bombed
The ranges by the desert or the shore,
Fired at towed targets, waited for our scores—
And turned into replacements and woke up
One morning, over England, operational.
It wasn't different: but if we died
It was not an accident but a mistake
(But an easy one for anyone to make).
We read our mail and counted up our missions—
In bombers named for girls, we burned
The cities we had learned about in school—
Till our lives wore out; our bodies lay among
The people we had killed and never seen.
When we lasted long enough they gave us medals;
When we died they said, "Our casualties were low."
They said, "Here are the maps"; we burned the cities.

It was not dying—no, not ever dying;
But the night I died I dreamed that I was dead,
And the cities said to me: "Why are you dying?
We are satisfied, if you are; but why did I die?"

Randall Jarrell   1944

RECONCILIATION

Word over all, beautiful as the sky,
Beautiful that war and all its deeds of carnage must in time
    be utterly lost,
That the hands of the sisters Death and Night incessantly softly
    wash again, and ever again, this soiled world;
For my enemy is dead, a man divine as myself is dead,
I look where he lies white-faced and still in the coffin—
    I draw near,
Bend down and touch lightly with my lips the white face
    in the coffin.

Walt Whitman 1865

BUTTONS

I have been watching the war map slammed up for advertising
    in front of the newspaper office.
Buttons—red and yellow buttons—blue and black buttons—
    are shoved back and forth across the map.

A laughing young man, sunny with freckles,
Climbs a ladder, yells a joke to somebody in the crowd,
And then fixes a yellow button one inch west
And follows the yellow button with a black button
    one inch west.

(Ten thousand men and boys twist on their bodies in a red
    soak along a river edge,
Gasping of wounds, calling for water, some rattling death
    in their throats.)
Who would guess what it cost to move two buttons one inch
    on the war map here in front of the newspaper office
    where the freckle-faced young man is laughing to us?

Carl Sandburg 1915

THE THREE RAVENS

There were three ravens sat on a tree,
They were as black as they might be.

Then one of them said to his mate,
"Where shall we our breakfast take?"

"Down in yonder green field
There lies a knight slain under his shield;

"His hounds they lie down at his feet,
So well they can their master keep;

"His hawks they fly so eagerly,
There's no fowl dare come him nigh."

Down there comes a fallow doe
As great with young as she might go.

She lifted up his bloody head
And kissed his wounds that were so red.

She got him up upon her back
And carried him to earthen lake.

She buried him before the prime;
She was dead herself ere even-song time.

God send every gentleman
Such hawks, such hounds, and such a leman.

Early English Ballad

HERE DEAD LIE WE BECAUSE WE DID NOT CHOOSE

Here dead lie we because we did not choose
    To live and shame the land from which we sprung.
Life, to be sure, is nothing much to lose;
    But young men think it is, and we were young.

A. E. Housman 1936

IN FLANDERS FIELDS

In Flanders fields the poppies blow
Between the crosses, row on row,
 That mark our place; and in the sky
 The larks, still bravely singing, fly
Scarce heard amid the guns below.

We are the Dead. Short days ago
We lived, felt dawn, saw sunset glow,
 Loved and were loved, and now we lie
 In Flanders fields.

Take up our quarrel with the foe:
To you from failing hands we throw
 The torch; be yours to hold it high.
 If ye break faith with us who die
We shall not sleep, though poppies grow
 In Flanders fields.

       John McCrae   1915

GRASS

Pile the bodies high at Austerlitz and Waterloo.
Shovel them under and let me work—
 I am the grass; I cover all.

And pile them high at Gettysburg
And pile them high at Ypres and Verdun.
Shovel them under and let me work.
Two years, ten years, and passengers ask the conductor:
 What place is this?
 Where are we now?

 I am the grass.
 Let me work.

       Carl Sandburg   1918

DOVER BEACH

The sea is calm tonight.
The tide is full, the moon lies fair
Upon the straits; on the French coast the light
Gleams and is gone; the cliffs of England stand,
Glimmering and vast, out in the tranquil bay.
Come to the window, sweet is the night air!
Only, from the long line of spray
Where the sea meets the moon-blanched land,
Listen! you hear the grating roar
Of pebbles which the waves draw back, and fling,
At their return, up the high strand,
Begin, and cease, and then again begin,
With tremulous cadence slow, and bring
The eternal note of sadness in.

Sophocles long ago
Heard it on the Aegean, and it brought
Into his mind the turbid ebb and flow
Of human misery; we
Find also in the sound a thought,
Hearing it by this distant northern sea.

The Sea of Faith
Was once, too, at the full, and round earth's shore
Lay like the folds of a bright girdle furled.
But now I only hear
Its melancholy, long, withdrawing roar,
Retreating, to the breath
Of the night wind, down the vast edges drear
And naked shingles of the world.

Ah, love, let us be true
To one another! for the world, which seems
To lie before us like a land of dreams,
So various, so beautiful, so new,
Hath really neither joy, nor love, nor light,
Nor certitude, nor peace, nor help for pain;
And we are here as on a darkling plain
Swept with confused alarms of struggle and flight,
Where ignorant armies clash by night.

Matthew Arnold   1867

RECESSIONAL

God of our fathers, known of old,
    Lord of our far-flung battle line,
Beneath whose awful hand we hold
    Dominion over palm and pine—
Lord God of Hosts, be with us yet,
Lest we forget—Lest we forget!

The tumult and the shouting dies;
    The Captains and the Kings depart:
Still stands Thine ancient sacrifice,
    An humble and a contrite heart.
Lord God of Hosts, be with us yet,
Lest we forget—lest we forget!

Far-called our navies melt away;
    On dune and headland sinks the fire:
Lo, all our pomp of yesterday
    Is one with Nineveh and Tyre!
Judge of the Nations, spare us yet,
Lest we forget—lest we forget!

If, drunk with sight of power, we loose
    Wild tongues that have not Thee in awe,
Such boasting as the Gentiles use,
    Or lesser breeds without the Law—
Lord God of Hosts, be with us yet,
Lest we forget—lest we forget!

For heathen heart that puts her trust
    In reeking tube and iron shard,
All valiant dust that builds on dust,
    And guarding, calls not Thee to guard,
For frantic boast and foolish word—
Thy mercy on Thy people, Lord!

Rudyard Kipling   1897

WHAT WERE THEY LIKE?

1) Did the people of Viet Nam use lanterns of stone?
2) Did they hold ceremonies to reverence the opening of buds?
3) Were they inclined to quiet laughter?
4) Did they use bone and ivory, jade and silver, for ornament?
5) Had they an epic poem?
6) Did they distinguish between speech and singing?

1) Sir, their light hearts turned to stone.
   It is not remembered whether in gardens stone lanterns
   illumined pleasant ways.
2) Perhaps they gathered once to delight in blossom, but after
   the children were killed there were no more buds.
3) Sir, laughter is bitter to the burned mouth.
4) A dream ago, perhaps. Ornament is for joy.
   All the bones were charred.
5) It is not remembered. Remember, most were peasants;
   their life was in rice and bamboo.
   When peaceful clouds were reflected in the paddies and
   the water buffalo stepped surely along terraces, maybe fathers
   told their sons old tales.
   When bombs smashed those mirrors there was time only
   to scream.
6) There is an echo yet of their speech which was like a song.
   It was reported their singing resembled the flight of moths in
   moonlight.
   Who can say? It is silent now.

Denise Levertov   1966

[I'M DREAMING THE MY LAI SOLDIER AGAIN]

I'm dreaming the My Lai soldier again,
I'm dreaming the My Lai soldier night after night.
He rings the doorbell like the Fuller Brush Man
and wants to shake hands with me
and I do because it would be rude to say no
and I look at my hand and it is green
with intestines.
And they won't come off,
they won't. He apologizes for this over and over.

The My Lai soldier lifts me up again and again
and lowers me down with the other dead women and babies
saying, *It's my job. It's my job.*
Then he gives me a bullet to swallow
like a sleeping tablet.

I am lying in this belly of dead babies
each one belching up the yellow gasses of death
and their mothers tumble, eyeballs, knees, upon me,
each for the last time, each authentically dead.
The soldier stands on a stepladder above us
pointing his red penis right at me and saying,
Don't take this personally.

Anne Sexton   1976

AND DID THOSE FEET IN ANCIENT TIME

And did those feet in ancient time
Walk upon England's mountains green?
And was the holy Lamb of God
On England's pleasant pastures seen?

And did the Countenance Divine
Shine forth upon our clouded hills?
And was Jerusalem builded here,
Among these dark Satanic Mills?

Bring me my bow of burning gold:
Bring me my arrows of desire:
Bring me my spear: O clouds unfold!
Bring me my Chariot of fire!

I will not cease from Mental Fight,
Nor shall my sword sleep in my hand,
Till we have built Jerusalem
In England's green & pleasant Land.

William Blake   1810

ONCE MORE UNTO THE BREACH

KING HENRY: Once more unto the breach, dear friends,
    once more;
Or close the wall up with our English dead.
In peace there's nothing so becomes a man
As modest stillness and humility:
But when the blast of war blows in our ears,
Then imitate the action of the tiger;
Stiffen the sinews, summon up the blood,
Disguise fair nature with hard-favored rage;
Then lend the eye a terrible aspect;
Let it pry through the portage of the head
Like the brass cannon; let the brow o'erwhelm it
As fearfully as doth a galled rock
O'erhang and jutty his confounded base,
Swilled with the wild and wasteful ocean.
Now set the teeth and stretch the nostril wide,
Hold hard the breath and bend up every spirit
To his full height. On, on, you noblest English,
Whose blood is fet from fathers of war-proof!
Fathers that, like so many Alexanders,
Have in these parts from morn till even fought
And sheathed their swords for lack of argument:
Dishonor not your mothers; now attest
That those whom you called fathers did beget you.
Be copy now to men of grosser blood,
And teach them how to war. And you, good yeomen,
Whose limbs were made in England, show us here
The mettle of your pasture; let us swear
That you are worth your breeding; which I doubt not;
For there is none of you so mean and base,
That hath not noble luster in your eyes.
I see you stand like greyhounds in the slips,
Straining upon the start. The game's afoot:
Follow your spirit, and upon this charge
Cry 'God for Harry, England, and Saint George!'

William Shakespeare   1599
King Henry V, Act III, Prologue

THE LAST WAR

The first country to die was normal in the evening,
Ate a good but plain dinner, chatted with some friends
Over a glass, and went to bed soon after ten;
And in the morning was found disfigured and dead.
    That was a lucky one.

At breakfast the others heard about it, and kept
Their eyes on their plates. Who was guilty? No one knew,
But by lunch time three more would never eat again.
The rest appealed for frankness, quietly cocked their guns,
    Declared "This can't go on."

They were right. Only the strongest turned up for tea:
The old ones with the big estates hadn't survived
The slobbering blindfold violence of the afternoon.
One killer or many? Was it a gang, or all-against-all?
    Somebody must have known.

But each of them sat there watching the others, until
Night came and found them anxious to get it over.
Then the lights went out. A few might have lived, even then;
Innocent, they thought (at first) it still mattered what
    You had or hadn't done.

They were wrong. One had been lenient with his servants;
Another ran an island brothel, but rarely left it;
The third owned a museum, the fourth a remarkable gun;
The name of the fifth was quite unknown, but in the end
    What was the difference? None.

Homicide, pacifist, crusader, tyrant, adventurer, boor
Staggered about moaning, shooting into the dark.
Next day, to tidy up as usual, the sun came in
When they and their ammunition were all finished,
    And found himself alone.

Upset, he looked them over, to separate, if he could,
The assassins from the victims, but every face
Had taken on the flat anonymity of pain;
And soon they'll all smell alike, he thought, and felt sick,
And went to bed at noon.

Kingsley Amis 1956

EARTH

"A planet doesn't explode of itself," said drily
The Martian astronomer, gazing off into the air—
"That they were able to do it is proof that highly
Intelligent beings must have been living there."

John Hall Wheelock 1961

THE WAY THROUGH THE WOODS

THE PASTURE

I'm going out to clean the pasture spring;
I'll only stop to rake the leaves away
(And wait to watch the water clear, I may):
I shan't be gone long—You come too.

I'm going out to fetch the little calf
That's standing by the mother. It's so young
It totters when she licks it with her tongue.
I shan't be gone long—You come too.

Robert Frost   1913

AFTER APPLE PICKING

My long two-pointed ladder's sticking through a tree
Toward heaven still,
And there's a barrel that I didn't fill
Beside it, and there may be two or three
Apples I didn't pick upon some bough.
But I am done with apple picking now.
Essence of winter sleep is on the night,
The scent of apples: I am drowsing off.
I cannot rub the strangeness from my sight
I got from looking through a pane of glass
I skimmed this morning from the drinking trough
And held against the world of hoary grass.
It melted, and I let it fall and break.
But I was well
Upon my way to sleep before it fell,
And I could tell
What form my dreaming was about to take.
Magnified apples appear and disappear,
Stem end and blossom end,
And every fleck of russet showing clear.
My instep arch not only keeps the ache,
It keeps the pressure of a ladder-round.
I feel the ladder sway as the boughs bend.
And I keep hearing from the cellar bin
The rumbling sound
Of load on load of apples coming in.
For I have had too much
Of apple picking: I am overtired
Of the great harvest I myself desired.
There were ten thousand thousand fruit to touch,
Cherish in hand, lift down, and not let fall.
For all
That struck the earth,
No matter if not bruised or spiked with stubble,
Went surely to the cider-apple heap
As of no worth.

One can see what will trouble
This sleep of mine, whatever sleep it is.
Were he not gone,
The woodchuck could say whether it's like his
Long sleep, as I describe its coming on,
Or just some human sleep.

Robert Frost 1914

ROOT CELLAR

Nothing would sleep in that cellar, dank as a ditch,
Bulbs broke out of boxes hunting for chinks in the dark,
Shoots dangled and drooped,
Lolling obscenely from mildewed crates,
Hung down long yellow evil necks, like tropical snakes.
And what a congress of stinks!
Roots ripe as old bait,
Pulpy stems, rank, silo-rich,
Leaf mold, manure, lime, piled against slippery planks.
Nothing would give up life:
Even the dirt kept breathing a small breath.

Theodore Roethke 1948

WHEN GREEN BUDS HANG IN THE ELM

When green buds hang in the elm like dust
    And sprinkle the lime like rain,
Forth I wander, forth I must,
    And drink of life again.

Forth I must by hedgerow bowers
    To look at the leaves uncurled,
And stand in the fields where cuckoo flowers
    Are lying about the world.

A. E. Housman 1936

THE ROAD NOT TAKEN

Two roads diverged in a yellow wood,
And sorry I could not travel both
And be one traveler, long I stood
And looked down one as far as I could
To where it bent in the undergrowth;

Then took the other, as just as fair,
And having perhaps the better claim,
Because it was grassy and wanted wear;
Though as for that, the passing there
Had worn them really about the same,

And both that morning equally lay
In leaves no step had trodden black.
Oh, I kept the first for another day!
Yet knowing how way leads on to way,
I doubted if I should ever come back.

I shall be telling this with a sigh
Somewhere ages and ages hence:
Two roads diverged in a wood, and I—
I took the one less traveled by,
And that has made all the difference.

Robert Frost   1916

THE WAY THROUGH THE WOODS

They shut the road through the woods
Seventy years ago.
Weather and rain have undone it again,
And now you would never know
There was once a path through the woods
Before they planted the trees.
It is underneath the coppice and heath
And the thin anemones.
Only the keeper sees
That, where the ring dove broods,
And the badgers roll at ease,
There was once a road through the woods.

Yet, if you enter the woods
Of a summer evening late,
When the night air cools on the trout-ringed pools
Where the otter whistles his mate,
(They fear not men in the woods
Because they see so few.)
You will hear the beat of a horse's feet
And the swish of a skirt in the dew,
Steadily cantering through
The misty solitudes,
As though they perfectly knew
The old lost road through the woods . . .
But there is no road through the woods.

Rudyard Kipling   1910

THE SONG OF THE WANDERING ÆNGUS

I went out to the hazel wood,
Because a fire was in my head,
And cut and peeled a hazel wand,
And hooked a berry to a thread;
And when white moths were on the wing,
And mothlike stars were flickering out,
I dropped the berry in a stream
And caught a little silver trout.
When I had laid it on the floor
I went to blow the fire aflame,
But something rustled on the floor,
And some one called me by my name:
It had become a glimmering girl
With apple blossoms in her hair
Who called me by my name and ran
And faded through the brightening air.

Though I am old with wandering
Through hollow lands and hilly lands,
I will find out where she has gone,
And kiss her lips and take her hands;
And walk among long dappled grass,
And pluck till time and times are done,
The silver apples of the moon,
The golden apples of the sun.

William Butler Yeats   1897

THE LAKE ISLE OF INNISFREE

I will arise and go now, and go to Innisfree,
And a small cabin build there, of clay and wattles made;
Nine bean rows will I have there, a hive for the honey bee,
And live alone in the bee-loud glade.

And I shall have some peace there, for peace comes
    dropping slow,
Dropping from the veils of the morning to where the
    cricket sings;
There midnight's all a glimmer, and noon a purple glow,
And evening full of the linnet's wings.

I will arise and go now, for always night and day
I hear lake water lapping with low sounds by the shore;
While I stand on the roadway, or on the pavements gray,
I hear it in the deep heart's core.

William Butler Yeats   1890

I TASTE A LIQUOR NEVER BREWED

I taste a liquor never brewed,
From tankards scooped in pearl;
Not all the vats upon the Rhine
Yield such an alcohol!

Inebriate of air am I,
And debauchee of dew,
Reeling through endless summer days,
From inns of molten blue.

When landlords turn the drunken bee
Out of the foxglove's door,
When butterflies renounce their drams,
I shall but drink the more!

Till seraphs swing their snowy hats,
And saints to windows run,
To see the little tippler
Leaning against the sun.

Emily Dickinson   1860

I WANDERED LONELY AS A CLOUD

I wandered lonely as a cloud
That floats on high o'er vales and hills,
When all at once I saw a crowd,
A host, of golden daffodils;
Beside the lake, beneath the trees,
Fluttering and dancing in the breeze.

Continuous as the stars that shine
And twinkle on the Milky Way,
They stretched in never-ending line
Along the margin of a bay:
Ten thousand saw I at a glance,
Tossing their heads in sprightly dance.

The waves beside them danced, but they
Outdid the sparkling waves in glee;
A poet could not but be gay,
In such a jocund company:
I gazed—and gazed—but little thought
What wealth the show to me had brought:

For oft, when on my couch I lie
In vacant or in pensive mood,
They flash upon that inward eye
Which is the bliss of solitude;
And then my heart with pleasure fills,
And dances with the daffodils.

William Wordsworth   1804

THE TIGER

Tiger! Tiger! burning bright
In the forests of the night,
What immortal hand or eye
Could frame thy fearful symmetry?

In what distant deeps or skies
Burnt the fire of thine eyes?
On what wings dare he aspire?
What the hand dare seize the fire?

And what shoulder and what art,
Could twist the sinews of thy heart?
And when thy heart began to beat,
What dread hand? and what dread feet?

What the hammer? what the chain?
In what furnace was thy brain?
What the anvil? what dread grasp
Dare its deadly terrors clasp?

When the stars threw down their spears,
And watered heaven with their tears,
Did he smile his work to see?
Did he who made the Lamb make thee?

Tiger! Tiger! burning bright
In the forests of the night,
What immortal hand or eye
Dare frame thy fearful symmetry?

William Blake   1794

THE LAMB

Little Lamb, who made thee?
Dost thou know who made thee?
Gave thee life, and bid thee feed,
By the stream and o'er the mead;
Gave thee clothing of delight,
Softest clothing, woolly, bright;
Gave thee such tender voice,
Making all the vales rejoice?
Little Lamb, who made thee?
Dost thou know who made thee?

Little Lamb, I'll tell thee,
Little Lamb, I'll tell thee:
He is called by thy name,
For He calls Himself a Lamb,
He is meek, and he is mild;

He became a little child.
I a child, and thou a lamb,
We are called by his name.
Little Lamb, God bless thee!
Little Lamb, God bless thee!

William Blake   1789

THE EAGLE

He clasps the crag with crooked hands;
Close to the sun in lonely lands,
Ringed with the azure world, he stands.

The wrinkled sea beneath him crawls;
He watches from his mountain walls,
And like a thunderbolt he falls.

Alfred, Lord Tennyson   1851

THE DALLIANCE OF EAGLES

Skirting the river road, (my forenoon walk, my rest,)
Skyward in air a sudden muffled sound, the dalliance of
    the eagles,
The rushing amorous contact high in space together,
The clinching, interlocking claws, a living, fierce, gyrating wheel,
Four beating wings, two beaks, a swirling mass tight grappling,
In tumbling, turning, clustering hoops, straight downward
    falling,
Till o'er the river poised, the twain yet one, a moment's lull,
A motionless still balance in the air, then parting, talons loosing,
Upward again on slow-firm pinions slanting, their separate
    diverse flight,
She hers, he his, pursuing.

Walt Whitman 1880

VULTURE

I had walked since dawn and lay down to rest on a bare hillside
Above the ocean. I saw through half-shut eyelids a vulture
    wheeling high up in heaven,
And presently it passed again, but lower and nearer, its orbit
    narrowing, I understood then
That I was under inspection. I lay death-still and heard the
    flight-feathers
Whistle above me and make their circle and come nearer.
I could see the naked red head between the great wings
Beak downward staring. I said, "My dear bird, we are
    wasting time here.
These old bones will still work; they are not for you." But how
    beautiful he'd looked, gliding down
On those great sails; how beautiful he looked, veering away in
    the sea light over the precipice. I tell you solemnly
That I was sorry to have disappointed him. To be eaten by
    that beak and become part of him, to share those wings and
    those eyes—
What a sublime end of one's body, what an enskyment;
    what a life after death.

Robinson Jeffers 1962

HURT HAWKS

1

The broken pillar of the wing jags from the clotted shoulder,
The wing trails like a banner in defeat,
No more to use the sky forever but live with famine
And pain a few days: cat nor coyote
Will shorten the week of waiting for death, there is game
    without talons.
He stands under the oak bush and waits
The lame feet of salvation; at night he remembers freedom
And flies in a dream, the dawns ruin it.
He is strong and pain is worse to the strong, incapacity
    is worse.
The curs of the day come and torment him
At distance, no one but death the redeemer will humble that
    head,
The intrepid readiness, the terrible eyes.
The wild God of the world is sometimes merciful to those
That ask mercy, not often to the arrogant.
You do not know him, you communal people, or you have
    forgotten him;
Intemperate and savage, the hawk remembers him;
Beautiful and wild, the hawks, and men that are dying,
    remember him.

2

I'd sooner, except the penalties, kill a man than a hawk;
    but the great redtail
Had nothing left but unable misery
From the bone too shattered for mending, the wing that
    trailed under his talons when he moved.
We had fed him six weeks, I gave him freedom,
He wandered over the foreland hill and returned in the
    evening, asking for death,
Not like a beggar, still eyed with the old
Implacable arrogance. I gave him the lead gift in the twilight.
    What fell was relaxed.
Owl-downy, soft feminine feathers; but what
Soared: the fierce rush: the night herons by the flooded river
    cried fear at its rising
Before it was quite unsheathed from reality.

Robinson Jeffers 1924

GOD'S WORLD

O world, I cannot hold thee close enough!
　　Thy winds, thy wide gray skies!
　　Thy mists that roll and rise!
Thy woods, this autumn day, that ache and sag
And all but cry with color! That gaunt crag
To crush! To lift the lean of that black bluff!
World, World, I cannot get thee close enough!

Long have I known a glory in it all,
　　But never knew I this:
　　Here such a passion is
As stretcheth me apart—Lord, I do fear
Thou'st made the world too beautiful this year;
My soul is all but out of me—let fall
No burning leaf; prithee, let no bird call.

Edna St. Vincent Millay   1913

SPRING

To what purpose, April, do you return again?
Beauty is not enough.
You can no longer quiet me with the redness
Of little leaves opening stickily.
I know what I know.
The sun is hot on my neck as I observe
The spikes of the crocus.
The smell of the earth is good.
It is apparent that there is no death.
But what does that signify?
Not only underground are the brains of men
Eaten by maggots.
Life in itself
Is nothing,
An empty cup, a flight of uncarpeted stairs.
It is not enough that yearly, down this hill,
April
Comes like an idiot, babbling and strewing flowers.

Edna St. Vincent Millay   1921

PIED BEAUTY

Glory be to God for dappled things—
 For skies of couple-color as a brinded cow;
  For rose-moles all in stipple upon trout that swim;
Fresh-firecoal chestnut-falls; finches' wings;
 Landscape plotted and pieced—fold, fallow, and plough;
  And áll trádes, their gear and tackle and trim.
All things counter, original, spare, strange;
 Whatever is fickle, freckled (who knows how?)
  With swift, slow; sweet, sour; adazzle, dim;
He fathers-forth whose beauty is past change:
   Praise Him.

      Gerard Manley Hopkins 1877

INVERSNAID

This darksome burn, horseback brown,
His rollrock highroad roaring down,
In coop and in comb the fleece of his foam
Flutes and low to the lake falls home.

A windpuff-bonnet of fáwn-fróth
Turns and twindles over the broth
Of a pool so pitchblack, féll-frówning,
It rounds and rounds Despair to drowning.

Degged with dew, dappled with dew
Are the groins of the braes that the brook treads through,
Wiry heathpacks, flitches of fern,
And the beadbonny ash that sits over the burn.

What would the world be, once bereft
Of wet and of wildness? Let them be left,
O let them be left, wildness and wet;
Long live the weeds and the wilderness yet.

      Gerard Manley Hopkins 1881

LOVE CALLS US TO THE THINGS OF THIS WORLD

The eyes open to a cry of pulleys,
And spirited from sleep, the astounded soul
Hangs for a moment bodiless and simple
As false dawn.
                    Outside the open window
The morning air is all awash with angels.

    Some are in bedsheets, some are in blouses,
Some are in smocks: but truly there they are.
Now they are rising together in calm swells
Of halcyon feeling, filling whatever they wear
With the deep joy of their impersonal breathing;

    Now they are flying in place, conveying
The terrible speed of their omnipresence, moving
And staying like white water; and now of a sudden
They swoon down into so rapt a quiet
That nobody seems to be there.
                    The soul shrinks

    From all that it is about to remember,
From the punctual rape of every blessed day,
And cries,
        "Oh, let there be nothing on earth but laundry,
Nothing but rosy hands in the rising steam
And clear dances done in the sight of heaven."

    Yet, as the sun acknowledges
With a warm look the world's hunks and colors,
The soul descends once more in bitter love
To accept the waking body, saying now
In a changed voice as the man yawns and rises,

    "Bring them down from their ruddy gallows;
Let there be clean linen for the backs of thieves;
Let lovers go fresh and sweet to be undone,
And the heaviest nuns walk in a pure floating
Of dark habits,
                    keeping their difficult balance."

                                        Richard Wilbur   1956

CHINOISERIES

REFLECTIONS

When I looked into your eyes,
I saw a garden
With peonies, and tinkling pagodas,
And round-arched bridges
Over still lakes.
A woman sat beside the water
In a rain-blue silken garment.
She reached through the water
To pluck the crimson peonies
Beneath the surface,
But as she grasped the stems,
They jarred and broke into white-green ripples;
And as she drew out her hand,
The water drops dripping from it
Stained her rain-blue dress like tears.

FALLING SNOW

The snow whispers about me,
And my wooden clogs
Leave holes behind me in the snow.
But no one will pass this way
Seeking my footsteps,
And when the temple bell rings again
They will be covered and gone.

HOAR-FROST

In the cloud-gray mornings
I heard the herons flying;
And when I came into my garden,
My silken outer garment
Trailed over withered leaves.
A dried leaf crumbles at a touch,
But I have seen many Autumns
With herons blowing like smoke
Across the sky.

Amy Lowell   1919

FERN HILL

Now as I was young and easy under the apple boughs
About the lilting house and happy as the grass was green,
    The night above the dingle starry,
        Time let me hail and climb
    Golden in the heydays of his eyes,
And honored among wagons I was prince of the apple towns
And once below a time I lordly had the trees and leaves
        Trail with daisies and barley
    Down the rivers of the windfall light.

And as I was green and carefree, famous among the barns
About the happy yard and singing as the farm was home,
    In the sun that is young once only,
        Time let me play and be
    Golden in the mercy of his means,
And green and golden I was huntsman and herdsman, the calves
Sang to my horn, the foxes on the hills barked clear and cold,
        And the sabbath rang slowly
    In the pebbles of the holy streams.

All the sun long it was running, it was lovely, the hay
Fields high as the house, the tunes from the chimneys, it was air
    And playing, lovely and watery
        And fire green as grass.
    And nightly under the simple stars
As I rode to sleep the owls were bearing the farm away,
All the moon long I heard, blessed among stables, the nightjars
        Flying with the ricks, and the horses
        Flashing into the dark.

And then to awake, and the farm, like a wanderer white
With the dew, come back, the cock on his shoulder: it was all
    Shining, it was Adam and maiden,
        The sky gathered again
    And the sun grew round that very day.
So it must have been after the birth of the simple light
In the first, spinning place, the spellbound horses walking warm
    Out of the whinnying green stable
        On to the fields of praise.

And honored among foxes and pheasants by the gay house
Under the new made clouds and happy as the heart was long,
   In the sun born over and over,
      I ran my heedless ways,
   My wishes raced through the house high hay
And nothing I cared, at my sky blue trades, that time allows
In all his tuneful turning so few and such morning songs
   Before the children green and golden
      Follow him out of grace.

Nothing I cared, in the lamb white days, that time would take me
Up to the swallow thronged loft by the shadow of my hand,
   In the moon that is always rising,
      Nor that riding to sleep
   I should hear him fly with the high fields
And wake to the farm forever fled from the childless land.
Oh as I was young and easy in the mercy of his means,
      Time held me green and dying
    Though I sang in my chains like the sea.

Dylan Thomas 1945

PURITAN SONNET

from "Wild Peaches"

Down to the Puritan marrow of my bones
There's something in this richness that I hate.
I love the look, austere, immaculate,
Of landscapes drawn in pearly monotones.
There's something in my very blood that owns
Bare hills, cold silver on a sky of slate,
A thread of water, churned to milky spate
Streaming through slanted pastures fenced with stones.

I love those skies, thin blue or snowy gray,
Those fields sparse-planted, rendering meager sheaves;
That spring, briefer than apple-blossom's breath,
Summer, so much too beautiful to stay,
Swift autumn, like a bonfire of leaves,
And sleepy winter, like the sleep of death.

Elinor Wylie 1921

FOG

The fog comes
on little cat feet.
It sits looking
over harbor and city
on silent haunches
and then moves on.

Carl Sandburg   1916

THE WANING MOON

And like a dying lady, lean and pale,
　Who totters forth, wrapped in a gauzy veil,
Out of her chamber, led by the insane
And feeble wanderings of her fading brain,
The moon arose up in the murky East
A white and shapeless mass.

　Art thou pale for weariness
Of climbing heaven and gazing on the earth,
　Wandering companionless
Among the stars that have a different birth,
And ever changing, like a joyless eye
That finds no object worth its constancy?

Percy Bysshe Shelley   1820

WHAT LIPS
MY LIPS
HAVE KISSED

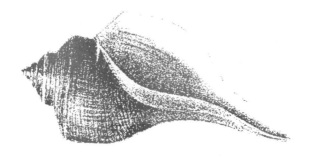

POLITICS

In our time the destiny of man presents its
meaning in political terms.—Thomas Mann

How can I, that girl standing there,
My attention fix
On Roman or on Russian
Or on Spanish politics?
Yet here's a traveled man that knows
What he talks about,
And there's a politician
That has read and thought,
And maybe what they say is true
Of war and war's alarms,
But O that I were young again
And held her in my arms!

William Butler Yeats   1939

I KNEW A WOMAN

I knew a woman, lovely in her bones,
When small birds sighed, she would sigh back at them;
Ah, when she moved, she moved more ways than one:
The shapes a bright container can contain!
Of her choice virtues only gods should speak,
Or English poets who grew up on Greek
(I'd have them sing in chorus, cheek to cheek).

How well her wishes went! She stroked my chin,
She taught me Turn, and Counter-turn, and Stand;
She taught me Touch, that undulant white skin;
I nibbled meekly from her proffered hand;
She was the sickle; I, poor I, the rake,
Coming behind her for her pretty sake
(But what prodigious mowing we did make).

Love likes a gander, and adores a goose:
Her full lips pursed, the errant note to seize;
She played it quick, she played it light and loose;
My eyes, they dazzled at her flowing knees;
Her several parts could keep a pure repose,
Or one hip quiver with a mobile nose
(She moved in circles, and those circles moved).

Let seed be grass, and grass turn into hay:
I'm martyr to a motion not my own;
What's freedom for? To know eternity.
I swear she cast a shadow white as stone.
But who would count eternity in days?
These old bones live to learn her wanton ways:
(I measure time by how a body sways).

Theodore Roethke   1954

NUDE DESCENDING A STAIRCASE

Toe upon toe, a snowing flesh,
A gold of lemon, root and rind,
She sifts in sunlight down the stairs
With nothing on. Nor on her mind.

We spy beneath the banister
A constant thresh of thigh on thigh
Her lips imprint the swinging air
That parts to let her parts go by.

One-woman waterfall, she wears
Her slow descent like a long cape
And pausing, on the final stair
Collects her motions into shape.

X. J. Kennedy   1960

PIAZZA DI SPAGNA, EARLY MORNING

I can't forget
How she stood at the top of that long marble stair
Amazed, and then with a sleepy pirouette
Went dancing slowly down to the fountain-quieted square;

Nothing upon her face
But some impersonal loneliness,—not then a girl,
But as it were a reverie of the place,
A called-for falling glide and whirl;

As when a leaf, petal, or thin chip
Is drawn to the falls of a pool and, circling a moment above it,
Rides on over the lip—
Perfectly beautiful, perfectly ignorant of it.

Richard Wilbur   1956

HER HEART

Her heart is always doing lovely things,
    Filling my wintry mind with simple flowers;
Playing sweet tunes on my untunèd strings,
    Delighting all my undelightful hours,

She plays me like a lute, what tune she will,
    No string in me but trembles at her touch,
Shakes into sacred music, or is still,
    Trembles or stops, or swells, her skill is such.

And in the dusty taverns of my soul
    Where filthy lusts drink witches' brew for wine,
Her gentle hand still keeps me from the bowl,
    Still keeps me man, saves me from being swine.

All grace in me, all sweetness in my verse,
Is hers, is my dear girl's, and only hers.

                                    John Masefield   1915

ON A CERTAIN LADY AT COURT

I know the thing that's most uncommon
    (Envy be silent, and attend!)
I know a reasonable woman,
    Handsome and witty, yet a friend.

Not warped by passion, awed by rumor,
    Not grave through pride, or gay through folly,
An equal mixture of good humor
    And sensible soft melancholy.

"Has she no faults, then (Envy says), sir?"
    Yes, she has one, I must aver:
When all the world conspires to praise her,
    The woman's deaf, and does not hear.

                                    Alexander Pope   1732

Delight in Disorder

A sweet disorder in the dress
Kindles in clothes a wantonness.
A lawn about the shoulders thrown
Into a fine distraction;
An erring lace, which here and there
Enthralls the crimson stomacher;
A cuff neglectful, and thereby
Ribbands to flow confusedly:
A winning wave, deserving note,
In the tempestuous petticoat;
A careless shoestring, in whose tie
I see a wild civility;
Do more bewitch me, than when art
Is too precise in every part.

Robert Herrick   1640

Preference

I likes a woman
six or eight and ten years older'n myself.
I don't fool with these young girls.
Young girl'll say,
  Daddy, I want so-and-so.
   I needs this, that, and the other.
But a old woman'll say,
  Honey, what does YOU need?
  I just drawed my money tonight
  and it's all your'n.
That's why I likes a older woman
who can appreciate me:
When she conversations you
it ain't forever, *Gimme!*

Langston Hughes   1951

THE GYPSY GIRL

"Come, try your skill, kind gentlemen,
A penny for three tries!"
Some threw and lost, some threw and won
A ten-a-penny prize.

She was a tawny gypsy girl,
A girl of twenty years,
I liked her for the lumps of gold
That jingled from her ears;

I liked the flaring yellow scarf
Bound loose about her throat,
I liked her showy purple gown
And flashy velvet coat.

A man came up, too loose of tongue,
And said no good to her;
She did not blush as Saxons do,
Or turn upon the cur;

She fawned and whined "Sweet gentleman,
A penny for three tries!"
—But, oh, the den of wild things in
The darkness of her eyes!

Ralph Hodgson   1911

NO IMAGES

She does not know
Her beauty,
She thinks her brown body
Has no glory.

If she could dance
Naked,
Under palm trees
And see her image in the river
She would know.

But there are no palm trees
On the street,
And dishwater gives back no images.

Waring Cuney   1931

THE HARLEM DANCER

Applauding youths laughed with young prostitutes
And watched her perfect, half-clothed body sway;
Her voice was like the sound of blended flutes
Blown by black players upon a picnic day.
She sang and danced on gracefully and calm,
The light gauze hanging loose about her form;
To me she seemed a proudly swaying palm
Grown lovelier for passing through a storm.
Upon her swarthy neck black, shiny curls
Profusely fell; and tossing coins in praise,
The wine-flushed, bold-eyed boys, and even the girls,
Devoured her with their eager, passionate gaze;
But looking at her falsely smiling face,
I knew her self was not in that strange place.

Claude McKay   1922

BLACKBERRY SWEET

Black girl black girl
lips as curved as cherries
full as grape bunches
sweet as blackberries

Black girl black girl
when you walk you are
magic as a rising bird
or a falling star

Black girl black girl
what's your spell to make
the heart in my breast
jump   stop   shake

Dudley Randall   1969

TO A DARK GIRL

I love you for your brownness
And the rounded darkness of your breast.
I love you for the breaking sadness in your voice
And shadows where your wayward eyelids rest.

Something of old forgotten queens
Lurks in the lithe abandon of your walk,
And something of the shackled slave
Sobs in the rhythm of your talk.

Oh, little brown girl, born for sorrow's mate,
Keep all you have of queenliness,
Forgetting that you once were slave,
And let your full lips laugh at Fate!

Gwendolyn Bennett   1931

NIGHT PIECE, TO JULIA

Her eyes the glowworm lend thee,
The shooting stars attend thee,
    And the elves also,
    Whose little eyes glow
Like the sparks of fire, befriend thee.

No will-o'-the-wisp mislight thee;
Nor snake or slow worm bite thee;
    But on, on thy way,
    Not making a stay,
Since ghost there's none to affright thee.

Let not the dark thee cumber;
What though the moon does slumber?
    The stars of the night
    Will lend thee their light,
Like tapers clear without number.

Then Julia, let me woo thee,
Thus, thus to come unto me;
    And when I shall meet
    Thy silvery feet,
My soul I'll pour into thee.

Robert Herrick   1648

To Celia

Drink to me only with thine eyes,
  And I will pledge with mine;
Or leave a kiss but in the cup,
  And I'll not look for wine.
The thirst that from the soul doth rise
  Doth ask a drink divine;
But might I of Jove's nectar sup,
  I would not change for thine.

I sent thee late a rosy wreath,
  Not so much honoring thee
As giving it a hope that there
  It could not withered be;
But thou thereon did'st only breathe,
  And sent'st it back to me;
Since when it grows and smells, I swear,
  Not of itself, but thee.

Ben Jonson   1616

To Helen

Helen, thy beauty is to me
  Like those Nicean barks of yore,
That gently, o'er a perfumed sea,
  The weary, way-worn wanderer bore
  To his own native shore.

On desperate seas long wont to roam,
  Thy hyacinth hair, thy classic face,
Thy Naiad airs have brought me home
  To the glory that was Greece,
And the grandeur that was Rome.

Lo! in yon brilliant window niche
  How statuelike I see thee stand,
  The agate lamp within thy hand!
Ah! Psyche, from the regions which
  Are Holy Land!

Edgar Allan Poe   1823

THE PASSIONATE SHEPHERD TO HIS LOVE

Come live with me and be my Love,
And we will all the pleasures prove
That hills and valleys, dales and fields,
Or woods or steepy mountain yields.

And we will sit upon the rocks,
And see the shepherds feed their flocks
By shallow rivers, to whose falls
Melodious birds sing madrigals.

And I will make thee beds of roses
And a thousand fragrant posies;
A cap of flowers, and a kirtle
Embroidered all with leaves of myrtle.

A gown made of the finest wool
Which from our pretty lambs we pull;
Fair-linèd slippers for the cold,
With buckles of the purest gold.

A belt of straw and ivy buds
With coral clasps and amber studs:
And if these pleasures may thee move,
Come live with me and be my Love.

The shepherd swains shall dance and sing
For thy delight each May morning;
If these delights thy mind may move,
Then live with me and be my Love.

Christopher Marlowe   1599

THE NYMPH'S REPLY TO THE SHEPHERD

If all the world and love were young
And truth in every shepherd's tongue,
These pretty pleasures might me move
To live with thee and be thy Love.

Time drives the flocks from field to fold
When rivers rage and rocks grow cold,
And Philomel becometh dumb;
The rest complain of cares to come.

The flowers do fade, and wanton fields
To wayward Winter reckoning yields;
A honey tongue, a heart of gall,
Is fancy's spring, but sorrow's fall.

Thy gowns, thy shoes, thy beds of roses,
Thy cap, thy kirtle, and thy posies
Soon break, soon wither—soon forgotten,
In folly ripe, in reason rotten.

Thy belt of straw and ivy buds,
Thy coral clasps and amber studs—
All these in me no means can move
To come to thee and be thy Love.

But could youth last and love still breed,
Had joys no date nor age no need,
Then these delights my mind might move
To live with thee and be thy Love.

Sir Walter Raleigh   1600

A SIMILE FOR HER SMILE

Your smiling, or the hope, the thought of it,
Makes in my mind such pause and abrupt ease
As when the highway bridgegates fall,
Balking the hasty traffic, which must sit
On each side massed and staring, while
Deliberately the drawbridge starts to rise:

Then horns are hushed, the oilsmoke rarefies,
Above the idling motors one can tell
The packet's smooth approach, the slip,
Slip of the silken river past the sides,
The ringing of clear bells, the dip
And slow cascading of the paddle wheel.

Richard Wilbur   1950

A RED, RED ROSE

O my love is like a red, red rose,
    That's newly sprung in June.
O my love is like the melody
    That's sweetly played in tune.

As fair art thou, my bonnie lass,
    So deep in love am I,
And I will love thee still, my dear,
    Till a' the seas gang dry.

Till a' the seas gang dry, my dear,
    And the rocks melt wi' the sun;
And I will love thee still, my dear,
    While the sands o' life shall run.

And fare thee well, my only love,
    And fare thee well awhile!
And I will come again, my love,
    Though it were ten thousand mile!

Robert Burns   1795

THAT TIME OF YEAR

That time of year thou mayst in me behold
When yellow leaves, or none, or few, do hang
Upon those boughs which shake against the cold,
Bare ruined choirs where late the sweet birds sang.
In me thou see'st the twilight of such day
As after sunset fadeth in the west,
Which by-and-by black night doth take away,
Death's second self, that seals up all in rest.
In me thou see'st the glowing of such fire
That on the ashes of his youth doth lie,
As the deathbed whereon it must expire,
Consumed with that which it was nourished by.
   This thou perceiv'st, which makes thy love more strong,
   To love that well which thou must leave ere long.

William Shakespeare 1594

IF I HAVE MADE,MY LADY

if i have made,my lady,intricate
imperfect various things chiefly which wrong
your eyes(frailer than most deep dreams are frail)
songs less firm than your body's whitest song
upon my mind—if i have failed to snare
the glance too shy—if through my singing slips
the very skillful strangeness of your smile
the keen primeval silence of your hair

—let the world say "his most wise music stole
nothing from death"—
      you only will create
(who are so perfectly alive)my shame:
lady through whose profound and fragile lips
the sweet small clumsy feet of April came

into the ragged meadow of my soul.

e. e. cummings 1926

LULLABY

Lay your sleeping head, my love,
Human on my faithless arm;
Time and fevers burn away
Individual beauty from
Thoughtful children, and the grave
Proves the child ephemeral:
But in my arms till break of day
Let the living creature lie,
Mortal, guilty, but to me
The entirely beautiful.

Soul and body have no bounds:
To lovers as they lie upon
Her tolerant enchanted slope
In their ordinary swoon,
Grave the vision Venus sends
Of supernatural sympathy,
Universal love and hope;
While an abstract insight wakes
Among the glaciers and the rocks
The hermit's carnal ecstasy.

Certainty, fidelity
On the stroke of midnight pass
Like vibrations of a bell
And fashionable madmen raise
Their pedantic boring cry:
Every farthing of the cost,
All the dreaded cards foretell,
Shall be paid, but from this night
Not a whisper, not a thought,
Not a kiss nor look be lost.

Beauty, midnight, vision dies:
Let the winds of dawn that blow
Softly round your dreaming head
Such a day of welcome show
Eye and knocking heart may bless,
Find our mortal world enough;
Noons of dryness find you fed

By the involuntary powers,
Nights of insult let you pass
Watched by every human love.

W. H. Auden   1937

A Line-Storm Song

The line-storm clouds fly tattered and swift.
  The road is forlorn all day,
Where a myriad snowy quartz stones lift,
  And the hoofprints vanish away.
The roadside flowers, too wet for the bee,
  Expend their bloom in vain.
Come over the hills and far with me,
  And be my love in the rain.

The birds have less to say for themselves
  In the wood-world's torn despair
Than now these numberless years the elves,
  Although they are no less there:
All song of the woods is crushed like some
  Wild, easily shattered rose.
Come, be my love in the wet woods, come,
  Where the boughs rain when it blows.

There is the gale to urge behind
  And bruit our singing down,
And the shallow waters aflutter with wind
  From which to gather your gown.
What matter if we go clear to the west,
  And come not through dry-shod?
For wilding brooch, shall wet your breast
  The rain-fresh goldenrod.

Oh, never this whelming east wind swells
  But it seems like the sea's return
To the ancient lands where it left the shells
  Before the age of the fern;
And it seems like the time when, after doubt,
  Our love came back amain.
Oh, come forth into the storm and rout
  And be my love in the rain.

Robert Frost   1913

THE LOST MISTRESS

All's over, then: does truth sound bitter
    As one at first believes?
Hark, 'tis the sparrows' good-night twitter
    About your cottage eaves!

And the leaf buds on the vine are woolly,
    I noticed that, today;
One day more bursts them open fully
    —You know the red turns gray.

Tomorrow we meet the same then, dearest?
    May I take your hand in mine?
Mere friends are we—well, friends the merest
    Keep much that I resign:

For each glance of the eye so bright and black.
    Though I keep with heart's endeavor—
Your voice, when you wish the snowdrops back,
    Though it stay in my soul forever!

Yet I will but say what mere friends say,
    Or only a thought stronger;
I will hold your hand but as long as all may,
    Or so very little longer!

Robert Browning   1845

IF THOU MUST LOVE ME

If thou must love me, let it be for naught
Except for love's sake only. Do not say,
"I love her for her smile—her look—her way
Of speaking gently—for a trick of thought
That falls in well with mine, and certes brought
A sense of pleasant ease on such a day"—
For these things in themselves, Belovèd, may
Be changed, or change for thee—and love, so wrought,
May be unwrought so. Neither love me for
Thine own dear pity's wiping my cheeks dry:
A creature might forget to weep, who bore
Thy comfort long, and lose thy love thereby!
But love me for love's sake, that evermore
Thou mayst love on, through love's eternity.

Elizabeth Barrett Browning   1850

I AM NOT YOURS

I am not yours, not lost in you,
     Not lost, although I long to be
Lost as a candle lit at noon,
     Lost as a snowflake in the sea.

You love me, and I find you still
     A spirit beautiful and bright,
Yet I am I, who long to be
     Lost as a light is lost in light.

Oh plunge me deep in love—put out
     My senses, leave me deaf and blind,
Swept by the tempest of your love,
     A taper in a rushing wind.

                    Sara Teasdale   1914

I WANT TO DIE WHILE YOU LOVE ME

I want to die while you love me,
     While yet you hold me fair,
While laughter lies upon my lips
     And lights are in my hair.

I want to die while you love me,
     And bear to that still bed,
Your kisses turbulent, unspent,
     To warm me when I'm dead.

I want to die while you love me,
     Oh! who would care to live
Till love has nothing more to ask,
     And nothing more to give!

I want to die while you love me
     And never, never see
The glory of this perfect day,
     Grow dim or cease to be.

     Georgia Douglas Johnson   1925

MY LAST DUCHESS
Ferrara

That's my last Duchess painted on the wall,
Looking as if she were alive. I call
That piece a wonder, now: Frà Pandolf's hands
Worked busily a day, and there she stands.
Will't please you sit and look at her? I said
"Frà Pandolf" by design, for never read
Strangers like you that pictured countenance,
The depth and passion of its earnest glance,
But to myself they turned (since none puts by
The curtain I have drawn for you, but I)
And seemed as they would ask me, if they durst,
How such a glance came there; so, not the first
Are you to turn and ask thus. Sir, 'twas not
Her husband's presence only, called that spot
Of joy into the Duchess' cheek: perhaps
Frà Pandolf chanced to say, "Her mantle laps
Over my lady's wrist too much," or "Paint
Must never hope to reproduce the faint
Half-flush that dies along her throat": such stuff
Was courtesy, she thought, and cause enough
For calling up that spot of joy. She had
A heart—how shall I say?—too soon made glad,
Too easily impressed; she liked whate'er
She looked on, and her looks went everywhere.
Sir, 'twas all one! My favor at her breast,
The dropping of the daylight in the west,
The bough of cherries some officious fool
Broke in the orchard for her, the white mule
She rode with round the terrace—all and each
Would draw from her alike the approving speech,
Or blush, at least. She thanked men—good! but thanked
Somehow—I know not how—as if she ranked
My gift of a nine-hundred-years-old name
With anybody's gift. Who'd stoop to blame
This sort of trifling? Even had you skill
In speech—which I have not—to make your will
Quite clear to such an one, and say, "Just this
Or that in you disgusts me; here you miss,

Or there exceed the mark"—and if she let
Herself be lessoned so, nor plainly set
Her wits to yours, forsooth, and made excuse,
—E'en then would be some stooping; and I choose
Never to stoop. Oh sir, she smiled, no doubt,
Whene'er I passed her; but who passed without
Much the same smile? This grew; I gave commands;
Then all smiles stopped together. There she stands
As if alive. Will't please you rise? We'll meet
The company below, then. I repeat,
The Count your master's known munificence
Is ample warrant that no just pretence
Of mine for dowry will be disallowed;
Though his fair daughter's self, as I avowed
At starting, is my object. Nay, we'll go
Together down, sir. Notice Neptune, though,
Taming a seahorse, thought a rarity,
Which Claus of Innsbruck cast in bronze for me!

Robert Browning   1842

PLAYBOY

High on his stockroom ladder like a dunce
The stock boy sits, and studies like a sage
The subject matter of one glossy page,
As lost in curves as Archimedes once.

Sometimes, without a glance, he feeds himself.
The left hand, like a mother bird in flight,
Brings him a sandwich for a sidelong bite,
And then returns it to a dusty shelf.

What so engrosses him? The wild décor
Of this pink-papered alcove into which
A naked girl has stumbled, with its rich
Welter of pelts and pillows on the floor,

Amidst which, kneeling in a supple pose,
She lifts a goblet in her farther hand,
As if about to toast a flower stand
Above which hovers an exploding rose

Fired from a long-necked crystal vase that rests
Upon a tasseled and vermilion cloth
One taste of which would shrivel up a moth?
Or is he pondering her perfect breasts?

Nothing escapes him of her body's grace
Or of her floodlit skin, so sleek and warm
And yet so strangely like a uniform,
But what now grips his fancy is her face,

And how the cunning picture holds her still
At just that smiling instant when her soul,
Grown sweetly faint, and swept beyond control,
Consents to his inexorable will.

Richard Wilbur   1968

REQUEST

Give me yourself one hour; I do not crave
    For any love, or even thought, of me.
Come as a Sultan may caress a slave
    And then forget forever, utterly.

Come! as west winds, that passing, cool and wet,
    O'er desert places, leave them fields in flower,
And all my life (for I shall not forget)
    Will keep the fragrance of that perfect hour!

Laurence Hope   1902

NON SUM QUALIS ERAM BONÆ
SUB REGNO CYNARÆ

Last night, ah, yesternight, betwixt her lips and mine
There fell thy shadow, Cynara! thy breath was shed
Upon my soul between the kisses and the wine;
And I was desolate and sick of an old passion,
    Yea, I was desolate and bowed my head:
I have been faithful to thee, Cynara! in my fashion.

All night upon mine heart I felt her warm heart beat,
Night-long within mine arms in love and sleep she lay;
Surely the kisses of her bought red mouth were sweet;
But I was desolate and sick of an old passion,
    When I awoke and found the dawn was gray;
I have been faithful to thee, Cynara! in my fashion.

I have forgot much, Cynara! gone with the wind,
Flung roses, roses riotously with the throng,
Dancing, to put thy pale, lost lilies out of mind;
But I was desolate and sick of an old passion,
    Yea, all the time, because the dance was long:
I have been faithful to thee, Cynara! in my fashion.

I cried for madder music and for stronger wine,
But when the feast is finished and the lamps expire,
Then falls thy shadow, Cynara! the night is thine;
And I am desolate and sick of an old passion,
    Yea, hungry for the lips of my desire:
I have been faithful to thee, Cynara! in my fashion.

Ernest Dowson 1891

SHALL I COMPARE THEE TO A SUMMER'S DAY

Shall I compare thee to a Summer's day?
Thou art more lovely and more temperate:
Rough winds do shake the darling buds of May,
And Summer's lease hath all too short a date:
Sometime too hot the eye of heaven shines,
And often is his gold complexion dimmed;
And every fair from fair sometime declines,
By chance or nature's changing course untrimmed:
But thy eternal Summer shall not fade
Nor lose possession of that fair thou owest;
Nor shall Death brag thou wanderest in his shade,
When in eternal lines to time thou growest:
   So long as men can breathe, or eyes can see,
   So long lives this, and this gives life to thee.

William Shakespeare   1594

SOME GLORY IN THEIR BIRTH, SOME IN THEIR SKILL

Some glory in their birth, some in their skill,
Some in their wealth, some in their body's force,
Some in their garments, though new-fangled ill,
Some in their hawks and hounds, some in their horse;
And every humor hath his adjunct pleasure,
Wherein it finds a joy above the rest,
But these particulars are not my measure,
All these I better in one general best.
Thy love is better than high birth to me,
Richer than wealth, prouder than garments' cost,
Of more delight than hawks or horses be;
And having thee, of all men's pride I boast:
   Wretched in this alone, that thou mayst take
   All this away and me most wretched make.

William Shakespeare   1594

WHEN, IN DISGRACE WITH FORTUNE AND MEN'S EYES

When, in disgrace with Fortune and men's eyes,
I all alone beweep my outcast state,
And trouble deaf heaven with my bootless cries,
And look upon myself, and curse my fate,
Wishing me like to one more rich in hope,
Featured like him, like him with friends possessed,
Desiring this man's art and that man's scope,
With what I most enjoy contented least;
Yet in these thoughts myself almost despising—
Haply I think on thee: and then my state,
Like to the Lark at break of day arising
From sullen earth, sings hymns at Heaven's gate;
    For thy sweet love remembered such wealth brings
    That then I scorn to change my state with Kings.

William Shakespeare   1594

NOT MARBLE, NOR THE GILDED MONUMENTS

Not marble, nor the gilded monuments
Of princes, shall outlive this powerful rhyme;
But you shall shine more bright in these contents
Than unswept stone, besmeared with sluttish time.
When wasteful war shall statues overturn,
And broils root out the work of masonry,
Nor Mars his sword nor war's quick fire shall burn
The living record of your memory.
'Gainst death and all-oblivious enmity
Shall you pace forth; your praise shall still find room
Even in the eyes of all posterity
That wear this world out to the ending doom.
    So, till the judgement that yourself arise,
    You live in this, and dwell in lovers' eyes.

William Shakespeare   1594

ADVICE TO A GIRL

Never love unless you can
Bear with all the faults of man!
Men sometimes will jealous be
Though but little cause they see,
And hang the head as discontent,
And speak what straight they will repent.

Men, that but one Saint adore,
Make a show of love to more;
Beauty must be scorned in none,
Though but truly served in one:
For what is courtship but disguise?
True hearts may have dissembling eyes.

Men, when their affairs require,
Must awhile themselves retire;
Sometimes hunt, and sometimes hawk,
And not ever sit and talk:
If these and such-like you can bear,
Then like, and love, and never fear!

Thomas Campion   1617

JOY

Let a joy keep you.
Reach out your hands
And take it when it runs by,
As the Apache dancer
Clutches his woman.
I have seen them
Live long and laugh loud,
Sent on singing, singing,
Smashed to the heart
Under the ribs
With a terrible love.
Joy always,
Joy everywhere—
Let joy kill you!
Keep away from the little deaths.

Carl Sandburg   1916

To the Virgins, To Make Much of Time

Gather ye rosebuds while ye may,
   Old Time is still a-flying;
And this same flower that smiles today,
   Tomorrow will be dying.

The glorious lamp of heaven, the sun,
   The higher he's a-getting,
The sooner will his race be run,
   And nearer he's to setting.

That age is best which is the first,
   When youth and blood are warmer;
But being spent, the worse, and worst
   Times still succeed the former.

Then be not coy, but use your time,
   And while ye may, go marry;
For having lost but once your prime,
   You may forever tarry.

Robert Herrick   1640

Love is not concerned

love is not concerned
with whom you pray
or where you slept
the night you ran away
from home
love is concerned
that the beating of your heart
should kill no one.

Alice Walker   1983

To His Coy Love

I pray thee, leave, love me no more,
    Call home the heart you gave me!
I but in vain that saint adore
    That can but will not save me.
These poor half-kisses kill me quite—
Was ever man thus servèd?
Amidst an ocean of delight
    For pleasure to be starvèd?

Show me no more those snowy breasts
    With azure riverets branchèd,
Where, whilst mine eye with plenty feasts,
    Yet is my thirst not stanchèd;
O Tantalus, thy pains ne'er tell!
    By me thou art prevented:
'Tis nothing to be plagued in Hell,
    But thus in Heaven tormented.

Clip me no more in those dear arms,
    Nor thy life's comfort call me,
O these are but too powerful charms,
    And do but more enthrall me!
        But see how patient I am grown
        In all this coil about thee:
        Come, nice thing, let my heart alone,
        I cannot live without thee!

                    Michael Drayton   1619

To His Coy Mistress

    Had we but world enough, and time,
This coyness, Lady, were no crime.
We would sit down, and think which way
To walk, and pass our long love's day.
Thou by the Indian Ganges' side
Shouldst rubies find; I by the tide
Of Humber would complain. I would
Love you ten years before the Flood,

And you should, if you please, refuse
Till the conversion of the Jews.
My vegetable love should grow
Vaster than empires and more slow;
An hundred years should go to praise
Thine eyes, and on thy forehead gaze;
Two hundred to adore each breast,
But thirty thousand to the rest;
An age at least to every part,
And the last age should show your heart.
For, Lady, you deserve this state,
Nor would I love at lower rate.

    But at my back I always hear
Time's wingèd chariot hurrying near;
And yonder all before us lie
Deserts of vast eternity.
Thy beauty shall no more be found,
Nor, in thy marble vault, shall sound
My echoing song; then worms shall try
That long-preserved virginity,
And your quaint honor turn to dust,
And into ashes all my lust:
The grave's a fine and private place,
But none, I think, do there embrace.

    Now therefore, while the youthful hue
Sits on thy skin like morning dew,
And while thy willing soul transpires
At every pore with instant fires,
Now let us sport us while we may,
And now, like amorous birds of prey,
Rather at once our time devour
Than languish in his slow-chapped power.
Let us roll all our strength and all
Our sweetness up into one ball,
And tear our pleasures with rough strife
Thorough the iron gates of life;
Thus, though we cannot make our sun
Stand still, yet we will make him run.

Andrew Marvell   1651

MEETING AT NIGHT

The gray sea and the long black land;
And the yellow half-moon large and low;
And the startled little waves that leap
In fiery ringlets from their sleep,
As I gain the cove with pushing prow,
And quench its speed i' the slushy sand.

Then a mile of warm sea-scented beach;
Three fields to cross till a farm appears;
A tap at the pane, the quick sharp scratch
And blue spurt of a lighted match,
And a voice less loud, through its joys and fears,
Than the two hearts beating each to each!

Robert Browning   1845

PARTING AT MORNING

Round the cape of a sudden came the sea,
And the sun looked over the mountain's rim:
And straight was a path of gold for him,
And the need of a world of men for me.

Robert Browning   1845

THAT DAY

This is the desk I sit at
and this is the desk where I love you too much
and this is the typewriter that sits before me
where yesterday only your body sat before me
with its shoulders gathered in like a Greek chorus,
with its tongue like a king making up rules as he goes,
with its tongue quite openly like a cat lapping milk,
with its tongue—both of us coiled in its slippery life.
That was yesterday, that day.

That was the day of your tongue,
your tongue that came from your lips,
two openers, half-animals, half-birds
caught in the doorway of your heart.
That was the day I followed the king's rules,
passing by your red veins and your blue veins,
my hands down the backbone, down quick like a firepole,
hands between legs where you display your inner knowledge,
where diamond mines are buried and come forth to bury,
come forth more sudden than some reconstructed city.
It is complete within seconds, that monument.
The blood runs underground yet brings forth a tower.
A multitude should gather for such an edifice.
For a miracle one stands in line and throws confetti.
Surely The Press is here looking for headlines.
Surely someone should carry a banner on the sidewalk.
If a bridge is constructed doesn't the mayor cut a ribbon?
If a phenomenon arrives shouldn't the Magi come bearing gifts?
Yesterday was the day I bore gifts for your gift
and came from the valley to meet you on the pavement.
That was yesterday, that day.

That was the day of your face,
your face after love, close to the pillow, a lullaby.
Half-asleep beside me letting the old fashioned rocker stop,
our breath became one, became a child-breath together,
while my fingers drew little o's on your shut eyes,
while my fingers drew little smiles on your mouth,
while I drew i love you on your chest and its drummer
and whispered, 'Wake up!' and you mumbled in your sleep,
'Sh. We're driving to Cape Cod. We're heading for the Bourne
Bridge. We're circling around the Bourne Circle.' Bourne!
Then I knew you in your dream and prayed of our time
that I would be pierced and you would take root in me
and that I might bring forth your born, might bear
the you or the ghost of you in my little household.
Yesterday I did not want to be borrowed
but this is the typewriter that sits before me
and love is where yesterday is at.

Anne Sexton   1969

STAYING AT ED'S PLACE

I like being in your apartment, and not disturbing anything.
As in the woods I wouldn't want to move a tree,
or change the play of sun and shadow on the ground.

The yellow kitchen stool belongs right there
against white plaster. I haven't used your purple towel
because I like the accidental cleft of shade you left in it.

At your small six-sided table, covered with mysterious
dents in the wood like a dartboard, I drink my coffee
from your brown mug. I look into the clearing

of your high front room, where sunlight slopes through bare
window squares. Your Afghanistan hammock,
     a man-sized cocoon
slung from wall to wall, your narrow desk and typewriter

are the only furniture. Each morning your light from the east
douses me where, with folded legs, I sit in your meadow,
a casual spread of brilliant carpets. Like a cat or dog

I take a roll, then, stretched out flat
in the center of color and pattern, I listen
to the remote growl of trucks over cobbles on
     Bethune Street below.

When I open my eyes I discover the peaceful blank
of the ceiling. Its old paint-layered surface is moonwhite
and trackless, like the Sea—of Tranquillity.

May Swenson   1974

IN MAY

In a nook
That opened south,
You and I
Lay mouth to mouth.

A snowy gull
And sooty daw
Came and looked
With many a caw;

"Such," I said,
"Are I and you,
When you've kissed me
Black and blue!"

    John Millington Synge   1908

GOLD

Pale gold of the walls, gold
of the centers of daisies, yellow roses
pressing from a clear bowl. All day
we lay on the huge bed, my hand
stroking the deep
gold of your things and your back.
We slept and woke
entering the golden room together,
lay down in it breathing
quickly, then
slowly again,
caressing and dozing, your hand sleepily
touching my hair now.

We made in those days
tiny identical rooms inside our bodies
which the men who uncover our graves
will find in a thousand years
shining and whole.

    Donald Hall   1971

A WOMAN WAITS FOR ME

A woman waits for me, she contains all, nothing is lacking,
Yet all were lacking if sex were lacking, or if the moisture of
   the right man were lacking.

Sex contains all, bodies, souls,
Meanings, proofs, purities, delicacies, results, promulgations,
Songs, commands, health, pride, the maternal mystery,
   the seminal milk,
All hopes, benefactions, bestowals, all the passions, loves,
   beauties, delights of the earth,
All the governments, judges, gods, followed persons of the earth,
These are contained in sex as parts of itself and justifications
   of itself.

Without shame the man I like knows and avows the deliciousness
   of his sex,
Without shame the woman I like knows and avows hers.

Now I will dismiss myself from impassive women,
I will go stay with her who waits for me, and with those
   women that are warm-blooded and sufficient for me,
I see that they understand me and do not deny me,
I see that they are worthy of me, I will be the robust husband
   of those women.

They are not one jot less than I am,
They are tanned in the face by shining suns and blowing winds,
Their flesh has the old divine suppleness and strength,
They know how to swim, row, ride, wrestle, shoot, run, strike,
   retreat, advance, resist, defend themselves,
They are ultimate in their own right—they are calm, clear,
   well-possessed of themselves.

I draw you close to me, you women,
I cannot let you go, I would do you good,
I am for you, and you are for me, not only for our own sake,
   but for others' sakes,
Enveloped in you sleep greater heroes and bards,
They refuse to awake at the touch of any man but me.

It is I, you women, I make my way,
I am stern, acrid, large, undissuadable, but I love you,

I do not hurt you any more than is necessary for you,
I pour the stuff to start sons and daughters fit for these States,
   I press with slow rude muscle,
I brace myself effectually, I listen to no entreaties,
I dare not withdraw till I deposit what has so long
   accumulated within me.

Through you I drain the pent-up rivers of myself,
In you I wrap a thousand onward years,
On you I graft the grafts of the best-beloved of me and America,
The drops I distill upon you shall grow fierce and athletic girls,
   new artists, musicians, and singers,
The babes I beget upon you are to beget babes in their turn,
I shall demand perfect men and women out of my
   love-spendings,
I shall expect them to interpenetrate with others, as I and you
   interpenetrate now,
I shall count on the fruits of the gushing showers of them,
   as I count on the fruits of the gushing showers I give now,
I shall look for loving crops from the birth, life, death,
   immortality, I plant so lovingly now.

Walt Whitman 1860

It is This Way with Men

They are pounded into the earth
like nails; move an inch,
they are driven down again.
The earth is sore with them.
It is a spiny fruit
that has lost hope
of being raised and eaten.
It can only ripen and ripen.
And men, they too are wounded.
They too are sifted from their loss
and are without hope. The core
softens. The pure flesh softens
and melts. There are thorns, there
are the dark seeds, and they end.

C. K. Williams 1969

MAY I FEEL SAID HE

may i feel said he
(i'll squeal said she
just once said he)
it's fun said she

(may i touch said he
how much said she
a lot said he)
why not said she

(let's go said he
not too far said she
what's too far said he
where you are said she)

may i stay said he
(which way said she
like this said he
if you kiss said she

may i move said he
is it love said she)
if you're willing said he
(but you're killing said she

but it's life said he
but your wife said she
now said he)
ow said she

(tiptop said he
don't stop said she
oh no said he)
go slow said she

(cccome?said he
ummm said she)
you're divine! said he
(you are Mine said she)

            e. e. cummings   1935

FOUR POEMS

An embrace at first and then a loving kiss
had been her losses in the gambling match.
Now when her lover asks again for stakes
she is silent, though the flesh upon her cheek
rises with suppressed excitement, and her hand
is sweating as she moves the piece.

Rājasekhara

•

As he came to bed the knot fell open of itself,
the dress held only somehow to my hips
by the strands of the loosened girdle.
So much I know, my dear;
but
when within his arms, I can't remember
who he was
or who I was, or what we did or how.

Vikatanitambā

•

The night was deep,
the lamp shone forth with heavy flame,
and that darling is an expert
in the rite which passion prompts;
but, my dear, he made love slowly,
slowly and with limbs constrained,
for the bed kept up a creaking
like an enemy with gnashing teeth.

Vidyā

•

Her dress is somewhat tarnished,
the flowers lie disheveled in her hair;
her eye is torpid, while her breast
is marked with the fresh track of nails;
her loins are lighted by a serpent jewel
that shines within her girdle's opening clasp:
such is the poison she has taken,
body pressed to body, from the many men who love her.

Vallana

Vidyakara's Treasury
translated by Daniel H. H. Ingalls
from the Eleventh-Century Sanskrit

LIGHTNING

I felt the lurch and halt of her heart
   Next my breast, where my own heart was beating;
And I laughed to feel it plunge and bound,
And strange in my blood-swept ears was the sound
   Of the words I kept repeating,
Repeating with tightened arms, and the hot blood's
   blindfold art.

Her breath flew warm against my neck,
   Warm as a flame in the close night air;
And the sense of her clinging flesh was sweet
Where her arms and my neck's blood-surge could meet.
   Holding her thus, did I care
That the black night hid her from me, blotted out
   every speck?

I leaned me forward to find her lips,
   And claim her utterly in a kiss,
When the lightning flew across her face,
And I saw her for the flaring space
   Of a second, afraid of the clips
Of my arms, inert with dread, wilted in fear of my kiss.

A moment, like a wavering spark,
   Her face lay there before my breast,
Pale love lost in a snow of fear,
And guarded by a glittering tear,
   And lips apart with dumb cries;
A moment, and she was taken again in the merciful dark.

I heard the thunder, and felt the rain,
   And my arm fell loose, and I was dumb.
Almost I hated her, she was so good,
Hated myself, and the place, and my blood,
   Which burned with rage, as I bade her come
Home, away home, ere the lightning floated forth again.

D. H. Lawrence 1911

LEDA AND THE SWAN

A sudden blow: the great wings beating still
Above the staggering girl, her thighs caressed
By the dark webs, her nape caught in his bill,
He holds her helpless breast upon his breast.

How can those terrified vague fingers push
The feathered glory from her loosening thighs?
And how can body, laid in that white rush,
But feel the strange heart beating where it lies?

A shudder in the loins engenders there
The broken wall, the burning roof and tower
And Agamemnon dead.
                              Being so caught up,
So mastered by the brute blood of the air,
Did she put on his knowledge with his power
Before the indifferent beak could let her drop?

William Butler Yeats   1928

IN BERTRAM'S GARDEN

Jane looks down at her organdy skirt
As if *it* somehow were the thing disgraced,
For being there, on the floor, in the dirt,
And she catches it up about her waist,
Smoothes it out along one hip,
And pulls it over the crumpled slip.

On the porch, green-shuttered, cool,
Asleep is Bertram, that bronze boy,
Who, having wound her around a spool,
Sends her spinning like a toy
Out to the garden, all alone,
To sit and weep on a bench of stone.

Soon the purple dark will bruise
Lily and bleeding heart and rose,
And the little Cupid lose
Eyes and ears and chin and nose,
And Jane lie down with others soon
Naked to the naked moon.

Donald Justice   1954

TWO SONGS

1

Sex, as they harshly call it,
I fell into this morning
at ten o'clock, a drizzling hour
of traffic and wet newspapers.
I thought of him who yesterday
clearly didn't
turn me to a hot field
ready for plowing,
and longing for that young man
piercèd me to the roots
bathing every vein, etc.
All day he appears to me
touchingly desirable,
a prize one could wreck one's peace for.
I'd call it love if love
didn't take so many years
but lust too is a jewel
a sweet flower and what
pure happiness to know
all our high-toned questions
breed in a lively animal.

2

That "old last act"!
Any yet sometimes
all seems post coitum triste
and I a mere bystander.
Somebody else is going off,
getting shot to the moon.
Or, a moon-race!
Split seconds after
my opposite number
lands
I make it—
we lie fainting together
at a crater-edge

heavy as mercury in our moonsuits
till he speaks—
in a different language
yet one I've picked up
through cultural exchanges. . .
we murmur the first moonwords:
Spasibo. Thanks. O.K.

Adrienne Rich   1964

MOCK ORANGE

It is not the moon, I tell you.
It is these flowers
lighting the yard.

I hate them.
I hate them as I hate sex,
the man's mouth
sealing my mouth, the man's
paralyzing body—

and the cry that always escapes,
the low, humiliating
premise of union—

In my mind tonight
I hear the question and pursuing answer
fused in one sound
that mounts and mounts and then
is split into the old selves,
the tired antagonisms. Do you see?
We were made fools of.
And the scent of mock orange
drifts through the window.

How can I rest?
How can I be content
when there is still
that odor in the world?

Louise Glück   1985

WOMAN'S CONSTANCY

Now thou hast loved me one whole day,
Tomorrow when thou leav'st, what wilt thou say?
Wilt thou then antedate some new-made vow?
   Or say that now
We are not just those persons which we were?
Or, that oaths made in reverential fear
Of Love, and his wrath, any may forswear?
Or, as true deaths true marriages untie,
So lovers' contracts, images of those,
Bind but till sleep, death's image, them unloose?
   Or, your own end to justify,
For having purposed change and falsehood, you
Can have no way but falsehood to be true?
Vain lunatic, against these 'scapes I could
   Dispute and conquer, if I would,
   Which I abstain to do,
For by tomorrow, I may think so too.

John Donne   1601

TO A LADY ASKING HIM HOW LONG HE WOULD LOVE HER

It is not, Celia, in our power
To say how long our love will last;
It may be we within this hour
May lose those joys we now do taste;
The Blessed, that immortal be,
From change in love are only free.
Then, since we mortal lovers are,
Ask not how long our love will last;
But while it does, let us take care
Each minute be with pleasure passed:
Were it not madness to deny
To live because we're sure to die!

Sir George Etherege   c. 1665

TO MY INCONSTANT MISTRESS

When thou, poor excommunicate
   From all the joys of love, shalt see
The full reward and glorious fate
   Which my strong faith shall purchase me,
   Then curse thine own inconstancy.

A fairer hand than thine shall cure
   That heart, which thy false oaths did wound;
And to my soul, a soul more pure
   Than thine, shall by Love's hand be bound,
   And both with equal glory crowned.

Then shalt thou weep, entreat, complain
   To Love, as I did once to thee;
When all thy tears shall be as vain
   As mine were then; for thou shalt be
   Damned for thy false apostacy.

Thomas Carew   1640

THE CONSTANT LOVER

Out upon it, I have loved
   Three whole days together!
And am like to love three more,
   If it prove fair weather.

Time shall moult away his wings
   Ere he shall discover
In the whole wide world again
   Such a constant lover.

But the spite on 't is, no praise
   Is due at all to me:
Love with me had made no stays,
   Had it any been but she.

Had it any been but she,
   And that very face,
There had been at least ere this
   A dozen dozen in her place.

Sir John Suckling   1642

FOR MY LOVER, RETURNING TO HIS WIFE

She is all there.
She was melted carefully down for you
and cast up from your childhood,
cast up from your one hundred favorite aggies.

She has always been there, my darling.
She is, in fact, exquisite.
Fireworks in the dull middle of February
and as real as a cast-iron pot.

Let's face it, I have been momentary.
A luxury. A bright red sloop in the harbor.
My hair rising like smoke from the car window.
Littleneck clams out of season.

She is more than that. She is your have to have,
has grown you your practical your tropical growth.
This is not an experiment. She is all harmony.
She sees to oars and oarlocks for the dinghy,

has placed wild flowers at the window at breakfast,
sat by the potter's wheel at midday,
set forth three children under the moon,
three cherubs drawn by Michelangelo,

done this with her legs spread out
in the terrible months in the chapel.
If you glance up, the children are there
like delicate balloons resting on the ceiling.

She has also carried each one down the hall
after supper, their heads privately bent,
two legs protesting, person to person,
her face flushed with a song and their little sleep.

I give you back your heart.
I give you permission—

for the fuse inside her, throbbing
angrily in the dirt, for the bitch in her
and the burying of her wound—
for the burying of her small red wound alive—

for the pale flickering flare under her ribs,
for the drunken sailor who waits in her left pulse,
for the mother's knee, for the stockings,
for the garter belt, for the call—

the curious call
when you will burrow in arms and breasts
and tug at the orange ribbon in her hair
and answer the call, the curious call.

She is so naked and singular.
She is the sum of yourself and your dream.
Climb her like a monument, step after step.
She is solid.

As for me, I am a watercolor.
I wash off.

Anne Sexton   1969

THE HOUSE GROWN SILENT

After he had gone the wind rose,
Buffeting the house and rumbling in the chimney,
And I thought: It will roar against him like a lion
As onward he goes.

Seven miles before him, all told—
Chilled will be the lips I kissed so warm at parting,
Kissed in vain; for he's forth into the wind, and kisses
Won't keep out the cold.

Closer should I have kissed, fondlier prayed:
Pleasant is the room in the wakeful firelight,
And within is the bed, arrayed with peace and safety.
Would he had stayed!

Sylvia Townsend Warner   1928

O WESTERN WIND

O western wind, when will thou blow,
    The small rain down can rain?
Christ, if my love were in my arms
    And I in my bed again!

Author unknown c. 1500

SIWASHING IT OUT ONCE IN SIUSLAW FOREST

I slept under   rhododendron
All night   blossoms fell
Shivering on   a sheet of cardboard
Feet stuck   in my pack
Hands deep   in my pockets
Barely able   to   sleep.
I remembered   when we were in school
Sleeping together   in a big warm bed
We were   the youngest lovers
When we broke up   we were still nineteen.
Now our   friends are married
You teach   school back east
I don't mind   living this way
Green hills   the long blue beach
But sometimes   sleeping in the open
I think back   when I had you.

Miyazawa Kenji
translated by Gary Snyder 1968

O THAT 'TWERE POSSIBLE

O that 'twere possible
After long grief and pain
To find the arms of my true love
Round me once again! . . .

A shadow flits before me,
Not thou, but like to thee:
Ah, Christ! that it were possible
For one short hour to see
The souls we loved, that they might tell us
What and where they be!

Alfred, Lord Tennyson   1855

SLEEPLESS

If I could have your arms tonight—
   But half the world and the broken sea
   Lie between you and me.

The autumn rain reverberates in the courtyard,
Beating all night against the barren stone,
The sound of useless rain in the desolate courtyard
Makes me more alone.

If you were here, if you were only here—
   My blood cries out to you all night in vain
   As sleepless as the rain.

Sara Teasdale   1919

BELLE ISLE, 1949

We stripped in the first warm spring night
and ran down into the Detroit River
to baptize ourselves in the brine
of car parts, dead fish, stolen bicycles,
melted snow. I remember going under
hand in hand with a Polish highschool girl
I'd never seen before, and the cries
our breath made caught at the same time
on the cold, and rising through the layers
of darkness into the final moonless atmosphere
that was this world, the girl breaking
the surface after me and swimming out
on the starless waters toward the lights
of Jefferson Ave. and the stacks
of the old stove factory unwinking.
Turning at last to see no island at all
but a perfect calm dark as far
as there was sight, and then a light
and another riding low out ahead
to bring us home, ore boats maybe, or smokers
walking alone. Back panting
to the gray coarse beach we didn't dare
fall on, the damp piles of clothes,
and dressing side by side in silence
to go back where we came from.

Philip Levine   1974

IF THERE BE SORROW

If there be sorrow
let it be
for things undone . . .
undreamed
   unrealized
      unattained
to these add one:
Love withheld . . .
   . . . restrained

Mari Evans   1970

WHERE HAVE YOU GONE

Where have you gone

with your confident
walk with
your crooked smile

why did you leave
me
when you took your
laughter
and departed

are you aware that
with you
went the sun
all light
and what few stars
there were?

where have you gone
with your confident
walk your
crooked smile the
rent money
in one pocket and
my heart
in another . . .

Mari Evans   1970

THE HEART ASKS PLEASURE FIRST

The heart asks pleasure first,
And then excuse from pain;
And then those little anodynes
That deaden suffering;

And then to go to sleep
And then, if it should be
The will of its Inquisitor,
The privilege to die.

Emily Dickinson   1862

LA BELLE DAME SANS MERCI

O what can ail thee, Knight at arms,
   Alone and palely loitering?
The sedge has withered from the Lake
   And no birds sing!

O what can ail thee, Knight at arms,
   So haggard and so woe begone?
The squirrel's granary is full,
   And the harvest's done.

I see a lily on thy brow
   With anguish moist and fever dew,
And on thy cheeks a fading rose
   Fast withereth too.

"I met a Lady in the Meads,
   Full beautiful, a faery's child,
Her hair was long, her foot was light,
   And her eyes were wild.

"I made a Garland for her head,
   And bracelets too, and fragrant Zone;
She looked at me as she did love,
   And made sweet moan.

"I set her on my pacing steed,
   And nothing else saw all day long,
For sidelong would she bend and sing
   A faery's song.

"She found me roots of relish sweet,
   And honey wild, and manna dew,
And sure in language strange she said,
   'I love thee true!'

"She took me to her elfin grot
   And there she wept and sighed full sore,
And there I shut her wild, wild eyes
   With kisses four.

"And there she lullèd me asleep,
  And there I dreamed, Ah! woe betide!
The latest dream I ever dreamed
  On the cold hill side.

"I saw pale Kings, and Princes too,
  Pale warriors, death-pale were they all;
They cried, 'La belle dame sans merci
  Hath thee in thrall!'

"I saw their starved lips in the gloam
  With horrid warning gapèd wide,
And I awoke and found me here
  On the cold hill's side.

"And this is why I sojourn here,
  Alone and palely loitering;
Though the sedge is withered from the Lake
  And no birds sing."

                              John Keats   1819

DOWN BY THE SALLEY GARDENS

Down by the salley gardens my love and I did meet;
She passed the salley gardens with little snow-white feet.
She bid me take love easy, as the leaves grow on the tree;
But I, being young and foolish, with her would not agree.
In a field by the river my love and I did stand,
And on my leaning shoulder she laid her snow-white hand.
She bid me take life easy, as the grass grows on the weirs;
But I was young and foolish, and now am full of tears.

                    William Butler Yeats   1889

THE HILL

Breathless, we flung us on the windy hill,
    Laughed in the sun, and kissed the lovely grass.
    You said, "Through glory and ecstasy we pass;
Wind, sun, and earth remain, the birds sing still,
When we are old, are old. . ." "And when we die
    All's over that is ours; and life burns on
Through other lovers, other lips," said I,
—"Heart of my heart, our heaven is now, is won!"

"We are Earth's best, that learned her lesson here.
    Life is our cry. We have kept the faith!" we said;
    "We shall go down with unreluctant tread
Rose-crowned into the darkness!" . . . Proud we were,
And laughed, that had such brave true things to say.
—And then you suddenly cried, and turned away.

                                    Rupert Brooke   1911

BECAUSE I LIKED YOU BETTER

Because I liked you better
    Than suits a man to say,
It irked you, and I promised
    To throw the thought away.

To put the world between us
    We parted, stiff and dry;
"Good-bye," said you, "forget me."
    "I will, no fear," said I.

If here, where clover whitens
    The dead man's knoll, you pass,
And no tall flower to meet you
    Starts in the trefoiled grass,

Halt by the headstone naming
    The heart no longer stirred,
And say the lad that loved you
    Was one that kept his word.

                        A. E. Housman   1936

ONE ART

The art of losing isn't hard to master;
so many things seem filled with the intent
to be lost that their loss is no disaster.

Lose something every day. Accept the fluster
of lost door keys, the hour badly spent.
The art of losing isn't hard to master.

Then practice losing farther, losing faster:
places, and names, and where it was you meant
to travel. None of these will bring disaster.

I lost my mother's watch. And look! my last, or
next-to-last, of three loved houses went.
The art of losing isn't hard to master.

I lost two cities, lovely ones. And, vaster,
some realms I owned, two rivers, a continent.
I miss them, but it wasn't a disaster.

—Even losing you (the joking voice, a gesture
I love) I shan't have lied. It's evident
the art of losing's not too hard to master
though it may look like (*Write* it!) like disaster.

Elizabeth Bishop   1969

ONLY TELL HER THAT I LOVE

Only tell her that I love:
   Leave the rest to her and Fate:
Some kind planet from above
May perhaps her pity move:
   Lovers on their stars must wait—
Only tell her that I love!

John, Lord Cutts   1707

LOVE

I have known what it is to love:
to walk among the midday mob,
and share the friendship of the faceless throng;
to laugh with children on the paths,
and chatter at a bright-eyed squirrel.
I have known what it is to love:
afraid to speak,
fearing it would be thought a lie;
afraid to breathe a smoke-ring dream
and watch it fade,
or see it ground beneath a careless toe.
I have known what it is to love
and hear a sigh—
soft as worn string that parts—
and not to know it as my own.
I have known what it is to love:
to walk the tower-shadowed streets
and seek one face;
to shudder at cacophony of horns and brakes,
and listen for one voice.
I have known what it is to love:
to seek to hide the thought
in Lethal wine and laughing eyes
and kisses from a dozen pairs
of painted lips.
I have known what it is to love,
and tongue the alum of
a lonely heart.

Darwin T. Turner   1974

SEPARATION

Your absence has gone through me
Like thread through a needle.
Everything I do is stitched with its color.

W. S. Merwin   1963

WHAT LIPS MY LIPS HAVE KISSED

What lips my lips have kissed, and where, and why,
I have forgotten, and what arms have lain
Under my head till morning; but the rain
Is full of ghosts tonight, that tap and sigh
Upon the glass and listen for reply,
And in my heart there stirs a quiet pain
For unremembered lads that not again
Will turn to me at midnight with a cry.
Thus in the winter stands the lonely tree,
Nor knows what birds have vanished one by one,
Yet knows its boughs more silent than before:
I cannot say what loves have come and gone,
I only know that summer sang in me
A little while, that in me sings no more.

Edna St. Vincent Millay   1923

I SHALL GO BACK

I shall go back again to the bleak shore
And build a little shanty on the sand,
In such a way that the extremest band
Of brittle seaweed will escape my door
But by a yard or two; and nevermore
Shall I return to take you by the hand;
I shall be gone to what I understand,
And happier than I ever was before.
The love that stood a moment in your eyes,
The words that lay a moment on your tongue,
Are one with all that in a moment dies,
A little under-said and over-sung.
But I shall find the sullen rocks and skies
Unchanged from what they were when I was young.

Edna St. Vincent Millay   1923

OH, WHEN I WAS IN LOVE WITH YOU

Oh, when I was in love with you,
    Then I was clean and brave,
And miles around the wonder grew
    How well did I behave.

And now the fancy passes by,
    And nothing will remain,
And miles around they'll say that I
    Am quite myself again.

A. E. Housman   1896

IF EVER TWO WERE ONE

TO MY DEAR AND LOVING HUSBAND

If ever two were one, then surely we.
If ever man were loved by wife, then thee;
If ever wife was happy in a man,
Compare with me, ye women, if you can.
I prize thy love more than whole mines of gold,
Or all the riches that the East doth hold.
My love is such that rivers cannot quench,
Nor ought but love from thee give recompense.
Thy love is such I can no way repay,
The heavens reward thee manifold, I pray.
Then while we live, in love let's so persevere,
That when we live no more, we may live ever.

Anne Bradstreet   1678

HOW DO I LOVE THEE?

How do I love thee? Let me count the ways.
I love thee to the depth and breadth and height
My soul can reach, when feeling out of sight
For the ends of Being and ideal Grace.
I love thee to the level of every day's
Most quiet need, by sun and candle light.
I love thee freely, as men strive for Right;
I love thee purely, as they turn from Praise.
I love thee with the passion put to use
In my old griefs, and with my childhood's faith.
I love thee with a love I seemed to lose
With my lost saints—I love thee with the breath,
Smiles, tears, of all my life—and, if God choose,
I shall but love thee better after death.

Elizabeth Barrett Browning   1846

MODERN DECLARATION

I, having loved ever since I was a child a few things,
      never having wavered
In these affections; never through shyness in the houses
      of the rich or in the presence of clergymen having denied
      these loves;
Never when worked upon by cynics like chiropractors having
      grunted or clicked a vertebra to the discredit of these loves;
Never when anxious to land a job having diminished them
      by a conniving smile; or when befuddled by drink
Jeered at them through heartache or lazily fondled the fingers
      of their alert enemies; declare

That I shall love you always.
No matter what party is in power;
No matter what temporarily expedient combination of allied
      interests wins the war;
Shall love you always.

Edna St. Vincent Millay   1939

LOVE IS NOT ALL

Love is not all: it is not meat or drink
Nor slumber nor a roof against the rain;
Nor yet a floating spar to men that sink
And rise and sink and rise and sink again;
Love cannot fill the thickened lung with breath,
Nor clean the blood, nor set the fractured bone;
Yet many a man is making friends with death
Even as I speak, for lack of love alone.
It may well be that in a difficult hour,
Pinned down by pain and moaning for release,
Or nagged by want past resolution's power,
I might be driven to sell your love for peace,
Or trade the memory of this night for food.
It may well be. I do not think I would.

Edna St. Vincent Millay 1931

PERMANENTLY

One day the Nouns were clustered in the street.
An Adjective walked by, with her dark beauty.
The Nouns were struck, moved, changed.
The next day a Verb drove up, and created the Sentence.

Each Sentence says one thing—for example, "Although it was
    a dark rainy day when the Adjective walked by, I shall
    remember the pure and sweet expression on her face until
    the day I perish from the green, effective earth."
Or, "Will you please close the window, Andrew?"
Or, for example, "Thank you, the pink pot of flowers on the
    window sill has changed color recently to a light yellow,
    due to the heat from the boiler factory which exists nearby."

In the springtime the Sentences and Nouns lay silently on the grass.
A lonely Conjunction here and there would call, "And! But!"
But the Adjective did not emerge.

As the adjective is lost in the sentence,
So am I lost in your eyes, ears, nose, and throat—
You have enchanted me with a single kiss
Which can never be undone
Until the destruction of language.

Kenneth Koch 1962

LOVE POEM

My clumsiest dear, whose hands shipwreck vases,
At whose quick touch all glasses chip and ring,
Whose palms are bulls in china, burs in linen,
And have no cunning with any soft thing

Except all ill-at-ease fidgeting people:
The refugee uncertain at the door
You make at home; deftly you steady
The drunk clambering on his undulant floor.

Unpredictable dear, the taxi drivers' terror,
Shrinking from far headlights pale as a dime
Yet leaping before red apoplectic streetcars—
Misfit in any space. And never on time.

A wrench in clocks and the solar system. Only
With words and people and love you move at ease;
In traffic of wit expertly maneuver
And keep us, all devotion, at your knees.

Forgetting your coffee spreading on our flannel,
Your lipstick grinning on our coat,
So gaily in love's unbreakable heaven
Our souls on glory of spilt bourbon float.

Be with me, darling, early and late. Smash glasses—
I will study wry music for your sake.
For should your hands drop white and empty
All the toys of the world would break.

John Frederick Nims   1947

OH! DEATH WILL FIND ME

Oh! Death will find me, long before I tire
     Of watching you; and swing me suddenly
Into the shade and loneliness and mire
     Of the last land! There, waiting patiently,

One day, I think, I'll feel a cool wind blowing,
     See a slow light across the Stygian tide,
And hear the Dead about me stir, unknowing,
     And tremble. And I shall know that you have died,

And watch you, a broad-browed and smiling dream,
 Pass, light as ever, through the lightless host,
Quietly ponder, start, and sway, and gleam—
 Most individual and bewildering ghost!

And turn, and toss your brown delightful head
Amusedly, among the ancient Dead.

       Rupert Brooke   1911

Long I thought that knowledge alone would suffice

Long I thought that knowledge alone would suffice me—
 O if I could but obtain knowledge!
Then my lands engrossed me—Lands of the prairies, Ohio's
 land, the southern savannas, engrossed me—For them
 I would live—I would be their orator;
Then I met the examples of old and new heroes—I heard
 of warriors, sailors, and all dauntless persons—And it seemed
 to me that I too had it in me to be as dauntless as any—
 and would be so;
And then, to enclose all, it came to me to strike up the songs
 of the New World—And then I believed my life must
 be spent in singing;
But now take notice, land of the prairies, land of the south
 savannas, Ohio's land,
Take notice, you Kanuck woods—and you Lake Huron—and
 all that with you roll toward Niagara—and you Niagara also,
And you, Californian mountains—That you each and all find
 somebody else to be your singer of songs,
For I can be your singer of songs no longer—One who loves me is
 jealous of me, and withdraws me from all but love,
With the rest I dispense—I sever from what I thought would
 suffice me, for it does not—it is now empty and tasteless to me,
I heed knowledge, and the grandeur of The States, and the
 example of heroes, no more,
I am indifferent to my own songs—I will go with him I love.
It is to be enough for us that we are together—We never
 separate again.

       Walt Whitman   1860

SAME IN BLUES

I said to my baby,
Baby, take it slow.
I can't, she said, I can't!
I got to go!
> *There's a certain*
> *amount of traveling*
> *in a dream deferred.*

Lulu said to Leonard,
I want a diamond ring.
Leonard said to Lulu,
You won't get a goddam thing!
> *A certain*
> *amount of nothing*
> *in a dream deferred.*

Daddy, daddy, daddy,
All I want is you.
You can have me, baby—
But my lovin' days is through
> *A certain*
> *amount of impotence*
> *in a dream deferred.*

Three parties
On my party line—
But that third party,
Lord, ain't mine!
> *There's liable*
> *to be confusion*
> *in a dream deferred.*

From river to river
Uptown and down
There's liable to be confusion
when a dream gets kicked around.

Langston Hughes   1951

50–50

I'm all alone in this world, she said,
Ain't got nobody to share my bed,
Ain't got nobody to hold my hand—
The truth of the matter's
I ain't got no man.

Big Boy opened his mouth and said,
Trouble with you is
You ain't got no head!
If you had a head and used your mind
You could have *me* with you
All the time.

She answered, Babe, what must I do?

He said, Share your bed—
And your money, too.

Langston Hughes   1942

Soiled Dove

Let us be honest; the lady was not a harlot until she married a
  corporation lawyer who picked her from a Ziegfeld chorus.
Before then she never took anybody's money and paid for her
  silk stockings out of what she earned singing and dancing.
She loved one man and he loved six women and the game
  was changing her looks, calling for more and more
  massage money and high coin for the beauty doctors.
Now she drives a long, underslung motor car all by herself,
  reads in the day's papers what her husband is doing to the
  interstate commerce commission, requires a larger corsage
  from year to year, and wonders sometimes how one man is
  coming along with six women.

Carl Sandburg   1916

LET ME NOT TO THE MARRIAGE OF TRUE MINDS

Let me not to the marriage of true minds
Admit impediments. Love is not love
Which alters when it alteration finds,
Or bends with the remover to remove:
O, no! it is an ever-fixèd mark,
That looks on tempests and is never shaken;
It is the star to every wand'ring bark,
Whose worth's unknown, although his height be taken.
Love's not Time's fool, though rosy lips and cheeks
Within his bending sickle's compass come;
Love alters not with his brief hours and weeks,
But bears it out even to the edge of doom—
　　If this be error and upon me proved,
　　I never writ, nor no man ever loved.

William Shakespeare　1594

WHEN I HAVE FEARS

When I have fears that I may cease to be
　　Before my pen has gleaned my teeming brain,
Before high-piled books, in charactery,
　　Hold like rich garners the full-ripened grain;
When I behold, upon the night's starred face,
　　Huge cloudy symbols of a high romance,
And think that I may never live to trace
　　Their shadows, with the magic hand of chance;
And when I feel, fair creature of an hour,
　　That I shall never look upon thee more,
Never have relish in the faery power
　　Of unreflecting love—then on the shore
Of the wide world I stand alone, and think
Till love and fame to nothingness do sink.

John Keats　1818

The River-Merchant's Wife: A Letter

While my hair was still cut straight across my forehead
I played about the front gate, pulling flowers.
You came by on bamboo stilts, playing horse,
You walked about my seat, playing with blue plums.
And we went on living in the village of Chokan:
Two small people, without dislike or suspicion.

At fourteen I married My Lord you.
I never laughed, being bashful.
Lowering my head, I looked at the wall.
Called to, a thousand times, I never looked back.

At fifteen I stopped scowling,
I desired my dust to be mingled with yours
Forever and forever and forever.
Why should I climb the look out?

At sixteen you departed,
You went into far Ku-to-yen, by the river of swirling eddies,
And you have been gone five months.
The monkeys make sorrowful noise overhead.

You dragged your feet when you went out.
By the gate now, the moss is grown, the different mosses,
Too deep to clear them away!
The leaves fall early this autumn, in wind.
The paired butterflies are already yellow with August
Over the grass in the west garden;
They hurt me. I grow older.
If you are coming down through the narrows of the river
    Kiang,
Please let me know beforehand,
And I will come out to meet you
        As far as Cho-fu-Sa.

Rihaku
translated by Ezra Pound   1915

LOVE ON THE FARM

What large, dark hands are those at the window
Grasping in the golden light
Which weaves its way through the evening wind
    At my heart's delight?

Ah, only the leaves! But in the west
I see a redness suddenly come
Into the evening's anxious breast—
    'Tis the wound of love goes home!

The woodbine creeps abroad
Calling low to her lover:
    The sunlit flirt who all the day
    Has poised above her lips in play
    And stolen kisses, shallow and gay
    Of pollen, now has gone away—
        She woos the moth with her sweet, low word;
And when above her his moth wings hover
Then her bright breast she will uncover
And yield her honey drop to her lover.

Into the yellow, evening glow
Saunters a man from the farm below;
Leans, and looks in at the low-built shed
Where the swallow has hung her marriage bed.
    The bird lies warm against the wall.
    She glances quick her startled eyes
    Toward him, then she turns away
    Her small head, making warm display
    Of red upon the throat. Her terrors sway
    Her out of the nest's warm, busy ball,
    Whose plaintive cry is heard as she flies
    In one blue swoop from out the sties
    Into the twilight's empty hall.

Oh, water-hen, beside the rushes,
Hide your quaintly scarlet blushes,
Still your quick tail, lie still as dead,
Till the distance folds over his ominous tread!

The rabbit presses back her ears,
Turns back her liquid, anguished eyes
And crouches low; then with wild spring
Spurts from the terror of his oncoming;
To be choked back, the wire ring
Her frantic effort throttling:
   Piteous brown ball of quivering fears!
Ah, soon in his large, hard hands she dies,
And swings all loose from the swing of his walk!
Yet calm and kindly are his eyes
And ready to open in brown surprise
Should I not answer to his talk
Or should he my tears surmise.

I hear his hand on the latch, and rise from my chair
Watching the door open; he flashes bare
His strong teeth in a smile, and flashes his eyes
In a smile like triumph upon me; then careless-wise
He flings the rabbit soft on the table board
And comes toward me: he! the uplifted sword
Of his hand against my bosom! and oh, the broad
Blade of his glance that asks me to applaud
His coming! With his hand he turns my face to him
And caresses me with his fingers that still smell grim
Of rabbit's fur! God, I am caught in a snare!
I know not what fine wire is round my throat;
I only know I let him finger there
My pulse of life, and let him nose like a stoat
Who sniffs with joy before he drinks the blood.

And down his mouth comes to my mouth! and down
His bright dark eyes come over me, like a hood
Upon my mind! his lips meet mine, and a flood
Of sweet fire sweeps across me, so I drown
Against him, die, and find death good.

D. H. Lawrence   1911

THE FARMER'S BRIDE

Three summers since I chose a maid,
Too young maybe—but more's to do
At harvest time than bide and woo.
   When us was wed she turned afraid
Of love and me and all things human;
Like the shut of a winter's day.
Her smile went out, and 'twasn't a woman—
    More like a little frightened fay.
      One night, in the Fall, she runned away.

"Out 'mong the sheep, her be," they said,
"Should properly have been abed";
But sure enough she wasn't there
Lying awake with her wide brown stare.
So over seven-acre field and up along across the down
We chased her, flying like a hare
Before our lanterns. To Church Town
    All in a shiver and a scare
We caught her, fetched her home at last
    And turned the key upon her, fast.
She does the work about the house
As well as most, but like a mouse:
    Happy enough to chat and play
    With birds and rabbits and such as they,
    So long as menfolk keep away.
"Not near, not near!" her eyes beseech
When one of us comes within reach.
    The women say that beasts in stall
    Look round like children at her call.
    I've hardly heard her speak at all.

Shy as a leveret, swift as he,
Straight and slight as a young larch tree,
Sweet as the first wild violets, she
To her wild self. But what to me?

The short days shorten and the oaks are brown,
   The blue smoke rises to the low gray sky,
One leaf in the still air falls slowly down,
   A magpie's spotted feathers lie
On the black earth spread white with rime,
The berries redden up to Christmas time.
   What's Christmas time without there be
Some other in the house than we!

   She sleeps up in the attic there
   Alone, poor maid. 'Tis but a stair
Betwixt us. Oh! my God! the down,
The soft young down of her, the brown,
The brown of her—her eyes, her hair, her hair . . .

               Charlotte Mew   1916

I HAVE BEEN THROUGH THE GATES

His heart, to me, was a place of palaces and pinnacles
   and shining towers;
I saw it then as we see things in dreams—I do not remember
   how long I slept;
I remember the trees, and the high, white walls, and how the
   sun was always on the towers;
The walls are standing today, and the gates: I have been
   through the gates, I have groped, I have crept
Back, back. There is dust in the streets, and blood;
   they are empty; darkness is over them;
His heart is a place with the lights gone out, forsaken by great
   winds and the heavenly rain, unclean and unswept,
Like the heart of the holy city, old, blind, beautiful Jerusalem,
Over which Christ wept.

               Charlotte Mew   1921

THE WIFE'S TALE

When I had spread it all on linen cloth
Under the hedge, I called them over.
The hum and gulp of the thresher ran down
And the big belt slowed to a standstill, straw
Hanging undelivered in the jaws.
There was such quiet that I heard their boots
Crunching the stubble twenty yards away.

He lay down and said "Give these fellows theirs.
I'm in no hurry," plucking grass in handfuls
And tossing it in the air. "That looks well."
(He nodded at my white cloth on the grass.)
"I declare a woman could lay out a field
Though boys like us have little call for cloths."
He winked, then watched me as I poured a cup
And buttered the thick slices that he likes.
"It's threshing better than I thought, and mind
It's good clean seed. Away over there and look."
Always this inspection has to be made
Even when I don't know what to look for.

But I ran my hand in the half-filled bags
Hooked to the slots. It was hard as shot,
Innumerable and cool. The bags gaped
Where the chutes ran back to the stilled drum
And forks were stuck at angles in the ground
As javelins might mark lost battlefields.
I moved between them back across the stubble.

They lay in the ring of their own crusts and dregs
Smoking and saying nothing. "There's a good yield,
Isn't there?"—as proud as if he were the land itself—
"Enough for crushing and for sowing both."
And that was it. I'd come and he had shown me
So I belonged no further to the work.
I gathered cups and folded up the cloth
And went. But they still kept their ease
Spread out, unbuttoned, grateful, under the trees.

Seamus Heaney   1969

MEDITATION AT KEW

Alas! for all the pretty women who marry dull men,
Go into the suburbs and never come out again,
Who lose their pretty faces, and dim their pretty eyes,
Because no one has skill or courage to organize.

What do these pretty women suffer when they marry?
They bear a boy who is like Uncle Harry,
A girl who is like Aunt Eliza, and not new,
These old, dull races must breed true.

I would enclose a common in the sun,
And let the young wives out to laugh and run;
I would steal their dull clothes and go away,
And leave the pretty naked things to play.

Then I would make a contract with hard Fate
That they see all the men in the world and choose a mate,
And I would summon all the pipers in the town
That they dance with Love at a feast, and dance him down.

From the gay unions of choice
We'd have a race of splendid beauty and of thrilling voice.
The World whips frank, gay love with rods,
But frankly, gaily shall we get the gods.

Anna Wickham   1921

HOW SWEET I ROAMED

How sweet I roamed from field to field
And tasted all the summer's pride,
Till I the Prince of Love beheld
Who in the sunny beams did glide!

He showed me lilies for my hair,
And blushing roses for my brow;
He led me through his gardens fair,
Where all his golden pleasures grow.

With sweet May dews my wings were wet,
And Phoebus fired my vocal rage;
He caught me in his silken net,
And shut me in his golden cage.

He loves to sit and hear me sing,
Then, laughing, sports and plays with me;
Then stretches out my golden wing,
And mocks my loss of liberty.

William Blake   1783

DANSE RUSSE

If when my wife is sleeping
and the baby and Kathleen
are sleeping
and the sun is a flame-white disc
in silken mists
above shining trees,
if I in my north room
dance naked, grotesquely
before my mirror
waving my shirt round my head
and singing softly to myself:

"I am lonely, lonely.
I was born to be lonely,
I am best so!"
If I admire my arms, my face,
my shoulders, flanks, buttocks
against the yellow drawn shades,
Who shall say I am not
the happy genius of my household?

William Carlos Williams 1917

What Wild Dawns There Were

What wild dawns there were
   in our first years here
when we would run outdoors naked
to pee in the long grass behind the house
     and see over the hills such streamers,
     such banners of fire and blue (the blue
     that is Lilith to full day's honest Eve)—
What feathers of gold under the morning star
   we saw from dazed eyes before
stumbling back to bed chilled with dew
to sleep till the sun was high!

Now if we wake early
   we don't go outdoors—or I don't—
and you if you do go
   rarely call me to see the day break.
I watch the dawn through glass: this year
     only cloudless flushes of light, paleness
     slowly turning to rose,
     and fading subdued.
We have not spoken of these tired
risings of the sun.

Denise Levertov 1970

STORM FEAR

When the wind works against us in the dark,
And pelts with snow
The lower-chamber window on the east,
And whispers with a sort of stifled bark,
The beast,
"Come out! Come out!"
It costs no inward struggle not to go,
Ah, no!
I count our strength,
Two and a child,
Those of us not asleep subdued to mark
How the cold creeps as the fire dies at length—
How drifts are piled,
Dooryard and road ungraded,
Till even the comforting barn grows far away,
And my heart owns a doubt
Whether 'tis in us to arise with day
And save ourselves unaided.

Robert Frost   1913

A WIFE WAITS

Will's at the dance in the Clubroom below.
    Where the tall liquor-cups foam;
I on the pavement up here by the Bow,
    Wait, wait, to steady him home.

Will and his partner are treading a tune,
    Loving companions they be;
Willy, before we were married in June,
    Said he loved no one but me;

Said he would let his old pleasures all go
    Ever to live with his Dear.
Will's at the dance in the Clubroom below,
    Shivering I wait for him here.

Thomas Hardy   1902

AFTER MAKING LOVE WE HEAR FOOTSTEPS

For I can snore like a bullhorn
or play loud music
or sit up talking with any reasonably sober Irishman
and Fergus will only sink deeper
into his dreamless sleep, which goes by all in one flash,
but let there be that heavy breathing
or a stifled come-cry anywhere in the house
and he will wrench himself awake
and make for it on the run—as now, we lie together,
after making love, quiet, touching along the length of our bodies,
familiar touch of the long-married,
and he appears—in his baseball pajamas, it happens,
the neck opening so small
he has to screw them on, which one day may make him wonder
about the mental capacity of baseball players—
and flops down between us and hugs us and snuggles himself
    to sleep,
his face gleaming with satisfaction at being this very child.

In the half darkness we look at each other
and smile
and touch arms across his little, startlingly muscled body—
this one whom habit of memory propels to the ground of his
    making,
sleeper only the mortal sounds can sing awake,
this blessing love gives again into our arms.

Galway Kinnell   1980

A QUESTION

I asked if I got sick and died, would you
With my black funeral go walking too,
If you'd stand close to hear them talk or pray
While I'm let down in that steep bank of clay.

And, No, you said, for if you saw a crew
Of living idiots pressing round that new
Oak coffin—they alive, I dead beneath
That board—you'd rave and rend them with your teeth.

John Millington Synge   1908

THE ACHE OF MARRIAGE

The ache of marriage:

thigh and tongue, beloved,
are heavy with it,
it throbs in the teeth

We look for communion
and are turned away, beloved,
each and each

It is leviathan and we
in its belly
looking for joy, some joy
not to be known outside it

two by two in the ark of
the ache of it.

Denise Levertov   1964

Man and Wife

It was late, we
talked   it all
came out   words
fell   we stuffed them
in each other's ears

I talked, she listened
and agreed.   Not
enough.   Don't shout
she yelled, Don't—I'm
not—.   Quietly: In other
words, I said—There are
no other words
she said.   *Think.* I
(thought) can't think.
Words she could not say
I said, then she
spoke for me.

Be a woman, I said.
What is a woman,
she asked, nakedly,
taking off her clothes. That
ended it.   The next night
we began again, as if
there were someone
who knew
the answer.

Mitchell Goodman   1968

SIX YEARS LATER

So long had life together been that now
the second of January fell again
on Tuesday, making her astonished brow
lift like a windshield wiper in the rain,
    so that her misty sadness cleared, and showed
    a cloudless distance waiting up the road.
So long had life together been that once
the snow began to fall, it seemed unending;
that, lest the flakes should make her eyelids wince,
I'd shield them with my hand, and they, pretending
    not to believe that cherishing of eyes,
    would beat against my palm like butterflies.

So alien had all novelty become
that sleep's entanglements would put to shame
whatever depths the analysts might plumb;
that when my lips blew out the candle flame,
    her lips fluttering from my shoulder, sought
    to join my own, without another thought.

So long had life together been that all
that tattered brood of paper roses went,
and a whole birch grove grew upon the wall,
and we had money, by some accident,
    and tonguelike on the sea, for thirty days,
    the sunset threatened Turkey with its blaze.

So long had life together been without
books, chairs, utensils—only that ancient bed—
that the triangle, before it came about,
had been a perpendicular, the head
    of some acquaintance hovering above
    two points which had been coalesced by love.

So long had life together been that she
and I, with our joint shadows, had composed
a double door, a door which, even if we
were lost in work or sleep, was always closed:
    somehow its halves were split and we went right
    through them into the future, into night.

                         Joseph Brodsky   1969
                    translated by Richard Wilbur

MAN AND WIFE

Tamed by *Miltown,* we lie on Mother's bed;
the rising sun in war paint dyes us red;
in broad daylight her gilded bedposts shine,
abandoned, almost Dionysian.
At last the trees are green on Marlborough Street,
blossoms on our magnolia ignite
the morning with their murderous five days' white.
All night I've held your hand,
as if you had
a fourth time faced the kingdom of the mad—
its hackneyed speech, its homicidal eye—
and dragged me home alive. . . . Oh my *Petite,*
clearest of all God's creatures, still all air and nerve:
you were in your twenties, and I,
once hand on glass
and heart in mouth,
outdrank the Rahvs in the heat
of Greenwich Village, fainting at your feet—
too boiled and shy
and poker-faced to make a pass,
while the shrill verve
of your invective scorched the traditional South.

Now twelve years later, you turn your back.
Sleepless, you hold
your pillow to your hollows like a child;
your old-fashioned tirade—
loving, rapid, merciless—
breaks like the Atlantic Ocean on my head.

Robert Lowell   1957

TO MY WIFE

And does the heart grow old? You know
In the indiscriminate green
Of summer or in earliest snow
A landscape is another scene,

Inchoate and anonymous,
And every rock and bush and drift
As our affections alter us
Will alter with the season's shift.

So love by love we come at last,
As through the exclusions of a rhyme,
Or the exactions of a past,
To the simplicity of time,

The antiquity of grace, where yet
We live in terror and delight
With love as quiet as regret
And love like anger in the night.

J. V. Cunningham   1958

COMING TO THIS

We have done what we wanted.
We have discarded dreams, preferring the heavy industry
of each other, and we have welcomed grief
and called ruin the impossible habit to break.

And now we are here.
The dinner is ready and we cannot eat.
The meat sits in the white lake of its dish.
The wine waits.

Coming to this
has its rewards: nothing is promised, nothing is taken away.
We have no heart or saving grace,
no place to go, no reason to remain

Mark Strand   1968

WE NEVER SAID FAREWELL

We never said farewell, nor even looked
  Our last upon each other, for no sign
Was made when we the linkèd chain unhooked
  And broke the level line.

And here we dwell together, side by side,
Our places fixed for life upon the chart.
Two islands that the roaring seas divide
  Are not more far apart.

Mary Coleridge   1896

SINCE THERE'S NO HELP,
COME LET US KISS AND PART

Since there's no help, come let us kiss and part—
Nay, I have done, you get no more of me;
And I am glad, yea, glad with all my heart,
That thus so cleanly I myself can free.
Shake hands for ever, cancel all our vows,
And when we meet at any time again,
Be it not seen in either of our brows
That we one jot of former love retain.
Now at the last gasp of Love's latest breath,
When, his pulse failing, Passion speechless lies,
When Faith is kneeling by his bed of death,
And Innocence is closing up his eyes:
  —Now if thou would'st, when all have given him over,
  From death to life thou might'st him yet recover.

Michael Drayton   1619

OH, OH, YOU WILL BE SORRY FOR THAT WORD!

Oh, Oh, you will be sorry for that word!
Give back my book and take my kiss instead.
Was it my enemy or my friend I heard,
"What a big book for such a little head!"
Come, I will show you now my newest hat,
And you may watch me purse my mouth and prink!
Oh, I shall love you still, and all of that.
I never again shall tell you what I think.
I shall be sweet and crafty, soft and sly;
You will not catch me reading any more:
I shall be called a wife to pattern by;
And some day when you knock and push the door,
Some sane day, not too bright and not too stormy,
I shall be gone, and you may whistle for me.

Edna St. Vincent Millay   1923

UNPUNISHED

The weapon that you fought with was a word,
    And with that word you stabbed me to the heart.
Not once but twice you did it, yet the sword
    Made no blood start.
They have not tried you for your life. You go
    Strong in such innocence as men will boast.
They have not buried me! They do not know
    Life from its ghost.

Mary Coleridge   1890

DIVORCE

A voice from the dark is calling me.
In the close house I nurse a fire.
Out in the dark, cold winds rush free
To the rock heights of my desire.
I smother in the house in the valley below,
Let me out to the night, let me go, let me go!

Spirits that ride the sweeping blast,
Frozen in rigid tenderness,
Wait! For I leave the fire at last
My little-love's warm loneliness.
I smother in the house in the valley below,
Let me out in the night, let me go, let me go!

High on the hills are beating drums.
Clear from a line of marching men
To the rock's edge the hero comes.
He calls me, and he calls again.
On the hill there is fighting, victory or quick death,
In the house is the fire, which I fan with sick breath.
I smother in the house in the valley below,
Let me out in the dark, let me go, let me go!

Anna Wickham   1911

A RENEWAL

Having used every subterfuge
To shake you, lies, fatigue, or even that of passion,
Now I see no way but a clean break.
I add that I am willing to bear the guilt.

You nod assent. Autumn turns windy, huge,
A clear vase of dry leaves vibrating on and on.
We sit, watching. When I next speak
Love buries itself in me, up to the hilt.

James Merrill   1958

MAG

I wish to God I never saw you, Mag.
I wish you never quit your job and came along with me.
I wish we never bought a license and a white dress
For you to get married in the day we ran off to a minister
And told him we would love each other and take care
    of each other
Always and always long as the sun and the rain lasts anywhere.
Yes, I'm wishing now you lived somewhere away from here
And I was a bum on the bumpers a thousand miles away
    dead broke.
        I wish the kids had never come
        And rent and coal and clothes to pay for
        And a grocery man calling for cash,
        Every day cash for beans and prunes.
        I wish to God I never saw you, Mag.
        I wish to God the kids had never come.

Carl Sandburg   1916

AH, YOU THOUGHT

Ah—you thought I'd be the type
You could forget,
And that praying and sobbing, I'd throw myself
Under the hooves of a bay.

Or I would beg from the witches
Some kind of root in charmed water
And send you a terrible gift—
My intimate, scented handkerchief.

Damned if I will. Neither by glance nor by groan
Will I touch your cursed soul,
But I vow to you by the garden of angels,
By the miraculous icon I vow
And by the fiery passion of our nights—
I will never return to you.

Anna Akhmatova   1921
translated by Judith Hemschemeyer

MEMENTOS, I

Sorting out letters and piles of my old
    Canceled checks, old clippings, and yellow note cards
That meant something once, I happened to find
    Your picture. *That* picture. I stopped there cold,
Like a man raking piles of dead leaves in his yard
    Who has turned up a severed hand.

Still, that first second, I was glad: you stand
    Just as you stood—shy, delicate, slender,
In that long gown of green lace netting and daisies
    That you wore to our first dance. The sight of you stunned
Us all. Well, our needs were different, then,
    And our ideals came easy.

Then through the war and those two long years
    Overseas, the Japanese dead in their shacks
Among dishes, dolls, and lost shoes; I carried
    This glimpse of you, there, to choke down my fear,
Prove it had been, that it might come back.
    That was before we got married.

—Before we drained out one another's force
    With lies, self-denial, unspoken regret
And the sick eyes that blame; before the divorce
    And the treachery. Say it: before we met. Still,
I put back your picture. Someday, in due course,
    I will find that it's still there.

W. D. Snodgrass   1967

IDOLATRY

You have been good to me, I give you this:
The arms of lovers empty as our own,
Marble lips sustaining one long kiss
And the hard sound of hammers breaking stone.

For I will build a chapel in the place
Where our love died and I will journey there
To make a sign and kneel before your face
And set an old bell tolling on the air.

Arna Bontemps   1949

PARTING

My life closed twice before its close;
It yet remains to see
If immortality unveil
A third event to me

So huge, so hopeless to conceive
As these that twice befell.
Parting is all we know of heaven,
And all we need of hell.

Emily Dickinson   c. 1863

TIME DOES NOT BRING RELIEF

Time does not bring relief; you all have lied
Who told me time would ease me of my pain!
I miss him in the weeping of the rain;
I want him at the shrinking of the tide;
The old snows melt from every mountainside,
And last year's leaves are smoke in every lane;
But last year's bitter loving must remain
Heaped on my heart, and my old thoughts abide.
There are a hundred places where I fear
To go—so with his memory they brim.
And entering with relief some quiet place
Where never fell his foot or shone his face
I say, "There is no memory of him here!"
And so stand stricken, so remembering him.

Edna St. Vincent Millay   1912

Seeing You Stand Once More Before My Eyes

Seeing you stand once more before my eyes
In your pale dignity and tenderness,
Wearing your frailty like a misty dress
Draped over the great glamour which denies
To years their domination, all disguise
Time can achieve is but to add a stress,
A finer fineness, as though some caress
Touched you a moment to a strange surprise.
Seeing you after these long lengths of years,
I only know the glory come again,
A majesty bewildered by my tears,
A golden sun spangling slant shafts of rain,
Moonlight delaying by a sick man's bed,
A rush of daffodils where wastes of dried leaves spread.

Amy Lowell 1925

Alzheimer's: The Wife

for Renée Mauger

She answers the bothersome telephone, takes the message,
    forgets the message, forgets who called.
One of their daughters, her husband guesses: the one with the
    dogs, the babies, the boy Jed?
Yes, perhaps, but how tell which, how tell anything when all
    the name tags have been lost or switched,
when all the lonely flowers of sense and memory bloom
    and die now in adjacent bites of time?
Sometimes her own face will suddenly appear with terrifying
    inappropriateness before her in a mirror.
She knows that if she's patient, its gaze will break, demurely,
    decorously, like a well-taught child's,
it will turn from her as though it were embarrassed by
    the secrets of this awful hide-and-seek.
If she forgets, though, and glances back again, it will still be
    in there, furtively watching, crying.

C. K. Williams 1987

THE WIDOW'S LAMENT IN SPRINGTIME

Sorrow is my own yard
where the new grass
flames as it has flamed
often before but not
with the cold fire
that closes round me this year.
Thirtyfive years
I lived with my husband.
The plumtree is white today
with masses of flowers.
Masses of flowers
load the cherry branches
and color some bushes
yellow and some red
but the grief in my heart
is stronger than they
for though they were my joy
formerly, today I notice them
and turned away forgetting.
Today my son told me
that in the meadows,
at the edge of the heavy woods
in the distance, he saw
trees of white flowers.
I feel that I would like
to go there
and fall into those flowers
and sink into the marsh near them.

William Carlos Williams   1921

AT LEAST, MY DEAR

At least, my dear,
You did not have to live to see me die.

Considering now how many things I did that must have
    caused you pain,
Sweating at certain memories, blushing dark blood, unable
To gather home my scattered thoughts that graze
    forbidden hills, cropping the mind-bane,
I cut from the hedge for crook the one disservice
I never did you—you never saw me die.

I find in my disorderly files among unfinished
Poems, and photographs of picnics on the rocks, letters
    from you in your bold hand.
I find in the pocket of a coat I could not bring myself
    to give away
A knotted handkerchief, containing columbine seeds.
A few more moments such as these and I shall have paid all.

Not that you ever—
O, love inflexible, O militant forgiveness, I know
You kept no books against me! In my own hand
Are written down the sum and the crude items of
    my inadequacy.

It is only that there are moments when for the sake of
    a little quiet in the brawling mind I must search out,
Recorded in my favor,
One princely gift.
The most I ever did for you was to outlive you.
But that is much.

Edna St. Vincent Millay   1940

COMPLAINT

She's gone. She was my love, my moon or more.
She chased the chickens out and swept the floor,
Emptied the bones and nutshells after feasts,
And smacked the kids for leaping up like beasts.
Now morbid boys have grown past awkwardness;
The girls let stitches out, dress after dress,
To free some swinging body's riding space
And form the new child's unimagined face.
Yet, while vague nephews, spitting on their curls,
Amble to pester winds and blowsy girls,
What arm will sweep the room, what hand will hold
New snow against the milk to keep it cold?
And who will dump the garbage, feed the hogs,
And pitch the chickens' heads to hungry dogs?
Not my lost hag who dumbly bore such pain:
Childbirth and midnight sassafras and rain.
New snow against her face and hands she bore,
And now lies down, who was my moon or more.

James Wright   1958

ON HIS DECEASED WIFE

Methought I saw my late espousèd Saint
    Brought to me like Alcestis from the grave,
    Whom Jove's great Son to her glad Husband gave,
    Rescued from Death by force, though pale and faint.
Mine, as whom washed from spot of childbed taint
    Purification in the old Law did save,
    And such, as yet once more I trust to have
    Full sight of her in Heaven without restraint,
Came vested all in white, pure as her mind:
    Her face was veiled, yet to my fancied sight
    Love, sweetness, goodness, in her person shined
So clear, as in no face with more delight.
    But, O as to embrace me she inclined,
    I waked, she fled, and day brought back my night.

John Milton   1658

HIGHLAND MARY

Ye banks and braes and streams around
    The castle o' Montgomery,
Green be your woods, and fair your flowers,
    Your waters never drumlie!
There Summer first unfold her robes,
    And there the langest tarry;
For there I took the last farewell
    O' my sweet Highland Mary.

How sweetly bloomed the gay green birk,
    How rich the hawthorn's blossom,
As underneath their fragrant shade
    I clasped her to my bosom!
The golden hours on angel wings
    Flew o'er me and my dearie;
For dear to me as light and life
    Was my sweet Highland Mary.

Wi' many a vow and lock'd embrace
    Our parting was full tender;
And, pledging aft to meet again,
    We tore ourselves asunder;
But oh! fell Death's untimely frost,
    That nipt my flower sae early!
Now green's the sod, and cold's the clay,
    That wraps my Highland Mary!

O pale, pale now, those rosy lips
    I aft hae kiss'd sae fondly!
And closed for aye the sparkling glance
    That dwelt on me sae kindly!
And moldering now in silent dust
    That heart that loved me dearly!
But still within my bosom's core
    Shall live my Highland Mary.

Robert Burns 1792

THE LAST DANCE

Midnight is past, and it is time to go:
Yet still I linger in the banquet hall
And with the dancers clap my hands and call
For one waltz more, although my step lags slow,
And my dark coachman waits for me I know
Upon the lowest stair. The petals fall
From the pale rose upon my breast, and all
The waxen tapers in their urns burn low.
Sweet partners in our all too brief quadrille,
Full loath am I to loose your clinging hands,
And so I dance again and tarry still
While on the stair my patient coachman stands.
And where he takes me when I go from here
Your arms are waiting for me, O my dear!

May Riley Smith   1893

WHEN YOU ARE OLD

When you are old and gray and full of sleep,
And nodding by the fire, take down this book,
And slowly read, and dream of the soft look
Your eyes had once, and of their shadows deep;

How many loved your moments of glad grace,
And loved your beauty with love false or true,
But one man loved the pilgrim soul in you,
And loved the sorrows of your changing face;

And bending down beside the glowing bars,
Murmur, a little sadly, how Love fled
And paced upon the mountains overhead
And hid his face amid a crowd of stars.

William Butler Yeats   1892

MY PAPA'S WALTZ

MORNING SONG

Love set you going like a fat gold watch.
The midwife slapped your footsoles, and your bald cry
Took its place among the elements.

Our voices echo, magnifying your arrival. New statue.
In a drafty museum, your nakedness
Shadows our safety. We stand round blankly as walls.

I'm no more your mother
Than the cloud that distils a mirror to reflect its own slow
Effacement at the wind's hand.

All night your moth-breath
Flickers among the flat pink roses. I wake to listen:
A far sea moves in my ear.

One cry, and I stumble from bed, cow-heavy and floral
In my Victorian nightgown.
Your mouth opens clean as a cat's. The window square

Whitens and swallows its dull stars. And now you try
Your handful of notes;
The clear vowels rise like balloons.

Sylvia Plath   1961

To L. B. S.

Sometimes, tired, I imagine your death:
By childish illness, reasonless accident
Stopped still forever, gone; until I loathe
Fool dramatizations of the brain—I won't,
Though I could, write them into pictures here.

My child, outlive me! Stay beyond my times
Which—how I see now—could be worse than these,
As they are worse for many who had sons.
Death I can bear for myself once, not twice.
I am out of bed at midnight to beg this.

Winfield Townley Scott   1945

PREFACE TO A TWENTY VOLUME SUICIDE NOTE
for Kellie Jones, born 16 May, 1959

Lately, I've become accustomed to the way
The ground opens up and envelopes me
Each time I go out to walk the dog.
Or the broad-edged silly music the wind
Makes when I run for a bus . . .

Things have come to that.

And now, each night I count the stars,
And each night I get the same number.
And when they will not come to be counted,
I count the holes they leave.

Nobody sings anymore.

And then last night, I tiptoed up
To my daughter's room and heard her
Talking to someone, and when I opened
The door, there was no one there . . .
Only she on her knees, peeking into

Her own clasped hands.

Amiri Baraka   1961

MILL DOORS

You never come back.
I say good-bye when I see you going in the doors,
The hopeless open doors that call and wait
And take you then for—how many cents a day?
How many cents for the sleepy eyes and fingers?

I say good-bye because I know they tap your wrists,
In the dark, in the silence, day by day,
And all the blood of you drop by drop,
And you are old before you are young.
You never come back.

Carl Sandburg   1916

THE ONE GIRL AT THE BOYS PARTY

When I take my girl to the swimming party
I see her down among the boys. They tower and
bristle, she stands there smooth and sleek,
her math scores unfolding in the air around her.
They will strip to their suits, her body hard and
indivisible as a prime number,
they'll plunge in the deep end, she'll subtract
her height from ten feet, divide it into
hundreds of gallons of water, the numbers
bouncing in her mind like molecules of chlorine
in the bright blue pool. When they climb out,
her ponytail will hang its pencil lead
down her back, her narrow silk suit
with hamburgers and french fries printed on it
will glisten in the brilliant air, and they will
see her sweet face, solemn and
sealed, a factor of one, and she will
see their eyes, two each,
their legs, two each, and the curves of their sexes,
one each, and in her head she'll be doing her
wild multiplying, as the drops
sparkle and fall to the power of a thousand from her body.

Sharon Olds   1983

35/10

Brushing out my daughter's dark
silken hair before the mirror
I see the gray gleaming on my head,
the silver-haired servant behind her. Why is it
just as we begin to go
they begin to arrive, the fold in my neck
clarifying as the fine bones of her
hips sharpen? As my skin shows
its dry pitting, she opens like a small
pale flower on the tip of a cactus;
as my last chances to bear a child
are falling through my body, the duds among them,
her full purse of eggs, round and
firm as hard-boiled yolks, is about
to snap its clasp. I brush her tangled
fragrant hair at bedtime. It's an old
story—the oldest we have on our planet—
the story of replacement.

Sharon Olds   1983

SPRING AND FALL

To a young child

Margaret, are you grieving
Over Goldengrove unleaving?
Leaves, like the things of man, you
With your fresh thoughts care for, can you?
Ah, as the heart grows older
It will come to such sights colder
By and by, nor spare a sigh
Though worlds of wanwood leafmeal lie;
And yet you *will* weep and know why.
Now no matter, child, the name:
Sorrow's springs are the same.
Nor mouth had, no nor mind, expressed
What heart heard of, ghost guessed:
It is the blight man was born for,
It is Margaret you mourn for.

Gerard Manley Hopkins   1880

PORTRAIT OF GIRL WITH COMIC BOOK

Thirteen's no age at all. Thirteen is nothing.
It is not wit, or powder on the face,
Or Wednesday matinées, or misses' clothing,
Or intellect, or grace.
Twelve has its tribal customs. But thirteen
Is neither boys in battered cars nor dolls,
Not *Sara Crewe,* or movie magazine,
Or pennants on the walls.

Thirteen keeps diaries and tropical fish
(A month, at most); scorns jumpropes in the spring;
Could not, would fortune grant it, name its wish;
Wants nothing, everything;
Has secrets from itself, friends it despises;
Admits none to the terrors that it feels;
Owns half a hundred masks but no disguises;
And walks upon its heels.

Thirteen's anomalous—not that, not this:
Not folded bud, or wave that laps a shore,
Or moth proverbial from the chrysalis.
Is the one age defeats the metaphor.
Is not a town, like childhood, strongly walled
But easily surrounded; is no city.
Nor, quitted once, can it be quite recalled—
Not even with pity.

Phyllis McGinley   1952

YOUNG GIRLS

Nothing, not even fear of punishment
can stop the giggle in a girl.
Oh mothers' trim
shapes on the chesterfield cannot dispel
their lolloping fatness.
Adolescence tumbles about in them
in cinder schoolyard or behind the expensive gates.

See them in class like porpoises
with smiles and tears
loosed from the same subterranean faucet; some
find individual adventure in
the obtuse angle, some in a phrase
that leaps like a smaller fish from a sea of words.
But most, deep in their daze, dawdle and roll,
their little breasts like wounds beneath their clothes.

A shoal of them in a room makes it a pool.
How can one teacher keep the water out,
or, being adult, find the springs and taps
of their tempers and tortures?
Who on a field filled with their female cries
can reel them in on a line of words
or land them neatly in a net?
On the dry ground they goggle, flounder, flap.

Too much weeping in them and unfamiliar blood
has set them perilously afloat.
Not divers these—but as if the waters rose in flood—
making them partially amphibious
and always drowning a little and hearing bells;
until the day the shoreline wavers less,
and caught and swung on the bright hooks of their sex,
earth becomes home, their natural element.

P. K. Page   1954

WHEN I WAS A BOY

Years and years and years ago, when I was a boy,
when there were wolves in Wales, and birds the color of red-
    flannel petticoats whisked past the harp-shaped hills,
when we sang and wallowed all night and day in caves that
    smelled like Sunday afternoons in damp front farmhouse
    parlors, and we chased, with the jawbones of deacons,
    the English and the bears,
before the motor car, before the wheel, before the duchess-
    faced horse, when we rode the daft and happy hills bareback,
    it snowed and it snowed.
But here a small boy says: "It snowed last year, too. I made a
    snowman and my brother knocked it down and I knocked
    my brother down and then we had tea."
"But that was not the same snow," I say. "Our snow was not
    only shaken from whitewash buckets down the sky, it came
    shawling out of the ground and swam and drifted out of the
    arms and hands and bodies of the trees;
snow grew overnight on the roofs of houses like a pure and
    grandfather moss, minutely white-ivied the walls and settled
    on the postman, opening the gate, like a dumb, numb
    thunderstorm of white, torn Christmas cards.
"Were there postmen then, too?"
"With sprinkling eyes and wind-cherried noses, on spread,
    frozen feet they crunched up to the doors and mittened on
    them manfully.
But all the children could hear was a ringing of bells."
"You mean that the postman went rat-a-tat-tat and the doors
    rang?"
"I mean that the bells that the children could hear were inside
    them."
"I only hear thunder sometimes, never bells."
"There were church bells, too."
"Inside them?"
"No, no, no, in the bat-black, snow-white belfries, tugged by
    bishops and storks. And they rang their tidings over the
    bandaged town, over the frozen foam of the powder and
    ice-cream hills, over the crackling sea.

Dylan Thomas 1954
from A Child's Christmas in Wales

BAUDELAIRE

When I fall asleep, and even during sleep,
I hear, quite distinctly, voices speaking
Whole phrases, commonplace and trivial,
Having no relation to my affairs.

Dear Mother, is any time left to us
In which to be happy? My debts are immense.
My bank account is subject to the court's judgment.
I know nothing. I cannot know anything.
I have lost the ability to make an effort.
But now as before my love for you increases.
You are always armed to stone me, always:
It is true. It dates from childhood.

For the first time in my long life
I am almost happy. The book, almost finished,
Almost seems good. It will endure, a monument
To my obsessions, my hatred, my disgust.

Debts and inquietude persist and weaken me.
Satan glides before me, saying sweetly:
"Rest for a day! You can rest and play today.
Tonight you will work." When night comes,
My mind, terrified by the arrears,
Bored by sadness, paralyzed by impotence,
Promises: "Tomorrow: I will tomorrow."
Tomorrow the same comedy enacts itself
With the same resolution, the same weakness.

I am sick of this life of furnished rooms.
I am sick of having colds and headaches:
You know my strange life. Every day brings
Its quota of wrath. You little know
A poet's life, dear Mother: I must write poems,
The most fatiguing of occupations.

I am sad this morning. Do not reproach me.
I write from a café near the post office,

Amid the click of billiard balls, the clatter of dishes,
The pounding of my heart. I have been asked to write
"A History of Caricature." I have been asked to write
"A History of Sculpture." Shall I write a history
Of the caricatures of the sculptures of you in my heart?

Although it costs you countless agony,
Although you cannot believe it necessary,
And doubt that the sum is accurate,
Please send me money enough for at least three weeks.

Delmore Schwartz   1954

THIS WORLD IS GRADUALLY BECOMING A PLACE

This world is gradually becoming a place
where I do not care to be any more. Can Delmore die?
I don't suppose
in all them years a day went ever by
without a loving thought for him. Welladay.
In the brightness of his promise,

unstained, I saw him thro' the mist of the actual
blazing with insight, warm with gossip
thro' all our Harvard years
when both of us were just becoming known
I got him out of a police station once, in Washington,
    the world is *tref*
and grief too astray for tears.

I imagine you have heard the terrible news,
that Delmore Schwartz is dead, miserably & alone,
in New York: he sang me a song
"I am the Brooklyn poet Delmore Schwartz
Harms & the child I sing, two parents' torts"
when he was young & gift-strong.

John Berryman   1968

MOMMA WELFARE ROLL

Her arms semaphore fat triangles,
Pudgy hands bunched on layered hips
Where bones idle under years of fatback
And lima beans.
Her jowls shiver in accusation
Of crimes clichéd by
Repetition. Her children, strangers
To childhood's toys, play
Best the games of darkened doorways,
Rooftop tag, and know the slick feel of
Other peoples' property.

Too fat to whore,
Too mad to work,
Searches her dreams for the
Lucky sign and walks bare-handed
Into a den of bureaucrats for
Her portion.
"They don't give me welfare.
I take it."

Maya Angelou   1978

TO MY MOTHER

Most near, most dear, most loved and most far,
Under the window where I often found her
Sitting as huge as Asia, seismic with laughter,
Gin and chicken helpless in her Irish hand,
Irresistible as Rabelais, but most tender for
The lame dogs and hurt birds that surround her,
She is a procession no one can follow after
But be like a little dog following a brass band.
She will not glance up at the bomber, or condescend
To drop her gin and scuttle to a cellar,
But lean on the mahogany table like a mountain
Whom only faith can move, and so I send
O all my faith, and all my love to tell her
That she will move from mourning into morning.

George Barker   1941

NIGHTINGALES IN AMERICA

The older women were Sunbeams and I guess we
were Cherubs or Lambs but our mothers were Nightingales.
Sunday mornings they prayed and sang in a niche
of the Methodist Church. They studied the sorrows of Jesus
and all who suffered in places like Abyssinia,
where there was still so much to be done.
There was much to be done everywhere, of course—
bake sales, suppers, altars, the homely chores
women were made for. Once a year, however,
they paused in their good works and took us all
to Cold Spring Park. After we skidded around
the roller rink maybe a million times,
seesawed, swang, got skinned and bitten, skittered
through poison ivy, fell in the creek, rode
the little train and ate our fill we lay back
blissfully in the grass and watched our blessed
mothers, their wings suddenly tinged with gold,
wheel overhead in the shape of a cross, singing
a wistful hymn we never could remember.

Jane Flanders   1988

PIANO

Softly, in the dusk, a woman is singing to me;
Taking me back down the vista of years, till I see
A child sitting under the piano, in the boom
     of the tingling strings
And pressing the small poised feet of a mother who
     smiles as she sings.

In spite of myself, the insidious mastery of song
Betrays me back, till the heart of me weeps to belong
To the old Sunday evenings at home, with winter outside
And hymns in the cozy parlor, the tinkling piano our guide.

So now it is vain for the singer to burst into clamor
With the great black piano appassionato. The glamour
Of childish days is upon me, my manhood is cast
Down in the flood of remembrance, I weep like a child
     for the past.

D. H. Lawrence   1918

MY PAPA'S WALTZ

The whiskey on your breath
Could make a small boy dizzy;
But I hung on like death:
Such waltzing was not easy.

We romped until the pans
Slid from the kitchen shelf;
My mother's countenance
Could not unfrown itself.

The hand that held my wrist
Was battered on one knuckle;
At every step you missed
My right ear scraped a buckle.

You beat time on my head
With a palm caked hard by dirt,
Then waltzed me off to bed
Still clinging to your shirt.

Theodore Roethke   1942

THOSE WINTER SUNDAYS

Sundays too my father got up early
and put his clothes on in the blueblack cold,
then with cracked hands that ached
from labor in the weekday weather made
banked fires blaze. No one ever thanked him.

I'd wake and hear the cold splintering, breaking.
When the rooms were warm, he'd call,
and slowly I would rise and dress,
fearing the chronic angers of that house,
Speaking indifferently to him,
who had driven out the cold
and polished my good shoes as well.
What did I know, what did I know
of love's austere and lonely offices?

Robert Hayden   1962

GRANDFATHER IN THE OLD MEN'S HOME

Gentle at last, and as clean as ever,
He did not even need drink any more,
And his good sons unbent and brought him
Tobacco to chew, both times when they came
To be satisfied he was well cared for.
And he smiled all the time to remember
Grandmother, his wife, wearing the true faith
Like an iron nightgown, yet brought to birth
Seven times and raising the family
Through her needle's eye while he got away
Down the green river, finding directions
For boats. And himself coming home sometimes
Well-heeled but blind drunk, to hide all the bread
And shoot holes in the bucket while he made
His daughters pump. Still smiled as kindly in
His sleep beside the other clean old men
To see Grandmother, every night the same,
Huge in her age, with her thumbed-down mouth, come
Hating the river, filling with her stare
His gliding dream, while he turned to water,
While the children they both had begotten,
With old faces now, but themselves shrunken
To child-size again, stood ranged at her side,
Beating their little Bibles till he died.

W. S. Merwin   1960

THE MOSS OF HIS SKIN

Young girls in old Arabia were often buried
alive next to their dead fathers, apparently as a
sacrifice to the goddesses of the tribes . . .
　　—Harold Feldman, "Children of the Desert"

It was only important
to smile and hold still,
to lie down beside him
and to rest awhile,
to be folded up together
as if we were silk,
to sink from the eyes of mother
and not to talk.　　•
The black room took us
like a cave or a mouth
or an indoor belly.
I held my breath
and daddy was there,
his thumbs, his fat skull,
his teeth, his hair growing
like a field or a shawl.
I lay by the moss
of his skin until
it grew strange. My sisters
will never know that I fall
out of myself and pretend
that Allah will not see
how I hold my daddy
like an old stone tree.

　　　　　　Anne Sexton   1958

WANDERER'S SONG

WANDERER'S SONG

I have had enough of women, and enough of love,
But the land waits, and the sea waits, and day and night is enough;
Give me a long white road and the gray wide path of the sea,
And the wind's will and the bird's will, and the heartache still in me.

Why should I seek out sorrow, and give gold for strife?
I have loved much and wept much, but tears and love are not life;
The grass calls to my heart, and the foam to my blood cries up,
And the sun shines and the road shines, and the wine's in the cup.

I have had enough of wisdom, and enough of mirth,
For the way's one and the end's one, and it's soon to the
    ends of the earth;
And it's then good-night and to bed, and if heels or heartache,
Well, it's sound sleep and long sleep, and sleep too deep to wake.

Arthur Symons   1889

241

THE WORLD IS TOO MUCH WITH US

The world is too much with us; late and soon,
Getting and spending, we lay waste our powers;
Little we see in Nature that is ours;
We have given our hearts away, a sordid boon!
This Sea that bares her bosom to the moon,
The winds that will be howling at all hours,
And are up-gathered now like sleeping flowers;
For this, for everything, we are out of tune;
It moves us not—Great God! I'd rather be
A Pagan suckled in a creed outworn;
So might I, standing on this pleasant lea,
Have glimpses that would make me less forlorn;
Have sight of Proteus rising from the sea;
Or hear old Triton blow his wreathèd horn.

William Wordsworth   1807

SEA FEVER

I must down to the seas again, to the lonely sea and the sky,
And all I ask is a tall ship and a star to steer her by,
And the wheel's kick and the wind's song and the
    white sail's shaking,
And a gray mist on the sea's face and a gray dawn breaking.

I must down to the seas again, for the call of the running tide
Is a wild call and a clear call that may not be denied;
And all I ask is a windy day with the white clouds flying,
And the flung spray and the blown spume, and
    the sea gulls crying.

I must down to the seas again to the vagrant gypsy life.
To the gull's way and the whale's way where the wind's
    like a whetted knife;
And all I ask is a merry yarn from a laughing fellow rover,
And quiet sleep and a sweet dream when the long trick's over.

John Masefield   1902

SAILING TO BYZANTIUM

That is no country for old men. The young
In one another's arms, birds in the trees,
—Those dying generations—at their song,
The salmon falls, the mackerel-crowded seas,
Fish, flesh, or fowl, commend all summer long
Whatever is begotten, born, and dies.
Caught in that sensual music all neglect
Monuments of unaging intellect.

An aged man is but a paltry thing,
A tattered coat upon a stick, unless
Soul clap its hands and sing, and louder sing
For every tatter in its mortal dress,
Nor is there singing school but studying
Monuments of its own magnificence;
And therefore I have sailed the seas and come
To the holy city of Byzantium.

O sages standing in God's holy fire
As in the gold mosaic of a wall,
Come from the holy fire, perne in a gyre,
And be the singing masters of my soul.
Consume my heart away; sick with desire
And fastened to a dying animal
It knows not what it is; and gather me
Into the artifice of eternity.

Once out of nature I shall never take
My bodily form from any natural thing,
But such a form as Grecian goldsmiths make
Of hammered gold and gold enameling
To keep a drowsy Emperor awake;
Or set upon a golden bough to sing
To lords and ladies of Byzantium
Of what is past, or passing, or to come.

William Butler Yeats 1927

ULYSSES

It little profits that an idle king,
By this still hearth, among these barren crags,
Matched with an agèd wife, I mete and dole
Unequal laws unto a savage race,
That hoard, and sleep, and feed, and know not me.
I cannot rest from travel; I will drink
Life to the lees: all times I have enjoyed
Greatly, have suffered greatly, both with those
That loved me, and alone; on shore, and when
Through scudding drifts the rainy Hyades
Vexed the dim sea. I am become a name;
For always roaming with a hungry heart
Much have I seen and known—cities of men
And manners, climates, councils, governments,
Myself not least, but honored of them all—
And drunk delight of battle with my peers,
Far on the ringing plains of windy Troy.
I am a part of all that I have met;
Yet all experience is an arch wherethrough
Gleams that untraveled world, whose margin fades
For ever and for ever when I move.
How dull it is to pause, to make an end,
To rust unburnished, not to shine in use!
As though to breathe were life! Life piled on life
Were all too little, and of one to me
Little remains: but every hour is saved
From that eternal silence, something more,
A bringer of new things; and vile it were
For some three suns to store and hoard myself,
And this gray spirit yearning in desire
To follow knowledge like a sinking star,
Beyond the utmost bound of human thought.

This is my son, mine own Telemachus,
To whom I leave the scepter and the isle,
Well-loved of me, discerning to fulfill
This labor, by slow prudence to make mild
A rugged people, and through soft degrees
Subdue them to the useful and the good.

Most blameless is he, centered in the sphere
Of common duties, decent not to fail
In offices of tenderness, and pay
Meet adoration to my household gods,
When I am gone. He works his work, I mine.

   There lies the port; the vessel puffs her sail;
There gloom the dark broad seas. My mariners,
Souls that have toiled, and wrought, and thought with me,
That ever with a frolic welcome took
The thunder and the sunshine, and opposed
Free hearts, free foreheads—you and I are old;
Old age hath yet his honor and his toil.
Death closes all; but something ere the end,
Some work of noble note, may yet be done,
Not unbecoming men that strove with gods.
The lights begin to twinkle from the rocks;
The long day wanes; the slow moon climbs; the deep
Moans round with many voices. Come, my friends,
'Tis not too late to seek a newer world.
Push off, and sitting well in order smite
The sounding furrows; for my purpose holds
To sail beyond the sunset, and the baths
Of all the western stars, until I die.
It may be that the gulfs will wash us down:
It may be we shall touch the Happy Isles,
And see the great Achilles, whom we knew.
Though much is taken, much abides; and though
We are not now that strength which in old days
Moved earth and heaven; that which we are, we are;
One equal temper of heroic hearts,
Made weak by time and fate, but strong in will
To strive, to seek, to find, and not to yield.

                              Alfred, Lord Tennyson   1833

DOLOR

I have known the inexorable sadness of pencils,
Neat in their boxes, dolor of pad and paper weight,
All the misery of manila folders and mucilage,
Desolation in immaculate public places,
Lonely reception room, lavatory, switchboard,
The unalterable pathos of basin and pitcher,
Ritual of multigraph, paper clip, comma,
Endless duplication of lives and objects.
And I have seen dust from the walls of institutions,
Finer than flour, alive, more dangerous than silica,
Silt, almost invisible, through long afternoons of tedium,
Dropping a fine film on nails and delicate eyebrows,
Glazing the pale hair, the duplicate gray standard faces.

Theodore Roethke   1943

DEPARTMENTAL

An ant on the tablecloth
Ran into a dormant moth
Of many times his size.
He showed not the least surprise.
His business wasn't with such.
He gave it scarcely a touch,
And was off on his duty run.
Yet if he encountered one
Of the hive's enquiry squad
Whose work is to find out God
And the nature of time and space,
He would put him onto the case.
Ants are a curious race;
One crossing with hurried tread
The body of one of their dead
Isn't given a moment's arrest—
Seems not even impressed.
But he no doubt reports to any
With whom he crosses antennae,
And they no doubt report
To the higher-up at court.
Then word goes forth in Formic:

"Death's come to Jerry McCormic,
Our selfless forager Jerry.
Will the special Janizary
Whose office it is to bury
The dead of the commissary
Go bring him home to his people.
Lay him in state on a sepal.
Wrap him for shroud in a petal.
Embalm him with ichor of nettle.
This is the word of your Queen."
And presently on the scene
Appears a solemn mortician;
And taking formal position
With feelers calmly atwiddle,
Seizes the dead by the middle,
And heaving him high in air,
Carries him out of there.
No one stands round to stare.
It is nobody else's affair.
It couldn't be called ungentle.
But how thoroughly departmental.

Robert Frost   1936

THE CAMBRIDGE LADIES WHO LIVE
IN FURNISHED SOULS

the Cambridge ladies who live in furnished souls
are unbeautiful and have comfortable minds
(also,with the church's protestant blessings
daughters,unscented shapeless spirited)
they believe in Christ and Longfellow,both dead,
are invariably interested in so many things—
at the present writing one still finds
delighted fingers knitting for the is it Poles?
perhaps.   While permanent faces coyly bandy
scandal of Mrs. N and Professor D
. . . . the Cambridge ladies do not care,above
Cambridge if sometimes in its box of
sky lavender and cornerless,the
moon rattles like a fragment of angry candy

e. e. cummings   1923

HE STARED AT RUIN

He stared at ruin. Ruin stared straight back.
He thought they was old friends. He felt on the stair
where her papa found them bare
they became familiar. When the papers were lost
rich with pals' secrets, he thought he had the
    knack of ruin. Their paths crossed

and once they crossed in jail; they crossed in bed;
and over an unsigned letter their eyes met,
and in an Asian city
directionless & lurchy at two & three,
or trembling to a telephone's fresh threat,
and when some wired his head

to reach a wrong opinion, "Epileptic."
But he noted now that: they were not old friends.
He did not know this one.
This one was a stranger, come to make amends
for all the imposters, and to make it stick.
Henry nodded, un-.

John Berryman   1969

MEMORIES OF WEST STREET AND LEPKE

Only teaching on Tuesdays, book-worming
in pajamas fresh from the washer each morning,
I hog a whole house on Boston's
"hardly passionate Marlborough Street,"
where even the man
scavenging filth in the back alley trash cans,
has two children, a beach wagon, a helpmate,
and is "a young Republican."
I have a nine months' daughter,
young enough to be my granddaughter.
Like the sun she rises in her flame-flamingo infants' wear.

These are the tranquilized *Fifties,*
and I am forty. Ought I to regret my seedtime?
I was a fire-breathing Catholic C.O.,

and made my manic statement,
telling off the state and president, and then
sat waiting sentence in the bull pen
beside a negro boy with curlicues
of marijuana in his hair.

Given a year,
I walked on the roof of the West Street Jail, a short
enclosure like my school soccer court,
and saw the Hudson River once a day
through sooty clothesline entanglements
and bleaching khaki tenements.
Strolling, I yammered metaphysics with Abramowitz,
a jaundice-yellow ("it's really tan")
and fly-weight pacifist,
so vegetarian,
he wore rope shoes and preferred fallen fruit.
He tried to convert Bioff and Brown,
the Hollywood pimps, to his diet.
Hairy, muscular, suburban,
wearing chocolate double-breasted suits,
they blew their tops and beat him black and blue.
I was so out of things, I'd never heard
of the Jehovah's Witnesses.
"Are you a C.O.?" I asked a fellow jailbird.
"No," he answered, "I'm a J.W."
He taught me the hospital "tuck,"
and pointed out the T-shirted back
of Murder Incorporated's Czar Lepke,
there piling towels on a rack,
or dawdling off to his little segregated cell full
of things forbidden the common man:
a portable radio, a dresser, two toy American
flags tied together with a ribbon of Easter palm.
Flabby, bald, lobotomized,
he drifted in a sheepish calm,
where no agonizing reappraisal
jarred his concentration on the electric chair—
hanging like an oasis in his air
of lost connections . . .

Robert Lowell 1957

SKUNK HOUR
for Elizabeth Bishop

Nautilus Island's hermit
heiress still lives through winter in her Spartan cottage;
her sheep still graze above the sea.
Her son's a bishop. Her farmer
is first selectman in our village;
she's in her dotage.

Thirsting for
the hierarchic privacy
of Queen Victoria's century,
she buys up all
the eyesores facing her shore,
and lets them fall.

The season's ill—
we've lost our summer millionaire,
who seemed to leap from an L.L. Bean
catalogue. His nine-knot yawl
was auctioned off to lobstermen.
A red fox stain covers Blue Hill.

And now our fairy
decorator brightens his shop for fall;
his fishnet's filled with orange cork,
orange, his cobbler's bench and awl;
there is no money in his work,
he'd rather marry.

One dark night,
my Tudor Ford climbed the hill's skull;
I watched for love-cars. Lights turned down,
they lay together, hull to hull,
where the graveyard shelves on the town . . .
My mind's not right.

A car radio bleats,
"Love, O careless Love . . ." I hear
my ill-spirit sob in each blood cell,
as if my hand were at its throat . . .
I myself am hell;
nobody's here—

only skunks, that search
in the moonlight for a bite to eat.
They march on their soles up Main Street:
white stripes, moonstruck eyes' red fire
under the chalk-dry and spar spire
of the Trinitarian Church.

I stand on top
of our back steps and breathe the rich air—
a mother skunk with her column of kittens swills
    the garbage pail.
She jabs her wedge-head in a cup
of sour cream, drops her ostrich tail,
and will not scare.

Robert Lowell   1957

MEN AT FORTY

Men at forty
Learn to close softly
The doors to rooms they will not be
Coming back to.

At rest on a stair landing,
They feel it
Moving beneath them now like the deck of a ship,
Though the swell is gentle.

And deep in mirrors
They rediscover
The face of the boy as he practices tying
His father's tie there in secret

And the face of that father,
Still warm with the mystery of lather.
They are more fathers than sons themselves now.
Something is filling them, something

That is like the twilight sound
Of the crickets, immense,
Filling the woods at the foot of the slope
Behind their mortgaged houses.

Donald Justice   1966

THIRD AVENUE IN SUNLIGHT

Third Avenue in sunlight. Nature's error.
Already the bars are filled and John is there.
Beneath a plentiful lady over the mirror
He tilts his glass in the mild mahogany air.

I think of him when he first got out of college,
Serious, thin, unlikely to succeed;
For several months he hung around the Village,
Boldly T-shirted, unfettered but unfreed.

Now he confides to a stranger, "I was first scout,
And kept my glimmers peeled till after dark.
Our outfit had as its sign a bloody knout,
We met behind the museum in Central Park.

Of course, we were kids." But still those savages,
War-painted, a flap of leather at the loins,
File silently against him. Hostages
Are never taken. One summer, in Des Moines,

They entered his hotel room, tomahawks
Flashing like barracuda. He tried to pray.
Three years of treatment. Occasionally he talks
About how he almost didn't get away.

Daily the prowling sunlight whets its knife
Along the sidewalk. We almost never meet.
In the Rembrandt dark he lifts his amber life.
My bar is somewhat further down the street.

Anthony Hecht   1959

THE HUNCHBACK IN THE PARK

The hunchback in the park
A solitary mister
Propped between trees and water
From the opening of the garden lock
That let the trees and water enter

Until the Sunday somber bell at dark,
Eating bread from a newspaper
Drinking water from the chained cup
That the children filled with gravel
In the fountain basin where I sailed my ship
Slept at night in a dog kennel
But nobody chained him up.

Like the park birds he came early
Like the water he sat down
And Mister they called hey Mister
The truant boys from the town
Running when he had heard them clearly
On out of sound

Past lake and rockery
Laughing when he shook his paper
Hunchbacked in mockery
Through the loud zoo of the willow groves
Dodging the park keeper
With his stick that picked up leaves.

And the old dog sleeper
Alone between nurses and swans
While the boys among willows
Made the tiger jump out of their eyes
To roar on the rockery stones

And the groves were blue with sailors
Made all day until bell time
A woman figure without fault
Straight as a young elm
Straight and tall from his crooked bones
That she might stand in the night
After the lock and chains

All night in the unmade park
After the railings and shrubberies
The birds the grass the trees the lake
And the wild boys innocent as strawberries
Had followed the hunchback
To his kennel in the dark.

Dylan Thomas   1941

THOUGHTS

Excuse me, isn't that you I see concealed underneath there
Inside the shield, or conning tower, of your head,
Your eyes looking out of the perforations in your flesh?
How can you think you can see from out of liquid, anyway?
     Are rain puddles watching me even now,
And can ducts which punctuate the underground of a field
Examine it at will for buried treasure? Is the rain outside your
     window a voyeur, then? Deep down under all that, though,
Underneath the liquids and the various unobservant stuffs
There is a spirit, shifting around from foot to foot.

Michael Benedikt   1967

MY EROTIC DOUBLE

He says he doesn't feel like working today.
It's just as well. Here in the shade
Behind the house, protected from street noises,
One can go over all kinds of old feeling,
Throw some away, keep others.
          The wordplay
Between us gets very intense when there are
Fewer feelings around to confuse things.
Another go-round? No, but the last things
You always find to say are charming, and rescue me
Before the night does. We are afloat
On our dreams as on a barge made of ice,
Shot through with questions and fissures of starlight
That keep us awake, thinking about the dreams
As they are happening. Some occurrence. You said it.

I said it but I can hide it. But I choose not to.
Thank you. You are a very pleasant person.
Thank you. You are too.

John Ashbery   1979

SONNET 115

As usual I'm up before the sun
begins to warm this intolerable place
and I have stared all night upon your face
but am not wiser thereby. Everyone
rattles his weakness or his thing undone,
I shake you like a rat. Open disgrace
yawns all before me: have I left a trace,
a spoor? Clouding it over, I look for my gun.

She's hidden it. I won't sing on of that.
Whiskey is bracing. Failures are my speed,
I thrive on ends, the dog is at the door
in heat, the neighborhood is male except one cat
and they thresh on my stoop. Prevent my need,
Someone, and come & find me on the floor.

John Berryman   1971

THE SOUL SELECTS HER OWN SOCIETY

The soul selects her own society
Then shuts the door
On her divine majority,
Present no more.

Unmoved, she notes the chariots pausing
At her low gate.
Unmoved, an emperor be kneeling
Upon her Mat.

I've known her from an ample nation
Choose one
Then close the valves of her attention
Like stone.

Emily Dickinson   1862

MUCH MADNESS IS DIVINEST SENSE

Much madness is divinest sense
To a discerning eye;
Much sense the starkest madness.
'Tis the majority
In this, as all, prevail.
Assent and you are sane;
Demur and you're straightaway dangerous
And handled with a chain.

Emily Dickinson   1862

HER KIND

I have gone out, a possessed witch,
haunting the black air, braver at night;
dreaming evil, I have done my hitch
over the plain houses, light by light:
lonely thing, twelve-fingered, out of mind.
A woman like that is not a woman, quite.
I have been her kind.

I have found the warm caves in the woods,
filled them with skillets, carvings, shelves,
closets, silks, innumerable goods;
fixed the suppers for the worms and the elves:
whining, rearranging the disaligned.
A woman like that is misunderstood.
I have been her kind.

I have ridden in your cart, driver,
waved my nude arms at villages going by,
learning the last bright routes, survivor
where your flames still bite my thigh
and my ribs crack where your wheels wind.
A woman like that is not ashamed to die.
I have been her kind.

Anne Sexton   1960

RINGING THE BELLS

And this is the way they ring
the bells in Bedlam
and this is the bell-lady
who comes each Tuesday morning
to give us a music lesson
and because the attendants make you go
and because we mind by instinct,
like bees caught in the wrong hive,
we are the circle of the crazy ladies
who sit in the lounge of the mental house
and smile at the smiling woman
who passes us each a bell,
who points at my hand
that holds my bell, E flat,
and this is the gray dress next to me
who grumbles as if it were special
to be old, to be old,
and this is the small hunched squirrel girl
on the other side of me
who picks at the hairs over her lip,
who picks at the hairs over her lip all day,
and this is how the bells really sound,
as untroubled and clean
as a workable kitchen,
and this is always my bell responding
to my hand that responds to the lady
who points at me, E flat;
and although we are no better for it,
they tell you to go. And you do.

Anne Sexton   1960

TOMORROW, AND TOMORROW, AND TOMORROW

MACBETH: Tomorrow, and tomorrow, and tomorrow,
Creeps in this petty pace from day to day
To the last syllable of recorded time,
And all our yesterdays have lighted fools
The way to dusty death. Out, out, brief candle!
Life's but a walking shadow, a poor player
That struts and frets his hour upon the stage
And then is heard no more: it is a tale
Told by an idiot, full of sound and fury,
Signifying nothing.

William Shakespeare   1606
Macbeth, Act V, Scene 5

PRELUDES

1

The winter evening settles down
With smell of steaks in passageways.
Six o'clock
The burnt-out ends of smoky days.
And now a gusty shower wraps
The grimy scraps
Of withered leaves about your feet
And newspapers from vacant lots;
The showers beat
On broken blinds and chimney-pots,
And at the corner of the street
A lonely cab-horse steams and stamps.
And then the lighting of the lamps.

2

The morning comes to consciousness
Of faint stale smells of beer
From the sawdust-trampled street
With all its muddy feet that press
To early coffee-stands.
With the other masquerades
That time resumes,
One thinks of all the hands
That are raising dingy shades
In a thousand furnished room

3

You tossed a blanket from the bed,
You lay upon your back and waited;
You dozed, and watched the night revealing
The thousand sordid images
Of which your soul was constituted;
They flickered against the ceiling.
And when all the world came back
And the light crept up between the shutters
And you heard the sparrows in the gutters,
You had such a vision of the street
As the street hardly understands;
Sitting along the bed's edge, where
You curled the papers from your hair,
Or clasped the yellow soles of feet
In the palms of both soiled hands.

4

His soul stretched tight across the skies
That fade behind a city block,
Or trampled by insistent feet
At four and five and six o'clock;
And short square fingers stuffing pipes,
And evening newspapers, and eyes
Assured of certain certainties,
The conscience of a blackened street
Impatient to assume the world.
I am moved by fancies that are curled
Around these images, and cling:
The notion of some infinitely gentle
Infinitely suffering thing.
Wipe your hand across your mouth, and laugh;
The worlds revolve like ancient women
Gathering fuel in vacant lots.

T. S. Eliot   1917

THE LOVE SONG OF J. ALFRED PRUFROCK

S'io credesse che mia riposta fosse
A persona che mai tornasse al mondo,
Questa fiamma staria senza più scosse.
Ma perciocche giammai di questo fondo
Non tornò vivo alcun, s'i'odo il vero,
Senza tema d'infamia ti rispondo.

Let us go then, you and I,
When the evening is spread out against the sky
Like a patient etherized upon a table;
Let us go, through certain half-deserted streets,
The muttering retreats
Of restless nights in one-night cheap hotels
And sawdust restaurants with oyster-shells:
Streets that follow like a tedious argument
Of insidious intent
To lead you to an overwhelming question . . .
Oh, do not ask, "What is it?"
Let us go and make our visit.

In the room the women come and go
Talking of Michelangelo.

The yellow fog that rubs its back upon the window-panes,
The yellow smoke that rubs its muzzle on the window-panes,
Licked its tongue into the corners of the evening,
Lingered upon the pools that stand in drains,
Let fall upon its back the soot that falls from chimneys,
Slipped by the terrace, made a sudden leap,
And seeing that it was a soft October night,
Curled once about the house, and fell asleep.

And indeed there will be time
For the yellow smoke that slides along the street,
Rubbing its back upon the window-panes;
There will be time, there will be time
To prepare a face to meet the faces that you meet;
There will be time to murder and create,
And time for all the works and days of hands
That lift and drop a question on your plate;

Time for you and time for me,
And time yet for a hundred indecisions,
And for a hundred visions and revisions,
Before the taking of a toast and tea.

In the room the women come and go
Talking of Michelangelo.

And indeed there will be time
To wonder, "Do I dare?" and, "Do I dare?"
Time to turn back and descend the stair,
With a bald spot in the middle of my hair—
[They will say: "How his hair is growing thin!"]
My morning coat, my collar mounting firmly to the chin,
My necktie rich and modest, but asserted by a simple pin—
[They will say: "But how his arms and legs are thin!"]
Do I dare
Disturb the universe?
In a minute there is time
For decisions and revisions which a minute will reverse.

For I have known them all already, known them all:
Have known the evenings, mornings, afternoons,
I have measured out my life with coffee spoons;
I know the voices dying with a dying fall
Beneath the music from a farther room.
So how should I presume?

And I have known the eyes already, known them all—
The eyes that fix you in a formulated phrase,
And when I am formulated, sprawling on a pin,
When I am pinned and wriggling on the wall,
Then how should I begin
To spit out all the butt-ends of my days and ways?
And how should I presume?

And I have known the arms already, known them all—
Arms that are braceleted and white and bare
[But in the lamplight, downed with light brown hair!]
Is it perfume from a dress
That makes me so digress?

Arms that lie along a table, or wrap about a shawl.
    And should I then presume?
    And how should I begin?
        . . . . .

    Shall I say, I have gone at dusk through narrow streets
And watched the smoke that rises from the pipes
Of lonely men in shirt-sleeves, leaning out of windows? . . .

    I should have been a pair of ragged claws
Scuttling across the floors of silent seas.
        . . . . .

    And the afternoon, the evening, sleeps so peacefully!
Smoothed by long fingers,
Asleep . . . tired . . . or it malingers,
Stretched on the floor, here beside you and me.
Should I, after tea and cakes and ices,
Have the strength to force the moment to its crisis?
But though I have wept and fasted, wept and prayed,
Though I have seen my head [grown slightly bald] brought in
    upon a platter,
I am no prophet—and here's no great matter;
I have seen the moment of my greatness flicker,
And I have seen the eternal Footman hold my coat, and snicker,
And in short, I was afraid.

    And would it have been worth it, after all,
After the cups, the marmalade, the tea,
Among the porcelain, among some talk of you and me,
Would it have been worth while,
To have bitten off the matter with a smile,
To have squeezed the universe into a ball
To roll it toward some overwhelming question,
To say: "I am Lazarus, come from the dead,
Come back to tell you all, I shall tell you all"—
If one, settling a pillow by her head,
    Should say: "That is not what I meant at all.
    That is not it, at all."

    And would it have been worth it, after all,
Would it have been worth while,
After the sunsets and the dooryards and the sprinkled streets,
After the novels, after the teacups, after the skirts that trail
    along the floor—

And this, and so much more?—
It is impossible to say just what I mean!
But as if a magic lantern threw the nerves in patterns on a
    screen:
Would it have been worth while
If one, settling a pillow or throwing off a shawl,
And turning toward the window, should say:
    "That is not it at all,
    That is not what I meant, at all."

    . . . . .

    No! I am not Prince Hamlet, nor was meant to be;
Am an attendant lord, one that will do
To swell a progress, start a scene or two,
Advise the prince; no doubt, an easy tool,
Deferential, glad to be of use,
Politic, cautious, and meticulous;
Full of high sentence, but a bit obtuse;
At times, indeed, almost ridiculous—
Almost, at times, the Fool.

    I grow old . . . I grow old . . .
I shall wear the bottoms of my trousers rolled.

    Shall I part my hair behind? Do I dare to eat a peach?
I shall wear white flannel trousers, and walk upon the beach.
I have heard the mermaids singing, each to each.

I do not think that they will sing to me.

I have seen them riding seaward on the waves
Combing the white hair of the waves blown back
When the wind blows the water white and black.

We have lingered in the chambers of the sea
By sea-girls wreathed with seaweed red and brown
Till human voices wake us, and we drown.

                                    T. S. Eliot   1911

TO BE, OR NOT TO BE

HAMLET: To be, or not to be: that is the question:
Whether 'tis nobler in the mind to suffer
The slings and arrows of outrageous fortune,
Or to take arms against a sea of troubles,
And by opposing end them? To die: to sleep;
No more; and by a sleep to say we end
The heartache and the thousand natural shocks
That flesh is heir to, 'tis a consummation
Devoutly to be wish'd. To die, to sleep;
To sleep: perchance to dream: ay, there's the rub;
For in that sleep of death what dreams may come
When we have shuffled off this mortal coil,
Must give us pause: there's the respect
That makes calamity of so long life;
For who would bear the whips and scorns of time,
The oppressor's wrong, the proud man's contumely,
The pangs of despised love, the law's delay,
The insolence of office and the spurns
That patient merit of the unworthy takes,
When he himself might his quietus make
With a bare bodkin? who would fardels bear,
To grunt and sweat under a weary life,
But that the dread of something after death,
The undiscovered country from whose bourn
No traveler returns, puzzles the will
And makes us rather bear those ills we have
Than fly to others that we know not of?
Thus conscience does make cowards of us all;
And thus the native hue of resolution
Is sicklied o'er with the pale cast of thought,
And enterprises of great pitch and moment
With this regard their currents turn awry,
And lose the name of action.

William Shakespeare   1601
Hamlet, Act III, Scene 1

THE ROOFWALKER

for Denise Levertov

Over the half-finished houses
night comes. The builders
stand on the roof. It is
quiet after the hammers,
the pulleys hang slack.
Giants, the roofwalkers,
on a listing deck, the wave
of darkness about to break
on their heads. The sky
is a torn sail where figures
pass magnified, shadows
on a burning deck.

I feel like them up there:
exposed, larger than life,
and due to break my neck.

Was it worth while to lay—
with infinite exertion—
a roof I can't live under?
—All those blueprints,
closing of gaps,
measurings, calculations?
A life I didn't choose
chose me: even
my tools are the wrong ones
for what I have to do.
I'm naked, ignorant,
a naked man fleeing
across the roofs
who could with a shade of difference
be sitting in the lamplight
against the cream wallpaper
reading—not with indifference—
about a naked man
fleeing across the roofs.

Adrienne Rich   1961

LYING IN A HAMMOCK AT WILLIAM DUFFY'S FARM IN PINE ISLAND, MINNESOTA

Over my head, I see the bronze butterfly,
Asleep on the black trunk,
Blowing like a leaf in green shadow.
Down the ravine behind the empty house,
The cowbells follow one another
Into the distances of the afternoon.
To my right,
In a field of sunlight between two pines,
The droppings of last year's horses
Blaze up into golden stones.
I lean back, as the evening darkens and comes on.
A chicken hawk floats over, looking for home.
I have wasted my life.

James Wright   1961

ABOVE THESE CARES

Above these cares my spirit in calm abiding
Floats like a swimmer at sunrise, facing the pale sky;
Peaceful, heaved by the light infrequent lurch of the
        heavy wave serenely sliding
Under his weightless body, aware of the wide morning,
        aware of the gull on the red buoy bedaubed with guano,
        aware of his sharp cry;
Idly athirst for the sea, as who should say:
In a moment I will roll upon my mouth and drink it dry.

Painfully, under the pressure that obtains
At the sea's bottom, crushing my lungs and my brains
(For the body makes shift to breathe and after a fashion flourish
Ten fathoms deep in care,
Ten fathoms down in an element denser than air
Wherein the soul must perish)
I trap and harvest, stilling my stomach's needs;
I crawl forever, hoping never to see
Above my head the limbs of my spirit no longer free
Kicking in frenzy, a swimmer enmeshed in weeds.

Edna St. Vincent Millay   1934

A Poem Some People Will Have to Understand

Dull unwashed windows of eyes
and buildings of industry. What
industry do I practice? A slick
colored boy, 12 miles from his
home. I practice no industry.
I am no longer a credit
to my race. I read a little,
scratch against silence slow spring afternoons.

       I had thought, before, some years ago
that I'd come to the end of my life.

       Watercolor ego. Without the preciseness
a violent man could propose.

       But the wheel, and the wheels,
wont let us alone. All the fantasy
       and justice, and dry charcoal winters
All the pitifully intelligent citizens
       I've forced myself to love.

We have waited the coming of a natural
phenomenon. Mystics and romantics, knowledgeable
workers
of the land.
But none has come.
(Repeat)
       but none has come.

Will the machinegunners please step forward?

                           Amiri Baraka   1969

IN A DARK TIME

In a dark time, the eye begins to see,
I meet my shadow in the deepening shade;
I hear my echo in the echoing wood—
A lord of nature weeping to a tree.

I live between the heron and the wren,
Beasts of the hill and serpents of the den.

What's madness but nobility of soul
At odds with circumstance? The day's on fire!
I know the purity of pure despair,
My shadow pinned against a sweating wall.
That place among the rocks—is it a cave,
Or winding path? The edge is what I have.

A steady storm of correspondences!
A night flowing with birds, a ragged moon,
And in broad day the midnight come again!
A man goes far to find out what he is—
Death of the self in a long, tearless night,
All natural shapes blazing unnatural light.

Dark, dark my light, and darker my desire.
My soul, like some heat-maddened summer fly,
Keeps buzzing at the sill. Which I is I?
A fallen man, I climb out of my fear.
The mind enters itself, and God the mind,
And one is One, free in the tearing wind.

                    Theodore Roethke   1960

THE LEADEN-EYED

Let not young souls be smothered out before
They do quaint deeds and fully flaunt their pride.
It is the world's one crime its babes grow dull,
Its poor are ox-like, limp and leaden-eyed.

Not that they starve, but starve so dreamlessly,
Not that they sow, but that they seldom reap,
Not that they serve, but have no gods to serve,
Not that they die, but that they die like sheep.

Vachel Lindsay   1914

ON HIS BLINDNESS

When I consider how my light is spent
    E're half my days in this dark world and wide,
    And that one Talent which is death to hide
    Lodged with me useless, though my Soul more bent
To serve therewith my Maker, and present
    My true account, lest He returning chide,
    "Doth God exact day labor, light denied?"
    I fondly ask. But Patience, to prevent
That murmur, soon replies, "God doth not need
    Either man's work or his own gifts. Who best
    Bear His mild yoke, they serve Him best. His state
Is kingly. Thousands at His bidding speed,
    And post o'er land and ocean without rest;
    They also serve who only stand and wait."

John Milton   1652

KUBLA KHAN
or Vision in a Dream. A Fragment

In Xanadu did Kubla Khan
A stately pleasure dome decree:
Where Alph, the sacred river, ran
Through caverns measureless to man
    Down to a sunless sea.
So twice five miles of fertile ground
With walls and towers were girdled round:
And here were gardens bright with sinuous rills,
Where blossomed many an incense-bearing tree;
And here were forests ancient as the hills,
Enfolding sunny spots of greenery.

But oh! that deep romantic chasm which slanted
Down the green hill athwart a cedarn cover!
A savage place! as holy and enchanted
As e'er beneath a waning moon was haunted
By woman wailing for her demon lover!
And from this chasm, with ceaseless turmoil seething,
As if this earth in fast thick pants were breathing,
A mighty fountain momently was forced:
Amid whose swift half-intermitted burst
Huge fragments vaulted like rebounding hail,
Or chaffy grain beneath the thresher's flail:
And 'mid these dancing rocks at once and ever
It flung up momently the sacred river.
Five miles meandering with a mazy motion
Through wood and dale the sacred river ran,
Then reached the caverns measureless to man.
And sank in tumult to a lifeless ocean:
And 'mid this tumult Kubla heard from far
Ancestral voices prophesying war!

The shadow of the dome of pleasure
Floated midway on the waves;
Where was heard the mingled measure
From the fountain and the caves.
It was a miracle of rare device,
A sunny pleasure dome with caves of ice!

A damsel with a dulcimer
In a vision once I saw:
It was an Abyssinian maid,
And on her dulcimer she played,
Singing of Mount Abora.
Could I revive within me,
Her symphony and song,
To such a deep delight 'twould win me.
That with music loud and long,
I would build that dome in air,
That sunny dome! those caves of ice!
And all who heard should see them there,
And all should cry, Beware! Beware!
His flashing eyes, his floating hair!
Weave a circle round him thrice,
And close your eyes with holy dread,
For he on honey dew hath fed,
And drunk the milk of Paradise.

Samuel Taylor Coleridge   1798

THE RUNES

These words were given me in a dream. In the dream I was a Finnish child of 8 or 9 who had been given by her teacher the task of writing out these three ancient runes of her people. This is how they went:

(1) Know the pinetrees. Know the orange dryness of sickness and death in needle and cone. Know them too in green health, those among whom your life is laid.

(2) Know the ship you sail on. Know its timbers. Deep the fjord waters where you sail, steep the cliffs, deep into the unknown coast goes the winding fjord. But what would you have? Would you be tied up to a sandwhite quay in perpetual sunshine, yards and masts sprouting little violet mandolins?

(3) In city, in suburb, in forest, no way to stretch out the arms— so if you would grow, go straight up or deep down.

Denise Levertov   1964

SO, WE'LL GO NO MORE A-ROVING

So, we'll go no more a-roving
    So late into the night,
Though the heart be still as loving,
    And the moon be still as bright.

For the sword outwears its sheath,
    And the soul wears out the breast,
And the heart must pause to breathe,
    And love itself have rest.

Though the night was made for loving,
    And the day returns too soon,
Yet we'll go no more a-roving
    By the light of the moon.

George Gordon, Lord Byron   1817

WEARINESS

Oh let me be alone, far from the eyes and faces,
    Let me be alone, awhile, even from you;
My soul is like a desert, sick of light-filled spaces,
    The urge of useless winds, the sky of pitiless blue;
Let me be alone, awhile, in twilit places,
    Waiting the merciful night, the stately stars and the dew.

Sara Teasdale   1916

ACQUAINTED WITH THE NIGHT

ACQUAINTED WITH THE NIGHT

I have been one acquainted with the night.
I have walked out in rain—and back in rain.
I have outwalked the furthest city light.

I have looked down the saddest city lane.
I have passed by the watchman on his beat
And dropped my eyes, unwilling to explain.

I have stood still and stopped the sound of feet
When far away an interrupted cry
Came over houses from another street,

But not to call me back or say good-bye;
And further still at an unearthly height
One luminary clock against the sky

Proclaimed the time was neither wrong nor right.
I have been one acquainted with the night.

Robert Frost   1928

273

STOPPING BY WOODS ON A SNOWY EVENING

Whose woods these are I think I know.
His house is in the village, though;
He will not see me stopping here
To watch his woods fill up with snow.

My little horse must think it queer
To stop without a farmhouse near
Between the woods and frozen lake
The darkest evening of the year.

He gives his harness bells a shake
To ask if there is some mistake.
The only other sound's the sweep
Of easy wind and downy flake.

The woods are lovely, dark, and deep,
But I have promises to keep,
And miles to go before I sleep,
And miles to go before I sleep.

Robert Frost   1923

THE DARK FOREST

Dark is the forest and deep, and overhead
Hang stars like seeds of light
In vain, though not since they were sown was bred
Anything more bright.

And evermore mighty multitudes ride
About, nor enter in;
Of the other multitudes that dwell inside
Never yet was one seen.

The forest foxglove is purple, the marguerite
Outside is gold and white,
Nor can those that pluck either blossom greet
The others, day or night.

Edward Thomas   1918

RELUCTANCE

Out through the fields and the woods
   And over the walls I have wended;
I have climbed the hills of view
   And looked at the world, and descended;
I have come by the highway home,
   And lo, it is ended.

The leaves are all dead on the ground,
   Save those that the oak is keeping
To ravel them one by one
   And let them go scraping and creeping
Out over the crusted snow,
   When others are sleeping.

And the dead leaves lie huddled and still,
   No longer blown hither and thither;
The last lone aster is gone;
   The flowers of the witch hazel wither;
The heart is still aching to seek,
   But the feet question "Whither?"

Ah, when to the heart of man
   Was it ever less than a treason
To go with the drift of things,
   To yield with a grace to reason,
And bow and accept the end
   Of a love or a season?

Robert Frost   1913

DIRECTIVE

Back out of all this now too much for us,
Back in a time made simple by the loss
Of detail, burned, dissolved, and broken off
Like graveyard marble sculpture in the weather,
There is a house that is no more a house
Upon a farm that is no more a farm
And in a town that is no more a town.
The road there, if you'll let a guide direct you
Who only has at heart your getting lost,
May seem as if it should have been a quarry—
Great monolithic knees the former town
Long since gave up pretense of keeping covered.
And there's a story in a book about it:
Besides the wear of iron wagon wheels
The ledges show lines ruled southeast-northwest,
The chisel work of an enormous Glacier
That braced his feet against the Arctic Pole.
You must not mind a certain coolness from him
Still said to haunt this side of Panther Mountain.
Nor need you mind the serial ordeal
Of being watched from forty cellar holes
As if by eye pairs out of forty firkins.
As for the woods' excitement over you
That sends light rustle rushes to their leaves,
Charge that to upstart inexperience.
Where were they all not twenty years ago?
They think too much of having shaded out
A few old pecker-fretted apple trees.
Make yourself up a cheering song of how
Someone's road home from work this once was,
Who may be just ahead of you on foot
Or creaking with a buggy load of grain.
The height of the adventure is the height
Of country where two village cultures faded
Into each other. Both of them are lost.
And if you're lost enough to find yourself
By now, pull in your ladder road behind you
And put a sign up CLOSED to all but me.
Then make yourself at home. The only field
Now left's no bigger than a harness gall.
First there's the children's house of make-believe,
Some shattered dishes underneath a pine,

The playthings in the playhouse of the children.
Weep for what little things could make them glad.
Then for the house that is no more a house,
But only a belilaced cellar hole,
Now slowly closing like a dent in dough.
This was no playhouse but a house in earnest.
Your destination and your destiny's
A brook that was the water of the house,
Cold as a spring as yet so near its source,
Too lofty and original to rage.
(We know the valley streams that when aroused
Will leave their tatters hung on barb and thorn.)
I have kept hidden in the instep arch
Of an old cedar at the waterside
A broken drinking goblet like the Grail
Under a spell so the wrong ones can't find it,
So can't get saved, as Saint Mark says they mustn't
(I stole the goblet from the children's playhouse.)
Here are your waters and your watering place.
Drink and be whole again beyond confusion.

Robert Frost   1947

BEREFT

Where had I heard this wind before
Change like this to a deeper roar?
What would it take my standing there for,
Holding open a restive door,
Looking downhill to a frothy shore?
Summer was past and day was past.
Somber clouds in the west were massed.
Out in the porch's sagging floor
Leaves got up in a coil and hissed,
Blindly struck at my knee and missed.
Something sinister in the tone
Told me my secret must be known:
Word I was in the house alone
Somehow must have gotten abroad,
Word I was in my life alone,
Word I had no one left but God.

Robert Frost   1928

TERMINUS

It is time to be old,
To take in sail
The god of bounds,
Who sets to seas a shore,
Came to me in his fatal rounds,
And said: "No more!
No farther spread
Thy broad ambitious branches, and thy root.
Fancy departs: no more invent,
Contract thy firmament
To compass of a tent.
There's not enough for this and that,
Make thy option which of two;
Economize the failing river,
Not the less revere the Giver,
Leave the many and hold the few.
Timely wise accept the terms,
Soften the fall with wary foot;
A little while
Still plan and smile,
And fault of novel germs
Mature the unfallen fruit.
Curse, if thou wilt, thy sires,
Bad husbands of their fires,
Who, when they gave thee breath,
Failed to bequeath
The needful sinew stark as once,
The Baresark marrow to thy bones,
But left a legacy of ebbing veins,
Inconstant heat and nerveless reins,
Amid the Muses, left thee deaf and dumb,
Amid the gladiators, halt and numb."

As the bird trims her to the gale,
I trim myself to the storm of time,
I man the rudder, reef the sail,
Obey the voice at eve obeyed at prime:
"Lowly faithful, banish fear,
Right onward drive unharmed;
The port, well worth the cruise, is near,
And every wave is charmed."

Ralph Waldo Emerson   1867

ON GROWING OLD

Be with me, Beauty, for the fire is dying,
My dog and I are old, too old for roving.
Man, whose young passion sets the spindrift flying,
Is soon too lame to march, too cold for loving.
I take the book and gather to the fire,
Turning old yellow leaves; minute by minute,
The clock ticks to my heart; a withered wire
Moves a thin ghost of music in the spinet.
I cannot sail your seas, I cannot wander
Your cornland, nor your hill-land nor your valleys,
Ever again, nor share the battle yonder
Where the young knight the broken squadron rallies.
Only stay quiet while my mind remembers
The beauty of fire from the beauty of embers.

Beauty have pity, for the strong have power,
The rich their wealth, the beautiful their grace,
Summer of man its sunlight and its flower,
Springtime of man all April in a face.
Only, as in the jostling in the Strand,
Where the mob thrusts or loiters or is loud,
The beggar with the saucer in his hand
Asks only a penny from the passing crowd,
So, from this glittering world with all its fashion,
Its fire and play of men, its stir, its march,
Let me have wisdom, Beauty, wisdom and passion,
Bread to the soul, rain where the summers parch.
Give me but these, and though the darkness close
Even the night will blossom as the rose.

John Masefield 1920

THE VILLAIN

While joy gave clouds the light of stars,
   That beamed where'er they looked;
And calves and lambs had tottering knees,
   Excited, while they sucked;
While every bird enjoyed his song,
Without one thought of harm or wrong—
I turned my head and saw the wind,
   Not far from where I stood,
Dragging the corn by her golden hair,
   Into a dark and lonely wood.

                  W. H. Davies   1924

YOU, ANDREW MARVELL

And here face down beneath the sun
And here upon earth's noonward height
To feel the always coming on
The always rising of the night:

To feel creep up the curving east
The earthly chill of dusk and slow
Upon those under lands the vast
And ever climbing shadow grow

And strange at Ecbatan the trees
Take leaf by leaf the evening strange
The flooding dark about their knees
The mountains over Persia change

And now at Kermanshah the gate
Dark empty and the withered grass
And through the twilight now the late
Few travelers in the westward pass

And Baghdad darken and the bridge
Across the silent river gone
And through Arabia the edge
Of evening widen and steal on

And deepen on Palmyra's street
The wheel rut in the ruined stone
And Lebanon fade out and Crete
High through the clouds and overblown

And over Sicily the air
Still flashing with the landward gulls
And loom and slowly disappear
The sails above the shadowy hulls

And Spain go under and the shore
Of Africa the gilded sand
And evening vanish and no more
The low pale light across that land

Nor now the long light on the sea:
And here face downward in the sun
To feel how swift how secretly
The shadow of the night comes on . . .

Archibald MacLeish   1930

DREAM VARIATIONS

To fling my arms wide
In some place of the sun,
To whirl and to dance
Till the white day is done.
Then rest at cool evening
Beneath a tall tree
While night comes on gently,
   Dark like me—
That is my dream!

To fling my arms wide
In the face of the sun,
Dance! Whirl! Whirl!
Till the quick day is done.
Rest at pale evening . . .
A tall, slim tree . . .
Night coming tenderly
   Black like me.

Langston Hughes   1926

LONDON

I wander through each chartered street,
Near where the chartered Thames does flow,
And mark in every face I meet
Marks of weakness, marks of woe.

In every cry of every Man,
In every Infant's cry of fear,
In every voice, in every ban,
The mind-forged manacles I hear.

How the Chimney sweeper's cry
Every blackening Church appalls;
And the hapless Soldier's sigh
Runs in blood down Palace walls.

But most through midnight streets I hear
How the youthful Harlot's curse
Blasts the new born Infant's tear,
And blights with plagues the Marriage hearse.

William Blake   1794

CLEAR NIGHT

Clear night, thumb-top of a moon, a back-lit sky.
Moon-fingers lay down their same routine
On the side deck and the threshold, the white keys
    and the black keys.
Bird hush and bird song. A cassia flower falls.

I want to be bruised by God.
I want to be strung up in a strong light and singled out.
I wanted to be stretched, like music wrung from a dropped seed.
I want to be entered and picked clean.

And the wind says "What?" to me.
And the castor beans, with their little earrings of death,
    say "What?" to me.
And the stars start out on their cold slide through the dark.
And the gears notch and the engines wheel.

Charles Wright   1983

SILVER

Slowly, silently, now the moon
Walks the night in her silver shoon;
This way, and that, she peers, and sees
Silver fruit upon silver trees;
One by one the casements catch
Her beams beneath the silvery thatch;
Couched in his kennel, like a log,
With paws of silver sleeps the dog;
From their shadowy cote the white breasts peep
Of doves in a silver-feathered sleep;
A harvest mouse goes scampering by,
With silver claws and a silver eye;
And moveless fish in the water gleam,
By silver reeds in a silver stream.

Walter de la Mare   1913

BEGINNING

The moon drops one or two feathers into the field.
The dark wheat listens.
Be still.
Now.
There they are, the moon's young, trying
Their wings.
Between trees, a slender woman lifts up the lovely shadow
Of her face, and now she steps into the air, now she is gone
Wholly, into the air.
I stand alone by an elder tree, I do not dare breathe
Or move.
I listen.
The wheat leans back toward its own darkness,
And I lean toward mine.

James Wright   1971

END OF SUMMER

An agitation of the air,
A perturbation of the light
Admonished me the unloved year
Would turn on its hinge that night.

I stood in the disenchanted field
Amid the stubble and the stones,
Amazed, while a small worm lisped to me
The song of my marrow-bones.

Blue poured into summer blue,
A hawk broke from his cloudless tower,
The roof of the silo blazed, and I knew
That part of my life was over.

Already the iron door of the north
Clangs open: birds, leaves, snows
Order their populations forth,
And a cruel wind blows.

Stanley Kunitz   1953

NIGHT IS MY SISTER

Night is my sister, and how deep in love,
How drowned in love and weedily washed ashore,
There to be fretted by the drag and shove
At the tide's edge, I lie—these things and more:
Whose arm alone between me and the sand,
Whose voice alone, whose pitiful breath brought near,
Could thaw these nostrils and unlock this hand,
She could advise you, should you care to hear.
Small chance, however, in a storm so black,
A man will leave his friendly fire and snug
For a drowned woman's sake, and bring her back
To drip and scatter shells upon the rug.
No one but Night, with tears on her dark face,
Watches beside me in this windy place.

Edna St. Vincent Millay   1931

WHAT IF A MUCH OF A WHICH OF A WIND

what if a much of a which of a wind
gives the truth to summer's lie;
bloodies with dizzying leaves the sun
and yanks immortal stars awry?
Blow king to beggar and queen to seem
(blow friend to fiend:blow space to time)
—when skies are hanged and oceans drowned,
the single secret will still be man

what if a keen of a lean wind flays
screaming hills with sleet and snow:
strangles valleys by ropes of thing
and stifles forests in white ago?
Blow hope to terror;blow seeing to blind
(blow pity to envy and soul to mind)
—whose hearts are mountains,roots are trees,
it's they shall cry hello to the spring

what if a dawn of a doom of a dream
bites this universe in two,
peels forever out of his grave
and sprinkles nowhere with me and you?
Blow soon to never and never to twice
(blow life to isn't:blow death to was)
—all nothing's only our hugest home;
the most who die,the more we live

                    e. e. cummings 1944

A DIRGE

Rough wind, that moanest loud
    Grief too sad for song;
    Wild wind, when sullen cloud
Knells all the night long;
Sad storm, whose tears are vain,
Bare woods, whose branches strain,
Deep caves and dreary main—
    Wail, for the world's wrong!

        Percy Bysshe Shelley 1822

THE SECOND COMING

Turning and turning in the widening gyre
The falcon cannot hear the falconer;
Things fall apart; the center cannot hold;
Mere anarchy is loosed upon the world,
The blood-dimmed tide is loosed, and everywhere
The ceremony of innocence is drowned;
The best lack all conviction, while the worst
Are full of passionate intensity.

Surely some revelation is at hand;
Surely the Second Coming is at hand.
The Second Coming! Hardly are those words out
When a vast image out of *Spiritus Mundi*
Troubles my sight: somewhere in sands of the desert
A shape with lion body and the head of a man,
A gaze blank and pitiless as the sun,
Is moving its slow thighs, while all about it
Reel shadows of the indignant desert birds.
The darkness drops again; but now I know
That twenty centuries of stony sleep
Were vexed to nightmare by a rocking cradle
And what rough beast, its hour come round at last,
Slouches toward Bethlehem to be born?

William Butler Yeats   1920

BLOW, WINDS, AND CRACK YOUR CHEEKS!

LEAR: Blow, winds, and crack your cheeks! rage! blow!
You cataracts and hurricanes, spout
Till you have drenched our steeples, drowned the cocks!
You sulphurous and thought-executing fires,
Vaunt couriers to oak-cleaving thunderbolts,
Singe my white head! And thou, all-shaking thunder,
Smite flat the thick rotundity o' the world!
Crack nature's molds, all germens spill at once,
That make ingrateful man!

William Shakespeare   1605
King Lear, Act III, Scene 1

ENGLAND IN 1819

An old, mad, blind, despised, and dying king,
Princes, the dregs of their dull race, who flow
Through public scorn—mud from a muddy spring;
Rulers who neither see, nor feel, nor know,
But leech-like to their fainting country cling,
Till they drop, blind in blood, without a blow;
A people starved and stabbed in the untilled field—
An army, which liberticide and prey
Makes as a two-edged sword to all who wield;
Golden and sanguine laws which tempt and slay;
Religion Christless, Godless—a book sealed;
A Senate—Time's worst statute unrepealed—
Are graves, from which a glorious Phantom may
Burst, to illumine our tempestuous day.

Percy Bysshe Shelley   1819

PROPHECY

I shall lie hidden in a hut
   In the middle of an alder wood,
With the back door blind and bolted shut,
   And the front door locked for good.

I shall lie folded like a saint,
   Lapped in a scented linen sheet,
On a bedstead striped with bright-blue paint,
   Narrow and cold and neat.

The midnight will be glassy black
   Behind the panes, with wind about
To set his mouth against a crack
   And blow the candle out.

Elinor Wylie   1923

SLEEP

Come, Sleep; O Sleep! the certain knot of peace.
The baiting-place of wit, the balm of woe,
The poor man's wealth, the prisoner's release,
Th' indifferent judge between the high and low;
With shield of proof shield me from out the prease
Of those fierce darts Despair at me doth throw:
O make in me those civil wars to cease;
I will good tribute pay, if thou do so.
Take thou of me smooth pillows, sweetest bed,
A chamber deaf to noise and blind of light,
A rosy garland and a weary head;
And if these things, as being thine by right,
    Move not thy heavy grace, thou shalt in me,
    Livelier than elsewhere, Stella's image see.

Sir Philip Sidney   1582

I HEAR AN ARMY

I hear an army charging upon the land,
    And the thunder of horses plunging, foam about their knees:
Arrogant, in black armor, behind them stand,
    Disdaining the reins, with fluttering whips, the charioteers.

They cry unto the night their battle-name:
    I moan in sleep when I hear afar their whirling laughter.
They cleave the gloom of dreams, a blinding flame,
    Clanging, clanging upon the heart as upon an anvil.

They come shaking in triumph their long, green hair:
    They come out of the sea and run shouting by the shore.
My heart, have you no wisdom thus to despair?
    My love, my love, my love, why have you left me alone?

James Joyce   1918

THE WATCH

I wakened on my hot, hard bed,
Upon the pillow lay my head;
Beneath the pillow I could hear
My little watch was ticking clear.
I thought the throbbing of it went
Like my continual discontent;
I thought it said in every tick:
I am so sick, so sick, so sick;
O Death, come quick, come quick, come quick,
Come quick, come quick, come quick, come quick. . . .

Frances Cornford   1910

SNOWFLAKES

Out of the bosom of the Air,
  Out of the cloud-folds of her garments shaken,
Over the woodlands brown and bare,
  Over the harvest-fields forsaken,
    Silent, and soft, and slow
    Descends the snow.

Even as our cloudy fancies take
  Suddenly shape in some divine expression,
Even as the troubled heart doth make
  In the white countenance confession,
    The troubled sky reveals
    The grief it feels.

This is the poem of the air,
  Slowly in silent syllables recorded;
This is the secret of despair,
  Long in its cloudy bosom hoarded,
    Now whispered and revealed
    To wood and field.

Henry Wadsworth Longfellow   1859

THE BIRD

Though the evening comes with slow steps
    and has signalled for all songs to cease;
Though your companions have gone to their rest
    and you are tired;
Though fear broods in the dark
    and the face of the sky is veiled;
Yet, bird, O my bird, listen to me,
    do not close your wings.

That is not the gloom of the leaves of the forest,
    that is the sea swelling like a dark black smoke.
That is not the dance of the flowering jasmine,
    that is flashing foam.
Ah, where is the sunny green shore,
    where is your nest?
Bird, O my bird, listen to me,
    do not close your wings.

The lone night lies along your path,
    the dawn sleeps behind the shadowy hills.
The stars hold their breath counting the hours,
    the feeble moon swims the deep night.
Bird, O my bird, listen to me,
    do not close your wings.

There is no hope, no fear for you.
There is no word, no whisper, no cry.
There is no home, no bed of rest.
There is only your own pair of wings and the pathless sky.
Bird, O my bird, listen to me,
    do not close your wings.

Rabindranath Tagore   1912

If—

If you can keep your head when all about you
    Are losing theirs and blaming it on you;
If you can trust yourself when all men doubt you,
    But make allowance for their doubting too;
If you can wait and not be tired by waiting,
    Or being lied about, don't deal in lies,
Or being hated don't give way to hating,
    And yet don't look too good, not talk too wise;

If you can dream—and not make dreams your master;
    If you can think—and not make thoughts your aim;
If you can meet with Triumph and Disaster
    And treat those two impostors just the same;
If you can bear to hear the truth you've spoken
    Twisted by knaves to make a trap for fools,
Or watch the things you gave your life to, broken,
    And stoop and build 'em up with worn-out tools;

If you can make one heap of all your winnings
    And risk it on one turn of pitch-and-toss,
And lose, and start again at your beginnings
    And never breathe a word about your loss;
If you can force your heart and nerve and sinew
    To serve your turn long after they are gone,
And so hold on when there is nothing in you
    Except the Will which says to them: "Hold on!"

If you can talk with crowds and keep your virtue,
    Or walk with Kings—nor lose the common touch;
If neither foes nor loving friends can hurt you;
    If all men count with you, but none too much;
If you can fill the unforgiving minute
    With sixty seconds' worth of distance run,
Yours is the Earth and everything that's in it,
    And—which is more—you'll be a Man, my son!

Rudyard Kipling 1910

INVICTUS

Out of the night that covers me,
    Black as the Pit from pole to pole,
I thank whatever gods may be
    For my unconquerable soul.

In the fell clutch of circumstance
    I have not winced nor cried aloud.
Under the bludgeonings of chance
    My head is bloody, but unbowed.

Beyond this place of wrath and tears
    Looms but the Horror of the shade,
And yet the menace of the years
    Finds and shall find me unafraid.

It matters not how strait the gate,
    How charged with punishments the scroll,
I am the master of my fate:
    I am the captain of my soul.

William Ernest Henley   1875

MEDICINE FORMULA

When the new moon appears it is shouted to:
I shall prosper,
I shall yet remain alive.
Even if people do say of me,
"Would that he died!"
Just like thee shall I do,
Again shall I arise.
Even if all sorts of evil beings devour thee,
When frogs eat thee up,
Many evil beings—lizards,
Even when those eat thee up,
Still dost thou rise again.
Just like you will I do in time to come.
Bo!

Takelma Indian song
translated by Edward Sapir

THE TWENTY-THIRD PSALM

The Lord is my shepherd; I shall not want.
He maketh me to lie down in green pastures: he leadeth me
    beside the still waters.
He restoreth my soul: he leadeth me in the paths of
    righteousness for his name's sake.
Yea, though I walk through the valley of the shadow of death,
    I will fear no evil: for thou art with me; thy rod and
    thy staff they comfort me.
Thou preparest a table before me in the presence of mine
    enemies: thou anointest my head with oil; my cup runneth
    over.
Surely goodness and mercy shall follow me all the days of my
    life: and I will dwell in the house of the Lord forever.

The King James Bible   1611

THE PEACE OF WILD THINGS

When despair for the world grows in me
and I wake in the night at the least sound
in fear of what my life and my children's lives may be,
I go and lie down where the wood drake
rests in his beauty on the water, and the great heron feeds
I come into the peace of wild things
who do not tax their lives with forethought
of grief. I come into the presence of still water.
And I feel above me the day-blind stars
waiting with their light. For a time
I rest in the grace of the world, and am free.

Wendell Berry   1968

WHEN EARTH'S LAST PICTURE IS PAINTED

When Earth's last picture is painted and the tubes are twisted
  and dried,
When the oldest colors have faded, and the youngest critic
  has died,
We shall rest, and, faith, we shall need it—lie down for an æon
  or two,
Till the Master of All Good Workmen shall put us to work anew.

And those that were good shall be happy: they shall sit in a
  golden chair;
They shall splash at a ten-league canvas with brushes of
  comets' hair.
They shall find real saints to draw from—Magdalene, Peter,
  and Paul;
They shall work for an age at a sitting and never be tired at all!

And only the Master shall praise us, and only the Master shall
  blame;
And no one shall work for money, and no one shall work
  for fame,
But each for the joy of the working, and each, in his
  separate star,
Shall draw the Thing as he sees It for the God of Things
  as They are!

Rudyard Kipling   1892

EPISTLE TO BE LEFT IN THE EARTH

. . . It is colder now,
            there are many stars,
                        we are drifting
North by the Great Bear,
                  the leaves are falling,
The water is stone in the scooped rocks,
                        to southward
Red sun gray air:
            the crows are
Slow on their crooked wings,
                  the jays have left us:

Long since we passed the flares of Orion.
Each man believes in his heart he will die.
Many have written last thoughts and last letters.
None know if our deaths are now or forever:
None know if this wandering earth will be found.
We lie down and the snow covers our garments.
I pray you,
           you (if any open this writing)
Make in your mouths the words that were our names.
I will tell you all we have learned,
               I will tell you everything:
The earth is round,
           there are springs under the orchards,
The loam cuts with a blunt knife,
                   beware of
Elms in thunder,
           the lights in the sky are stars—
We think they do not see,
                we think also
The trees do not know nor the leaves of the grasses hear us:
The birds too are ignorant.
                 Do not listen.
Do not stand at dark in the open windows.
We before you have heard this:
             they are voices:
They are not words at all but the wind rising.
Also none among us has seen God.
(. . . We have thought often
The flaws of sun in the late and driving weather
Pointed to one tree but it was not so.)
As for the nights I warn you the nights are dangerous:
The wind changes at night and the dreams come.

It is very cold,
           there are strange stars near Arcturus,

Voices are crying an unknown name in the sky
                  Archibald MacLeish 1930

The End of the World

Quite unexpectedly as Vasserot
The armless ambidextrian was lighting
A match between his great and second toe
And Ralph the lion was engaged in biting
The neck of Madame Sossman while the drum
Pointed, and Teeny was about to cough
In waltz-time swinging Jocko by the thumb—
Quite unexpectedly the top blew off:

And there, there overhead, there, there, hung over
Those thousands of white faces, those dazed eyes,
There in the starless dark the poise, the hover,
There with vast wings across the canceled skies,
There in the sudden blackness the black pall
Of nothing, nothing, nothing—nothing at all.

Archibald MacLeish   1926

Good-bye

The last of last words spoken is Good-bye—
The last dismantled flower in the weed-grown hedge,
The last thin rumor of a feeble bell far ringing,
The last blind rat to spurn the mildewed rye.

A hardening darkness glasses the haunted eye,
Shines into nothing the watcher's burnt-out candle,
Wreathes into scentless nothing the wasting incense,
Faints in the outer silence the hunting-cry.

Love of its muted music breathes no sigh,
Thought in her ivory tower gropes in her spinning,
Toss on in vain the whispering trees of Eden,
Last of all last words spoken is Good-bye.

Walter de la Mare   1921

DEATH
BE NOT
PROUD

THE LAST INVOCATION

At the last, tenderly,
From the walls of the powerful fortressed house,
From the clasp of the knitted locks, from the keep
   of the well-closed doors,
Let me be wafted.

Let me glide noiselessly forth;
With the key of softness unlock the locks—with a whisper,
Set ope the doors O soul.

Tenderly—be not impatient,
(Strong is your hold O mortal flesh,
Strong is your hold O love.)   *Walt Whitman   1868*

ALL THE WORLD'S A STAGE

JAQUES: All the world's a stage,
And all the men and women merely players:
They have their exits and their entrances;
And one man in his time plays many parts,
His acts being seven ages. At first the infant,
Mewling and puking in the nurse's arms.
And then the whining school boy, with his satchel
And shining morning face, creeping like snail
Unwillingly to school. And then the lover,
Sighing like furnace, with a woeful ballad
Made to his mistress' eyebrow. Then a soldier,
Full of strange oaths and bearded like the pard,
Jealous in honor, sudden and quick in quarrel,
Seeking the bubble reputation
Even in the cannon's mouth. And then the justice,
In fair round belly with good capon lined;
With eyes severe and beard of formal cut,
Full of wise saws and modern instances;
And so he plays his part. The sixth age shifts
Into the lean and slippered pantaloon,
With spectacles on nose and pouch on side,
His youthful hose, well saved, a world too wide
For his shrunk shank; and his big manly voice,
Turning again toward childish treble, pipes
And Whistles in his sound. Last scene of all,
That ends this strange eventful history,
Is second childishness and mere oblivion,
Sans teeth, sans eyes, sans taste, sans everything.

William Shakespeare   1599
As You Like It, Act II, Scene Seven

REQUIESCAT

Tread lightly, she is near
　　Under the snow,
Speak gently, she can hear
　　The daisies grow.

All her bright golden hair
　　Tarnished with rust,
She that was young and fair
　　Fallen to dust.

Lily-like, white as snow,
　　She hardly knew
She was a woman, so
　　Sweetly she grew.

Coffin board, heavy stone,
　　Lie on her breast;
I vex my heart alone,
　　She is at rest.

Peace, Peace, she cannot hear
　　Lyre or sonnet,
All my life's buried here,
　　Heap earth upon it.

Oscar Wilde   1875

WITH RUE MY HEART IS LADEN

With rue my heart is laden
　　For golden friends I had,
For many a rose-lipped maiden
　　And many a lightfoot lad.

By brooks too broad for leaping
　　The lightfoot boys are laid;
The rose-lipped girls are sleeping
　　In fields where roses fade.

A. E. Housman   1896

DO NOT GO GENTLE INTO THAT GOOD NIGHT

Do not go gentle into that good night,
Old age should burn and rave at close of day;
Rage, rage against the dying of the light.

Though wise men at their end know dark is right,
Because their words had forked no lightning they
Do not go gentle into that good night.

Good men, the last wave by, crying how bright
Their frail deeds might have danced in a green bay,
Rage, rage against the dying of the light.

Wild men who caught and sang the sun in flight,
And learn, too late, they grieved it on its way,
Do not go gentle into that good night.

Grave men, near death, who see with blinding sight
Blind eyes could blaze like meteors and be gay,
Rage, rage against the dying of the light.

And you, my father, there on the sad height,
Curse, bless, me now with your fierce tears, I pray.
Do not go gentle into that good night.
Rage, rage against the dying of the light.

Dylan Thomas   1946

THE EMPEROR OF ICE-CREAM

Call the roller of big cigars,
The muscular one, and bid him whip
In kitchen cups concupiscent curds.
Let the wenches dawdle in such dress
As they are used to wear, and let the boys
Bring flowers in last month's newspapers.
Let be be finale of seem.
The only emperor is the emperor of ice-cream.

Take from the dresser of deal,
Lacking the three glass knobs, that sheet
On which she embroidered fantails once
And spread it so as to cover her face.
If her horny feet protrude, they come
To show how cold she is, and dumb.
Let the lamp affix its beam.
The only emperor is the emperor of ice-cream.

Wallace Stevens   1923

STOP ALL THE CLOCKS

Stop all the clocks, cut off the telephone,
Prevent the dog from barking with a juicy bone,
Silence the pianos and with muffled drum
Bring out the coffin, let the mourners come.

Let airplanes circle moaning overhead
Scribbling on the sky the message He Is Dead,
Put crêpe bows round the white necks of the public doves,
Let the traffic policemen wear black cotton gloves.

He was my North, my South, my East and West,
My working week and my Sunday rest,
My noon, my midnight, my talk, my song;
I thought that love would last forever: I was wrong.

The stars are not wanted now: put out every one;
Pack up the moon and dismantle the sun;
Pour away the ocean and sweep up the wood,
For nothing now can ever come to any good.

W. H. Auden   1938

BREAK, BREAK, BREAK

Break, break, break,
On the cold gray stones, O Sea!
And I would that my tongue could utter
The thoughts that arise in me.

O, well for the fisherman's boy,
That he shouts with his sister at play!
O, well for the sailor lad,
That he sings in his boat on the bay!

And the stately ships go on
To their haven under the hill;
But O for the touch of a vanished hand,
And the sound of a voice that is still!

Break, break, break,
At the foot of thy crags, O Sea!
But the tender grace of a day that is dead
Will never come back to me.

Alfred, Lord Tennyson   1834

BELLS FOR JOHN WHITESIDE'S DAUGHTER

There was such speed in her little body,
And such lightness in her footfall,
It is no wonder her brown study
Astonishes us all.

Her wars were bruited in our high window.
We looked among orchard trees and beyond
Where she took arms against her shadow,
Or harried unto the pond

The lazy geese, like a snow cloud
Dripping their snow on the green grass,
Tricking and stopping, sleepy and proud,
Who cried in goose, Alas,

For the tireless heart within the little
Lady with rod that made them rise

From their noon apple-dreams and scuttle
Goose-fashion under the skies!

But now go the bells, and we are ready,
In one house we are sternly stopped
To say we are vexed at her brown study,
Lying so primly propped.

John Crowe Ransom   1924

O CAPTAIN! MY CAPTAIN!

O Captain! my Captain! our fearful trip is done,
The ship has weathered every rack, the prize we sought is won,
The port is near, the bells I hear, the people all exulting,
While follow eyes the steady keel, the vessel grim and daring;
 But O heart! heart! heart!
  O the bleeding drops of red!
   Where on the deck my Captain lies,
    Fallen cold and dead.

O Captain! my Captain! rise up and hear the bells;
Rise up—for you the flag is flung—for you the bugle trills,
For you bouquets and ribboned wreaths—for you the shores
 crowding,
For you they call, the swaying mass, their eager faces turning;
 Here, Captain! dear father!
  This arm beneath your head!
   It is some dream that on the deck,
    You've fallen cold and dead.

My Captain does not answer, his lips are pale and still,
My father does not feel my arm, he has no pulse nor will,
The ship is anchored safe and sound, its voyage closed and done,
From fearful trip the victor ship comes in with object won;
 Exult, O shores! and ring O bells!
  But I with mournful tread,
   Walk the deck my Captain lies,
    Fallen cold and dead.

Walt Whitman   1865

PUNISHMENT

I can feel the tug
of the halter at the nape
of her neck, the wind
on her naked front.

It blows her nipples
to amber beads,
it shakes the frail rigging
of her ribs.

I can see her drowned
body in the bog,
the weighing stone,
the floating rods and boughs.

Under which at first
she was a barked sapling
that is dug up
oak-bone, brain-firkin:

her shaved head
like a stubble of black corn,
her blindfold a soiled bandage,
her noose a ring

to store
the memories of love.
Little adulteress,
before they punished you

you were flaxen-haired,
undernourished, and your
tar-black face was beautiful.
My poor scapegoat,

I almost love you
but would have cast, I know,
the stones of silence.
I am the artful voyeur

of your brain's exposed
and darkened combs,
your muscles' webbing
and all your numbered bones:

I who have stood dumb
when your betraying sisters,
cauled in tar,
wept by the railings,

who would connive
in civilized outrage
yet understand the exact
and tribal, intimate revenge.

Seamus Heaney   1975

ELEGY FOR JANE
My Student, Thrown by a Horse

I remember the neckcurls, limp and damp as tendrils;
And her quick look, a sidelong pickerel smile;
And how, once startled into talk, the light syllables
    leaped for her,
And she balanced in the delight of her thought,
A wren, happy, tail into the wind,
Her song trembling the twigs and small branches.
The shade sang with her;
The leaves, their whispers turned to kissing;
And the mold sang in the bleached valleys under the rose.

Oh, when she was sad, she cast herself down into
    such a pure depth,
Even a father could not find her:
Scraping her cheek against straw;
Stirring the clearest water.

My sparrow, you are not here,
Waiting like a fern, making a spiny shadow.
The sides of wet stones cannot console me,
Nor the moss, wound with the last light.

If only I could nudge you from this sleep,
My maimed darling, my skittery pigeon.
Over this damp grave I speak the words of my love:
I, with no rights in this matter,
Neither father nor lover.

Theodore Roethke   1950

TO AN ATHLETE DYING YOUNG

The time you won your town the race
We chaired you through the marketplace;
Man and boy stood cheering by,
And home we brought you shoulder-high.

Today, the road all runners come,
Shoulder-high, we bring you home,
And set you at your threshold down,
Townsman of a stiller town.

Smart lad, to slip betimes away
From fields where glory does not stay
And early though the laurel grows
It withers quicker than the rose.

Eyes the shady night has shut
Cannot see the record cut,
And silence sounds no worse than cheers
After earth has stopped the ears:

Now you will not swell the rout
Of lads that wore their honors out,
Runners whom renown outran
And the name died before the man.

So set, before its echoes fade,
The fleet foot on the sill of shade,
And hold to the low lintel up
The still-defended challenge cup.

And round that early-laureled head
Will flock to gaze the strengthless dead,
And find unwithered on its curls
The garland briefer than a girl's.

A. E. Housman   1896

IS MY TEAM PLOWING?

"Is my team plowing,
   That I was used to drive
And hear the harness jingle
   When I was man alive?"

Ay, the horses trample,
   The harness jingles now;
No change though you lie under
   The land you used to plow.

"Is football playing
   Along the river shore,
With lads to chase the leather,
   Now I stand up no more?"

Ay, the ball is flying,
   The lads play heart and soul;
The goal stands up, the keeper
   Stands up to keep the goal.

"Is my girl happy,
   That I thought hard to leave,
And has she tired of weeping
   As she lies down at eve?"

Ay, she lies down lightly,
   She lies not down to weep:
Your girl is well contented.
   Be still, my lad, and sleep.

"Is my friend hearty,
   Now I am thin and pine,
And has he found to sleep in
   A better bed than mine?"

Yes, lad, I lie easy,
   I lie as lads would choose;
I cheer a dead man's sweetheart,
   Never ask me whose.

        A. E. Housman   1896

CROSSING THE BAR

Sunset and evening star,
   And one clear call for me!
And may there be no moaning of the bar,
   When I put out to sea,

But such a tide as moving seems asleep,
   Too full for sound and foam,
When that which drew from out the boundless deep
   Turns again home.

Twilight and evening bell,
   And after that the dark!
And may there be no sadness of farewell,
   When I embark;

For though from out our bourne of Time and Place
   The flood may bear me far,
I hope to see my Pilot face to face
   When I have crossed the bar.

Alfred, Lord Tennyson   1889

MUSIC
After Sully Prudhomme

Kindly watcher by my bed, lift no voice in prayer,
Waste not any words on me when the hour is nigh,
Let a stream of melody but flow from some sweet player,
And meekly will I lay my head and fold my hands to die.

Sick I am of idle words, past all reconciling,
Words that weary and perplex and pander and conceal,
Wake the sounds that cannot lie, for all their sweet beguiling;
The language one need fathom not, but only hear and feel.

Let them roll once more to me, and ripple in my hearing
Like waves upon a lonely beach where no craft anchoreth
That I may steep my soul therein, and craving naught,
   nor feeling,
Drift on through slumber to a dream, and through a dream
   to death.

George du Maurier   c. 1865

PROSPICE

Fear death?—to feel the fog in my throat,
    The mist in my face,
When the snows begin, and the blasts denote
    I am nearing the place,
The power of the night, the press of the storm,
    The post of the foe;
Where he stands, the Arch Fear in a visible form,
    Yet the strong man must go:
For the journey is done and the summit attained,
    And the barriers fall,
Though a battle's to fight ere the guerdon be gained,
    The reward of it all.
I was ever a fighter, so—one fight more,
    The best and the last!
I would hate that death bandaged my eyes and forbore,
    And bade me creep past.
No! let me taste the whole of it, fare like my peers
    The heroes of old,
Bear the brunt, in a minute pay glad life's arrears
    Of pain, darkness and cold.
For sudden the worst turns the best to the brave,
    The black minute's at end,
And the elements' rage, the fiend-voices that rave,
    Shall dwindle, shall blend,
Shall change, shall become first a peace out of pain,
    Then a light, then thy breast,
O thou soul of my soul! I shall clasp thee again,
    And with God be the rest!

Robert Browning   1861

LADY LAZARUS

I have done it again.
One year in every ten
I manage it—

A sort of walking miracle, my skin
Bright as a Nazi lampshade,
My right foot

A paperweight,
My face a featureless, fine
Jew linen.

Peel off the napkin
O my enemy.
Do I terrify?

The nose, the eye pits, the full set of teeth?
The sour breath
Will vanish in a day.

Soon, soon the flesh
The grave cave ate will be
At home on me

And I a smiling woman.
I am only thirty.
And like the cat I have nine times to die.

This is Number Three.
What a trash
To annihilate each decade.

What a million filaments.
The peanut-crunching crowd
Shoves in to see

Them unwrap me hand and foot—
The big strip tease.
Gentlemen, ladies

These are my hands
My knees.
I may be skin and bone,

Nevertheless, I am the same, identical woman.
The first time it happened I was ten.
It was an accident.

The second time I meant
To last it out and not come back at all.
I rocked shut

As a seashell.
They had to call and call
And pick the worms off me like sticky pearls.

Dying
Is an art, like everything else.
I do it exceptionally well.

I do it so it feels like hell.
I do it so it feels real.
I guess you could say I've a call.

It's easy enough to do it in a cell.
It's easy enough to do it and stay put.
It's the theatrical

Comeback in broad day
To the same place, the same face, the same brute
Amused shout:

"A miracle!"
That knocks me out.
There is a charge

For the eyeing of my scars, there is a charge
For the hearing of my heart—
It really goes.

And there is a charge, a very large charge
For a word or a touch
Or a bit of blood

Or a piece of my hair or my clothes.
So, so, Herr Doktor.
So, Herr Enemy.

I am your opus,
I am your valuable,
The pure gold baby

That melts to a shriek.
I turn and burn.
Do not think I underestimate your great concern.

Ash, ash—
You poke and stir.
Flesh, bone, there is nothing there—

A cake of soap,
A wedding ring,
A gold filling.

Herr God, Herr Lucifer
Beware
Beware.

Out of the ash
I rise with my red hair
And I eat men like air.

Sylvia Plath   1963

AFTER GREAT PAIN, A FORMAL FEELING COMES

After great pain, a formal feeling comes.
The nerves sit ceremonious like tombs.
The stiff heart questions was it He that bore,
And yesterday or centuries before?

The feet, mechanical, go round
Of ground, or air, or ought—
A wooden way
Regardless grown,
A quartz contentment, like a stone.

This is the hour of lead.
Remembered, if outlived,
As freezing persons recollect the snow.
First chill, then stupor, then the letting go.

Emily Dickinson   1862

BECAUSE I COULD NOT STOP FOR DEATH

Because I could not stop for Death
He kindly stopped for me.
The carriage held but just ourselves
And Immortality.

We slowly drove. He knew no haste
And I had put away
My labor and my leisure too,
For his civility.

We passed the school where children strove
At recess, in the ring.
We passed the fields of gazing grain.
We passed the setting sun.

Or rather, he passed us.
The dews drew quivering and chill,
For only gossamer, my gown.
My tippet, only tulle.

We paused before a house that seemed
A swelling of the ground.
The roof was scarcely visible,
The cornice in the ground.

Since then 'tis centuries, and yet
Feels shorter than the day
I first surmised the horses' heads
Were toward eternity—

Emily Dickinson   1863

QUESTION

Body my house
my horse my hound
what will I do
when you are fallen
Where will I sleep
How will I ride
What will I hunt

Where can I go
without my mount
all eager and quick
How will I know
in the thicket ahead
is danger or treasure
when Body my good
bright dog is dead

How will it be
to lie in the sky
without roof or door
and wind for an eye

With cloud for shift
how will I hide?

May Swenson   1954

I STROVE WITH NONE
from The Last Fruit Off an Old Tree

I strove with none, for none was worth my strife:
    Nature I loved, and next to Nature, Art:
I warmed both hands before the fire of life;
    It sinks; and I am ready to depart.

Walter Savage Landor   1849

WHEN I AM DEAD

When I am dead, my dearest,
    Sing no sad songs for me;
Plant thou no roses at my head,
    Nor shady cypress tree:
Be the green grass above me
    With showers and dewdrops wet:
And if thou wilt, remember,
    And if thou wilt, forget.

I shall not see the shadows,
    I shall not feel the rain;
I shall not hear the nightingale
    Sing on, as if in pain:
And dreaming through the twilight
    That doth not rise nor set,
Haply I may remember,
    And haply may forget.

                    Christina Rossetti   1848

REMEMBER

Remember me when I am gone away,
    Gone far away into the silent land;
    When you can no more hold me by the hand,
Nor I half turn to go yet turning stay.
Remember me when no more day by day
    You tell me of our future that you planned:
    Only remember me; you understand
It will be late to counsel then or pray.
Yet if you should forget me for a while
    And afterwards remember, do not grieve:
    For if the darkness and corruption leave
    A vestige of thoughts that once I had,
Better by far you should forget and smile
    Than that you should remember and be sad.

                    Christina Rossetti   1858

INVOCATION

Let me be buried in the rain
In a deep, dripping wood,
Under the warm wet breast of Earth
Where once a gnarled tree stood.
And paint a picture on my tomb
With dirt and a piece of bough
Of a girl and a boy beneath a round, ripe moon
Eating of love with an eager spoon
And vowing an eager vow.
And do not keep my plot mowed smooth
And clean as a spinster's bed,
But let the weed, the flower, the tree,
Riotous, rampant, wild and free,
Grow high above my head.

Helene Johnson   1931

WHEN GOD LETS MY BODY BE

when god lets my body be

From each brave eye shall sprout a tree
fruit that dangles therefrom

the purpled world will dance upon
Between my lips which did sing

a rose shall beget the spring
that maidens whom passion wastes

will lay between their little breasts
My strong fingers beneath the snow

Into strenuous birds shall go
my love walking in the grass

their wings will touch with her face
and all the while shall my heart be

With the bulge and nuzzle of the sea

e. e. cummings   1923

THE REBEL

When I
die
I'm sure
I will have a
Big Funeral . . .

Curiosity
seekers . . .

coming to see
if I
am really
Dead

or just
trying to make
Trouble . . . .

Mari Evans   1970

DEATH BE NOT PROUD

Death be not proud, though some have called thee
Mighty and dreadful, for thou art not so;
For those whom thou think'st thou dost overthrow
Die not, poor Death; nor yet canst thou kill me.
From rest and sleep, which but thy pictures be,
Much pleasure, then from thee much more must flow;
And soonest our best men with thee do go,
Rest of their bones and souls' delivery!
Thou art slave to Fate, Chance, kings, and desperate men,
And dost with poison, war, and sickness dwell;
And poppy or charms can make us sleep as well,
And better than thy stroke. Why swell'st thou then?
One short sleep past, we wake eternally,
And death shall be no more; death, thou shalt die!

John Donne   1607

MADRIGAL

This world a hunting is:
The prey, poor man; the Nimrod fierce is Death;
His speedy greyhounds are
Lust, Sickness, Envy, Care,
Strife that ne'er falls amiss,
With all those ills which haunt us while we breathe.
Now if, by chance, we fly
Of these the eager chase,
Old age with stealing pace
Casts up his nets, and there we panting die.

William Drummond   1649

REQUIEM

Under the wide and starry sky,
Dig the grave and let me lie.
Glad did I live and gladly die,
　　And I laid me down with a will.

This be the verse you grave for me:
Here he lies where he longed to be;
Home is the sailor, home from sea,
　　And the hunter home from the hill.

Robert Louis Stevenson   1880

DREGS

The fire is out, and spent the warmth thereof,
(This is the end of every song man sings!)
The golden wine is drunk, the dregs remain,
Bitter as wormwood and as salt as pain;
And health and hope have gone the way of love
Into that drear oblivion of lost things.
Ghosts go along with us until the end;
This was a mistress, this, perhaps, a friend.
With pale, indifferent eyes, we sit and wait
For the dropped curtain and the closing gate:
This is the end of all the songs man sings.

Ernest Dowson   1899

AND DEATH SHALL HAVE NO DOMINION

And death shall have no dominion.
Dead men naked they shall be one
With the man in the wind and the west moon;
When their bones are picked clean and the clean bones gone,
They shall have stars at elbow and foot;
Though they go mad they shall be sane,
Though they sink through the sea they shall rise again;
Though lovers be lost love shall not;
And death shall have no dominion.
And death shall have no dominion.

Under the windings of the sea
They lying long shall not die windily;
Twisting on racks when sinews give way,
Strapped to a wheel, yet they shall not break;
Faith in their hands shall snap in two,
And the unicorn evils run them through;
Split all ends up they shan't crack;
And death shall have no dominion.

And death shall have no dominion.
No more may gulls cry at their ears
Or waves break loud on the seashores;
Where blew a flower may a flower no more
Lift its head to the blows of the rain;
Though they be mad and dead as nails,
Heads of the characters hammer through daisies;
Break in the sun till the sun breaks down,
And death shall have no dominion.

Dylan Thomas 1933

OUR REVELS NOW ARE ENDED

Our revels now are ended. These our actors,
As I foretold you, were all spirits and
Are melted into air, into thin air:
And, like the baseless fabric of this vision,
The cloud-capped towers, the gorgeous palaces,
The solemn temples, the great globe itself,
Yea, all which it inherit, shall dissolve
And, like this insubstantial pageant faded,
Leave not a rack behind. We are such stuff
As dreams are made on, and our little life
Is rounded with a sleep.

William Shakespeare   1611
The Tempest, Act IV, Scene 1

INDEX OF AUTHORS

INDEX OF TITLES AND FIRST LINES

ACKNOWLEDGMENTS

Grateful acknowledgment is made for permission to reprint the following previously published poems:

Anna Akhmatova: "Ah, You Thought," copyright © 1990, 1992 by Judith Hemschemeyer. From *The Complete Poems of Anna Akhmatova* (second edition, 1992). Reprinted by permission of the Zephyr Press of Somerville, Massachusetts.

Kingsley Amis: "The Last War," copyright © 1956 by Kingsley Amis. From *Collected Poems*. Reprinted by permission of Jonathan Clowes Ltd.

Maya Angelou: "Momma Welfare Roll," copyright © 1978 by Maya Angelou. From *And Still I Rise*. Reprinted by permission of Random House, Inc.

John Ashbery: "My Erotic Double," copyright © 1979 by John Ashbery. From *As We Know*. Reprinted by permission of Random House, Inc. "Paradoxes and Oxymorons," copyright © 1981 by John Ashbery. From *Shadow Train*. Reprinted by permission of the author and Georges Borchardt, Inc.

W. H. Auden: "The Unknown Citizen" and "Lullaby," copyright © 1940, 1968 by W. H. Auden. From *Collected Poems*. "Stop all the clocks," copyright © 1976 by Edward Mendelson, William Meredith and Monroe K. Spears. Reprinted by permission of Random House, Inc.

Amiri Baraka: "A Poem Some People Will Have to Understand" and "Preface to a Twenty Volume Suicide Note," copyright © 1961 and 1969 by Amiri Baraka. Reprinted by permission of the author and Sterling Lord Literistic, Inc.

George Barker: "To My Mother," copyright © 1941 by George Barker. From *Collected Poems,* published by Criterion Books.

Stephen Vincent Benét: "The Ballad of William Sycamore," copyright © 1922, 1950 by Stephen Vincent Benét. From *Ballads and Poems*. Reprinted by permission of Brandt & Brandt Literary Agents, Inc.

Michael Benedikt: "Thoughts," copyright © 1968 by Michael Benedikt. From *The Body*. Reprinted by permission of the author.

Gwendolyn Bennett: "To a Dark Girl," copyright © 1931 by Gwendolyn Bennet. Reprinted by permission of the Estate of Gwendolyn Bennet and the Schomburg Center for Research in Black Culture, The New York Public Library.

Wendell Berry: "The Peace of Wild Things," copyright © 1968 by Wendell Berry. From *Openings*. Reprinted by permission of Harcourt Brace & Company.

John Berryman: "He stared at ruin" and "This world is gradually becoming a place," copyright © 1969 by John Berryman. From *The Dream Songs*. "Sonnet 115," copyright © 1952, 1967 by John Berryman. From *Berryman's Sonnets*. Reprinted by permission of Farrar, Straus & Giroux, Inc.

Elizabeth Bishop: "One Art," copyright © 1979, 1983 by Alice Helen Methfessel. From *The Complete Poems 1927–1979* by Elizabeth Bishop. Reprinted by permission of Farrar, Straus & Giroux, Inc.

Joseph Brodsky: "Six Years Later," copyright © 1980 by Farrar, Straus & Giroux, Inc. From *A Part of Speech*. Reprinted by permission of Farrar, Straus & Giroux, Inc.

Countee Cullen: "Yet Do I Marvel," copyright © 1925 by Countee Cullen. From *Color*. Reprinted by permission of Amistad Research Center, Tulane University and James R. Rhone, Esq.

e. e. cummings: "if i have made,my lady," "may I feel said he," "next to of course god america i," "what if a much of a which of a wind," "when god lets my body be," and "the Cambridge ladies who live in furnished souls," copyright © 1923, 1926, 1935, 1944, 1951, 1963, 1972, 1991 by the Trustees for the E. E. Cummings Trust. From *Complete Poems 1904–1962*. Reprinted by permission of Liveright Publishing Corporation.

J. V. Cunningham: "To My Wife," copyright © 1960 by J. V. Cunningham. From *The Exclusions of a Rhyme*. Reprinted by permission of Jessie Cunningham.

W. H. Davies: "The Villain," copyright © 1924 by W. H. Davies. From *Selected Poems,* published by Harcourt Brace, 1924.

James Dickey: "The Performance," copyright © 1967 by James Dickey. From *Poems 1957–1967*. Reprinted by permission of University Press of New England.

A. E. Housman: "Because I liked you better," "Here dead lie we because we did not choose," and "When green buds hang in the elm," copyright © 1939, 1940 by Henry Holt and Co., Inc. Copyright © 1967 by Robert E. Symons. From *The Collected Poems of A. E. Housman.* Reprinted by permission of Henry Holt and Co., Inc.

Langston Hughes: "50–50," "Dream Variations," "I, too, sing America," "Night Funeral in Harlem," "Preferences," and "Same as Blues," copyright © 1944 by the Estate of Langston Hughes. From *The Collected Poems of Langston Hughes.* Reprinted by permission of Alfred A. Knopf, Inc.

Randall Jarrell: "Losses" and "The Death of the Ball Turret Gunner," copyright © 1969 by Mrs. Randall Jarrell. From *The Complete Poems.* Reprinted by permission of Farrar, Straus & Giroux, Inc.

Robinson Jeffers: "Hurt Hawks," copyright © 1928, 1956 by Robinson Jeffers. "Antrim," copyright © 1931, 1959 by Robinson Jeffers. "New Mexican Mountain," copyright © 1932, 1960 by Robinson Jeffers. "Vulture," copyright © 1963 by Robinson Jeffers. From *The Selected Poetry of Robinson Jeffers.* Reprinted by permission of Random House, Inc.

James Weldon Johnson: "The Creation," copyright © 1927 by The Viking Press, Inc., renewed 1955 by Grace Nail Johnson. From *God's Trombones.* Reprinted by permission of Viking Penguin, a division of Penguin Books USA, Inc.

Donald Justice: "In Bertram's Garden," copyright © 1954 by Donald Justice. From *The Summer Anniversaries.* "Men at forty," copyright © 1966 by Donald Justice. From *Night Light.* Reprinted by permission of the author.

X. J. Kennedy: "Nude Descending a Staircase," copyright © 1961 by X. J. Kennedy, renewed. From *Nude Descending a Staircase.* Reprinted by permission of the author and Curtis Brown Ltd.

Galway Kinnell: "After Making Love We Hear Footsteps," copyright © 1980, 1983 by Galway Kinnell. From *Three Books.* Reprinted by permission of Houghton Mifflin Co.

Etheridge Knight: "For Black Poets Who Think of Suicide" and Hard Rock Returns to Prison . . . ," copyright © 1968 by Etheridge Knight. From *Poems from Prison.* Reprinted by permission of The University of Pittsburgh Press.

Kenneth Koch: "Permanently," copyright © 1962, 1995 by Kenneth Koch. From *Selected Poems.* Reprinted by permission of the author.

W. S. Merwin: "Grandfather in the Old Men's Home," copyright © 1960 by W. S. Merwin. From *The Drunk in the Furnace.* "Separation," copyright © 1963 by W. S. Merwin. From *The Moving Target.* Reprinted by permission of the author.

Edna St. Vincent Millay: "Above these cares," copyright © 1934, 1962 by Edna St. Vincent Millay and Norma Millay Ellis. "At least, my dear," copyright © 1940, 1968 by Edna St. Vincent Millay and Norma Millay Ellis. "I shall go back," "Oh, Oh, you will be sorry for that word!," and "What lips my lips have kissed," copyright © 1923, 1951 by Edna St. Vincent Millay and Norma Millay Ellis. "Love is not all" and "Night is My Sister," copyright © 1931, 1958 by Edna St. Vincent Millay and Norma Millay Ellis. "Modern Declaration," copyright © 1939, 1967 by Edna St. Vincent Millay and Norma Millay Ellis. "Spring," Copyright © 1921, 1948 by Edna St. Vincent Millay. From *Collected Poems,* HarperCollins Publishers, Inc. Reprinted by permission of Elizabeth Barnett, literary executor.

John Frederick Nims: "Love Poem," copyright © 1947 by John Frederick Nims. From *Selected Poems.* Reprinted by permission of The University of Chicago Press.

Sharon Olds: "35/10" and "The One Girl at the Boys Party," copyright © 1983 by Sharon Olds. From *The Dead and the Living.* Reprinted by permission of Alfred A. Knopf, Inc.

P. K. Page: "Young Girls," copyright © 1954 by P. K. Page. Reprinted by permission of the author.

Sylvia Plath: "Lady Lazarus," copyright © 1963 by Ted Hughes. "Morning Song," copyright © 1961 by Ted Hughes. From *Ariel.* Reprinted by permission of Harper Collins Publishers, Inc.

Dudley Randall: "Blackberry Sweet," copyright © 1969 by Dudley Randall. Reprinted by permission of the author. John Crowe Ransom: "Bells for John Whiteside's Daughter," copyright © 1924 by Alfred A. Knopf, Inc. and renewed 1952 by John Crowe Ransom. From *Selected Poems.* Reprinted by permission of the publisher.

Henry Reed: "Naming of Parts," copyright © 1946 by Henry Reed. From *A Map of Verona.* Reprinted by permission of Jonathan Cape, Ltd.

Charles Reznikoff: "I will write songs against you" and "Let other people come as streams," copyright © 1959 by Charles Reznikoff. From *By*